MODERNITY
FOR THE MASSES

*Lateral Exchanges: Architecture, Urban Development,
and Transnational Practices*
A series edited by Felipe Correa, Bruno Carvalho, and Alison Isenberg

Also in the series:

Tara A. Dudley, *Building Antebellum New Orleans: Free People of Color
    and Their Influence*

Burak Erdim, *Landed Internationals: Planning Cultures, the Academy,
    and the Making of the Modern Middle East*

Mary P. Ryan, *Taking the Land to Make the City: A Bicoastal History
    of North America*

Fabiola López-Durán, *Eugenics in the Garden: Transatlantic Architecture
    and the Crafting of Modernity*

MODERNITY FOR THE MASSES

Ana María León

ANTONIO BONET'S DREAMS FOR BUENOS AIRES

UNIVERSITY OF TEXAS PRESS *Austin*

Copyright © 2021 by the University of Texas Press
All rights reserved
Printed in the United States of America
First edition, 2021

Requests for permission to reproduce material from this work should be sent to:
 Permissions
 University of Texas Press
 P.O. Box 7819
 Austin, TX 78713–7819
 utpress.utexas.edu/rp-form

⊖ The paper used in this book meets the minimum requirements of
ANSI/NISO Z39.48–1992 (R1997) (Permanence of Paper).

Library of Congress Cataloging-in-Publication Data

Names: León, Ana María, author.
Title: Modernity for the masses : Antonio Bonet's dreams for Buenos Aires /
Ana María León.
Description: First edition. | Austin : University of Texas Press, 2021. | Series:
 Lateral exchanges : architecture, urban development, and transnational
 practices | Includes bibliographical references and index.
Identifiers: LCCN 2020001529 (print) | LCCN 2020001530 (ebook)
 ISBN 978-1-4773-2178-2 (cloth)
 ISBN 978-1-4773-2179-9 (library ebook)
 ISBN 978-1-4773-2180-5 (non-library ebook)
Subjects: LCSH: Architecture and society—Argentina—Buenos Aires—
History—20th century. | Unbuilt architectural projects—Argentina—Buenos
Aires—History—20th century. | Housing—Political aspects—Argentina—Buenos
Aires—History—20th century. | Bonet Castellana, Antoni, 1913–1989—Criticism
and interpretation.
Classification: LCC NA2543.S6 L45 2020 (print) | LCC NA2543.S6 (ebook) |
 DDC 720.1/03—dc23
LC record available at https://lccn.loc.gov/2020001529
LC ebook record available at https://lccn.loc.gov/2020001530

doi:10.7560/321782

CONTENTS

INTRODUCTION

The decisive weight of coloniality in the constitution of the European
paradigm of modernity/rationality is clearly revealed in the actual crisis
of that cultural complex.

> ANÍBAL QUIJANO,
> "Coloniality and Modernity/Rationality,"
> *Cultural Studies*, Vol. 21, Nos. 2–3
> March/May 2007

On October 17, 1945, thousands of union workers poured into the city center
of Buenos Aires. These Porteños (citizens of Buenos Aires) came from the
edges of the city, from the low-income neighborhoods of the periphery, and
took over the downtown, converging on the Plaza de Mayo—the main public square in front of the Casa Rosada, the Presidential Palace. These crowds
demanded the liberation of a young general under arrest, Juan Domingo Perón,
the only member of the ruling military dictatorship who had maintained close
relationships with the workers' unions. An iconic photograph captures their
occupation of the plaza (FIGURE 0.01). In the heat of the southern spring, men
sit with their pant legs rolled up, dipping their feet in the neoclassical fountain at its center. Several men and women in the background stand inside the
fountain. The photograph was given the derogatory popular name "Las patas
en la fuente" (The hooves in the fountain). The conflation of these daring
crowds and a herd of cows, the basis of one of Argentina's primary economies,
was no accident. The vast plains of the countryside were a source of wealth

FIGURE 0.01. (*opposite*)
"The hooves in the
fountain." AR, AGN DDF/
Consulta INV: 47810.

and also of the large migrations that contributed to the growth of the Buenos Aires periphery. Overwhelmed by the masses, the regime freed Perón, who subsequently ran for office and was elected president in 1946, ending years of conservative rule and changing the country—from a land ruled by the few to a land with a populist government addressed to the many.

Ten years after this episode, members of the Argentinian navy and air force bombarded Buenos Aires, targeting strategic locations including the Plaza de Mayo. Hundreds of civilians were killed; thousands were injured. The attack was one of several military actions against Perón that eventually led to his removal from power by an alliance of conservative right-wing military factions who took over the country, installing a dictatorship and sending him into exile. These two episodes in the Plaza de Mayo—its physical occupation and subsequent destruction—were the context in which Catalan architect Antoni Bonet i Castellana's modern housing projects were designed, developed, and eventually discarded. As a site of congregation and ultimately violent removal of the populations that these projects were meant to house, the plaza serves as a foil to modern architecture's obsession with cleared ground. Understood as products of these totalitarian states, Bonet's unbuilt projects reveal the role of architecture as an instrument of mass deception.

Antoni Bonet i Castellana (Barcelona, 1913–1989, hereafter Antonio Bonet) was born, raised, and trained as an architect in Barcelona, where he attended the Escuela Superior de Arquitectura (ESA, Superior School of Architecture) from 1929 to 1936.[1] The traditional training that he received there greatly contrasted with his simultaneous apprenticeship in modern architecture at the office of Josep Lluís Sert and Josep Torres Clavé (1932–1936). Bonet's formation as an architect coincided with the aggravating conflict of the Spanish Civil War as well as with a productive moment for the Catalonian art and architecture avant-garde, particularly in relation to Catalan surrealism. He was close to these developments through his connection with Sert: he participated in the Congrès Internationaux d'Architecture Moderne (CIAM: International Congresses of Modern Architecture) conversations, worked as the site architect in the Pavilion of the Spanish Republic, and spent some time in the atelier of Le Corbusier (Charles-Edouard Jeanneret) in 1937–1938, where he met Chilean architect Roberto Matta Echaurren and Argentinians Jorge Ferrari Hardoy and Juan Kurchan. Persuaded by Ferrari and Kurchan to escape the dire situation in Europe by relocating to Argentina, he collaborated with them in the formation of Austral, a modern architecture group that mobilized their experience at Le Corbusier's office to generate similar conversations in Argentina. Their collective design of the BKF (Bonet, Kurchan, Ferrari) chair is their best-known contribution to the modern design lexicon.

Bonet developed a successful architectural practice based in Buenos Aires, designing and building single-family houses, a few small projects and a private resort in Uruguay, and several high-rises in Mar del Plata. Throughout his time in Argentina, he participated in the design of several housing projects, which, as this book recounts, were never built. In the late 1950s, as the political situation in the country deteriorated, he returned to Spain in the middle of the so-called Spanish Miracle. There he designed and built several beach resorts and high-rise apartment buildings. He also continued to work on larger urban plans, mostly unbuilt, and a nuclear power center in Tarragona. He passed away in his native Barcelona.

As a European architect who worked with José Luis Sert and Le Corbusier in Barcelona and Paris, Bonet embodies the desire to transfer European modernism to the American continent. He was an eager advocate of the CIAM, which he negotiated through his own developing interpretations of an architecture of surrealism. They were sparked by his admiration of Antonio Gaudí; his contact with Catalan surrealists Salvador Dalí, Joan Miró, and Pablo Picasso; and his collaboration with Roberto Matta. Working in collaboration with Argentinian and European artists, architects, and intellectuals, Bonet was called on to design a series of housing projects for the growing Buenos Aires masses and the states that sought to control them. These projects reveal the disconnect between modern architecture's discourse and the societies that it intended to house as well as the limits of the European model when translated to Argentina and its expansive landscapes (especially its large crowds, given the racial complexities of a settler colonial society). The physical presence and tragic death of *el pueblo* (the people), as Perón described them, in the Plaza de Mayo underscore their absence in the conversations among the architects who wanted to house them and the states that claimed to protect them. Bonet and the architects he worked with, I argue, constructed these populations as an imaginary other: ever present in the architectural projects, in their illustrated representations, and in the ways in which they advertised them to different publics but absent as an active constituency.

While the masses were not invited to participate in these conversations, their imposing presence shaped Buenos Aires, which is the second protagonist in this story. In the first decades of the twentieth century, successive migrations from overseas and from the countryside had changed the cultural and racial composition of the capital city. The masses occupied its public spaces and increased the demand for housing, which led to a confrontation with the landowning elites who ruled them. These changes elicited different reactions from intellectuals, artists, and the modern architects in their milieu, ranging from anxiety and fear of their otherness to pragmatic confrontation of the problems that they posed. The Argentinian state, wavering between totalitarian dictatorships and the populist rule of Perón, mobilized the housing shortage to pursue different agendas. As the main target of these projects, the politically active population of Buenos Aires was seen as a threat, whose power needed to be harnessed, displaced, or destroyed.

Many modern architects, strongly influenced by the CIAM, argued for a pragmatic approach to housing mathematically quantifiable bodies. Bonet, however, sought to modify what he saw as cold rationality by arguing in favor of a "collective psychology," a surrealist-inspired concept that he believed would assist architects in understanding the masses.[2] Yet his modern projects and their representations (in the drawings, photomontages, models, and promotional film examined here) also reveal a complicated fascination with, and ultimately fear of, the latent irrational power that the masses were understood to possess. This fear culminated in a return to the technocratic rationality that Bonet had originally renounced. His thinking as an architect was further complicated by the involvement of opposing regimes that viewed the masses as either an opportunity or a threat. As a collaboration between modern architecture and the state, Bonet's housing projects reveal the ensuing contradictory discourses, agendas, and anxieties of the different actors involved in their production. By containing, managing, and eventually controlling the bodies that they sought to house, these projects ultimately embody the architect's own unconscious thoughts and desires in regard to those populations as well as his complicity with the states he served and the violence they deployed.

Modernity for the Masses explores the fractious relationship among modern architects, the people they meant to house, and the states they courted by studying one built project and three unbuilt housing projects designed by Bonet in Buenos Aires between 1938 and 1960. Trained with the avant-gardes of Barcelona and Paris, Bonet arrived in Buenos Aires to find different modernization processes at work, informing other modernisms. His discourse and practice of modern architecture were transformed as he negotiated the social, cultural, and political landscape of Argentina in the mid-twentieth century. Bonet's dreams for Buenos Aires give us insights into the different modernities contained by the city. Following Aníbal Quijano, I peel back the discourses behind these various modernities in order to reveal the ways in which the coloniality of power is constitutive of these projects—and of the Argentinian state itself.

Using Bonet's creative production as a narrative thread, each chapter centers on one of his projects and addresses a different set of discourses and disciplines, a different scale of intervention, and a different relationship between city center and periphery. My research examines literary insights related to

Buenos Aires and its growing population, journals and publications, correspondence, drawings, models, photographs, state propaganda, and popular magazines that solicited their readers' dreams for psychoanalytic interpretation. These sources allow me to trace links among political systems, the people they govern, and how their bodies are regulated in space. The book follows two interrelated lines of inquiry. First, how did the spatial politics between the monumental core of Buenos Aires—centered on the Plaza de Mayo—and its growing periphery inform the modern project of housing the masses? Second, did states construct a collective unconscious that represented its population in order to control it?

In Buenos Aires the notion of the city center stood in dialectical tension with the pampas, the expansive, horizontal plains that are part of both the landscape and the imaginary of the country. The dichotomy between city and countryside was invoked by Argentinian politician and writer Domingo Sarmiento in his critique of the ruthless leadership of Juan Manuel de Rosas (1793–1877).[3] Sarmiento mapped ethical implications onto the Argentinian geography, opposing the civilizing, republican, and ultimately European values of the city to the barbaric impulses of the pampas. When large migrations from the plains contributed to the expansion of Buenos Aires in the early twentieth century, many of the city's elite, influenced by Sarmiento, associated the incoming masses with myths related to their place of origin: the savage, primitive pampas. The influx of the masses resulted in a struggle for the city's center and its expansion toward the countryside as the migrants settled into sprawling slums that pushed against the city's legally constituted limits. Guided by the tenets of the CIAM, Bonet's housing projects engaged both the city and the region by shifting scales from the building to the city and the encompassing pampas. The growing scale, changing locations, and various politics at work in his proposed interventions, I argue, reflect the struggle for the city center between older hierarchies and the rising working class.

Stressing the imbrications of architecture and politics, *Modernity for the Masses* links the increased political power and agency of the city's crowds to discourses informed by their presence and to the state-funded housing projects designed to discipline them. These masses, increasingly threatening to the ruling landowning elite, were different from them in terms of race and class. Argentina has long been constructed as a racially homogeneous, white settler colonial nation whose Indigenous population was violently eradicated in the nineteenth-century appropriation of the valuable pampas and replaced with a mostly southern European population. More recent analysis has challenged this perception, suggesting that Indigenous people and African descendants continued to exist, but not necessarily as distinct communities. They joined the nation's poorer sections, who were traditionally considered racially white but whose darker hair and skin tone were linked to lower economic and cultural status.[4] In their anthology on race in Argentina, Paulina Alberto and Eduardo Elena argue that the category of "white" was broadened to include an array of origins and racial variations, virtually eliminating other racial categories. This flattening of racial difference also helps explain the lack of race-based movements and politics in Buenos Aires, where the poorer sections of the city coalesced into an artificially homogeneous but nevertheless "othered" population. The growth of this population coincided with the modernization of the country's industry and infrastructure, creating a large working class that organized itself around neighborhood and employment-based associations and unions. Perón's enactment of women's suffrage in 1949 effectively doubled the electoral power of these groups, further challenging the position of the conservative landowning classes that had long governed the country.

This growing population and its latent power were the focus of literary, psychoanalytic, and architecture circles, who examined it in the context of the rise of fascism in Europe. I compare José Ortega y Gasset's fear of the masses and their potential for revolt with Le Corbusier's exhortation for architects to educate rulers on the discipline's potential to control crowds by appealing to their emotions.[5] Both of these authors discouraged revolution and proposed alternative ways to manage or harness the crowds. They visited and were inspired by Argentina in their writing, which made their texts particularly important to intellectuals working there. I also examine the discourse of members of the intellectual circle Sur (South), including Jorge Luis Borges's allegories of the city as a container of crowds and lectures by French renegade surrealist Roger Caillois, who opposed totalitarian governments and saw monumental architecture as a way to resist them by educating and edifying the public. These circles developed in the context of the popularity of psychoanalysis in Buenos Aires, which prompted artists and architects to experiment with representations of the unconscious but also extended to more popular forums, including magazines, film, and other types of media.

In this sense, Bonet's early evocation of an "architecture of surrealism" resonated with the Buenos Aires avant-garde, which was both repelled by and fascinated with the obscure, the mythical, and the primitive. In Buenos Aires, I argue, the origin of this impulse lies in the perceived threat of a growing population and its governance. With the advent of Peronist populism, the surrealist project of accessing the unconscious was displaced by Perón's ability to harness the masses. Further, the populist construction of a collective unconscious was mobilized to promote different state projects, informed by current theories on crowd behavior and management. Due to the Argentinian army's connection with Nazi Germany and fascist Italy, both Perón and the military dictatorships that preceded and followed him included traces of these totalitarian ideologies.[6] Their efforts to control the crowds through housing projects reveal the inevitable entanglements of modern actors with these types of regimes.

Public housing, a particular interest of modern architects, is the site where the spatial politics of the city and the construction of its collective unconscious converge.[7] The dynamics of rural migration to Buenos Aires, on the one hand, and the complicity of the avant-garde with the state, on the other, led to a confrontation between the tenets of modern architecture as an avant-garde discourse and modern architecture as a professional service discipline. A detailed reading of Bonet's projects and the discourses that surrounded them reveals how he wavered between a definition of architecture as a sensory, surreal experience or as a technical, rational field of expertise. He also wavered between serving the masses that he meant to house or serving the state that funded the projects. The restless growing population gave increased urgency to his proposals, while political and intellectual forces complicated their ultimate objectives. On a broader level, Bonet's projects trace a history of modern architecture's complicity with totalitarian states. His formal strategies may be seen as interventions in the city that evolved from an idealist celebration of the masses to their manipulation and eventually to the repression of their political power.

Despite Bonet's modernist credentials, this book is not an effort to insert him into the modern architecture canon. Rather, I argue for the insights into the history of architecture that can be gleaned from the housing projects that he designed and their failure. While Bonet benefited from generously funded state commissions for large housing projects, these projects were never built. He never achieved the international reputation he desired. In that sense, this study of Bonet in Buenos Aires reconstructs a minor history. Art historian Branden Joseph's reading of the work of Mike Kelley, alongside Gilles Deleuze and Félix Guattari, prompts him to think about the productive historiographical labor produced by minor histories, a useful methodology for narratives that elide established categories and major events. If so-called major histories are marked by patterns of domination that establish a set of characters and events as superior, minor histories bypass these developments, to which they are proximate or even parasitic. Joseph theorizes the minor as "not the qualitatively or quantitatively inferior, but what is marked by an irreducible or uncontainable difference."[8] While appearing underdeveloped, heterogeneous, and not quite fitting established categories, Joseph argues, minor histories have the capacity to open these categories to their outside.

Rather than transforming Bonet into a major character, we can productively discuss him as a minor actor, operating in close proximity to figures like Le Corbusier and José Luis Sert but not quite able to build or publish at their international scale; often affected by major events in Argentinian history but never a protagonist in them. It is precisely the failure of Bonet's unbuilt projects and his inability to become a so-called major figure that I examine in this book. While the history of Bonet presents one of the major triangulations in the history of modernism's dissemination outside Europe, I am less interested in strengthening the canonical hierarchies that he is a part of and more interested in the ways in which understanding this narrative as a "minor history" opens up the categories established by more traditional historiographies of modernism.

This book considers the history of the housing projects that Bonet designed for Buenos Aires but never built in terms of the ways in which they describe a vision for the growing populations of a city. Their failure is a repeating trope in the history of architecture in South America, a region where projects were often conceived and dismissed due to economic stress or political upheaval. This failure itself is an important lacuna in the scholarship. Why are these projects significant today? It seems to me that this question is asked most productively in the very societies whose precariousness often results in projects left on the drafting table. The considerable labor and capital invested in them reveal a conversation between architects and the different states that sponsored them that shaped the discourse and production of modern architecture in the region and beyond. Bonet's unbuilt projects and the discourse around them reveal the chasm between the discourse of modern architecture and the realities of population growth and political upheaval, a legacy that still mars the cities of the South.

To examine the relationship between modern architecture and the state, I examine four projects in four chapters: the Artists' Ateliers (1939), Bonet's first built project in Buenos Aires; the unbuilt Casa Amarilla (1943), a modern housing project south of downtown Buenos Aires designed with a team for the 1943 dictatorship; Bajo Belgrano (1949), an unbuilt Peronist housing project led by Bonet's colleague Jorge Ferrari (the team included Bonet as an important actor, German photographer Grete Stern as graphic designer, and Italian surrealist Enrico Gras as film director); and Barrio Sur (1957), an unbuilt project sponsored by the dictatorial regime that overthrew Perón (FIGURE 0.02). These case studies provide opportunities to align the specifics of mass housing with different political contexts and scales of intervention.

While prior scholarship on Bonet has been either comprehensive or focused on isolated projects, this study takes a transnational and interdisciplinary

FIGURE 0.02. (opposite) Bonet's housing projects in Buenos Aires. Site plans from OVRA, Casa Amarilla (1943), FABC, © copyright AHCOAC (Bonet); EPBA, Bajo Belgrano, (1949), JFHA, courtesy FLL, Harvard University GSD; Bonet, Barrio Sur (1956), FABC, © copyright AHCOAC (Bonet). Montage by Linda Lee under the direction of the author.

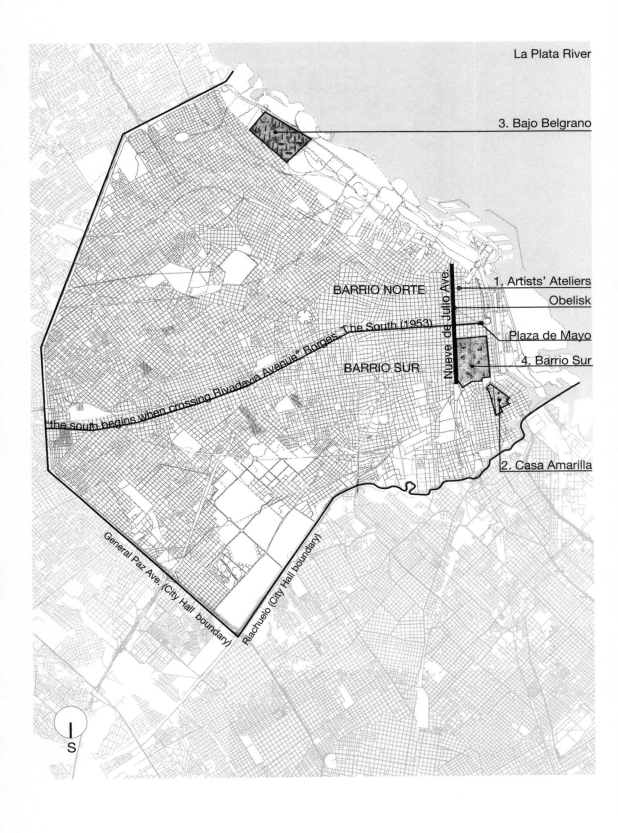

La Plata River

3. Bajo Belgrano

BARRIO NORTE

1, Artists' Ateliers

Obelisk

Plaza de Mayo

4. Barrio Sur

BARRIO SUR

Nueve de Julio Ave.

"The South (1953)

Borges,

Rivadavia Avenue"

when crossing

the south begins

2. Casa Amarilla

General Paz Ave. (City Hall boundary)

Riachuelo (City Hall boundary)

S

approach, emphasizing both connections and misalignments. In doing so, I build on the studies of historians Ernesto Katzenstein, Fernando Álvarez Prozorovich, and Jorge Nudelman, who established the groundwork for scholarship on Bonet, as well as subsequent historians who have centered their attention on Bonet and his work.[9] This book also engages with Jorge Francisco Liernur's research on Austral. Liernur documents the work of the group, with more attention to Argentinian figures and narratives, focusing on the architecture discipline.[10] On a broader level, I look closely at the 1940s, a decade that has been largely neglected in the history of architecture, except for the early surveys of Latin American work by Henry-Russell Hitchcock and Francisco Bullrich.[11] More recent contributions by Andrew Shanken, Jean Louis Cohen, and Lucia Allais examine broad histories but center their narratives on Europe or the United States.[12] My work examines this period from both inside and outside Argentina through Bonet's ambiguous status as a foreigner working for nationalist regimes wary of outside influence, and expands on a broader cast of characters linked to him in Spain, France, and the United States. Bonet's career in Buenos Aires developed as modern architecture boomed throughout Latin America, culminating in the construction of large modern projects, most notably the University City in Caracas by Carlos Raúl Villanueva (1945–1967), the Campus of the National Autonomous University of Mexico in Mexico City by Mario Pani and Enrique del Moral (1954), and the city of Brasilia by Lucio Costa with buildings by Oscar Niemeyer (1956–1960). Bonet's work reveals the longer shadows of these projects in the failed attempts of other states to emulate their scope and monumentality.

This book examines the intersection between the discourse of modern architecture applied to social housing and the Argentinian historical and political context within which Bonet attempted to operate. Rather than presenting a comprehensive history of mass housing in Buenos Aires or the architecture of Peronism, such as the work of historians Anahí Ballent, Jorge Francisco Liernur, and Ramón Gutiérrez,[13] this study is intended to complement more detailed histories that examine state housing policies and plans in Argentina. My interdisciplinary approach, including architecture, literature, aesthetics, and visual culture, takes cues from Beatriz Colomina's scholarship on modern architecture and mass media. However, my work goes beyond canonical European figures and examines political complicities more closely.[14]

Furthermore, the cultural context that shaped these events prompts me to engage with the work of scholars beyond the discipline of architecture, in particular historians Adrián Gorelik and Graciela Silvestri's important work on the pampas and the city.[15] My research overlaps and extends intellectual histories on the literary group Sur in Argentina and the Collège de

Sociologie in France.[16] While these groups are usually considered separately, my research looks into their overlaps, in particular the writings of *Sur* contributor Roger Caillois in Argentina in the context of his transformation from renegade surrealist to member of the United Nations Educational, Scientific and Cultural Organization (UNESCO) and advocate of the cult of monuments.[17] The unique intersection of psychoanalysis culture and aesthetics in Argentina has been researched by art historians Luis Priamo and Paula Bertúa as well as cultural historian Mariano Ben Plotkin. My work engages with their research and extends it to architecture. Finally, I tackle the problematic links between the pragmatics of architecture and the dream world of surrealism, a topic examined by Thomas Mical, Anthony Vidler, and Neil Spiller.[18] While these authors explore the potential of surrealism in architecture, I examine its potential downfalls. In Bonet's attempts at an architecture of surrealism, I argue, the insights into the unconscious that this movement strove to provide ultimately came to serve the totalitarian politics that surrealism wished to resist. The revolutionary potential of surrealism remains an illusory promise.

In each of these four projects I explore a different aspect of the discourse of modern architecture: ship, void, dream, and nostalgia. This summary elaboration deliberately counters modern architecture's self-definition through the tenets of the CIAM, instead foregrounding the more irrational aspects of its discourse. In doing so, I find common ground between modern architecture's supposedly rational claims and the discourse of surrealism. Bonet's involvement is a loose but continuous chronological thread along which projects and themes engage various groups of actors and collaborators, different sets of disciplines, and an increasingly larger scale of intervention into the city. Bonet himself often recedes into the background as the book explores architecture's intersections with literature, photography, film, and politics.

Chapter 1, "A Wandering Ship," focuses on the Artists' Ateliers (1939) as a project that combined ideas, methods, and organizations from Barcelona, Paris, and Buenos Aires in the years immediately preceding World War II. I highlight the importance of Catalonian culture in these developments, which a very recently arrived Bonet was eager to explore in Buenos Aires. In Catalan avant-garde circles the order and rationality prescribed by modern architecture found itself in tension with surrealism's desire to delve into the forces of the irrational. The Spanish Civil War (1936–1939) and the impending conflict of World War II gave particular urgency to this struggle. Bonet's involvement with Catalan surrealist circles, working on the 1937 Pavilion of the Spanish Republic in Paris, and his collaboration with architect-turned-artist Roberto

Matta in Le Corbusier's office are products of this charged environment. Building on these European encounters, Bonet's first contact with Buenos Aires was inflected, on the one hand, by his new architecture contacts, and, on the other, by the city itself as a formal system with its own grid and ordinances. He also remained attuned to his mentors Le Corbusier and Sert. These different experiences came together in the Artists' Ateliers, a small building anchored on a downtown corner, containing ideas that traveled and collected passengers and discourses in Barcelona, Paris, and Buenos Aires. Most importantly, this metaphorically moored ship was meant to advertise these ideas to potential clients.

Chapter 2, "The Machine in the Pampas," examines the avant-garde's anxiety over the accelerating growth of Buenos Aires, compounded by the city's increasingly blurry edges, which stretched into the figurative void of the pampas from which the migrations came. The interrelated phenomena of population growth and the notion of the pampas as a sublime void came to haunt the literary and aesthetic production of the city in the late 1930s and early 1940s. As large migrations from the pampas extended the limits of the city toward this ominous void, monumental structures were built in the center of Buenos Aires, sponsored by conservative elites. I examine this phenomenon through the discourse on the masses and their governance by intellectuals living in Argentina, comparing it to contemporaneous discourse on architecture and its capacity to channel the emotions of crowds. I argue that the demolition of several blocks in the center of the dense Buenos Aires grid is indicative of the unease about the void. It is a reminder of the pampas and the population that they represented.

In this context, Bonet led a team that designed Casa Amarilla (1943), a modern housing project south of downtown. It was meant to guide the state—a dictatorship that took over the country in 1943—in the implementation of modern solutions. Attending to the void in the urban grid, this project proposed a series of monumental buildings to house the city's growing population. By borrowing the characteristics of monumental scale and central location from the elites to identify the disenfranchised masses, and inserting them into the middle of the city, Casa Amarilla attempted to counter the rising authoritarian power of the Argentinian state. But while the architects initially meant to elevate the crowds, the project ultimately echoed the state's mandate to contain and control them. It was never built, but Bonet's career was taking off. He moved to Uruguay to build a resort community in Punta Ballena (1945–1947) but returned to a Peronist Argentina when the Buenos Aires city hall engaged his associate Ferrari to design a modern plan for the city, following Perón's liberation at the Plaza de Mayo and ascent to the presidency.

Chapter 3, "The Peronist Unconscious," looks at the mobilization of avant-garde aesthetics in the service of Peronist propaganda, which included the promotion of the Bajo Belgrano (1949) housing project. After his rise to the presidency in 1946, Perón built a formidable propaganda platform to advance the task of inventing a new country. I compare his tactics with those of the *invencionistas*, an avant-garde group in 1940s Argentina that sought to bring together abstraction and revolutionary leftist politics. I argue that Perón—a populist who opposed communism—was the greatest *invencionista* of all, as seen in everything from his construction of celebratory rituals to the saturation of mass media. This was particularly evident in the reproduction of the voices and images of himself and his wife, the iconic Eva "Evita" Duarte de Perón. In his visual aesthetic Perón represented everything that the *invencionistas*, who promoted abstraction, argued against. He favored kitsch and the figurative and mined the symbolic and narrative potential of the image. But at the same time his tactics were modern, celebrating the voice of the expert and the promise of utopia, compressed into concrete, wave-emanating objects, infinitely reproduced through mass media. Like Casa Amarilla six years earlier, however, Bajo Belgrano was never built.

The architects used Peronist tactics to promote this failed project. Grete Stern's "Dreams" (photomontages made to illustrate female dreams, deciphered by a sociologist and a publisher who were posing as a psychoanalyst) are informative when considering her graphic design work for Bajo Belgrano. Stern introduces another dimension in the promotional material for Bajo Belgrano, including printed material and a film, *La ciudad frente al río* (The city in front of the river), directed by Italian filmmaker Enrico Gras, a self-proclaimed surrealist who had worked for Italian fascist dictator Benito Mussolini. I argue that these projects all shared similar tactics and goals, whether they were kitschy political propaganda, women's journals, or modern architecture. All reached back to an imaginary past in order to give concrete shape to the elusive dream of the modern city and modern city dweller. Drawing on Jacques Lacan's and Fredric Jameson's theories of the unconscious, I call this collective political imaginary a "Peronist unconscious." Multiple cultural forms were independently reproduced within this paradigm, amplifying the project of the state, which I describe as a pastoral modernity. Bonet's involvement in this production reveals how easily the discourse of modern architecture was molded to the Peronist project. It would be eight years before Bonet received another opportunity to house the masses.

Chapter 4, "Eternal Returns," studies the period immediately following the violent military coup d'état that deposed Perón in September 1955. The new government, led by Eduardo Lonardi and later Pedro Eugenio Aramburu

(1955–1958), embarked on a campaign to discredit Perón, painting him as old, outdated, and morally corrupt. Bonet's Barrio Sur (1957), a state-sponsored urban development plan meant to replace the old neighborhood of San Telmo, can be understood as commensurate with this effort. Through Barrio Sur, the last large-scale housing project that Bonet worked on in Argentina, the Argentinian state intended to rebuild itself in the image of technocratic, efficient modernity. While the project failed, its formal and discursive ambiguity was mined by Bonet, who used it as his presentation card to return to Spain in the late 1950s. After being flaunted in Argentina as the image of modernity, Barrio Sur was rebranded in Spain in line with growing trends toward Mediterranean nostalgia. I problematize this nostalgia in the context of the so-called Spanish Miracle of the late 1960s, which conflated Francisco Franco's nationalism with his strategic political opening toward the United States and his adoption of neoliberal financial mechanisms. The aesthetic of a nationalist tradition, particularly exploited by tourism, was a tool of global capitalism. In Bonet's case, this anxiety resolved itself in a final transformation, from embracing the CIAM aspiration to house the masses to his acceptance of the postwar world of the resort. Bonet's final turn to a Mediterranean modernity of consumption, nostalgia, and tourism points to broader shifts in modern architecture's assumed role, from an agent of change to a subject of capital.

At the core of this narrative is the relationship among modern architects, the states within which they operate, and the populations that these states are meant to govern, which architects claim to serve. These populations are largely absent from the relationship between architecture and the state, but they assert their presence in different and ultimately more meaningful ways. "A Wandering Ship" looks at the tension between a more utopian or idealist vein of modern architecture and more pragmatic approaches. "The Machine in the Pampas" addresses the masses as the populations to be housed by these projects, although they are constantly abstracted and elided. "The Peronist Unconscious" shifts to the state and its operations, alternatively controlling, manipulating, and orchestrating populations and agents. Finally, "Eternal Returns" turns back to the modern architect as a figure who in this case "returns" to a failed and compromised project in Europe.

The four projects illustrate the ways in which links among political regimes, the people they govern, and the location of projects are always embodied and influence the design of buildings and cities. They also point to the politics inherent in the way architects think about people, where they live in the city, and the relative density of their housing. Throughout the twentieth century it became a common trope in South America to understand large state projects as electoral tools, promoted for their ability to provide jobs. As the housing question shifted from the public sector to private enterprise in the second half of the twentieth century, these jobs and their populations were increasingly pushed to the edges of cities. Spaces of congregation like the iconic Plaza de Mayo have been replaced with private spaces of consumption such as shopping malls and the internet. These changes reveal the neoliberal state as the logical conclusion of the dictatorships that oppressed the continent in the second half of the twentieth century. Ultimately, what is at stake in these visions is the control of populations, a mandate in which the anxieties and desires of modern architects such as Bonet coincided with those of totalitarian states. The resurgence of totalitarianism in our contemporary moment leads us to question the loyalties and complicities of architects and the interests they serve.

A NOTE ON TRANSLATION AND TERMINOLOGY

Translations from original correspondence are mine unless otherwise noted. In the case of nuanced quotations I have included the original language in the notes. I occasionally use some terms that might be more "Argentinian" than Spanish, such as pampas (plains), arrabal (area of small houses in the periphery), and Porteño (citizen of Buenos Aires). Translations are given in the text. Argentinians are fond of acronyms, so it seemed appropriate to leave them in their original language, along with a translation. I include a list of abbreviations at the end of the text.

The actors in this narrative often invoke "America" to refer to the American continent, understood as what is separately called North, Central, and South America and the Caribbean in the United States. This usage had specific importance in the 1940s, both in supporting the United States after the attack on Pearl Harbor and in comparing Europe to America as continents. It continues to have political resonance in a region that is otherwise designated as the South American or Latin American equivalent to a perceived "actual" America assumed to be the United States. I come from the South and choose to follow its conventions.

AUSTRAL

chapter one

A WANDERING SHIP

We begin with a back cover. Published in 1939 in Argentina, the last issue of the architecture journal *Austral* features a photograph of Antonio Bonet, sitting on the garden terrace of the Artists' Ateliers, his first built work in Buenos Aires, completed that year in collaboration with Abel López Chas and Ricardo Vera Barros (FIGURE 1.01). In the foreground a small arrangement of succulents in a roof garden (*toit-jardin*) and a round column (*piloti*) affirm the Corbusian roots of this mise-en-scène. Bonet's back is to the camera. The sun creates stark shadows on the ground, highlighting the curves of a wrought-iron chair beside him. Bonet sits informally on the gravel floor, with his sleeves rolled up, ready to work, but his casual posture and attire are contradicted by the careful framing of the scene, revealed by the angle of the photograph. In order to take this picture, the photographer had to climb up to a small ledge on the edge of the building's audacious curved roof, a barrel vault extended along the curve of a parabola. It is not a difficult climb, as I learned, but it does take some effort. The photograph's angle obscures what Bonet is looking at, but it is easy to figure out. Perched in this corner as if on the bow of a ship, he studies the intersection of Suipacha and Paraguay streets below. The photograph is framed by a map of the city that surrounds Bonet and constitutes his milieu. The high vantage point of the photograph and the tight grid of the plan that surrounds it suggest the strategy of "planning from above," the detached operation that so often characterized modern architecture's urban approach. Having just arrived in Buenos Aires, Bonet is already sitting on top of his first built work, both looking down and floating over the city. If modern architecture is linked to the image of the ship (through formal traits borrowed by modernism as well as from the 1933 CIAM meeting on the ss *Patris II*, which sailed from Marseilles to Athens), this building was the ship on which Bonet arrived on the Buenos Aires architectural scene. As a product of the Spanish and French

FIGURE 1.01. (*opposite*) Back cover, *Austral* 3 (December 1939). CD BMIN, FADU-UBA.

architecture avant-garde, he embodied the shift of the modern architecture project from Europe to the Americas. As he moved from Barcelona to Paris and then to Buenos Aires, he participated in different groups and collaborated in key projects, collecting experiences and gaining insights. Settling in Buenos Aires, Bonet sought to emulate the path to success of his European masters, José Luis Sert and Le Corbusier, by promoting his work through the creation of architecture associations and publications. His activity culminated in this building, designed and built shortly after he arrived in Buenos Aires: the Artists' Ateliers.

Numerous groups and projects informed Bonet's thinking on housing the masses, a mandate related to the urban project of the CIAM, which required a close relationship with the state in this context. Following his mentors Sert and Le Corbusier, Bonet knew that it was advantageous to emulate the image of the avant-garde artist as someone who could communicate and persuade the masses, ideally mediating between them and the state. Through the use of publications, manifestos, and ultimately architecture as propaganda, the architect could become a figure with authority and power. In relation to his previous work as the site architect of José Luis Sert and Luis Lacasa Navarro's Pavilion of the Spanish Republic (Paris, 1937) and his collaboration with Roberto Matta at Le Corbusier's office, we can conclude that Bonet approached the design of the Artists' Atelier as a propaganda machine: the ultimate objective was to acquire urban commissions from the Argentinian state.

THE PATH LEADS TO A STAR

GATCPAC WITH A "C"

The importance of Catalonia in the production and dissemination of modern art and architecture remains underestimated, partly because of the actors and the way they presented themselves. Throughout his career in Buenos Aires, Antoni Bonet i Castellana strategically emphasized the few months that he spent in Le Corbusier's atelier in Paris instead of his development as an architect in Catalonia on the eve of the Spanish Civil War. In the mid-1930s Catalan politics were led by representatives of large industries, syndicalists, workers, and anarchists, a complicated alliance that came together for greater independence from the central government in Madrid. Its main nationalist bourgeois party, the Lliga Regionalista, was pressured from the left by coalitions of workers and peasants pushing for agrarian and social revolution. This alliance between militantly committed revolutionaries and more pragmatic and business-minded groups was reflected in Bonet's mentors and employers in Barcelona, Josep Torres Clavé and Josep Lluís Sert. These men also linked him to a wealthy bourgeoisie of industrialists and business owners, to artists including Pablo Picasso, Joan Miró, and Salvador Dalí, and to Dalí's strong infatuation with the architecture of *modernisme*, a distinctive Catalan modernism that flourished between 1888 and 1911.

All of this informed the figure of the modern architect in Barcelona as someone who might bridge art and commerce, architecture and revolution, and surrealism and modernity. Circling among these groups, Bonet was intrigued by the romantic and aspirational potential of the figure of the avant-garde artist and the revolutionary but was ultimately closer to the pragmatic, business-minded leanings of his mentor Sert, for whom he started working while still an architecture student from 1932 to 1936.

The declaration of the Catalan Republic in 1931—a few hours before the proclamation of the Second Spanish Republic in Madrid—held the promise of a renewed and progressive state. It was quickly followed by the creation of the Grup d'Artistes i Tècnics Catalans per al Progrés de l'Arquitectura Contemporània (GATCPAC, Group of Catalan Artists and Technicians for the Progress of Contemporary Architecture), an entity eager to emphasize its independence from the Spanish group, the Grupo de Artistas y Técnicos Españoles para el Progreso de la Arquitectura Contemporánea (GATEPAC, Group of Spanish Artists and Technicians for the Progress of Contemporary Architecture).[1] Naming the group in Catalan and replacing the "E" of Spain with the "C" of Catalonia—as well as using the names "Antoni" instead of "Antonio" and "Josep" instead of "José"—were an important reminder of the importance of the Catalan language in marking both the identity of the group and the audience being addressed.[2] This separation was short lived. Three days after, Catalonia joined the Spanish Republic in order to resist the more immediate threat of Gen. Francisco Franco. But the GATCPAC continued to operate, shifting to GATEPAC (GE)—meaning eastern group—when addressing a Spanish audience. This oscillating identity came to mask, particularly to foreign eyes, the leading role of Catalonia and the GATCPAC in the discourse of modern architecture in Spain.

Both groups were explicitly established as CIAM representatives and sought to promote modern architecture. Their members eagerly followed the discourse of modern architecture coming from publications and architects from France, Italy, Germany, and even the Soviet Union and were strongly influenced by Le Corbusier's visits and his connection to Sert, who had established his modern credentials by working in the Swiss architect's office. To fund its activities in Barcelona, the GATCPAC courted the support of industrialists and wealthy business owners. Its offices, which were effectively Sert and Torres Clavé's offices, accommodated multiple additional functions. They acted as a site for architectural collaborations, a storefront for the sale of modern industrial products, and a working space for the GATEPAC's journal, *A.C.: Documentos de Actividad Contemporánea* (Documents of Contemporary Activity), the leading journal of Spanish modern architectural discourse, which was edited by Torres Clavé and published from 1931 to 1937. They also provided an exhibition space for the fellow modern art group Amics de l'Art Nou (ADLAN, Friends of the New Art). ADLAN was founded by Sert with Joan Prats and Joaquim Gomis, wealthy men eager to promote the work of established Catalan artists, including Pablo Picasso, Joan Miró, and Salvador Dalí as well as American sculptor Alexander Calder, who was close to the group.[3] Thus Spanish modern architectural discourse was led by Catalonia through a multiple-pronged approach: an architectural avant-garde group, the journal, a retail store, an architecture office, and the art association.

The GATCPAC's aspiration to reconcile business interests with the social good also characterized the different personalities of its leaders, Sert and Torres Clavé. Bonet followed suit, becoming a student member of the GATCPAC in 1934. He remembered his mentors as a study in contrasts:

> Torres Clavé was an extraordinary character. He was a very spontaneous man, very passionate, an exceptional human being. As an architect he was less creative than Sert, but he was indispensable to him. They complemented each other stupendously. Torres Clavé was the person who worked hard, a laborer of architecture. Sert was the person who was there to provide ideas. With the war, Torres Clavé was named president of the Society of Architects in Barcelona and of the journal. At the last moment he decided to go to the front. He died there. It was because of an excess of passion.[4]

Torres Clavé's militant socialism was eloquently articulated in the editorial line of the journal *A.C.*, which paid close attention to socialist aesthetic production, regularly featuring Soviet constructivist films and Ernst May's housing projects in the Soviet Union. Torres Clavé would become an active member of the Partit Socialista Unificat de Catalunya (PSUC, Unified Socialist Party of Catalunya), created in 1936. His political commitment extended across the spectrum from practice to action. Though he died fighting in the Civil War in 1939, he remained an important presence throughout Bonet's career. Torres Clavé's passionate politics complemented Sert's more businesslike approach to architecture, while at the same time impressing the young Bonet with the heroic potential of modern architecture and the tragic consequences of political investment.

In stark contrast to his partner, Sert was closer to the liberalism of philosopher José Ortega y Gasset, whose articles he read carefully and cited for many years. Ortega edited the journal *Revista de Occidente*, which was critical of the monarchy and in favor of a republic led by "the most prepared and capable Spaniards,"[5] an enlightened elite that would guide the ungovernable masses. Here modern art played a key role. Accessible only to a few, it had the potential to help the elite "to know and recognize each other amid the grayness of the crowd, and to learn their role, which consists of being the few who have to struggle against the many."[6] Following Ortega's thinking, Sert belonged to a series of elite intellectual groups operating close to sources of power but more detached in their politics. This thinking was reinforced in Bonet when the young architecture student attended the Universidad Internacional de Verano de Santander (Santander Summer International University) in 1934, organized by Francisco Giner de los Ríos through the Institución Libre de Enseñanza (ILE, Free Teaching Institution) and supported by Ortega.[7] The ILE was a progressive pedagogical initiative of the Spanish Republic to separate education from religion or morals and create an "aristocracy of the spirit" by cultivating small elite groups that would eventually enlighten society.[8]

Through the journal *A.C.*, and later as director of the Escola Tècnica Superior d'Arquitectura de Barcelona (ETSAB, Technical Higher School of Architecture of Barcelona), from 1936 to 1939, Torres Clavé's socialism was the leading voice of modern architecture in Spain, while Sert's liberal politics guided the development of their architectural practice, which embodied these contradictions between revolutionary discourse and bourgeois comfort. The bulk of their work was designing comfortable upper-middle-class apartment buildings. The contrast between Torres Clavé's idealism and Sert's more pragmatic and business-oriented approach is paradigmatic of the type of alliances that were forming in the years between the creation of the Spanish Republic in 1931 and the outbreak of the Spanish Civil War in 1936. Trained in these years, Bonet was the product of these contradictory influences. Like Torres Clavé, he was an enthusiastic hard worker and a dedicated student, in contrast to Sert, who graduated with average grades and enjoyed the comfortable life associated with an aristocratic background. Bonet also shared Torres Clavé's idealism, an idea that modern architecture might be part of larger social change. But his politics were closer to Sert's—detached and pragmatic. Situated between these two role models, Bonet gave Torres Clavé his unreserved admiration and friendship but modeled his career after Sert, who remained a more distant acquaintance.

CATALONIAN MODERNITIES

This combination of revolutionary idealism and business acumen produced a specific discourse for modern architecture in Catalonia. The GATCPAC was initially influenced by discussions Sert had heard at CIAM 3 in Brussels (1930). This led Sert and Torres Clavé to apply Walter Gropius's arguments on rationality as common sense. They embraced and promoted the aesthetics, themes, and projects of the Soviet and German architectural avant-garde, but in their practice they applied these ideas to the Catalan bourgeoisie. As the editor of *A.C.*, Torres Clavé openly attacked the Spanish system of architectural training, based on the dictates of the Escuela Superior de Arquitectura (ESA). He dismissed the ESA's conservative teachings, heavily reliant on beaux-arts traditions, as a superficial and stylistic emulation of the past. However, Catalonia's regionalism and aspirations for political autonomy did not favor a movement that looked to foreign influences, prompting *A.C.* to search for local roots for the modernity they sought to promote. Torres Clavé found this ideal precedent in the Mediterranean coast, describing its architecture, objects, and traditions as the source of Catalonian modernity. While their first efforts had looked elsewhere in Europe for inspiration and emulation, Torres Clavé's proposal of the Mediterranean as protomodern allowed *A.C.* and the GATCPAC to claim a modernity of their own. Bonet would one day engage the Mediterranean as a post-Corbusian professional upon his return to Spain in the 1960s.

In an essay on Ibiza *A.C.* describes the architecture of the island through an enumeration of modern virtues: "simplicity, clarity, order, cleanliness, absolute absence of concerns over decoration or originality."[9] For the journal, these traits were also markers of Ibiza's *latinidad*, a word pointing to a regional community of Latin ancestry that preceded and transcended the nation-state, echoing the journal's Catalan loyalties and separatist tendencies and integrating the region to the broader Mediterranean region, including Egypt, Greece, Italy, and the northern coast of Africa (the issue of *hispanidad* vs. *latinidad* is taken up in chapter 4). The close connection between Catalonia and this broader Mediterranean community was highlighted in a special issue dedicated to popular Mediterranean architecture, highlighting the common heritage of traditional construction techniques employed in these different locales. Torres Clavé claimed that all these places had developed a similar set of "standard" construction solutions, with "a human scale and its absolute absence of superfluous decorated motifs and absurd artifices."[10] He argued that Mediterranean plans were the rational result of function and need, rather than the studious compositions developed in contemporaneous Spanish academic architecture. By claiming the Mediterranean vernacular as protomodern, Torres Clavé found a Catalonian source to validate modern architecture to a Spanish audience.

But while Torres Clavé was eager to put forward ideals of scarcity and economy for modern architecture, he had to contend with the constant presence of *modernisme*, a specifically Catalonian modernism that is still an important part of Barcelona's identity and visibly distinguishes the city from the rest of Spain. *Modernisme* had its strongest expression in architecture, particularly in the work of Lluís Domènech i Montaner and most famously in the delirious productions of Antoni Gaudí i Cornet. Gaudí's mystical, conservative Catholicism made him a problematic figure for the Spanish Republic, which was eager to distance itself from religion. Further complicating his legacy, the formal and structural audacity of his buildings was admired by more radical and complicated figures, in particular the budding surrealist Dalí, who was fascinated by *modernisme*'s organic folds, bulging curves, and elastic pleats for their potential to liberate the unconscious.[11] This antirational position was implicitly supported by Sert through ADLAN, which exhibited, promoted, and sold the work of Dalí, Picasso, and Miró as representatives of Catalan surrealism. Operating within ADLAN, Sert was less interested in the mental and political revolution to come from liberating the unconscious and more eager to explore these insights privately, by organizing brief, one-night exhibitions that were more akin to semiprivate spectacles, more conducive to personal titillation than to political revolution.[12] In turn these events were promoted and covered in the pages of the journal *A.C.*, completing a cycle of mutual support involving modern art, modern architecture, and the commercialization of both.

Thus the pages of *A.C.* contained both Torres Clavé's idealism for a Mediterranean modernity of austere materials and economy of means and Sert's exploration of the possibilities of surrealism for personal insight and enjoyment, uprooted from its revolutionary premises. Dalí stood at the crux of this conflict. Reacting to ADLAN's exhibition of the artist in December 1933, Torres Clavé penned a letter from the GATCPAC officially admonishing the group for the exhibition as "an insalubrious manifestation, in total disagreement with the tendencies upheld by our group."[13] ADLAN defended its decision to exhibit Dalí, marking an internal disagreement within the group that highlighted Dalí's complicated relationship both with politics and with modern architecture. ADLAN's alliance between avant-garde art and business was suspect for more radical artists like Dalí, who was increasingly engaged in mining Sigmund Freud's writings and turning the free associations of the unconscious into ambiguous political critiques mediated by oil on canvas.[14]

Dalí's work was doubly troubling to the architects of the GATCPAC. On the one hand, his paintings veered dangerously close to the imagery of fascism by including swastikas in ambiguous depictions. On the other, his writing pointed out their bourgeois roots through a devastating critique of modern architecture in Barcelona. In an incisive response to Le Corbusier's 1928 visit to the city, Dalí mocked the architect's affinity for the "industrial mechanical world," stating:

Beware the false appearance of modernity!—sad caricatures of the most superficial appearance of cubist art. Cubism is a product of its time, and resembles it,
but does not have anything to do with the decorativist, anecdotal, and picturesque
influence that it might have had in superficial, snob spirits.[15]

Dalí's critique of modern architecture was based on its contradictions: while
claiming to be driven by function and structure, he suggests, it is just as deco-
rative and superficial as the works it critiques. Dalí claimed that modern architecture's sleek rationality constituted a false appearance. He skillfully turned
modern architecture's claims upside down by demonstrating their seductive
qualities. While giving backhanded praise to the anonymity of mechanically
produced objects, the artist pointedly disparaged the beauty of handcraft and
ornament. While his convoluted language playfully invites misreadings, his
parting lament on the "hateful enamels, wrought iron, fire-stamped leather,
goldsmiths" clearly points to the essay's underlying valorization of the absur-
dity and beauty of the handmade, highly decorated object over the mechanically reproduced *objet-types* advocated by Le Corbusier.[16] It was also an
inversion of Adolf Loos's canonical "Ornament and Crime" essay of 1908, the
basis for many functionalist arguments in modern architecture.[17]

Dalí's critique of the Corbusian modern *objet-type* highlights the concerns with another part of the GATCPAC's operations: its use of the premises
for the exhibition, advertisement, and selling of modern materials and furniture. The GATCPAC was installed in a storefront that allowed it to display
the journal along with the objects advertised in its pages, modern household
items such as radiators, fans, and chrome tube furniture.[18] The group also had
what it called "industrial partners": industrial firms both local and international, including Catalana de Gas, Siemens, and Frigidaire. These objects,
artists, and distributors created a web of capital exchange, whereby modern
living was deployed as an assemblage of functional technical objects to be
sold and purchased. Modern art and modern design were thus components
of an aesthetic lifestyle, rather than part of an aesthetic revolution.[19] This
emphasis on commerce and bourgeois comfort was far from Torres Clavé's
politics, but the internal contradiction within the office was resolved when
the group began to focus on the city, aligning architectural and political
revolution by directing the architects to a more enticing client than the
bourgeoisie: the state.

As already noted, Sert's ambitions were closely linked to his connection with the CIAM, which was founded in 1928 by twenty-eight European architects led by Le Corbusier, Hélène de Mandrot, and Sigfried Giedion. Sert participated in CIAM meetings starting in 1929 and would serve as its president from 1947 to 1956. Throughout the 1930s the CIAM expanded the purview of its discussions from the building to the city, envisioning an orderly modern city designed in relationship to its region. Distinctly separate programmatic zones separated its basic functions (housing, work, recreation [during leisure], and traffic).[20] The architects were reacting against what they viewed as the chaos and insalubrity of the European city, which they considered to be a result of the primacy of private interests over the interests of the larger public.

These principles were summarized in 1933 in the Athens Charter, a document that consolidated these prior efforts as well as the conversations held in CIAM 4 aboard the SS *Patris II*, which Bonet had attended as a student when he began his apprenticeship with Sert.[21] This document, "The Functional City," emphasized tall apartment blocks as the preeminent modern solution to city planning. In this proposal for an understanding of architecture, the organization included a broad range of thought. While some architects focused on maximizing rationality in large housing solutions, others argued for more lyrical solutions in collaboration with art and poetry. The more rationally oriented architects eventually abandoned the group, leaving its leadership to Le Corbusier and Sigfried Giedion, who purposefully reached out to burgeoning avant-garde groups in different parts of the globe. Sert and Torres Clavé were a receptive and attentive audience for this outreach. Their approach to the urban was largely informed by the CIAM mandates and projects, lectures, and Le Corbusier's leadership. Paradigmatic projects would reject what they viewed as the repetitiveness and density of traditional cities in favor of elegant geometric compositions floating in large clean voids with clearly demarcated programmatic zones, which Bonet would emulate.

Eager to follow in his mentor's steps, Sert had courted Le Corbusier in 1932 to design a modern plan for Barcelona, with Sert leading the local team. This was the year Bonet started working with Sert. Le Corbusier proposed naming the project Plan Macià after the government of President Francesc Macià i Llussà, of the Esquerra Republicana de Catalunya (ERC, Republican Left of Catalonia).[22] It was never commissioned, but it established Sert and Torres Clavé's first attempt to collaborate with the state and led to their first social housing project, Casa Bloc (1932–1936), designed in collaboration with Joan Baptista Subirana and the GATCPAC. This exposed Bonet to the design and construction of his first social housing project. Casa Bloc upheld the ideals of collective living for the working class that were ostensibly one of the basic tenets of the group but until then had remained aspirational.[23] Its success suggested the possibility of a broader field of action in collaboration with the city and its inhabitants.

The idea of a self-appointed avant-garde figure leading the charge to design larger urban programs was problematic—it meant that architects were positioning themselves as mediators between the state and the masses. This raised the question of who the modern architect was supposed to serve: the bureaucracy of city and state officials enforcing the ideology of the state or the expanding populations in need of housing? Le Corbusier's eagerness to work with leaders ranging from Macià on the left to Italy's Mussolini (to whom he had sent his book) and Brazil's Getúlio Vargas on the right points to his preference for strong regimes that would lend stability to the large urban projects that he was intent on building.[24] Ultimately, Le Corbusier's priorities were not with the state or with the people but with his own ambitions to build and shape a modern world. Torrés Clavé and Sert would have had different approaches, but the larger commissions promised by a collaboration with the state satisfied Torres Clavé's revolutionary zeal and his interest in social programs and satisfied Sert's ambition because of the authority attaining such a program would grant him within the CIAM.

This Catalonian context had thus laid the ground for Bonet's formation as an architect, but it developed in tension with the strong authority and self-promotion of Le Corbusier in Paris, with whom he would soon work. Sert had spent a year working with Le Corbusier after his own architectural development and returned to Spain to become a leading voice in the cause of modern architecture. Bonet expected that his career would equally benefit from some time with the renowned Swiss architect. Although he was a dedicated architecture student at the ESA, his formation as a modern architect had really been through the world of the GATCPAC, where he spent four out of his seven years of architectural education. Through the GATCPAC, he first listened to accounts of CIAM meetings and eventually attended the congresses, as Sert was taking on an increasingly protagonist role. In all of these activities Le Corbusier was a distant but important figure who granted approval, inspiration, and validation to Sert's voice in Barcelona. Sert carefully courted Le Corbusier's friendship and mentorship throughout the 1930s, as Bonet observed.

In 1933 the GATCPAC sent five delegates, including Bonet as a "student member," to CIAM 4, where Sert presented the Plan Macià. Traveling from Marseille to Athens and back on board the ss *Patris II*, the twenty-year-old Bonet immersed himself in the discourse of the CIAM, later remembering the Athens Charter as "the most important document on urbanism of the prewar."[25] There he met important architects including Alvar Aalto and Walter Gropius, but he was most impressed by Le Corbusier. He remembers: "In that moment I told him that when I finished my career I would go to his studio. That meant a total change in my life. I graduated fifteen days before the Civil war started."[26] In 1936 Bonet finished his architecture studies and, without waiting for his diploma, headed for Paris in search of his next master. But he was not there. Le Corbusier had departed to Brazil on July 6, 1936, eager to court the large-scale commissions that he glimpsed across the Atlantic.[27]

THE PAVILION OF THE SPANISH REPUBLIC

On July 17, 1936, Franco invaded Spain from Morocco and started the Spanish Civil War. Bonet had just arrived in Paris and was quickly followed by Sert.[28] The two Catalans, who left as the conflict worsened, would soon lead the design and building of the most important architectural monument to the cause. In collaboration with Luis Lacasa, Sert designed the pavilion of the Spanish Republic in the Paris International Exhibition of Arts and Technology of 1937.[29] He delegated the construction supervision and some design components to Bonet.[30] Although the building was paradigmatic of Spanish modern architecture, its architects prioritized other agendas. Lacasa was more committed to the politics of the republic than to the ideology of modern architecture, and Sert was eager to mobilize his close collaboration with Picasso, Miró, and Calder, all formerly sponsored and promoted by ADLAN. The success of this project was another key moment in the development of Bonet's thinking. To understand the insights that he extracted, let us now turn to the pavilion and the collaboration between Catalan surrealism and modern architecture that it embodies.[31]

The Paris International Exhibition of 1937, with its large monumental displays, was a powerful and memorable translation of political tension between nation-states into built space, particularly what was occurring between the war in Spain and the start of World War II. As their later texts on monumentality show, it would haunt Sert and Giedion as a reminder of the power of architecture to assert the politics of states and human groups.[32] Though overshadowed in scale by the neoclassical monumentality of the rival Germany and USSR pavilions, the small Pavilion of the Spanish Republic had a strong presence: its modern art and architecture were deployed to promote the cause of the Second Republic, the democratic government established in Spain in 1931. Sert remembers:

The objective of the pavilion was to expose to the world the situation of the country at war, to inform about the true conditions and the heroic fight of a people defending their rights. This, with the purpose of countering the many false rumors that the press was circulating at that point.[33]

However, the political objectives of the structure were not as straightforward as Sert claimed. According to Sert, the pavilion continued the work of the Spanish Embassy in Paris, which had started as an information and exhibition center in the Boulevard de la Madeleine. A photograph among the pictures of the pavilion saved in Sert's archive shows an image of a young woman in uniform in the middle of giving a speech.[34] She is perched on some sort of stage and surrounded by uniformed men. The background seems to correspond to the corner of the Boulevard de la Madeleine. This small snapshot gives us a sense of Sert's attention to the ways in which propaganda, public speech, and aesthetics fluidly interacted at this moment on the eve of the war. The Spanish Republic's participation in the exhibition was confirmed shortly before the outbreak of the Spanish Civil War. It involved a large contingent of curators, artists, and architects, led by artist and graphic designer Josep Renau, who was appointed as director of the Dirección General de Bellas Artes (DGBA, General Fine Arts Department).[35] While the pavilion was being built, the Spanish Republic transitioned away from the more radical government of prime minister and minister of war Francisco Largo Caballero (1936–1937), which supported trade unions and anarchist groups, to the more dictatorial leadership style of Juan Negrín, who was closer to Joseph Stalin and the Soviet Union. Caballero and Negrín were part of the Partido Socialista Obrero Español (PSOE, Spanish Socialist Workers' Party). This shift meant that the pavilion was initially supposed to include a broad political spectrum united under the banner of the Second Spanish Republic but ended up presenting a more rigid national identity against a common enemy.[36]

The pavilion itself was a deceptively simple three-story box along the main axis of the Jardins de Trocadéro, in front of the fountain and just one pavilion away from the towering German pavilion.[37] The metal structure, painted in appropriately leftist dark red, was three floors high, eight spans wide, and two spans deep (FIGURE 1.02). The whole second floor front and back façades were covered in glass, with the exception of the last module on the right of the front facade. The blank panels there turned the corner and wrapped to the other side. They were used to mount photomontages designed by Renau. These large images advertised the cause of the republic, turning the building into a three-dimensional journal whose pages were changed periodically during public hours, throughout the duration of the exhibition.[38] Murals, sculptures,

FIGURE 1.02.
Exterior. José Luis Sert
and Luis Lacasa, Pavilion
of the Spanish Republic
(1937). JLSC, courtesy
FLL, Harvard University
GSD.

photographs, and artisanal objects were inserted within the walls of the pavilion or fitted specifically to it, with a series of stairs and ramps snaking their way through them. But the building was not only a container for these objects. It was an intrinsic part of a narrative organized around an architectural promenade that deliberately positioned its spectators to orchestrate and maximize their reception of strategically situated artworks.

The promenade started outside the building with a tall, totemlike sculpture by Spanish artist Alberto Sánchez Pérez, titled *El pueblo español tiene un camino que conduce a una estrella* (The Spanish people have a road that leads to a star).[39] Although Sánchez was from Toledo, Spain, his piece referenced Catalan *modernisme* through its organic shape covered with the characteristic *trencadís* (broken ceramic pieces) favored by Gaudí. The title pointed to the metaphorical road to revolution, which was played out in the pavilion as a literal architectural promenade.

The sculpture signaled the main access to the open ground floor, which was dominated by two key works: in the center by Alexander Calder's *Fountain of Mercury*, an homage to the mercury miners of Almadén and their struggle against the forces of Franco,[40] and Picasso's *Guernica*, meant to represent the horror and destruction caused by the very recent fascist bombardment of the small town on April 26, 1937.[41] On the opposite side of the main space, a glass case dedicated to the memory of Federico García Lorca reminded visitors of the poet's recent death at the hands of a fascist death squad—it also hit a personal note, as the poet had been a close friend of several of the artists involved in the pavilion. These artworks were built into the floors and walls of the pavilion or fitted specifically to it. Calder's fountain required special coordination. Bonet was in charge of installing its complex moving mechanism, including a deposit of mercury in an underground cistern.[42] *Guernica* had been commissioned as a mural but was done on canvas because Picasso wanted to work in his studio.[43] The architects provided the artist with the dimensions for the work (3.45 meters × 7.70 meters) so it would fit exactly within its assigned space in the building, which framed it by curving slightly inward in a gentle protective gesture. Together, these pieces illustrated the pain and violence caused by Franco's forces throughout Spain, but they also pointed to the collaboration between artists and architects, artworks and architectural spaces, in the assemblage of a promenade that went beyond Le Corbusier's self-centered circulation. Bonet extracted insights from all these aspects of the work.

Attentive visitors would have noted that a structural column was missing in front of *Guernica*'s canvas (**FIGURE 1.03**). The structural grid was broken

FIGURE 1.03.
View from the back. José Luis Sert and Luis Lacasa, Pavilion of the Spanish Republic. JLSC, courtesy FLL, Harvard University GSD.

between the fountain and the painting to allow for a better view of Picasso's work—a decision that Sert later admitted was made, impulsively and perilously, on the eve of the inauguration.[44] Historian Josep Rovira describes the moment as architecture accepting "its role as a means to an end... it can disappear without a trace."[45] The absence of the column points more likely to the intimate, often improvised relationship between artworks and building. Furthermore, by slightly curving the walls on both sides of *Guernica*, the architects increased the impression that the painting was a mural. As the wall with curved edges pulled back from the metallic structure, from the outside it hinted at a Corbusian free plan. More importantly, this adjustment distinguished it from Renau's panels on the façade above. This special treatment of Picasso's work actually extended to the spatial organization of the entire pavilion, turning the building into an actor in constant dialogue with the artworks, accommodating them, but also shaping their reception and arranging them into a unified procession through a series of specific spatial tactics.

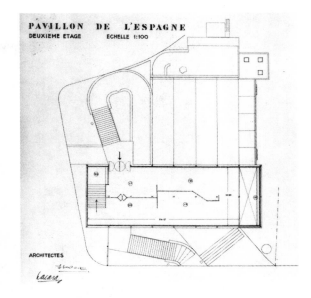

FIGURE 1.04.
Second floor plan. José Luis Sert and Luis Lacasa, Pavilion of the Spanish Republic (1937). JLSC, courtesy FLL, Harvard University GSD.

Beyond the ground floor, the visitor would have found a courtyard culminating in a small amphitheater, dedicated to a film series curated by surrealist film director Luis Buñuel. A large U-shaped combination of ramp and stair led visitors away from the building, wrapping around a tree and returning to deposit them directly on the second floor (FIGURE 1.04). Here the ramp's handrail continued on the other side of a wall featuring Miró's mural *The Reaper*. However, many visitors would have missed it, since the direction of travel led away from the mural and toward a series of Picasso sculptures, turned to greet the perambulating crowd.[46] The whole floor was illuminated by a glass ceiling filtering the light from windows above. The hallway led to the opposite end of the building, where a double-height space, open to the floor below, presented a large map of Spain framed by the seals of Catalonia and Euzkadi, which proclaimed these regions' right to autonomous government within the Spanish Republic.[47] The Euzkadi people populate the Basque country where Guernica is located, so arriving at this mural by walking past Picasso's sculptures was a deliberate reminder of the painting, which was located directly underneath the map. With this charged double-height void, the building referenced the painting as absence, expanding and enhancing its powerful presence below.

Following this experience, visitors continued the circulation away from the double-height space and through a section on popular art, followed by a display of the Basque country and war photographs and maps. At the start of this section, a life-sized mannequin represented a Catalan peasant in traditional garb including the *barretina*, a Phrygian cap. At the end of the corridor, panels depicting the war effort blocked the view of the stair to the first floor. Only upon turning the corner and reaching this stair were visitors confronted with Miró's mural, *The Reaper*: the Catalan peasant that it depicted was easily recognized after the encounter with the mannequin.[48] At this moment, careful observers would discover that the ramp they had previously used appeared to punch "through" the mural and then terminated in a star, toward which Miró's peasant was reaching—the star at the end of the road that had been referenced by Sánchez (FIGURE 1.05).[49] A sickle in the peasant's hand hinted at the significance of this architectural promenade: the path of the Spanish people led to the Communist revolution.[50]

The pavilion left a strong memory in the young Bonet. It must have confirmed that politically committed avant-garde artists could be recruited in the service of a revolutionary state but also in the service of the modern architect who wanted to gain authority and commissions from that state or for that matter any state. Beyond its spatial arrangement, experiential approach, and positioning of the artworks, the pavilion was ultimately a propaganda device: a media machine with the ability to entice and impress different publics. This ability to reach out to the masses connected the pavilion with the urban plan. Further, by demonstrating the architect's capacity to persuade an audience, the pavilion suggested the potential of larger projects in which the architect might effectively mediate between the state and its constituents. Le Corbusier understood this potential well and mobilized it in the Pavillon des Temps Nouveaux (Pavilion of the New Times), also in the Paris exhibition. Both pavilions were inaugurated together on July 12, 1937, the one-year anniversary of the start of the Spanish Civil War and several weeks after the official start of the exhibition, marking the inauguration itself as a political event.[51] The capacity of these pavilions to operate as media machines, reaching out to the masses with the message of the state, informed Bonet of their important function for the architects: securing commissions from the state. The star at the end of these architects' path was not the Communist revolution. It was the architectural commission.

"WE NEED WALLS LIKE WET SHEETS"

ARCHITECTURE AND SURREALISM

After the pavilion was completed in 1937, Bonet went to work at Le Corbusier's atelier, where he had a formative collaboration with Roberto Matta, a young Chilean architect. Matta was part of the loose circle of Spanish artists, architects, and writers working in Paris and would soon join the surrealist avant-garde. He was less enthusiastic than Bonet about working with the Swiss architect:

> The agency had no heating, it was rented to a convent in the rue de Sèvres, a hallway with a few chairs. Le Corbusier arrived always around five and looked around; his cousin Jeanneret was with us. In reality we worked for his book, we made drawings. There was no money and no works being built. We studied among ourselves. Sometimes he looked at the drawings we made for the Ville Radieuse. He did not teach and in terms of practice, there was none.[52]

Prior to arriving in Paris, Matta had spent some time in Madrid, where he met García Lorca and Dalí. In the spring of 1936 he volunteered to take Le Corbusier's Centrosoyuz plans to Moscow and spent most of the summer traveling around Europe, arriving in Barcelona two days after the start of the Spanish Civil War.[53] Somehow he made his way back to Paris and met the architects and artists involved with the Spanish Pavilion.

Matta and the Spaniards were undoubtedly united in solidarity with the struggle back home, although they experienced this period differently depending on their personality and political investment. Sert remembers that they met "almost every night" and jovially lists which people attended which cafés in Saint Germain or Montparnasse.[54] In contrast, Matta remembers the period as a depressing time and has no kind words for Sert: "The construction was late. Spain was in a civil war, the architect was bad, everything was sad."[55] Bonet also wrote down his memories of that time, and it is there that we see his connection with Matta and their common interest in surrealism:

> In Paris I would frequently see the collaborators of the Spanish Pavilion, who were close friends: Picasso, Miró, Calder, Alberto, etc., and Dalí, whom I met specially for his continuous visits to the construction site of the pavilion, in which he wanted to participate. In parallel manner I met a young Chilean, in theory an architect but really a painter, Roberto Matta Echaurren, and we became very good friends, since both he and I were immersed in a certain way in the surrealist movement, for which Dalí had fought in the preceding years in Barcelona.[56]

An undated letter to Sert confirms that Dalí solicited inclusion in the pavilion,[57] but Sert was not willing to sponsor the artist's ambiguous work. While Sert distanced himself from Dalí, Bonet continued to admire him. Bonet was further stimulated by his friendship with the talented Matta, whose paintings and drawings opened up new possibilities for architecture. Working together, and excited by the possibilities offered by the Spanish Pavilion's intermingling of Catalan surrealist art and modern architecture, the young architects began experimenting with the possibility of an architecture of surrealism.

Surrealism aligned with the goals of the Spanish Pavilion because the fight for surrealism was, at least rhetorically, the fight for revolutionary social change and against the reification produced by capitalism. As such it combined the interrelated models of Karl Marx and Sigmund Freud, both distorted through the lens of the surrealist leader André Breton.[58] Thus surrealists looked to Marx for a socioeconomic explanation of how capitalism increased inequality and produced social fragmentation, isolated individuals, and ultimately an alienated, commodified world. This alienation could be understood through Freudian psychoanalysis, which explained how psychic trauma splits the individual's mental psyche into the conscious and the unconscious, two aspects constantly at war with each other. Through interventions in both visual and verbal language, the surrealists meant to reconcile these two aspects of the alienated psyche and prompt a crisis in bourgeois consciousness. They also sought to learn from instances of "otherness" that they believed to be free from the alienation of capitalism and the constraints of civilization, including women, the so-called archaic past, and the so-called primitive societies of Africa and Latin America, as well as the supposedly irrational minds of children and individuals assumed insane or disturbed. These inherently racist, misogynistic positions, undoubtedly due to their privileged position as white European men, have come to define and undermine the main thrust of the movement. Ultimately, surrealism meant to operate on two scales, liberating individual human consciousness and provoking larger social revolution. Its problematic approach to specific societies and human groups was an attempt at examining the possibility of collective liberation.

In its search for "the ways to penetrate the deepest layers of the mental," artists sought and produced what Breton called surrealist objects.[59] These objects were meant to aid in "the systematic derangement of all the senses," as the result of "the cultivation of the effects of a systematic bewildering."[60] Following Marx, commodities constitute their value as socially necessary labor time represented by a nominal exchange value. The disconnect between the labor required for the production of a commodity and its exchange value produces what Marx calls "the fetishism of commodities," in which the social relations between people assume "the fantastic form of a relation between things."[61] By reconciling perception and representation, Breton argued, the surrealist object reveals the true nature of beings and objects, sublating the fetish character of commodities and reinforcing social relations between individuals.

A skeptical admirer of surrealism, Walter Benjamin was attentive to Breton's work and viewed surrealism as a "profane illumination."[62] Benjamin was keen on mining what he viewed as the "revolutionary energies" of the "outmoded," which could mean the rapidly outdated modernity of the first iron buildings or first factories or the no longer fashionable clothes or restaurants of yesteryear.[63] Benjamin also noted the surrealist attention to aging railway journeys, proletarian neighborhoods, deteriorated interiors, and ultimately the city itself, as noted in Breton's novel and homage to Paris, *Nadja*.[64] Benjamin was interested in how these objects revealed the putrefaction of wealth. By combining ruination and past glory, decay was able to exteriorize the workings of capitalism. While objects and utensils were part of this process, both Breton and Benjamin became increasingly interested in how decay is manifested in large buildings and in the city itself. Thus in exploring surrealist objects, they each turned to explorations of architecture and the city and considered the possibility of an architecture of surrealism.

Breton was particularly interested in the notion of the city as a large found object that might reveal the processes of the unconscious, which might be explored through aimless wandering—an interest shared with Benjamin, who wrote about the aimless stroller or *flâneur*.[65] Walking through Paris in pursuit of the elusive Nadja in the eponymous novel, Breton portrayed the city as a site of urban modernity subverted by the primitive and archaic traces of the past—a surrealist simile of the psyche, no doubt, but of a collective and multitudinous psyche. The city is conflated with Nadja herself in the novel (in both French and Spanish, the word "city" is female). Nadja and Paris elude Breton, leaving small traces in their wake: scribbled sketches, anodyne buildings, and forgotten corners. City and woman operate here as devices through which the artist can access the unconscious as the repository of repressed, forgotten memories, the locus of implicit knowledge. Within this urban landscape, the edges and nooks that have escaped the impetus of modernity become active triggers of surrealist desire. In his analysis of surrealism, Benjamin reads Nadja as an exponent of the masses and the neighborhoods of Paris as the spaces that "one must overrun and occupy in order to master their fate and—in their fate, in the fate of their masses—one's own."[66]

However, Benjamin remains skeptical of the surrealist project, which he describes as no more than an attempt "[t]o win the energies of intoxication for the revolution."[67] Ultimately, he finds it undialectical. For him, surrealism prioritizes the exploration of the occult, the trance of hashish, or the world of dreams over the "profane illumination of thinking" that a dialectical reading might extract from it. This seductive quality of the objects of interest of the surrealists' world—the danger of idealism—constantly threatens to override its revolutionary goals with superficial titillations. Such might be the case of the work of ADLAN and its private events. The exclusive nature of these events and the fascination with the potential to scandalize or titillate ultimately sidestepped any potential to transform aesthetic disruption into political consciousness, divesting them of any revolutionary politics.

By the mid-1930s Breton had turned his attention from the city to architecture. As a discipline that understands itself as both a service rendered and an art meant to affect the human senses, architecture has the potential to occupy a unique position within the catalog of surrealist objects. Following Hegel, Breton viewed architecture as the most elementary of the arts because of its dependence on the external material world. However, he was interested in precisely how this "elementary" art could reveal the powers of the spiritual life to consciousness like no other art.[68] He first noted this in the so-called

Palais Idéal, an elaborate construction by a postman named Ferdinand Cheval, who spent thirty-three years of his life building his ideal palace.[69] Remembering how he came to build the castle, Cheval describes dreaming about building, stumbling on a stone and admiring its beauty, and then gathering more stones during his daily deliveries and starting to arrange them to create this fantasy building.[70] The dreams, chance, and unplanned, protracted design process embodied in this account echoed Breton's own approach to accessing the unconscious. A photograph of Cheval's building was published as an example of automatic processes in the French surrealist journal *Minotaure*. Two pages later, in Dalí's article "De la beauté terrifiante et comestible de l'architecture 'modern' style" (On the terrifying and edible beauty of "modern" style architecture), the Spanish artist likened the rippling balconies of Gaudí's Casa Milà to a confectioner's cake, transforming that building into an edible object of desire and ecstasy.[71] The voluptuous curves of *modernisme* buildings were, for him, part of a catalog of real-world objects that provoked the "blind lucidity of desire."[72]

Together these two buildings outlined what an architecture of surrealism might be: for Breton, Cheval's castle pointed to an irrational, unplanned process that followed the whims of its creator, while for Dalí, Gaudí's more deliberate formalism prompted multiple associations with both sensual and sensory pleasure, from the edible to the erotic. While Cheval's work might reveal the workings of the unconscious as a type of architectural automatic drawing, Gaudí's edible architecture, via Dalí's reading, prompted its users to access their own unconscious thoughts and liberate the repression caused by the authority upon which civilization was built. Gaudí's devout, strict Catholicism—never mentioned in the essay but familiar to Catalans—supported Dalí's argument by confirming the repressed nature of desire. Breton observed a similar dialectic of repression and liberation in Le Corbusier's Swiss Pavilion at the Cité Universitaire (Paris, 1930): despite its exterior appearance of "rationality and coldness," it was originally intended to include a hall with what Breton misread as "irrationally wavy" walls.[73] Matta's drawings would soon take these types of gestures to new heights. In this context, surrealism's pursuit of revolutionary social change reveals Dalí's embrace of Gaudí and his rejection of the Corbusian *objet-type* as two sides of the same coin, embracing the former as a liberation of the repressed and rejecting the latter as a fetishized set of bourgeois commodities.

While Matta was eagerly engaged with surrealism's revolutionary potential, Bonet was more interested in the formal and sensorial experimentation it allowed. Influenced by their understanding of Dalí, Picasso, and Miró's Catalonian surrealism, Bonet and Matta viewed the Spanish Pavilion as a demonstration of the possibilities of surrealist art and modern architecture working together for the cause of the Spanish Republic. Inspired by this collaboration, they started exploring the possibilities of extending the insights of surrealism into architecture. But they wanted to distance themselves from the more orthodox, rational variant of modern architecture as practiced by Sert and embrace the potential for interplay between art and space that they had witnessed in the Spanish Pavilion as well as Dalí's enthusiastic embrace of *modernisme*. Their collaboration took place when they worked together at Le Corbusier's office, where they overlapped by a few months. This unrealized architectural project was designed by the pair on November 1937, a few months before Bonet moved to Buenos Aires.[74]

Le Corbusier asked Matta and Bonet to design a weekend country house known as the Jaoul House (not to be confused with the Maisons Jaoul in Neuilly-sur-Seine, 1954–1956), based on a preliminary project that did not fully satisfy him.[75] The Swiss architect's original design was a variant of his growing interest in the vernacular: a simple framework elevated on pine logs, organized around a central ramp.[76] A few service spaces were laid out on one side of the ramp on the ground floor, and the rest of the space was left open under a grid of *pilotis*. The upper floor included rooms for the parents and four children as well as a living room and a large balcony (*galerie plein air*). A large butterfly roof covered the entire structure.[77] Bonet and Matta kept a similar distribution of spaces and dimensions for the plan, with the same four- by five-*piloti* grid, but shifted the ramp away from the grid and transformed it into a more sculptural element (FIGURE 1.06). More strikingly, they turned the roof into an undulating wave hovering over the house (FIGURE 1.07).

For his only other project at Le Corbusier's office, the Water Pavilion at Liège, Bonet had rigorously drawn complex curves with regular, exacting geometry. For the Jaoul House, the curve is drawn freehand with colored pencils on tracing paper.[78] It strongly resembles the undulated roof of Antonio Gaudí's school for the Sagrada Familia church in Barcelona, a building that Bonet, Matta, and Le Corbusier knew well. The reference to Gaudí, in the context of Dalí's explicit praise, suggests that the architects were familiar with the surrealist artist's thoughts on edible architecture published in *Minotaure*. Interestingly, the gesture contrasts sharply with Sert and Torres Clavé's more rigorous, clean modern lines. Instead of the typical modern

FIGURE 1.06. (*top right*) Ground floor plan. Bonet and Matta, Maison de week-end Jaoul (1937). FABC, © copyright AHCOAC (Bonet and Matta).

FIGURE 1.07. (*bottom right*) Façade. Bonet and Matta, Maison de week-end Jaoul (1937). FABC, © copyright AHCOAC (Bonet and Matta).

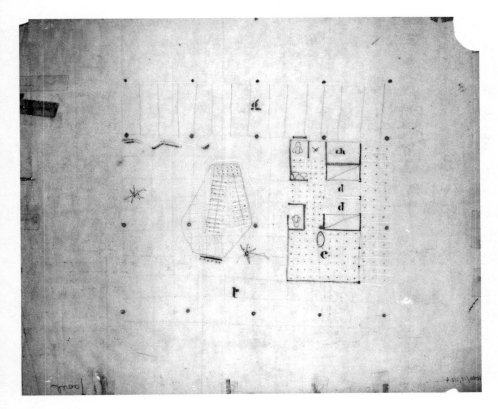

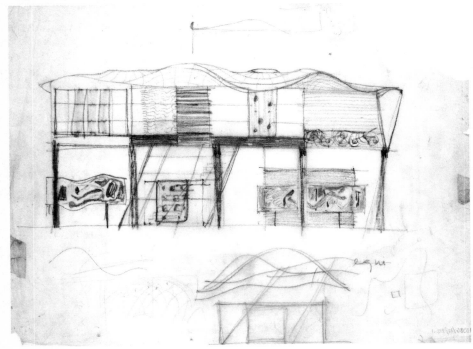

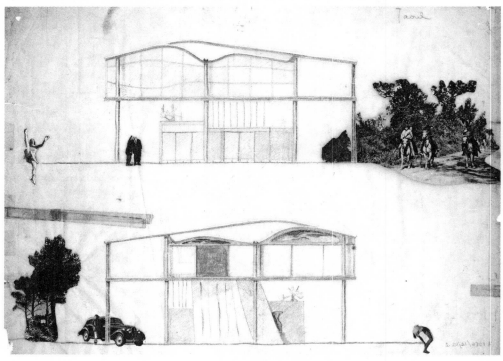

interiors, the elevation includes a series of panels with either paintings or graphic designs, some attached to the walls and some becoming the walls themselves, reminiscent of Renau's photo-murals at the Spanish Pavilion.

In addition to this first schematic elevation, the architects drew four sections with a more clearly defined geometry in the curves in the roof (FIGURES 1.08, 1.09). Here the roof consists of two parallel curved vaults covered by a larger vault. Bonet's affinity for curved roofs and Catalan vaults (suggested by his university projects and later work) is evident. These four sections are covered with drawings and textures similarly denoting paintings and painted panels as well as a series of curious cut-and-pasted photographs of trees, people, cars, and a dog. Altogether, although some details such as the gymnasts and car point to Corbusian tropes, the design and the presentation diverge from them. The architectural plans and sections were highlighted with colored pencils, and the murals hint at contemporaneous drawings by Matta (of which more later). The playful, quirky human bodies and plants inhabiting these spaces have been carefully pasted over the drawing, serving as scale figures in an architectural representation. But this would change in the next set of drawings.

The two sections that cut across the curved roof were drawn twice, and different photographs were pasted on them. The last two sections have slightly different qualities (FIGURES 1.10, 1.11). Here "nature" is represented with amorphous, independent blobs—a view of the ocean, a landscape with trees (FIGURE 1.10). Two men in swimsuits sit on top of the roof, while another blob cutout of a view of the ocean floats by like an unlikely cloud. A little girl coming from the beach runs toward the house with her sun hat and pail (FIGURE 1.11). The atmosphere is light and playful, but the crashing waves hint at violence. The curves of these nature blobs echo the curves of the roof: the ocean waves might be a direct allusion to them, as if nature were curving and shaping architecture in its image, moves that might be interpreted as an emerging surrealism. The human figures include Michelangelo's David, operating ambiguously between human-scale figure and sculpture. These figures are not always used to denote scale but rather to suggest a one-point, exaggerated perspective, with larger images in the foreground.

In a gesture unusual in architecture, both architects signed the drawings with the same colored pencils that they used to trace the lines of the sections and split the drawings (Matta kept the last two sections; Bonet kept the more architectural plans and sections). Although Bonet stated later that Le Corbusier was very interested in the project, the Swiss architect did not keep the drawings or request further design development. Bonet, however, remembered the design as an important moment in his development as an architect, in which he and Matta developed "all the things that for some time we had been preaching."[79]

FIGURE 1.08. (top left) Section. Bonet and Matta, Maison de week-end Jaoul (1937). FABC, © copyright AHCOAC (Bonet and Matta).

FIGURE 1.09. (bottom left) Section. Bonet and Matta, Maison de week-end Jaoul, (1937). FABC, © copyright AHCOAC (Bonet and Matta).

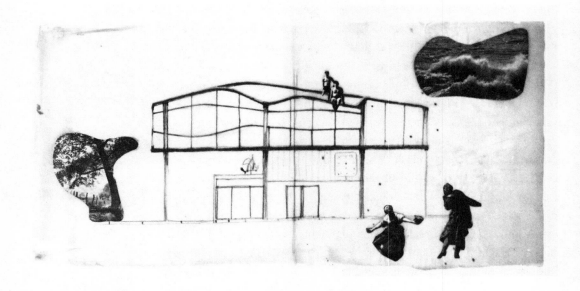

FIGURE 1.10.
Section. Matta and Bonet,
Maison de week-end
Jaoul (1937). FABC, ©
copyright 2019 ARS, New
York/ADAGP, Paris.

FIGURE 1.11.
Section. Matta and Bonet,
Maison de week-end
Jaoul (1937). FABC, ©
copyright 2019 ARS,
New York/ADAGP, Paris.

MODERNITY FOR THE MASSES

The artwork that Matta was producing at this time is helpful in understanding the significance of his collaboration with Bonet and the divergence in their later careers. Matta had been interested in the corporeal, organic possibilities of architecture since his days as an architecture student in Chile. In his graduation project, the League of Religions (1932), he literally modeled architectural spaces after female bodies, in a move akin to the casual surrealist objectification of women. Matta's formation as an architect led him to experiment with the depiction of space in later years. For instance, in *Fauteuils souples, pneumatiques* (1936), we observe a wall contorting and opening up a window, and a plane twisting and flexing to become a sofa. Other drawings have no reference to architecture and are populated by strange, biomorphic creatures resembling organs, fluids, and vegetation endowed with menacing, active postures. Bodies are broken, mangled, and distorted, particularly in two 1937 drawings that allude to the war in their titles, *The War as Civil* and *That Naked War*.[80] One of them clearly references Picasso's *Guernica*. The mangled and broken bodies depicted in these works speak to the violence that power exerts over populations, as revealed by the Spanish Civil War. Matta's friend, the surrealist artist Gordon Onslow Ford, remembers encountering Matta and his drawings in Paris in 1937:

> he invited me to his room, where, to my astonishment, amidst the banal *chinoiserie* of our hostess, were pinned his most exciting drawings, made with coloured pencils— the most extraordinary landscapes, full of maltreated nudes, strange architecture, and vegetation. . . . Matta regarded these drawings as a casual hobby and seemed astonished that I was so flabbergasted by them—I left that room a different person.[81]

Matta met Breton in the fall of 1937, a few months before working on the Jaoul House, and was encouraged by the surrealist leader. Only a few months later, four of his paintings were exhibited in the Exposition Internationale du Surréalisme, held on January and February 1938 at the Galerie Beaux-Arts, Paris, organized by Breton with Paul Éluard.[82] Before leaving architecture to become an artist, Matta produced one last work, an essay and collage prompted by Breton and published in *Minotaure* 11 (May 1938), under the title "Mathématique sensible—Architecture du temps" (Mathematics of the senses—Architecture of the times/of time), a loaded title alluding to several influences (FIGURE 1.12). The piece was prompted by Breton. In the midst of his 1938 visit to Mexico and in the context of his conversations with Diego Rivera and Leon Trotsky, he wrote a telegram to *Minotaure*, stating: "It is very important that Matta writes about architecture."[83]

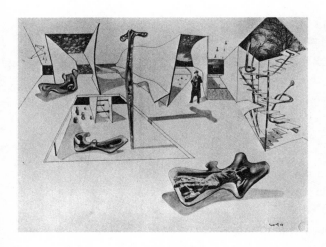

FIGURE 1.12.
Roberto Matta Echaurren, "Mathématique sensible— Architecture du temps," *Minotaure* 11 (Spring 1938): 43. © copyright 2019 ARS, New York/ ADAGP, Paris.

The use of "mathematics" points to the surrealist fascination with the idea of "mathematical objects." Between 1934 and 1936 surrealist artist and photographer Man Ray had photographed several *objets mathématiques* from the collection of the Institut Henri Poincaré. These objects transported the cold, rational world of mathematics into a sensuous, non-Euclidian realm. To Breton, mathematical objects could be part of the catalog of surrealist objects because they contributed to the derangement of the senses by showing seemingly equivocal, troubling spatial relationships in contrast to the ones perceived in our daily life.[84] They were incorporated in various surrealist exhibitions. Matta's title reinforces Breton's definition of the mathematical object. He sets up these theories of mathematics as the starting point for an architecture of surrealism, extracted from rationality and transformed into a spatial experience meant to "bewilder sensation" and operate like a surrealist object.[85]

This essay includes an image and a text by Matta. The image is captioned: "One's own space to become aware of human verticality. Different planes, stairs without railings to master the void. Ionic psychologic column. Flexible, pneumatic sofas. Materials employed: inflated rubber, cork, various papers, concrete, plaster, the armature of rational architecture."[86]

As in the Jaoul project, here architecture is depicted as a landscape of surrealist objects that echoes and amplifies their qualities. The collage depicts an interior space populated by amorphous blobs, with several openings suggesting double heights and long horizontal bands, probably taking cues from Le Corbusier's vocabulary. Through these openings we glimpse what might be a dark starry sky or bits of rough vegetation—a mystical representation of nature. But as the walls peel away toward this dark void, they lose their rigidity, warping and curving. Matta's text evokes a call to action: "We need walls like wet sheets that deform and marry our psychological fears; arms hanging between the switches that shed a light barking at the shapes and their colored shadows, susceptible of awakening the gums themselves as sculptures for lips."[87]

The sinuous, warped shapes of the walls are revealed as aids in the derangement of the senses: they are surrealist architectural objects that bewilder vision, hearing, smell, taste, and touch. Matta goes beyond the formal attributes of the object to give architecture semianimistic, biomorphic qualities that reach out to its inhabitants and their inner psyche. In both the text and the drawing, these qualities seem to emanate from "nature," increasingly a signifier for the dark forces of the unconscious mind.[88]

Around 1938 Matta began calling his paintings "inscapes" or "psychological morphologies," describing them as analogies for the artist's psyche and giving them spatial qualities.[89] In contrast to the hard materials of built form, here architecture starts becoming inhabitable "nature" or at least organic— soft, pliable, living-body organisms. Per the title, this is the way in which an architecture of the times would be a "mathematics of the senses": this architecture would embrace and provoke the humans that populate it, awakening their desires, hungers, and producing dreamlike images.

Who are these inhabitants? A solitary man stands in the threshold of one of the openings in the image. With his back to the outdoors, he seems to be pondering, taking in the space. A tall sculpted object described as an "ionic, psychologic column" slices vertically through the image, echoed on the right by a stair that seems to lead to an undefined outdoor area.[90] The organic, elongated vertical shape recalls Sánchez's sculpture at the entrance of the Spanish Pavilion. Sánchez had spent many nights wandering around Paris with Matta, while working at the pavilion. The gesture might be an homage to him and to the Catalan *modernisme* that he referenced in his work.[91] The curvy, sensuous outline of the column projects a straight shadow, similar to an architect's T-square. Landing near the man's feet, the shadow seems to mark him as an architect—indeed, his posture and dress resemble those of Le Corbusier. Here the representation of repressed rational thought is embodied in a modernist figure. Having worked for Le Corbusier for a few years, Matta was probably aware that he read *Minotaure*.[92] We can interpret this portrayal as a final goodbye to the discipline and an employer whom he did not appreciate.

While nature in the form of blobby clouds floated around the proposed Jaoul House drawings, echoing and maybe shaping its wavy roof, in the *Minotaure* collage we are placed within the interior of an unknown space: the openings to the outside show an infinite expanse. The night sky pulls us outside and seems to warp the walls and paths into the interior, while the curvy sofas respond with their softness. The surrealist dichotomies at play here suggest nature as an irrational force, pushing and pulling against the rational mind of the architect, Le Corbusier. However, Matta's title suggests another architecture ruled not by conscious decisions but by a turn to the sensorial. Following Breton, Matta was eager to explore the possibilities of disruption in the pursuit of a revolution that would be both personal and political. Eventually, the search for this revolution led him to abandon architecture to become an artist.[93]

But while such a revolution, artistic or political, was not part of Bonet's plans, Matta's enthusiasm for surrealism made a lasting impression.

LEAVING PARIS

Although sympathetic to the Spanish Republic's politics and to surrealist aesthetics, Bonet was eager to start his architectural career. His interest in surrealism, however, was related to the possibility of loosening the rational qualities of modern architecture. We can read Bonet's thoughts about potential new paths in architecture in a letter he wrote to Torres Clavé on February 11, 1938, a few weeks before the closing of the Surrealist International Exhibition. Here he explained his work and thoughts while living in Paris, which he describes as an initially sad and disappointing experience, stating that he had "almost forgotten his discipline." But then things took a turn, Bonet writes, particularly when he started working at Le Corbusier's office, where he began thinking about architecture "in philosophical terms":

> Hence we get into the psychological field (arriving in a certain sense at surrealism). This might be the philosophical sense of our architecture. Plastically try to give maximum sculptural value to architectural forms and to give primordial importance to color.[94]

Bonet was a poor writer. His description is no match for Matta's heaving sofas and walls with moist lips. Yet we should keep in mind that Bonet is writing to the architect who had admonished ADLAN for supporting Salvador Dalí. Eager to reassure his friend that he is not "one of those who run along Montparnasse," Bonet explains that he discussed these ideas at length with Le Corbusier, who was very interested despite opposing some of them. Sert, in contrast, knew nothing about this kind of thinking, being "as separate from me as I think he is from you." The letter is a reminder of Bonet's close friendship with Torres Clavé, who would die in the trenches of the Spanish Civil war the following year, and his more distant relationship with Sert, who would nevertheless continue to be an important presence throughout his career.[95] Bonet concludes his letter with news of his decision to leave Paris:

> I think I am very ready to decide to start a new life in a more stable manner, and here in Paris you know everything is temporary and theoretical. As an architect I want to start building, and you know here there is nothing to do. For all this and a whole series of reasons I have decided to go to Buenos Aires. There I have family and friends. And, above all, there things are being built.

…I feel confidence and enthusiasm. I already have some friends among young architects like me from there and enthusiasts. I think we will make great things. If we never get to make something using the GATCPAC system, I think we will make it better because I know all the things that did not work in Barcelona and I will try to avoid them (I suppose you know more or less what I'm talking about).[96]

Bonet gave Torres Clavé his address in Buenos Aires and asked him to send him the GATCPAC statutes and copies of the journal: "naturally I expect you to send me the journal. If I do something I'll send it to you too."[97]

As the political situation in Europe worsened, artists and architects started looking abroad. Many moved to New York, including Breton, Matta, Sert, and Miró. We will return to this expatriate community and their ties to South America in the coming chapters. In contrast to Sert, who had connections in New York and Boston and was fluent in English, Bonet was not.[98] Further, the growing Catalan community in South America promised more similarities to Europe, in particular to Spain and France, than the United States or Mexico. A strong Spanish and specifically Catalan migration to Argentina had increased with the Civil War. Bonet had some older relatives there.[99] But it was Argentina's youth that appealed to his European modern sensibilities: both the young architects who received him and what he perceived, as a European, as the relative youth of the country and the New World itself.

Years later, Argentinian writer and intellectual María Rosa Oliver described the members of the diaspora of the Spanish Civil War in Buenos Aires by saying they were "very proud of being red, although some were barely pink."[100] Bonet's architecture credentials rested firmly in projects that might be perceived as "red"—the image of the GATCPAC presented by Torres Clavé through the journal *A.C.*, which had circulated in Argentina, and the outspoken politics of the Pavilion for the Spanish Republic. But even though he joined other Spanish republicans in exile, his migration was prompted by his architectural ambition and his desire to build—and his politics were barely pink.

"NOW BUENOS AIRES!"

BUENOS AIRES MODERNITY

In Le Corbusier's office, Bonet had met two young Argentinian architects, Jorge Ferrari and Juan Kurchan, who had been set to work on an almost forgotten project: the plan for Buenos Aires, a commission that Le Corbusier had courted on his 1929 visit to Argentina and still aspired to secure.[101] Their enthusiastic description of the building activity going on in that city turned both

Bonet's and Le Corbusier's eyes toward Argentina.[102] Ferrari and Kurchan thus returned to Argentina with a mission: to get the commission for the Buenos Aires plan, which would give Le Corbusier a large-scale urban design project in a country that was not at war. These were the contacts that assured Bonet an introduction into the architectural world of Buenos Aires. They were also key in reminding him of the importance of large commissions from the state as the modern architect's strategy for success.

Bonet traveled alone across the Atlantic and arrived in Buenos Aires on April 9, 1938.[103] Ferrari and Kurchan joined him some months later but wrote in advance to their colleagues in Argentina about Bonet's arrival. Representatives of his Catalan past and Argentinian future waited for him at the port: a great aunt and uncle and three young Argentinian architects.[104] These architects were part of Ferrari and Kurchan's close circle of friends and colleagues, who had been alerted in advance of Bonet's arrival. In his first letters to his Argentinian colleagues still in Paris, Bonet writes full of enthusiasm and optimism for this almost instantaneous warm circle of friends.[105] He happily recounts meeting each one of these architecture colleagues and getting to know Buenos Aires, "a pleasant city, with a weather like mine, with friends waiting for me …I automatically felt adapted."[106] Buenos Aires reminded Bonet of Barcelona, but it was a very different city.

Kurchan's impression upon arriving back to Buenos Aires from Paris illustrates some of the contrasts between these two cities and between Europe and America: "Now BUENOS AIRES! Immense, feverish, colorless, building is done in such quantity, that you have to see it to believe it (but construction is bad, very bad, cold, rigid, sad)."[107]

Far from the violence and suffering taking place in Spain, Argentina was a country in the throes of growth and expansion, embarking on large infrastructure projects, with an active trade and a booming construction industry. Yet while experiencing this thriving modernization, the country was anchored to the past. It was governed by a combination of old landowning families and strong military that kept a tight grip on power and capital and gazed with nostalgia toward Europe as origin, while being intent on controlling a growing working class. Argentina's experience of modernity was different than Europe's, but Bonet's optimist vision focused on the similarities.

By the late 1930s Argentina had become a large-scale exporter of cereals, wool, and meat, which entailed the creation of a large network of refrigerated storage facilities, the development of sea transport, and the expansion of an impressive web of train tracks that covered much of the national territory, all converging in the capital city of Buenos Aires.[108] Goods were brought into Buenos Aires and shipped to England, the head of this economic empire. Between

1880 and 1913 British capital in Argentina increased by a factor of twenty.[109] This accelerated expansion required the elimination of the Indigenous population in order to appropriate their land and the aspiration of replacing these groups with a docile European population. We will return to the politics of this settler colonial operation and its consequences. European groups migrated to Argentina throughout the nineteenth century in waves that accelerated toward 1880, thanks to both demographic growth in Europe and Argentinian support for immigration through subsidies and propaganda. While these groups were directed to opportunities in the countryside, the wealth of landowners and investors was invested in the cities and most of all in the nation's capital.

As a result of this economic and social context, Buenos Aires had gone through an urban and architectural transformation. Large office buildings were built in downtown Buenos Aires, filling the center of the city with modern, well-appointed monuments to private capital.[110] Among these, the most notable was the Kavanagh (1934–1936), an art deco skyscraper built by Gregorio Sánchez, Ernesto Lagos, and Luis María de la Torre. It was celebrated at the time as the tallest building in South America.[111] These buildings combined an eclectic range of influences from art deco interiors to Italian and German rationalist and modernist exteriors, often focusing on the pragmatic study of city ordinances to maximize space. They were usually six- to ten-story middle-class apartment buildings or slightly taller office buildings for wealthy businesses. They were almost invariably white or neutral colored, with clean straight lines and repetitive fenestration (for offices) or balconies (for housing). Modern architecture in Argentina was formally present but discursively absent—it lacked the polemics of Le Corbusier or the militant politics of architect and Bauhaus director Hannes Meyer. Instead, it quietly and efficiently served the interests of private capital.

It was this building activity and openness to modernist aesthetics—rationality tied to the efficiency of capitalism—that had attracted Bonet to Buenos Aires in the first place. If the building industry had all but stopped in Europe, in Argentina it was booming.[112] This intense activity was recorded and promoted by two architecture journals, *Nuestra Arquitectura* (*NA*, Our Architecture) and *Revista de Arquitectura* (*RdA*, Journal of Architecture).[113] *A.C.* was very popular in Argentina (the country was its biggest client overseas) until its print run ended in 1937, leaving more space for local journals.[114] *Nuestra Arquitectura*, led by Walter Hylton Scott, evolved from a more eclectic and critical journal to an advocate of modern architecture in the 1930s. The journal openly supported both local and foreign modern architects, suggesting that the "our" in its name referred not to national affiliation but to modern dogma. Hylton Scott's progressive mentality was outlined in the journal's editorials, which throughout the 1930s advocated for the state's intervention in mass housing. Issues from the late 1930s feature clean white modern apartment buildings by Alberto Prebisch, Antonio Vilar, the firm Sánchez, Lagos y de la Torre, and Alfredo Joselevich, alternating with foreign architects including Gio Ponti (Italy), Frank Lloyd Wright (United States), and the California single-family houses of Richard Neutra and R. M. Schindler (Austria, relocated to the United States).

Nuestra Arquitectura's modern and international orientation contrasted with the orientations of *Revista de Arquitectura*, the journal of the Sociedad Central de Arquitectos (SCA, Central Society of Architects), the main architecture association of Buenos Aires. Although *RdA* also included modern work, in the 1930s it leaned toward slightly more conservative projects, with a preference for German and Italian architects such as Ludwig Hilberseimer and Marcelo Piacentini, echoing the Axis sympathies of the Argentinian state (examined in chapter 2).[115] *Nuestra Arquitectura* was a natural ally for the Corbusian team, but the architecture society's journal had the ties to the state that they might need for the scale they were eager to tackle. This is the architecture context that greeted Bonet, as he, in return, tried to inject his personal version of surrealism. He remembers:

> I was leaving Le Corbusier's studio full of rationalist architectural ideas and infused with the urban mysticism of the CIAM, to which I wanted to incorporate, enthusiastically, a surrealist essence. I considered that it was up to surrealism, the task of humanizing and individualizing that sort of Germanic architecture that was emerging from the different European groups. The cultural, social, and political reality of Argentina in that moment was a reflection of the intensely conflictive situation Europe was going through. Through a conservative government that intermixed with both liberal and pro-fascist politicians, the old oligarchy kept the control of the country; that cultured and Frenchified oligarchy that kept clinging to a luxurious and academicist architecture.[116]

Two assumptions in this quotation need unpacking. First, by assigning surrealism the task of "humanizing and individualizing" Germanic architecture, Bonet conflates the rationality and functionalism of modern architecture with Marxist notions of commodification. If the house is to become a machine for living, there is a danger that this machine might also come to replicate the processes of the factory line. Less interested in revolutionary processes, he focuses on surrealism as an entry point into the individual's unconscious and dismisses the need for collective change. The problematic result is a transformation of surrealism's tactics of shock into instruments of comfort. Second, while Bonet describes Buenos Aires as a reflection of Europe, his language points specifically to his native Barcelona, conflating his old and new homes. He describes how power is in the hands of a conservative government and an old oligarchy and identifies these forces with a "luxurious and academicist architecture." This language echoes Torres Clavé's editorials in *A.C.* and his critique of Barcelona's eclectic attitude toward architectural styles. Bonet viewed Buenos Aires as a Catalan and was more attentive to the similarities with his own background than to the differences of the new context.

AUSTRAL

Working at Le Corbusier's Paris office, Bonet, Ferrari, and Kurchan had planned on creating a modern architecture group in Buenos Aires called Austral, to be led by themselves.[117] It was officially started on November 23, 1938. The group's name, which means "Southern" in Spanish, emphasized its geographic location, a point of pride and identity in the Southern Cone region of Argentina, Uruguay, and Chile.[118] This desire to lead from the South, however, was complicated by the architects' avowed admiration for Le Corbusier, whose visit to Argentina in 1929 had left a strong impression. The ambitious architects courted any advantage they might gather from their association with the Swiss architect but ultimately sought to emulate their master in order to gain success of their own. Austral was founded with Bonet as president and Ferrari as secretary. Although these posts were soon forgotten, in pragmatic terms the group operated under their leadership, with Kurchan as a loyal collaborator.[119]

The founding document included architects Bonet, Ferrari, Kurchan, Alberto Le Pera, Abel López Chas, Samuel Sánchez de Bustamante, Simón Ungar, Ricardo Vera Barros, Itala Fulvia Villa, and Hilario Zalba. Villa (1913–1991) was the only woman in the group. She was part of Ferrari and Kurchan's generation and sent them the Buenos Aires plan that they used while working with Le Corbusier.[120] Her story, and the story of other early women architects like her, still remains to be told in architectural historiography.[121] Except for Bonet, the architects of Austral received their disciplinary formation at the School of Architecture in Buenos Aires, which like the ESA in Barcelona perpetuated a classicist tradition. They had been part of Ferrari and Kurchan's tight-knit group of friends, and many of them had participated in the European trip that brought them to Le Corbusier's studio.[122] The professor leading the trip, Alfredo Villalonga, described it in *Revista de Arquitectura* as a "return to Europe" and made repeated allusions to the benefits of reviewing "our architectural history,"[123] language that points to the relationship that wealthy conservative Argentinians had with Europe as a place of cultural and aesthetic origin. In contrast, members of this younger generation who founded Austral—Bonet among them—saw in Argentina an opportunity to go beyond the authority of the European legacy. They wished to break with what they viewed as the more passive stylistic reproduction and combination of architectural styles. At the same time, they looked carefully to the Corbusian model, in terms of both design and strategic self-promotion. In this context Bonet, Ferrari, and Kurchan's direct relationship with the master placed them in a privileged, leading position within the group.

Bonet also brought his Barcelona experience. His first impulse was to propose a set of businesslike statutes for Austral emulating those of the GATCPAC. To Bonet, Austral was "inspired by the GATCPAC of Barcelona, which had been guided by José Luis Sert and in which I had been formed."[124] The GATCPAC's statutes, adopted article by article by Austral, reflected the contradictions of a group that viewed itself as a part of the avant-garde but still needed its members to act within professional constraints.[125] The biggest change was in article 2, which modified the GATCPAC's intent to gather different professionals and promote and divulge contemporary architecture. They proposed a more heroic goal: "to fight for the progress of Architecture."[126] Like the GATCPAC, the architects designated themselves representatives of the CIRPAC (Comité International pour la Résolution des Problèmes de l'Architecture Contemporaine, International Committee for the Resolution of the Problems of Contemporary Architecture), the elected executive body of the CIAM, ambitiously self-situating themselves in this selected group. They vowed not to intervene in the particular activities of its members and declared themselves free of any political tendency or religion (statutes 4 and 5). The architects established a hierarchy of members (directors or active members, protectors, collaborators, students, and industrial members), based on the degree of education, background discipline, and economic collaboration or support. Additional posts including a delegate president, secretary, treasurer, librarians, archivists, redactors, and a delegate for industrial relationships were to be "renewed annually by secret and obligatory vote," lending a further air of mystery and exclusivity, though with the hierarchical structure and labor subdivision of a business enterprise.[127]

However, the situation in Argentina in 1939 was very different from the circumstances in prewar Spain, in which the GATCPAC had thrived. While members needed approval to both join and leave the Catalan group, Austral members seem to have attended sporadically, often avoiding paying their dues or missing meetings. Former member Jorge Vivanco explained in an interview that there were several groups, with architects and students flowing in and out.[128] The layered hierarchical structure did not work in such a small, shifting group—positions seem to have been assigned and forgotten. Furthermore, the war soon started depriving Argentina of its European markets and tightening the economy. The group had no journal for advertising revenues, had no building to display or sell goods, and depended on its members for income. The statutes were quickly forgotten. The attempt to reproduce the GATCPAC model points to Bonet's lack of understanding of the complicated economic and cultural realities of Argentina. It also illustrates the ways in which European models often needed to be transformed in different contexts and conditions.

By the end of 1939 Austral was trying to develop two projects: one for a University City (a university campus), led by Bonet, and another focused on workers' housing, led by Ferrari. A third project was an "Exhibition Pavilion" meant to advertise these projects as components of the Buenos Aires Plan originally designed at Le Corbusier's office.[129] The pavilion would also include additional city plans designed by members of the CIRPAC and CIAM. Zalba, Le Pera, and Bonet were ostensibly in charge of the project. Some sketches, probably drawn by Bonet, emulated Le Corbusier's Pavillon des Temps Nouveaux at the Paris Exhibition of 1937. Like that pavilion and the one for the Spanish Republic, this project was meant to garner public support and secure an eventual commission for the Buenos Aires Plan from the Argentinian state.[130] This idea later turned into a permanent building more akin to the GATCPAC offices. The group's minutes read: "The group's pavilion must be attention-seeking, façade panels to be replaced each year. It is necessary to make the exhibition more entertaining. Maybe a confectionery."[131] The rotating façades of the Pavilion of the Spanish Republic would be transformed to advertise Austral's projects, and the building would be designed to attract the public's attention through its architecture and a candy store. Neither this pavilion nor the other projects came to fruition. The Artists' Ateliers would eventually take up some of its intended functions, becoming both the meeting place and built architectural manifesto for the group. But first this manifesto had to be written and published in *Nuestra Arquitectura*.

AUSTRAL'S SURREALISM

Austral's mix of urban-scale commissions and avant-garde aspirations was best enunciated in a small publication that it produced, following in the footsteps of its role models (the GATCPAC's *A.C.*, Le Corbusier's *Esprit Nouveau*, and surrealism's *Minotaure*). Lacking the funds for a full journal, the group was able to publish an insert in *Nuestra Arquitectura* thanks to the sponsorship of editor Hylton Scott. Only three issues were published, in June, September, and December 1939. The back cover of the last issue featured the image of Bonet described at the beginning of this chapter. The three issues describe the group's goals and lingering ambiguities. It sought a clear break with the past while still depending on prior models and seeking Le Corbusier's approval. Moreover, the group positioned itself as both an avant-garde revolutionary group and a business-oriented association of professionals. These contradictions were intensified by Bonet, Ferrari, and Kurchan's decision explicitly to advocate for surrealism as one of Austral's models, despite the reluctance of their colleagues.

Austral's meeting notes describe the group's intentions for the journal's first cover: "a composition with photographs or the contrast between a Picasso thing and a technical object (an electric light bulb or something like that)."[132] This juxtaposition of art and technology summarizes the desired content of the journal, which displaced the more professional, pragmatic aims modeled after the GATCPAC with an attempt at surrealist language mediated with Corbusian rhetoric. The final cover combined an image of one of Picasso's head sculptures, similar to the ones exhibited in the Spanish Pavilion, an electric generator, the outline of a green square, and a photo of a row of men leaning against a low wall to create a horizontal line at the bottom (FIGURE 1.13). The Corbusian font of the title was one of several nods to their former employer. By representing art (Picasso), technology (the electric apparatus), geometry (the square), and people (as a geometric, orderly line), the cover articulated Austral's multiple interests: a union of art, industry, architecture, and an orderly, obedient population, lined up and ready to inhabit its buildings. The conflation of human bodies and the horizontal line also evokes the horizontal plains of the countryside, the pampas, from which the masses flooding into Buenos Aires came. But these masses were not the expected readers of the journal, who were instead the growing middle classes.

The back cover presented an extract of Austral's main statutes, highlighting a disagreement within the group. Here the initial goal of fighting for the progress of architecture, noted in the draft of the meeting minutes, had been scratched in favor of the original, less contentious goals of the GATCPAC, calling on members in other countries—architects,

FIGURE 1.13.
Front cover. *Austral* 1 (June 1939). CD BMIN, FADU-UBA.

engineers, builders, and industrialists as well as painters, sculptors, writers, doctors, lawyers, economists, sociologists, and pedagogues—to collaborate in the formation of the group. This was Austral's public: the growing upper middle class of Buenos Aires—ideally, wealthy professionals who might be interested in sponsoring their projects. From the outset, Austral was split on whether it should define itself as a revolutionary group—that would, at least metaphorically, fight for architecture—or a more pragmatic, businesslike association.

This ambivalence continued within the pages of the insert journal, which contained a manifesto titled "Will and Action" in both Spanish and French.[133] The text was complemented by a vertical line of photographs decorated with the black edges of photographic film and displaying a series of architecture icons, including the Eiffel Tower under construction, the Egyptian pyramids, Le Corbusier's Swiss Pavilion, Walter Gropius's Bauhaus, Filippo Brunelleschi's Florence cathedral dome, and the towers of San Gimignano, among others. While A.C. had avoided Gaudí, the journal Austral published two of his buildings: the roof at La Pedrera and the towers of Sagrada Familia. The lack of Argentinian images and the use of French suggest that the roots and audience of the architects lay in Europe, despite their name.[134]

The manifesto framed by these images took a polemical stance. The first part establishes continuities and ruptures with prior influences, echoing Torres Clavé's language in A.C., particularly his feud with the Spanish schools of architecture and their eclecticism. But it goes beyond local critique to denounce a moment of stagnation that they believed turned modern architecture into a style. The word "style" here is used derisively as an excessive trust in functionalism that has resulted in a new academicism promulgated by the schools of architecture. The architects argue that modern style, rather than modern architecture, has become one of many styles that architects could choose from, an "epidermic" (meaning skin deep), easy solution for mediocre architects that avoids the real, complex realities that architecture should confront. These complex realities, described as "the individual human and the social collective," help the architect bridge the scale of the building and the city.[135]

What is needed, they argue, is more contact with the plastic arts, in particular surrealism, not technical solutions that overwhelm architects: "The complete freedom that has allowed painting to reach surrealism, denouncing established truths and proposing psychological problems, has not been understood by the architect, slave of his formation." This dismal panorama, the manifesto continues, is the opposite of the fighting spirit of masters such as "Wright, Gaudí, Eiffel, Perret, and Le Corbusier."[136]

The second part of the manifesto proposes that architecture should follow the example of painting, which has "freed itself from all moral, social, and aesthetic PREJUDICE." Furthermore, young architects should revise old legacies and learn from surrealism:

> Surrealism makes us get to the bottom of individual life. Profiting from its lesson, we will stop despising the "protagonist" of the house to realize the true "machine à habiter."

> This same knowledge of the individual leads us to study collective problems not as the function of a unit repeated to infinity, but as a sum of elements considered until understood, the only way to arrive at the true collective psychology. Through these considerations we will reach a new and free concept of the Standard.

> The union of Urbanism, Architecture, and Interior Architecture is finally achieved.[137]

One cannot help but wonder why the modern architect should despise the protagonist of the house and whom the creative liberty of surrealism might ultimately serve—this despised protagonist or the architects themselves. The manifesto concludes with a salute to the CIAM and CIRPAC and the resolution to join "their spirit and their fight" in the study of architecture, humankind, plastic integration, and the solution of "the great urban problems of Argentina." With this language, the manifesto attempts to marry the Corbusian turn to the city with our three architects' interest in surrealism. They arrive at a synthesis and agreement through the idea of a "collective psychology." By studying this abstract entity, they argue, the repetitiveness of mass social housing, "the unit repeated to the infinite," would be transformed into a "sum of elements" leading to a less quantitative, more holistic understanding of the housing program.

The emphasis on psychology was prompted by the strong roots that surrealism already had in Argentina, matched by an even stronger fascination with psychoanalysis. The country had hosted the first surrealist group in Latin America, a short-lived association founded in 1926 by Aldo Pellegrini. Another surrealist group, Orión, organized exhibitions between 1939 and 1940 in Buenos Aires. The origins of Uruguayan Isidore Ducasse (who wrote as the Comte de Lautréamont) created a particular fascination with this surrealist figure in the region.[138] Freud was translated into Spanish in 1923, with an introduction by José Ortega y Gasset, a respected figure in Argentina. Moreover, while psychoanalysis in Europe renounced surrealism, in Argentina it did not: Enrique Pichon Rivière, a central figure in Argentinian psychoanalysis with a strong interest in surrealist art, even incorporated artists in the treatment of mental patients (for one of these artists, Grete Stern, see chapter 3).[139] Furthermore, psychoanalysis had ties to Austral. In 1942 Pichon Rivière and his colleagues Arnaldo Rascovsky, Guillermo Ferrari Hardoy (brother of Austral architect

Jorge), Ángel Garma (who became a close friend of Bonet),[140] Celes Cárcamo, and Marie Langer would found the Asociación Psicoanalítica Argentina (APA, Argentinian Psychoanalytic Association).[141] Ferrari himself was an advocate of psychoanalysis and kept a private record of his own insights.[142] Psychoanalysis and surrealism were close interlocutors in Argentina and part of a familiar discourse for the architects of Austral.

Yet architecture was viewed as a professional endeavor, distant from the vague and deliberately provocative claims made in the manifesto. Indeed this text was far from the strict statutes and businesslike attitude of Austral, and the rest of the group refused to sign it. Bonet remembers:

> In a certain way, the manifesto broke away from the principles of functional and rationalist architecture, incorporating for the first time the possibility of injecting the creative liberty of surrealism. This fact took some of the members of the group by surprise, which was why this manifesto was only signed by Bonet, Kurchan, and Ferrari.[143]

Austral's meeting notes show that other members of the group were reluctant to subscribe to the manifesto and its commitment to surrealism. Some members publicly distanced themselves from the journal and were later asked to quit the group.[144] This disagreement speaks to the conservative nature of architecture in Argentina, despite the modernity of some of its infrastructure, cities, and buildings.

The manifesto was illustrated with photographs of Buenos Aires by Argentinian photographer Horacio Coppola juxtaposed with a quotation from Le Corbusier (I discuss this image in more detail in chapter 2). Together these images present Buenos Aires as a chaotic urban entity in need of planning. This was followed by a selection of paintings by Picasso, Dalí, Miró, Henri Rousseau, and Marc Chagall. Two additional paintings that seem to be by Fernand Léger and Giorgio de Chirico point back to surrealism. In the middle of the spread, a series of quotations from Picasso, Novalis (Georg Philipp Friedrich Freiherr von Hardenberg), Le Corbusier, Breton, and others complement these images with surrealist allusions.[145]

Bonet described the layout as a collage intended to "make our new position more aggressive."[146] But there is nothing really transgressive in the form or content of the composition. The images are neatly lined up with the text floating in the middle, pointing to a dreamlike, poetic, somewhat nostalgic imaginary, with one exception. Perhaps unknown to our architects, the inclusion of Dalí's *The Weaning of Furniture-Nutrition* (1933–1934), which had prompted Breton to accuse him of "glorifying Hitler's fascism," was a return to Dalí's complicated prewar politics. This painting had initially included a swastika in the nurse's armband, a reference to the Catalan bourgeoisie's links to fascism. Was Bonet, who had admired the way Dalí "had fought so much" for surrealism in Barcelona, aware of these connections and perhaps intent on redeeming Dalí's reputation?[147] Bonet knew that Sert had decided to keep the artist out of the Spanish Pavilion. He not only included Dalí in the journal but expressly wrote to him and sent him a copy in the name of the group. Neatly placed between works by Picasso and Léger, Dalí's painting becomes one more allusion to a dreamlike, seductive world whose hidden motives remain covered, just like the swastika. The inclusion of this painting in the journal was a subconscious cipher of the contradictory statements of the members of the group. Despite choosing to steer away from politics, their allusions to surrealism and to a collective unconscious, as well as their desire to operate at the urban level, had political implications. In the context of the impending war, in which contemporaneous political strategies were looking to rally the masses by appealing to nationalism, neutrality was an increasingly untenable posture. These accidental affinities remained unacknowledged and unexplored but came to the surface in their architectural practice.

GENERAL DROWSINESS

The publication was Austral's first tangible output. Bonet, Ferrari, and Kurchan considered it a great success. Copies of the complete *Nuestra Arquitectura* journal, with the *Austral* insert, were sent to Le Corbusier as well as to local art, architecture, and engineering student associations and to influential Porteños, including Eduardo Mallea, Victoria Ocampo, and Enrique Bullrich, who had played an important role in Le Corbusier's first visit to the country.[148] Copies of Austral's insert were sent to CIAM representatives, including Cornelis Van Eesteren, Walter Gropius, Sigfried Giedion, Alvar Aalto, Gino Pollini, Piero Bottoni, Richard Neutra, and others. Tellingly, it was not sent to Sert, an omission that points to the long-standing distance between Bonet and his old master. Copies of Austral's insert were also sent to Dalí, Breton, de Chirico, Miró, Picasso, the journals *Cahiers d'Art* and *Minotaure*, and Matta. But this enthusiastic call to art and architecture would not be answered. The timing was unfortunate—the addresses in Paris that Austral was using were already or were about to become outdated. Many of the recipients might have never gotten the journal, which was mailed as the war was starting and many were scrambling to leave the city. Both foreign and local recipients were also caught in the fog of war, with local attention focused on Argentina's European trade ties and complicated neutrality. The lack of response dispirited the group.

Austral's momentum was unfortunately arrested from the start. Meeting minutes show the dwindling enthusiasm of its participants when jobs failed to materialize, donors did not show up, and the journal failed to find a local or international audience. In the first days of October 1939 the First Panamerican Congress of Popular Housing took place in Buenos Aires. It was attended by Argentine president Roberto Marcelino Ortiz and included delegations from the United States, Brazil, and Mexico among others, yet there is no record of Austral's attendance or participation.[149] The Sociedad Central de Arquitectos presented a project for workers' housing led by Fermín Bereterbide, an architect who had dedicated his practice to the design of such housing since the 1920s and had successfully built the Barrio Los Andes in 1931, a complex of four-story apartment buildings in Buenos Aires.[150] Austral's modern architects lacked the rigor and experience of figures like Bereterbide, who had already been working on the housing question for several years. At the same time, their firm insistence on a Corbusian approach to the city distanced them from other Argentinian architects.

Austral focused on publishing the third *Nuestra Arquitectura* insert and finishing the architectural project included in its pages. Two meetings in November 1939 further point to some lack of engagement. On November 13 the notes announce the start of a second phase for the group, only one year after its original formation. The minutes discuss filling vacant positions, propose new members, and establish a schedule of work meetings every fifteen days.[151] Despite this burst of enthusiasm, the next meeting on November 27 returns to general inertia: enthusiasm and willingness, but no action. When the architects wondered what happened with the issues of *Austral* that were sent out, someone notes: "There was no answer. Ask some of the institutions about what happened." The session concludes on a somber note: "9. Because of general drowsiness among the members, the session is adjourned at 12:30."[152]

Plans to display materials and reach out to industrialists got complicated as the state curtailed imports, limiting the availability of construction materials. Some of Austral's architects participated in architectural contests and placed well, but their success and their gradual consolidation as professional architects also distanced them from the group's objectives.[153]

Austral was meant to be a gateway to architectural commissions that would in turn allow members to produce work and gain prominence on the international scene. They had reached out to industrialists and business leaders for financial support and patronage and to international artists and architects for avant-garde credibility, but their call went unheeded amid the anxiety over the increasingly complicated international situation. Only one completed architectural project resulted from this initial burst of activity, and it would become Austral and Bonet's most important presentation card. It incorporated many of the ideas that he had picked up in Paris while working with Sert, Matta, and Le Corbusier. Appropriately, the architects gave it a French name: the Ateliers.

THE ARTISTS' ATELIERS (1939)

THE GRID AND THE PATIO

During his first months in Buenos Aires, and while Austral was taking shape, Bonet had enthusiastically sought and secured some architectural commissions. He designed these first projects in Buenos Aires in collaboration with Argentinian architects cognizant of the city's history, ordinances, and traditions. These projects combined his European ideas with Argentinian building practices. While collaboration was partially necessitated by the fact that Bonet was not able to validate his architectural diploma until 1954,[154] his enthusiastic letters to Ferrari and Kurchan, still in Paris, reveal a story of the quick friendships and affinities he was establishing with their mutual colleagues in Buenos Aires.[155] Similarly, these architects also write about Bonet's eagerness to collaborate and exchange ideas. Through this network of architects, Bonet secured projects to design and build in the first month of his arrival. These projects blend his experiences in Barcelona and Paris and his collaborators' expertise in the building typologies of the city.

In his first year Bonet designed four projects in quick succession: two small structures and two housing projects, all of which recall, in one way or another, his work in Barcelona and Paris. With Zalba and Le Pera, he designed a pavilion for Austral.[156] The design includes details from the two pavilions at the Paris exhibition that Bonet was familiar with. The tensile structure is reminiscent of the Pavillon des Temps Nouveaux of 1937 by Le Corbusier: the façade was meant to be changed on a regular basis, like the changing panels of the Pavilion of the Spanish Republic. The building was intended to function, like the GATCPAC store, as both a meeting space for Austral and an exhibition space for industrialist partners to display their products. Bonet also designed Terrazas del Sel, a set of parasols, of which little trace remains.[157] The single surviving photograph of this small structure shows a geometry similar to the Water Pavilion at Liège, a project that Bonet worked on with Pierre Jeanneret during his short stay at Le Corbusier's office.

The final two projects that Bonet designed that year were apartment buildings: the Cramer Street Apartments (unbuilt) and the Artists' Ateliers. Here Bonet's design ideas and precedents ran into the particulars of the Buenos

Aires grid, its building typologies, and the city ordinance. While Bonet's first two projects show how he adapted prior formal concepts, the Artists' Ateliers reveal the intersection of his European training with the formal restrictions and traditions of Buenos Aires. In contrast to the Jaoul project, which was situated in the middle of the countryside, the Artists' Ateliers were located in the center of Buenos Aires and thus were set in dialogue with the city's downtown and its inhabitants. The project and its publication also point to the ways in which Bonet attempted to incorporate his ideas about surrealism through a building that, like the Pavilion for the Spanish Republic, was meant to operate as an advertisement for its architects and their efficacy in manipulating the reactions of their audience.

The first challenge for Bonet was to gain a full understanding of the local building typologies and regulations. The *casa chorizo* (chorizo house) is an Argentinian urban housing type first developed in the eighteenth century. The typology was prompted by the city's long, narrow lots (hence the reference to sausage) and the lack of lateral setback requirements. Long and thin, it is organized along an open corridor, with a row of rooms on one side and a long patio on the other.[158] The type evolved toward the end of the nineteenth century: stacking the plan vertically allowed architects to turn it into an apartment building organized under the property regime of *casas de renta* (apartment buildings), a law that regulated housing until 1948 and created rental apartments. This was a common housing solution for the city's middle class.[159] The specifics of the municipal ordinance created a particular spatial approach for these apartment buildings.[160] In order to avoid overcrowding, the ordinance regulated building massing and ventilation through interior patios and permitted only one proprietor per building, so that most apartments in the city were rented not owned.[161] It determined the heights and front setbacks of buildings but did not require lateral or back setbacks. The only regulation in regard to the inside was to use a percentage of the surface of the lot for one or more interior patios (the percentage varied depending on the lot surface).

The combination of these regulations, the earlier typology of the long, narrow *casa chorizo*, and the single proprietor regime led designers to maximize profitable area with a specific geometry. Buildings extended all the way to the back edge of the lot and to both sides and extruded upward, creating one or two lateral inside patios to one side of the lot. The building typology in which a long ground floor lobby reaches to the end of the lot and gives access to two or three building towers, separated by interior patios, is still known in Argentina as the *casa de renta*.[162] The lateral walls (*medianeras*) are completely closed, as they usually butt right up to the neighboring building. The patios are transformed into long, tall light wells, which are the only source of light and air for the apartments in the back towers. These *casas de renta*, which populated the pages of *Nuestra Arquitectura* and *Revista de Arquitectura*, were increasing the density and changing the face of urban living in Buenos Aires.

This configuration contrasted with the Corbusian idea of isolated towers amid a large green expanse, but in these early works Bonet had to accommodate his work to the realities of the city. It also differed from the configuration of blocks in Barcelona, where Ildefons Cerdà's famous *ensanche* (expansion) project included a void in the middle of each city block, effectively creating a second, interior façade toward a more private space in the center, also conceived as a park. The lack of "air" (so to speak) in the *casas de renta*, compounded by the absence of lateral setbacks, created the need for interior patios and light wells. This gives the city a high density and long continuous façades along its streets.

A third formal component that Bonet had to address in Buenos Aires resonated with the Barcelona grid. The Buenos Aires ordinance determined specific conditions for corner lots, which still have to comply with a small chamfer known as the *ochava* (eighth). Within the city, most corner buildings use the ochava for a shop or store entry, creating a specific corner condition in which street intersections have facing shop storefronts. These chamfered corners are similar to but much smaller than the ones in Cerdà's ensanche in Barcelona. Furthermore, while the Barcelona sidewalk is chamfered, in Buenos Aires the corners of the sidewalks are only slightly rounded: the building itself shapes the geometry of the corner. While the Barcelona lot determines the geometry of the whole building, in Buenos Aires only the ground floor must be chamfered. The upper stories can terminate in a sharp corner. These subtle details thus create different spatial perceptions in the street intersections of these two cities: more expansive and open in Barcelona, closer and sharper in Buenos Aires. The apparent similarity and ultimate divergence between these two cities recalls Bonet's first impression of familiarity. Buenos Aires resembles Barcelona in some ways, but it is not the same city.

Bonet's other apartment building project, his first, was an unbuilt design for Cramer Street. The drawings are dated April to October 1938, meaning that Bonet started working on the project the same month he arrived in the city.[163] This was his first encounter with the city ordinance. In contrast to most *casas de renta*, Bonet took advantage of a particularly wide lot (most likely a combination of two lots), and chose to situate the vertical circulation on the middle axis instead of on the side of the building, creating a larger patio by sharing it between two buildings. This design was effectively a doubled *casa de renta* plan, mirrored along the circulation axis. Not surprisingly, the roof was solved through a regular system of Catalan vaults, and the typical modern double-height mezzanine was given an expressive curve. These characteristics were echoed in the design for the Artists' Ateliers, with a more regular mezzanine curve in plan, and a more daring roof section that points back to Bonet's work with Matta and their surrealist explorations.

A MACHINE FOR BACHELORS

In later lectures Bonet boasted of how the ateliers had been "the first polemical work in the country, which also shocked all the municipal ordinances."[164] The drawings tell a different story, one of careful knowledge and negotiation with the imposed regulations. The architects were cautious to label the lot's size as just under 10 by 20 meters, so that it would qualify for a smaller percentage of patio area, 12 percent. The ordinance required only habitable spaces to look onto a patio, so they used the whole ground floor for shops and moved the patio to the second floor, a conventional arrangement in downtown Buenos Aires. These moves point to a familiarity with the ordinances that probably came from the Argentinian architects who collaborated on the project, Ricardo Vera Barros and Abel López Chas, pointing to their participation in the project. In private correspondence to Ferrari, Kurchan attributed the project's more imaginative ideas to Bonet.[165]

The program designation itself might have helped with loosening the ordinance requirements. The architects avoided the denomination *casa de departamentos* (apartment building), defined by the ordinance as four or more complete, independent housing units with at least a bedroom, a kitchen, and a bathroom. Instead, they cleverly defined the program as artists' studios, which were not listed in the ordinance and thus had no specific requirements.[166] Bonet explained that this designation allowed them to take more formal liberties than they could with standard housing.[167] However, the only direct violation of the housing ordinances was the reduced height of the mezzanines. In a later interview Bonet boasted that his own "anarchist tendency" had led him to dismiss the building code and that the city official in charge was so excited about the project that he signed off on these relatively small transgressions.[168] Situating himself in the role of the avant-garde artist, Bonet wanted to shock. While certainly innovative for the time, however, his work was not as disruptive as he liked to claim.

Artists' studios were not common in Buenos Aires, but a few similar ateliers were being built around this time. The program for artists' ateliers might have been informed by a lesser-known building by Italian architects Luigi Figini and Gino Pollini, Villa-Studio per un Artista (Milan, 1933), which Bonet cited in later lectures.[169] In 1937 the firm of Sánchez, Lagos y de la Torre finished the Ateliers Tres Sargentos, a programmatically similar small set of apartment rooms around the corner from their better-known masterpiece, the Kavanagh building

(1934–1936).[170] Coincidentally, Bonet's first home in Buenos Aires was in Ateliers Tres Sargentos, perhaps inspiring the project. Two months after arriving, he moved to a studio in the attic, which he decorated in bright Corbusian colors.[171] The term "artist" here was more an aspiration to bohemianism than an occupational reality—these were *garçonnières*, bachelor flats for single men who could afford to live independently.[172] Thus they were neither *casas de renta* (apartment buildings) nor *casas colectivas* (collective houses dedicated to low-income families, of which more later) but a third, rarely used building type.[173]

The programmatic slippage from bachelor flats to artists' ateliers illustrates Bonet's slippage in his own understanding of surrealist aims and tactics: he was himself a professional and a bachelor, exploring both the methods and the life of the artist. The architects' description of the program explained the four shops on the ground floor as necessary due to the building's neighborhood, but the seven studios in the upper floors were explicitly proposed as an essential way to foster dialogue among artists in the city, even if their bohemian appearance masked the privileged life of the single male bachelor.

FIGURE 1.14.
Exterior. Bonet, Vera, and López, Artists' Ateliers.
Author's photo
© copyright 2014.

A LIVING MACHINE

The Artists' Ateliers spatially followed some of the characteristics of a *casa de renta*, with shops on the ground floor and studios above (FIGURE 1.14). They were

rented out by owners Ramón Vera Barros and his wife, M.C. Lavarello de Vera Barros, parents of collaborating architect Ricardo Vera Barros: the family connection explains the quick commission. The building is sited on a small lot on the corner of Suipacha and Paraguay streets, in downtown Buenos Aires. The corner site suggested the use of the *ochava*, which received the traditional chamfered treament as the front entry of a store. Contrary to the usual layout, here the corner pops out through an ingenious use of curves along the ground floor plan: following Suipacha Street, running north to south, a series of small store fronts undulates in and out (FIGURE 1.15). These waves recall the curves of the Jaoul House, here transposed from section to plan, prompting the storefronts to push in and out, activating the city sidewalks: the ripples in the storefronts seem to greet and tease pedestrians, turning toward them as they display their wares. They are echoed by the two barrel-vaulted paraboloid roofs that crown the building, another echo of the Jaoul House, but here molded to the corner site (FIGURE 1.16).

FIGURE 1.15.
Shops on Florida Street.
Bonet, Vera, and López,
Artists' Ateliers. *Austral* 3
(December 1939): 5. CD
BMIN, FADU-UBA.

A small, unobtrusive door on Paraguay Street leads up to the second floor, which is organized as a *casa chorizo* coiled into a C-shape, creating a small patio on the inside (FIGURES 1.17, 1.18). This patio, here transformed into a garden, puts "nature" at the core of the project. Most Buenos Aires buildings leave this space as a terrace to avoid the problems of the soil draining to the ground floor. But this lush green garden surprises the visitor as she enters the first floor gallery (FIGURE 1.19). At night it is illuminated from above by a strategically placed light fixture. A playful metal staircase climbs up to this light source, ostensibly for maintenance purposes, and highlights the double height of the space revealing the light source as the central point of the composition.

In the Jaoul collages, ocean waves and roof waves were juxtaposed with each other, suggesting that their similar shapes were both the result of natural forces. Here this external force is absorbed into the patio, transformed into a double-height interior garden open to the sky, right at the center of the building. This "natural" core ripples outward, prompting the storefront walls and vaulted paraboloid roof to ripple and warp in much the same way that the cut and paste "nature" that Bonet and Matta inserted in their collages. The vertical louvers in the round corner on the second floor open up to the

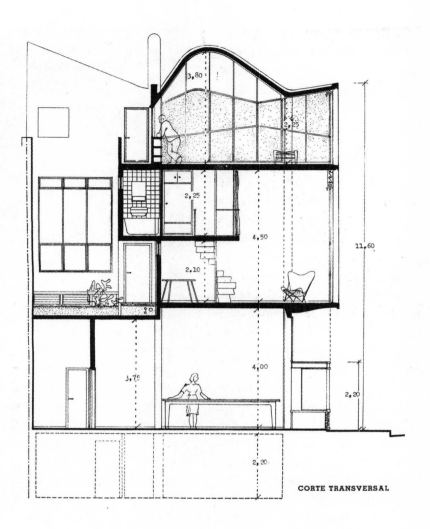

CORTE TRANSVERSAL

FIGURE 1.16.
Section. Bonet, Vera, and
López, Artists' Ateliers.
Austral 3 (December
1939): 9. CD BMIN,
FADU-UBA.

street intersection. As they form the louvered corner, they open up to provide the living space with an outdoor terrace that contrasts with the typical tight chamfers of the Buenos Aires corner or close to become a large curtain for the corner window (FIGURE 1.20). The different transparencies of the façade made with louvers, glass, and glass blocks create diffuse shadows at night, teasing Porteño *flâneurs* with the tantalizing theater of the building's inhabitants. The building reaches out to the street like a giant machine with parts that move or suggest movement.

The gallery corridor along the patio combines the traditional *casa de renta* typology with the modern double-height layout. Entering through a small bar-kitchen, the ateliers on the first floor open up to a double-height living space with generous windows onto the street. A circular staircase leads up to a bedroom

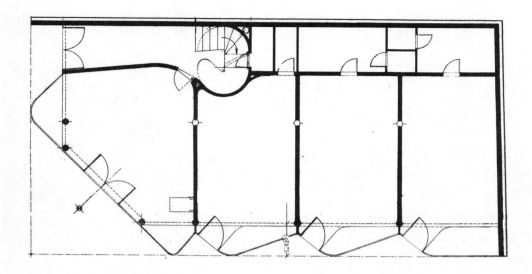

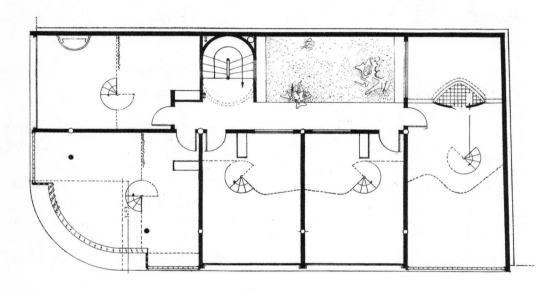

FIGURE 1.17.
Ground floor plan.
Bonet, Vera, and López,
Artists' Ateliers, *Austral* 3
(December 1939): 4.
Text deleted by author
for clarity. CD BMIN,
FADU-UBA.

FIGURE 1.18.
First floor plan. Bonet,
Vera, and López, Artists'
Ateliers, *Austral* 3
(December 1939): 4.
Text deleted by author
for clarity. CD BMIN,
FADU-UBA.

and bathroom that extend over the gallery circulation below (FIGURE 1.21). The curve of the mezzanine's floor plan here unravels down the spiral staircase, in a different resolution of this free-flowing line. Each apartment employs the same elements in different configurations, a variation that points to Austral's reflection on developing a nonrepetitive standard. The bathrooms are outfitted with vertical ducts that turn into playful chimneylike stacks on the roof, with a slightly anthropomorphic quality similar to Gaudí's chimney soldiers on the roof at Casa Milà. The top floor has two larger studios, each covered by a barrel vault with a parabola section, held in place by tensors underneath (FIGURES 1.22). The vaults stop short of the corner, creating an open terrace, a small, private roof garden split between the two units by a playful corrugated metal screen.

Several elements of the building's interior also move, pivot, and fold, recalling the mechanics of Calder's fountain at the Spanish Pavilion as well as the surrealist fascination with lifelike automata. Large doors in the penthouse apartment pivot open to allow passage into the bedroom space (FIGURE 1.23). The sinuous stairways and their handrails continue the theme, with the suggestion of movement. Built-in furniture elements operate as wall pieces, as objects, and in the biggest apartment as a closet that is also a door, rotating to provide access to the bathroom—a playful, surprising element that recalls secret passages. In a maritime allusion, the side door panels of the top apartment include

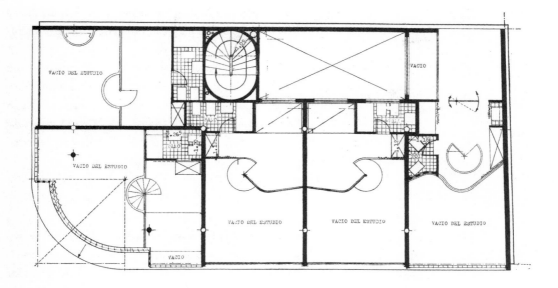

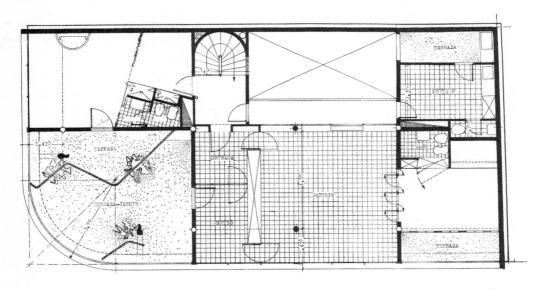

FIGURE 1.21.
Mezzanine floor plan.
Bonet, Vera, and López,
Artists' Ateliers. *Austral*
3 (December 1939): 6.
Text deleted by author for
clarity. CD BMIN, FADU-
UBA.

FIGURE 1.22.
Third floor plan. Bonet,
Vera, and López, Artists'
Ateliers. *Austral* 3
(December 1939): 6.
Text deleted by author for
clarity. CD BMIN, FADU-
UBA.

operable shiplike portholes. Another image of the corner apartment includes a rowing machine, playfully reinforcing the nautical connection. These elements invite us to reach out, move, and interact with them.

Moreover, the building's architectural elements flex, curve, warp, and acquire visible and tactile properties that stimulate the senses and recall references close to Bonet. Materials and finishes invite tactile exploration through their textures and colors. On the top floor, a reminder of Gaudí's *trencadís* shows up in a chimney in the front apartment, finished with red broken ceramics highlighting the hearth. The use of glass block and the curve in the corner recall Joyería Roca (1934), a shop in Barcelona that Bonet worked on while at Sert's office. They may also have been inspired by Pierre Chareau's Maison de Verre (Paris, 1928–1932), not far from Le Corbusier's atelier,[174] or by the glass block in Le Corbusier's own apartment building, the Immeuble Molitor (Paris, 1931–1934), an apartment with curved roofs that Bonet would have appreciated. It contains a niche bedroom similar to the one that Bonet designed for the top-floor apartment. Through the rippling and warping of the façade walls and turning louvers, and the pivots, folds, and rotating parts of the interior, the building as a whole is not quite a machine for living but rather a living machine, a surrealist automaton of sorts. Like surrealist objects such as Hans Bellmer's mechanical dolls, the building suggests the appearance of movement as much as realizes it. But if the Bellmer dolls became an erotic fetish, the only fetish within the ateliers is their own status as commodities, as tangentially discussed in the editorial of *Austral* 3, the last issue.

The Artists' Ateliers were the main focus of *Austral* 3, showcased as a combination of art and industry, modernity and surrealism. The graphic layout experimented with these qualities, punching blob-shaped holes through the cover, which featured six views of interior and exterior spaces of the project so that the reader gets a glimpse of the materials' textures (FIGURE 1.24). Hylton Scott, *Nuestra Arquitectura*'s editor, introduced the work, highlighting the use of industrial materials and its experimental nature and situating the building's modernity in the way it formally, materially, and programmatically challenged the traditional building conventions of the city. In this context, little attention is given to the ways in which the building molded itself to some of these conventions. The facing page reveals that the images glimpsed through the holes in the cover are the building's materials: cork, glass blocks, fiberglass, and reinforced concrete as well as two additional views. The first one is a photograph of the interior furnishings of a zeppelin, put forward as an ideal aesthetic that the architects aspired to but could not build with the resources at their disposal. The second is an image of a tall metallic structure under construction, suggesting that the project's ideas could easily be incorporated

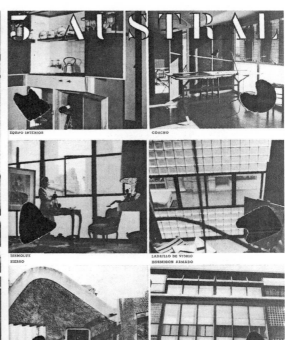

into bigger buildings—a reminder of the group's desire to work on a larger scale. A detailed construction section, juxtaposed with images of the corresponding windows, highlights the movement and openness of the building to the outside and reminds us how these materials are to be assembled. This collage of industrial materials, organic shapes, and small playful moments of surprise echoes both the building itself and the ideas put forth by the architects in their manifesto.

The publication, the building, and the manifesto all propose an architecture of the senses—Matta's challenge in *Minotaure*. This architecture is meant to be touched, moved, looked at, and listened to, poking and prodding its human inhabitants into interaction. But it also suggests that the attention of these senses can be recruited by architects to sell the materials featured within it, through the elaborate cover-display of *Austral* 3. The Artists' Ateliers might be a living machine, but it was also a machine for selling.

Austral 3 also included a page dedicated to one of Austral's most enduring designs: the BKF chair, named after its three designers, Bonet, Kurchan, and Ferrari (FIGURE 1.25). Its curved skeletal metal structure and organic leather sling summed up the combination of pragmatic functionality and organic

FIGURE 1.23.
Operable partitions on top floor. Bonet, Vera, and López, Artists' Ateliers. *Austral* 3 (December 1939): 11. CD BMIN, FADU-UBA.

FIGURE 1.24.
Front cover. *Austral* 3. CD BMIN, FADU-UBA.

FIGURE 1.25.
BKF chair. *Austral* 3
(December 1939): 10. CD
BMIN, FADU-UBA.

expression that the group preached. Sited in the large top-floor studio, the curves of the chair echo the curves of the roof. The rest of the issue alluded to modernity's shared aesthetic with the objects produced by so-called primitive cultures, which were posited as the intense expression of a private, interior world. To illustrate these thoughts, it included a few pages dedicated to modern sculpture, with examples by Jacques Lipchitz, Robert Laurent, and Constantin Brancusi (among other uncredited works). Additional examples by Calder and others were displayed side by side with some ancient objects of unknown origin, pointing back to the fascination with the so-called primitive shared by Breton and the surrealists as well as Sert and Torres Clavé in his editorials for *A.C.*[175]

The BKF chair carried within it not the lure of the exotic but the familiarity of the local. The leather sling that receives the human body came from one of Argentina's main exports: cattle. This detail reminds us that, in contrast to France and Spain, in Argentina references to the "primitive" embodied a different set of politics. Cattle are not native to America, having been brought over by the Spaniards. But by the twentieth century they were an important export and a source of Argentinian pride and identity. For the architects, the leather was not only thoroughly Argentinian, it was also modern: Le Corbusier kept an Argentinian cowhide rug in his apartment in Paris.

Austral 3's focus on materials also reminds us of the extent to which the group and its journal modeled itself after the GATCPAC and *A.C.*, particularly as they sought the patronage and sponsorship of industrialists, building component providers, and other businesses related to the construction industry. The entrepreneurial aspirations of their work was thus at odds with their avowed surrealist aims. Was the Artists' Ateliers a surrealist object or a vehicle for capitalist commodities? At least the architects thought it might be both. But the economic circumstances surrounding Austral ultimately frustrated their capitalist aims. Argentina imported ceramic tiles, timber, marble, rebar, plumbing, and other construction materials from Europe. But toward the end of 1939 the war interrupted all imports from across the Atlantic, prompting a return to reliance on Argentinian products and a reorganization of many of the country's industries to meet increasing demand. In this context, interest in the material experimentation and innovation advocated by the group waned and disappeared. In meeting minutes from October 3, 1939, the group agreed to use the top floor of the Artists' Ateliers—initially the studio of Bonet, Vera Barros, and López Chas—as its official meeting site.[176] Bonet's association with these two other architects, while successful at first, did not lead to more commissions. In the end, he moved into the top apartment of the Artists' Ateliers. On the back cover of *Austral* 3 we see him sitting on the floor of the terrace, with his back to the camera, looking over downtown Buenos Aires, perhaps contemplating this next move.

SHIP, TOY, ADVERTISEMENT

Bonet's accomplishments in Buenos Aires so far—the organization of the group Austral, the publication of a short-lived journal, and the construction of the Artists' Ateliers—were influenced by his Barcelona and Paris experiences. They include the GATCPAC and its journal *A.C.* as well as the influence of ADLAN and Catalan surrealism, not to mention the revolutionary environment surrounding the design and construction of the Pavilion of the Spanish Republic in Paris and Bonet's collaboration with Roberto Matta in Le Corbusier's office. Both in his collaboration with Bonet and in his own drawings, Matta engaged the dark untamable forces codified as "nature." Matta hoped that transferring the properties of these forces to architectural elements would appeal to the human senses. This "architecture of the senses" was also meant to shock and disrupt its occupants out of their complacency. Bonet attempted to do the same in his first built project in Buenos Aires, as we have seen.

But there is nothing unsettling in the Artists' Ateliers. Here Matta's attempts at disruption have been domesticated into a set of moving parts, an automaton that imitates movement in an effort to please rather than to shock. No one is bewildered. Instead of creating disruption, this architecture of the senses was mobilized to advertise its own materials and ultimately the work of Austral and Bonet himself. While surrealism aimed to bewilder the senses in order to reveal the commodified rule of capital, for Bonet this bewildering was only meant to return the individual to a more "humanized" state, away from cold rationality. The inherent contradiction of an apolitical surrealism is a conundrum that did not concern him. Instead, he sought to embody both the efficient businessman with elaborate rules and group statutes and the passionate drive and shock tactics of the avant-garde artist. These tactics, as it turned out, were more of an impersonation that presented him to an Argentinian audience as a prestigious member of the European avant-garde.

How the building was used tells a similar story. Rather than housing transgressive artists, it ended up housing bachelors, eventually including Bonet himself. In both the building and the architect, the desire to transgress yielded to the pragmatics of convention. Using a strategy based on Matta's architecture of the senses, Bonet meant to mobilize surrealism into an apolitical "humanizing" force in the Artists' Atelier. The project invites the senses to alertness: furniture asks to be swiveled, walls and roofs ripple and warp, windows and furnishings pivot in a graceful dance. But there is no transgression, only play. The building's movements are closer to those of a carefully articulated toy. As he distanced himself from the dramatic events taking place in Europe, Bonet was free to engage in playful experimentation. Surrealism's fascination with the dark forces of the unconscious had found different avenues for exploration in Europe. One of Ferrari's photographs from his Europe graduation trip shows that the Argentinians attended a Nazi rally at Albert Speer's Zeppelinfeld in Nuremberg, foreshadowing the dangers that lurked under this experimentation.[177] The Argentinian's pictures seem naively curious about these early events, but Argentina was also entangled in a complicated global geopolitical situation, with local repercussions that would soon affect and redirect this creative freedom.

In their poetic amalgam of surrealist phrases and paintings, Bonet, Ferrari, and Kurchan positioned themselves as avant-garde artists, but they were actually echoing the strategies of their mentors and using the tools at their

FIGURE 1.26.
Terrace. Bonet, Vera,
and López, Artists'
Atelier. Author's photo ©
copyright 2014.

disposal to advertise their presence: the group, the journal, and the building. In order to truly engage with the city, however, they would need to interact with the state; and in order to reach "a true collective psychology," they would need to reach a broader public of citizens. The public façade of the Artists' Ateliers and the journal can also be read as introductory efforts made to connect with this public.[178] Surrealism's sensorial tactics here would be a tool to demonstrate the architects' ability to communicate with broader publics and eventually lead to the larger commissions and to the city as an expanded site for modern architecture as put forth by the CIAM. Austral's detachment from the difficult politics that surrounded it hinted at the complications that this plan, like those of many modern architects of the time, would come to face. By 1939 the days of the ss *Patris II* and the dream of modern utopia were fading under the urgent realities of war. Atop the Artists' Ateliers in Buenos Aires, however, Bonet still believed that he could navigate that ship and use it to conquer the architectural landscape of Buenos Aires, a city he did not really know or understand (FIGURE 1.26). Let us now expand our focus to Buenos Aires and its mythic surroundings, the vast Argentinian plains known as the pampas.

chapter two

THE MACHINE IN THE PAMPAS

On June 4, 1943, a military coup d'état deposed president Ramón Castillo Barrionuevo, ending the so-called Infamous Decade, a period of fraudulently elected weak or de facto governments that had ruled Argentina since 1930.[1] Less than two months after the coup, Austral's architects met to discuss a call by the Sociedad Central de Arquitectos (SCA, Central Society of Architects), prompted by the new regime, to study the housing shortage. The result was Casa Amarilla, a monumental housing project with Bonet in charge designed for the new regime. The project, which was never built, was meant to guide the state in solving the city's housing problem. A photograph of the model shows how Casa Amarilla would have risen above Buenos Aires, a radical intervention completely disrupting the scale of the city and breaking away from its tight grid (FIGURE 2.01). While Casa Amarilla seems completely alien to Buenos Aires, it is a product of the large urban operations that were carving up the city's downtown area and expanding its edges, of the incoming crowds who were increasingly gaining visibility and power, and of the surrounding plains with which these crowds were associated, the pampas.

Buenos Aires's growth and layout developed in relationship to its blurry edges, extending into the large plains that surround it, a seemingly infinite landscape. The complicated history of this realm of the pampas includes its status as the last refuge of Argentina's Indigenous peoples, the wars waged against them by the state, and the importation of a European population lured to take over this mythic landscape. Despite attempts to eradicate Indigenous populations and replace them with Europeans, the two groups mingled, resulting in a countryside population inextricably connected to the emergence of Argentina as an imagined community.[2] It was this population that migrated to Buenos Aires in increasingly larger numbers in the 1930s, changing the composition of the city and becoming a source of fascination and anxiety for

FIGURE 2.01. (*opposite*) Photograph of model. OVRA (Organización de la Vivienda Integral en la República Argentina): Antonio Bonet, Amancio Williams, Hilario A. Zalba, Eduardo Sacriste, Ricardo Ribas, and Horacio Caminos. Casa Amarilla (1943). FABC, © copyright AHCOAC (OVRA).

the Porteño avant-garde. Groups of writers, artists, and architects increasingly focused on the city, its increasing expansion, and the crowds beginning to populate the edges. Their conversations quickly turned to the matter of governing these crowds. Facing the growing threat of a totalitarian state, these groups favored the idea of enlightened elites who might be able to guide the masses and their rulers. I follow these discussions as they relate to architecture discourse at the time, where the issue of monumentality and its role in guiding or controlling the masses was promoted within a network of journals and publications linking Paris, New York, and Buenos Aires.

In this chapter I explore Buenos Aires and its relationship with the landscape that surrounds it as the source of a series of cultural tropes related to its urban growth. We can relate this fascination with the pampas to the growing anxiety over the growing population of the city and its potential political power. These concerns were reflected in architectural discussions on how architects might mediate between these crowds and the state through monumental events and spaces by imposing buildings. In addition, two interrelated cases in which the center of the city was cleared reveal how the condition of the edges was brought into its very core. This occurred with the demolition of several blocks to create the Nueve de Julio, a large thoroughfare to celebrate the state, and the monumental Casa Amarilla, which Bonet and his team inserted into the center of the city. Casa Amarilla both contains and reveals the multiple relationships between center and periphery, between a powerful core of elites and the growing population that they struggled to control. Casa Amarilla was thus a stand-in for the machinery of a totalitarian state struggling to contain and control an increasingly resistant population that would take over the city in 1946, reversing these processes and ushering in the mythical birth of Peronism.

FROM PAMPA TO BABEL

PAMPAS AND *ARRABALES*

To understand Buenos Aires, we must think of it as situated within the pampas, the source of Argentina's wealth, where cattle and grain are raised. This link to capital generation was translated into a set of cultural signifiers that came to fill the literal and metaphorical void of these plains. In efforts to construct an Argentinian identity, Argentinian writers and artists repeatedly turned to this metaphorical space, inflecting it with their own artistic, cultural, and political agendas.[3] The most important of these interpretations is by the writer, journalist, and later president Domingo Sarmiento, who in 1845 wrote the essay

"Facundo: Civilización y barbarie" (Facundo: Civilization and barbarism), a key text of Argentinian nationalism that reflected on the early years of the Argentinian republic and the political struggles between the city and the countryside. In contrast to Walter Benjamin's later assessment on the inextricable link between both terms, Sarmiento polarizes the Argentinian city and countryside. He describes a clash between the cultured, European-like metropolis and the savage, barbaric pampas, with orientalist references to nomadic tribes and allusions to the Asian landscape. To Sarmiento, the sparse, "flat and hairy" (*lisa y velluda*) nature of the pampas discourages any type of society yet at the same time gives the Argentinian people a uniquely poetic nature:

> What impressions must the inhabitant of the Republic of Argentina receive with the simple act of gazing into the horizon and seeing . . . seeing nothing; because the more he sinks his eyes in that uncertain horizon, vaporous, indefinite, the more it retreats from him, the more it fascinates him, confuses him, and sinks him in contemplation and doubt? Where does that world end that he wishes in vain to penetrate? He doesn't know! What is beyond what he can see? Loneliness, danger, the savage, death!!![4]

Following Edmund Burke, Immanuel Kant, and other discourses on the sublime, Sarmiento transforms the pampas into a menacing, awe-inspiring presence of the infinite, invading and infecting the whole country with simultaneous feelings of attraction and repulsion. His description particularly echoes Kant's analysis of the power of nature as might, inspiring overwhelming fear and awe in fascinated humans, coupled with a feeling of impotence derived from our inability to resist its dominance. To this irresistible force, Sarmiento juxtaposes the metropolis, proposing that the nation might resist the barbaric impulse of the plains through the civilizing agency of the city.[5] And yet to him the "inhabitant of the Republic of Argentina" is the inhabitant of the pampas as a true representative of its history and culture.[6]

In the 1870s Argentina waged war against the native populations of the pampas through a series of military campaigns meant to eradicate them, take control of the land, and turn it into a site of extraction and capital generation.[7] Although these campaigns are known as the "Conquest of the Desert," the land was fertile, ideal for cultivating grain crops and raising cattle. The lands were redistributed to the military elite and colonized through an extensive railroad network funded by British capital. This connected the pampas to the docks and ports in and near Buenos Aires that shipped most of the goods extracted from them to England, helping to fuel the Industrial Revolution. To maintain control of the pampas, the state promoted them to Europeans, offering incentives to emigrate in the hope of changing the racial composition of the country and, following Sarmiento, turning it into a more "civilized" nation.

Between 1880 and 1916 about 2.9 million immigrants settled in Argentina, most of them coming from Italy and Spain.[8] While the goal of the campaign was to populate the countryside, most of these immigrants remained in or eventually moved to the cities, especially Buenos Aires. Between 1869 and 1914 the population of Argentina multiplied by 4.5, but the population of Buenos Aires multiplied by 8.6, reaching 1,575,814.[9] By 1914 Buenos Aires contained 46 percent of the total population of the country.[10] As the city grew, the myth of the pampas as its "other" was strengthened. It became the uncontaminated site of pure values, personified by the Argentinian gaucho. This mythical figure was the inhabitant of the pampas that Sarmiento had alluded to, based on the skilled yet unruly horsemen who tended to cattle and lived a nomadic existence in the plains. Gauchos became the focus of folklore and national identity, most strikingly through José Hernández's epic poem *Martín Fierro*,[11] which describes the racially mixed inhabitants of the plains where the last Indigenous populations struggled to survive. The gauchos' link to these populations hinted at their own tragic destiny: they were recruited into the very military campaigns charged with eradicating them. By the early twentieth century the gaucho had all but disappeared, but large groups of this racially mixed population gradually migrated to the city, determining its growth and eventually the politics of the country itself.

As the regional rail infrastructure improved and travel became more affordable, low-income populations found housing farther from the downtown area, on the south and west edges of the city. In 1888 the city limits were officially expanded from 4,000 hectares to 18,000 hectares, including a large swath of sparsely populated territory.[12] Historian Adrian Gorelik explains how the development of the urban growth plan of 1898 organized this territory into a square-based, uniform grid, a "homogenizing mesh laid on the plain" well before its actual occupation.[13] The city would not be completely urbanized and populated until the mid-1930s. The city's grid was complemented by a network of parks where public services and community initiatives such as hospitals, schools, theaters, sports facilities, and the first public housing projects were often concentrated. This suggested a more democratic and equitable form of urban growth. The small, sprawling neighborhoods growing on the city's periphery were known as the *arrabales*.

By the turn of the century the dichotomy between civilized metropolis and barbaric pampas was translated into the dichotomy between the center and periphery of the city itself. Through the 1910s and 1920s the pampas skewed impressions of the sprawling growth of Buenos Aires, leading writers to extend the qualities of the pampas to the *arrabales*.[14] Italian Massimo Bontempelli, visiting Buenos Aires in the 1930s with Pietro Maria Bardi as Mussolini's envoys, incisively read the grid as emulating the seemingly infinite horizontality of the pampas:

> Buenos Aires is a piece of the pampa translated into a city. This explains the construction in "blocks." . . . Repeating blocks to the infinite, one makes a city, with no boundaries needed. . . . The principle of repetition to the infinite, showed by nature with the Pampa, was scrupulously respected by men when they had to build the human world in front of the natural world.[15]

Bontempelli's language suggests mechanical reproducibility and the tabula rasa, both recurring themes of European modernity. Architects and urban planners were similarly quick to find modern qualities in both landscapes. Dismissing the Buenos Aires downtown as too crowded and chaotic, Le Corbusier praised the small cubic constructions of the *arrabales*, interpreting them as an unconscious modernity.[16] Picking up on avant-garde discourses encountered in Argentina, he summed up the whole country through a metaphorical reading of the pampa: "green and flat, and its destiny is violent."[17] These qualities were also embraced by German city planner Werner Hegemann, who visited in 1931 and proposed an expansion of the grid.[18] Overall, the European avant-garde eagerly picked up on the modern traits of the Argentinian urban and rural landscape—the infinite horizontality of the pampas and the cubic constructions and repetitive grid of the *arrabales*—and ultimately conflated them. The *arrabales* took on the sublime, menacing qualities of the pampas.

While attentive to their European counterparts, the Porteño avant-garde read the *arrabales* with a closer understanding of the city's geography. While the grid united the whole, the density and scale of the built environment revealed a cultural and social division between the northern half of the city, where older power and money resided, and the expanding *arrabales* to the south. Writer Jorge Luis Borges went as far as to locate the juncture between north and south in the long, east-west thoroughfare of Rivadavia Avenue, which leads to the Plaza de Mayo, directly in front of the presidential palace. Surrounding the plaza and the palace on the eastern edge of the city, a small downtown core represents the political power and capital that separates and governs both halves of the city (FIGURE 0.02). In common parlance, Buenos Aires is divided in half by this avenue into Barrio Norte and Barrio Sur (literally northern and southern neighborhoods), a division with important political, economic, and cultural implications.[19]

According to Borges, to cross Rivadavia Avenue into Barrio Sur was to enter "an older and firmer world."[20] Throughout the twentieth century the northern neighborhood was the site of a conservative, economically secure upper class.[21] In contrast, Barrio Sur was the site of the *arrabales* expanding toward the pampas and only technically bound by the ordinance of 1888, thus housing a working class loosely organized under various unions and the source of some of the city's more radical politics. The lack of north-south avenues connecting these neighborhoods reinforced their separation (I will return later to this physical and symbolic disconnect).

Aesthetic and political groups identified themselves with these neighborhoods, mapping local discourse into the very geography of the city and activating it with particular resonances. There were two main avant-garde groups: Florida, which met in Florida Street, north of Rivadavia; and Boedo, in Boedo Street, to the south.[22] While the two groups mingled and shared members and audiences, their geographic location and the journals they produced point to their diverging interests.[23] Florida sponsored an aesthetic and cultural agenda promoting European modernism with a detached political agenda, while Boedo was committed to the diffusion of radical leftist politics, although its engagement with art was in most cases relegated to the covers of its journals. Florida promoted several literary journals, most notably *Martín Fierro* (1924–1927).[24] Despite its title's reference to Hernández's epic poem, it argued for a break with the past and a new sensibility based on European modernism, although its models were often already outdated across the Atlantic and divested of their radical politics.[25] The journal's attitude toward the past aligned with the position of futurist Filippo Tommaso Marinetti, who visited Argentina in 1926 and was celebrated by the publication. While Florida members opposed the nationalism of the Argentinian state, many had close links to the country's economic elites. Boedo considered these attitudes conservative and elitist.

Returning from Europe in 1921, Borges was fascinated by the city's growth, though not interested in the politics underlying it. He was particularly drawn to the *arrabales*, where the empty grids laid out in 1888 were gradually being filled in with small houses. In a series of poems, most notably "Arrabal" (published in 1921), he captured the images of repetitive blocks and small houses, so different from the large avenues and monuments of the city center:

> and I was between the houses,
> [which were] scared and humiliated
> judicious like sheep in a flock
> jailed in blocks
> different and identical
> as if they were all
> shuffled, overlapping reminders
> of a single block.[26]

FIGURE 2.02.
Horacio Coppola, Florida
y Bartolomé Mitre (1936).
© copyright The Estate
of Horacio Coppola,
courtesy Galería Jorge
Mara—La Ruche, Buenos
Aires, Argentina.

Here Borges seems both attracted and repelled by the monotonous repetition: the cautious sheeplike houses, "different and identical," seem to stand for their inhabitants, similarly held in place by the repetitive, jail-like grip of the grid. Through his poetry, Borges transforms the small scale of the peripheral neighborhoods into harmless and repetitive blocks, devoid of any associations with the overcrowding, sickness, or political unrest characteristic of the more radical politics of the Boedo group. The forthright language and alienated characters amid urban chaos of writers like Roberto Arlt contrasted with Borges's more nostalgic characterizations. Borges occasionally wandered around the *arrabales* with photographer Horacio Coppola, who usually depicts them as empty, clean white blocks without streets, people, or traffic. These pictures contrast with his photographs of the frenetic downtown, with diagonal avenues accentuated by tilted compositions, illuminated signs captured at night, and wandering urbanites (FIGURE 2.02). Clearly many in the downtown crowds lived in the *arrabales*, but the dissonance between a seemingly empty periphery and the crowded downtown created a starker contrast.

Borges's image of 1920s Buenos Aires slowly evolved as the loose, empty grid of the city was eventually filled. The tranquil nostalgia of these small cubic constructions, scattered on an infinite plain that emulated the pampas, gave way in the 1930s to the overwhelming repetition of identical blocks. The relaxed atmosphere of 1920s Argentina had also given way to a military coup that started the Infamous Decade. An increasingly corrupt state resulted in the Roca-Runciman pact, signed with England in 1933, which guaranteed low prices and preferential treatment for British meat buyers, while secretly granting Great Britain the concession for all Argentinian public transportation. The bleak economic outlook produced by this arrangement was compounded by an increasingly authoritarian and repressive state, which echoed the rise of fascism in Europe. Economic uncertainty prompted massive migrations from the countryside to the cities, in particular Buenos Aires. The empty periphery where Borges had wandered in the 1920s filled in rapidly. The population of the city grew from 1.5 million in 1914 to 3.5 million in 1935.[27] While the city welcomed those fleeing European conflicts, by the end of the decade the bulk of its population growth came from the pampas.[28] *Provincianos* (immigrants "from the interior," the provinces or countryside) made their way to the city from the South, settling in the more affordable neighborhoods expanding along the rail infrastructure.

The war in Europe complicated an already volatile situation by reducing the demand for Argentina's agricultural goods and blocking the source of its industrial goods. Agriculture declined as the state took measures to improve local industries. With the decrease of jobs in the countryside and the need for workers in the industrial zones near Buenos Aires, the population grew exponentially and was diverse in origin, gender, and occupation, though consistently lacking political representation.[29] The upper classes in Buenos Aires, however, perceived these people as uniform and unified and met their arrival with suspicion and alarm. The anxiety produced by this incoming population was reflected in the discourse of the avant-garde and the way in which its various groups and politics were ostensibly mapped onto the very geography of the city.

Several writers discussed their apprehension toward the growing periphery in the pages of *Sur* (South, 1931–1970). This literary journal was started by Victoria Ocampo, a wealthy heiress who came into contact with the European avant-garde through her travels to Europe and as the hostess of foreign intellectuals, including Bengali poet Rabindranath Tagore, Baltic German philosopher Hermann von Keyserling, and José Ortega y Gasset. Ocampo was inspired to start *Sur*, which espoused the idea of a meritocratic ideal or a spiritual aristocracy, by Ortega's journal *Revista de Occidente* and was encouraged by novelist Waldo Frank. In 1931 her close friend and *Sur* co-founder Eduardo Mallea published "Sumersión" (Submersion), a short story about an anguished man lost in Buenos Aires, conveying a European man's horror in confronting the city's new arrivals.

> Possessed by a thirst for immediate conquest, seven thousand immigrants arrived weekly. They all had to traverse a neighborhood before arriving at the center of the city. In this region they habituated themselves, so as not to suffer shock, to the powerful buildings, the clime of powerful activity. Also in this region, submission to the law of the promised land began for the wretched. . . . The strongest later entered the city, but the weak ones remained encrusted in this neighborhood, people who would never enter the labyrinth, Ariadne's pale and unwanted beings.[30]

One might say Mallea extrapolated Sarmiento's dichotomy of civilization and barbarism to a global scale: here Europe is civilization, and the Americas are dominated by the barbaric—cold, hostile, and unintelligible beings. The more Buenos Aires absorbs the barbaric hordes of the countryside, the more it distances itself from the civilizing agency of Europe. The story ends with the migrant returning to his boat and glancing back at the city, relieved to be abandoning it.

Mallea's identification with an illusory European past has some racist connotations. The Porteño elites were predominantly French and English, while the people moving in from the countryside included the progeny of Indigenous peoples and the descendants of the large Italian migration from the turn of the century. They would eventually be known collectively as *cabecitas negras* (little black heads, formerly the name for an Argentine bird), which was used in the 1940s to highlight the dark skin and black hair of recent migrants coming from the provinces into the cities and settling in shantytowns that came to be known as *villas miseria* (misery villages).[31] This racial difference distanced the country from its European aspirations.[32] In the same issue of the journal, architect Alberto Prebisch, the former art critic for the journal *Martín Fierro*, notes the role of immigration in the changing appearance of the city:

> There was a moment in which Buenos Aires had a definite character, that is, a physical appearance perfectly in accordance with its spiritual reality, its characteristics were not negative as today, it corresponded admirably to its own destiny, it was a city with the beauty of things that are exactly what they seem. Immigration's advance had not yet altered society's hierarchical order or the moral physiognomy of its people. Today the rumbling parvenu has extended, along our streets, the most absurd varieties of architectural folly.[33]

Prebisch fluidly equates the population's physical appearance with morality and the beauty of the city with the order of society. He conflates morality and physical appearance, using them to describe both the city's architecture and its inhabitants.

Less racist, perhaps, but equally affected by what she perceived as growing vulgarity, Ocampo recorded her impressions of traveling from her family's summer retreat in San Isidro to downtown Buenos Aires in 1935.[34] "What a desolate spectacle: houses, houses small and big, recently built and profoundly dissonant . . . this unspeakable ugliness, . . . this indecorous mix of distinctly bad tastes, of the uncultured who have assumed the right to express themselves with bricks."[35] For Ocampo and *Sur*, the humble and repetitive architecture of the rural migrations was perceived as a disruption of the European aesthetic that they aspired to. They saw vulgarity and ugliness where Bontempelli and Le Corbusier had seen modernity.

The weak democracy of the Infamous Decade, which began in 1930, had given increasing power to the German-trained military elite, who favored the Axis governments of Nazi Germany and fascist Italy.[36] Argentina's large Italian population and Italy's sympathies with Germany at the beginning of the twentieth century soon made it another logical training ground. These loyalties had an economic component as well: the markets for Argentina's grain and cattle were in Europe, principally England. But Argentina was cut off from these markets at the start of the war. The economy went into crisis, further stressing an already weak state.

About this time Borges, now publishing regularly in *Sur*, addressed the transformations in both the city and the state in the short story "The Library of Babel" (1941).[37] He describes an infinite library composed of identical repetitive cells, in which all the books have "a uniform format" that conceals complete chaos. Multiple iterations of similar books are included in complete disarray, with no way to find them. Borges's library suggests that a hidden chaos lurks under the omnipresent grid. At the end of the story, he reveals that the library is both "unlimited and periodic," its infinite repetition suggesting the presence of a singular controlling order.[38] In this sense the library parallels the growth of the city, denouncing the chaos behind its seemingly infinite growth. Additional similarities can be found in Buenos Aires's octagonal blocks, which, with their chamfered corners, resembled the description of the hexagonal cells of the fictional library. The city's repetitive blocks were gradually filled. The sporadic houses described in Borges's earlier stories also gradually took over the whole grid, turning the isolated *arrabales* into a confusing and crowded Babel of faces and voices. Like Buenos Aires, the library of Babel combines infinite reproduction and a singular order, prompting us to read the story as a layered allegory. The infinite repetitive cells mimic the expansion of the Buenos Aires grid and its increasing population—identical, anonymous blocks *and* bodies.

The absolute rule of chance over this milieu points to the arbitrary decisions of an increasingly authoritarian state.[39] This reading is further clarified in the less-known prologue of the text. Borges's "The Library of Babel" was originally the second half of a longer text titled "Assyrians," with a prologue titled "The Lottery of Babylonia."[40] This prologue posits the idea of chance within a closed system told through the story of a lottery that rules human destinies. While this lottery includes the possibility of financial gain, it can also lead to penalties through monetary fees, jail time, and physical punishment. If "The Library of Babel" focuses on the endless repetition of identical cells and bodies, "The Lottery of Babylonia" looks at the unpredictable disciplining of those bodies. Borges's descriptions of the futility of understanding the library, its random, arbitrary nature, and the disciplining of bodies that it might entail if left to the whim of the oppressor, and the final discovery of an underlying absolute order all have parallels within the chaotic Argentinian government and its increasing polarization.[41]

Ultimately, Borges's interest in human limits and the failure of rationality offers an ambiguous critique in the story. He seems both captivated by the possibilities of an endless library and resigned to its inevitable failure. His parting solace when he discovers a singular order anticipates his later problematic complicities. His opposition to Perón eventually led him to support some of the dictatorships that followed the demagogue's ousting.[42] In the context of the war in Europe and the rise of authoritarian tendencies at home, the Argentinian avant-garde's discomfort with the increasing population of Buenos Aires shifted to more urgent fears of how fascism might harness its own political power, the power of the masses. Housing these populations, in order to keep them content and contained, was clearly a political imperative. This was the complicated landscape that Bonet, and modern architecture at large, had to maneuver, and it was further complicated by an increasingly chaotic political situation.

A RIGID MACHINE

THE MASSES AND TOTALITARIAN REGIMES

At the end of the nineteenth century the growing populations of cities and the institutionalization of suffrage (initially only for the male population) led many intellectuals in Europe and beyond to turn the crowd or the masses into a near-mythical creature that was irrational and easily led. French anthropologist Gustave Le Bon, addressing a bourgeois readership and focusing on the crowd's inability to reason and submission to the leader, was one of the first writers to sound the alarm (*Psychologie des foules*, 1895).[43] German philosopher Oswald Spengler viewed the masses as symptomatic of the decline of civilization (*Der Untergang des Abendlandes*, 1918).[44] US writer Walter Lippmann elaborated on the idea of the masses as a "bewildered herd" that needed to be guided by elites, lest it fall prey to mass-media advertising (*Public Opinion*, 1922).[45] Furthermore, Sigmund Freud theorized on the psychology of the masses, a term used in both the original German title and Spanish title of what would be called in English "Group Psychology and the Analysis of the Ego" (*Massenpsychologie und Ich-Analyse*, 1921).[46] Building on Le Bon's work on mental regression, he further analyzed the crowd's "herd instinct" concept, positing that the mental ability of the crowd regressed to that of "savages or children."[47] This approximated the crowd to the same groups admired by surrealism, given their close contact with the unconscious, bringing together these seemingly disparate conversations.

The attitude of these intellectuals toward the masses also shared the surrealists' condescending attitudes toward women, children, and so-called primitive societies, turning these groups into objects of study while dismissing their intellectual capacities and political agency. But while surrealists mined these groups for their insights into the unconscious, intellectuals turning to mass psychology were worried about the political consequences of this irrational behavior, which they identified in the growth of fascism. The following discussion examines the discourse of two Europeans stranded in Argentina during the war, José Ortega y Gasset and Roger Caillois, whose thoughts on the masses and totalitarian governments were inflected by their time in this country. In turn, they were key protagonists among the Porteño avant-garde: their thoughts on the ever-increasing population of the city resonated with the work of the modern architects who were eager to house the masses.

At the start of the Spanish Civil War, Ortega left Spain and moved to Argentina, where he remained until 1942.[48] As mentioned earlier, his ideas on the conformist nature of the masses and the need for enlightened minorities to lead them had been important to Sert, Bonet's mentor. Ortega had developed these ideas by observing crowds in both Europe and Argentina, where he lectured in 1928. These lectures, along with an article that appeared in the Spanish newspaper *El Sol*, were published in 1929 as *La rebelión de las masas* (The Revolt of the Masses). Because of its references to the Porteño crowds, Ortega's presence in Argentina, and his strong connection to Ocampo, the book was widely read. Ortega spoke of what he called the "mass-man," who lacked culture and education and thought of himself only as part of a crowd. He saw this as "constitutive of the American continent" and sought to elucidate from the crowds of the New World's large cities the antidote to their rise in Europe. Ortega found these crowds were growing not only larger but bolder. They no longer kept to the edges of society. He warned: "The multitude has suddenly become visible, installing itself in the preferential positions in society."[49] This occupation was both physical and political and had a particular resonance in Buenos Aires, where the incoming migrant crowds were being housed on the edges of the city but could be seen increasingly roaming through the center of town.[50]

In the late 1930s political organizers took to convening large crowds in the city's expanded public spaces, making the growth of the city's population unmistakable. Photographs of these large crowds, featured in the country's newspapers, echoed Ortega's words—the multitude had indeed "suddenly become visible." In a country immersed in the fragile democracy of the Infamous Decade, the shift in political power from small elite groups to these large populations made liberal intellectuals uncomfortable. Could these "menacing" masses be guided or controlled? Ortega proposed that the only way to manage them within a democratic system was through the guidance of public intellectuals. The untenable alternative, he argued, was fascism—a system that capitalized on the mentality of the mass-man. While *Sur* had expressed concern for the infiltrating masses who polluted culture and aesthetics, Ortega articulated this phenomenon as an outright political threat. The only path of resistance, he argued, was the public intellectual—in other words, himself, although he lacked the self-awareness to point out the contradictions in this presumed position. Placing an elite group of intellectuals in a leadership role was also acceptable to *Sur*, whose laudatory review of *La rebelión de las masas* agreed with Ortega. The journal saw its writers taking on this role as the political situation in both the country and the world worsened.[51]

While Ortega focused on the mass-man as a disoriented, easily influenced individual who only understood himself as part of the crowd (this individual was always male), Caillois was interested in how power, myth, and the sacred as mechanisms also manipulated by elites could guide or control crowds. His approach was carefully to explore phenomena that at first appeared to be magical or spontaneous. The control of the crowd through sacred ritual and the "delirium of the multitude" in response to a charismatic leader were to Caillois objects of study that needed to be dissected and understood. However, his proposed solution of delivering power into the hands of a selected meritocracy had troubling similarities to fascism. In 1939 Ocampo had invited him to Buenos Aires after hearing his lectures in Paris, but the war prevented him from returning to Europe until 1945.

In "The Nature and Structure of Totalitarian Regimes," a series of lectures delivered in Buenos Aires and published by *Sur* in 1940, Caillois tries to clarify his opposition to fascism by tasking elites with resisting it.[52] He defines totalitarian regimes as political systems "in which a disinterested individual stance has become impossible; which tolerate no opposition or indifference toward the state. . . . Thus, a regime is totalitarian when it holds the nation as the supreme value to which it seeks to subordinate everything else."[53] He describes the totalitarian nation in suffocating terms, as a structure that organizes a tight and enclosed world:

> In a liberal regime, liberty basically only derives from the structures' pluralism and mutual antagonism and from the variety of outlooks they reflect. The totalitarian regime, on the contrary, unifies and organizes the structures, turning them into a ruthless and rigid machine.[54]

Caillois proposed that "organic elites" and small collectives would operate as a moral authority, independent of the state and of both the "opinions of the majority" (which rule democracies) and the "unanimity of a terrorized mass" (characteristic of dictatorships).[55] These elites would oppose nationalism with universal values and counter the state's manipulation of the masses with intellect and lucidity. *Sur* members' responses to the lectures were collected in the journal. They were skeptical of Caillois's solutions, which they saw as either elitist or, at best, utopian, but they did not question the underlying idea of enlightened groups guiding the masses in order to avoid the mass-man produced by totalitarian regimes. Caillois, Ortega, and the members of *Sur* shared an unresolvable contradiction: similar to the totalitarian regimes they sought to resist, they assumed the superiority of the main group that they were promoting over the masses: themselves. Thus it fell upon these elites, in their proposal, to prevent the fascists' control of the masses by gently but firmly guiding these masses to the proper conduct.

The study of totalitarianism held particular urgency for *Sur*. Confronted with the growing power of the Argentinian army, and mindful of its connections to Germany and Italy, the discussions in this literary journal were relentlessly inflected by the fear and distrust prompted by what it perceived as a new and menacing population taking over the city. If the ruthless efficiency of the military was a threat, the large unknown crowds that were moving in seemed to be an untenable alternative. They brought the infinite pampas into the city and extended the city itself into the pampas. From the other side of the political divide, the right-wing newspaper *Crisol* dismissed Caillois's ideas entirely, defending totalitarianism as a regime that gave its proper rank to talent and virtue and that corrected the defects of democracy, which, it argued, makes "human society into a herd."[56] This effectively turned the critique of the masses into a critique of democracy itself.

We can look at Caillois's description of the totalitarian state and Borges's construction of "The Library of Babel" and "The Lottery of Babylonia" as complementary descriptions of both the city and its governance. If the uniformity of the grid is akin to the physical manifestation of the rule of a singular order, a uniform measure for infinite expansion, then the rigid machine of Caillois's totalitarian state gives that order a concrete shape: a closed system with no tolerance for difference. The allegories of the grid and the machine describe two sides of the same problem. They are physical manifestations of a concentration of power that cannot be escaped.

At the time, *Sur* also interpreted Borges's "Assyrians" as a political statement: Ocampo and Caillois selected "Assyrians" for an issue of *Lettres Françaises*, the French journal that Caillois edited in Buenos Aires. Caillois translated the story to French. In October 1944 he and Ocampo had this translated story flown over the sky of recently liberated Paris, suggesting that the forces defeated that day in Paris were also present in Argentina.

If the spatial equivalence of the crowds was the growing city, these authors were broaching another topic: the spatial representation of authority—the monument. One year after Borges's "The Library of Babel," Caillois published "Sociología de la novela" (Sociology of the novel, 1942) in *Sur*. Here he speculates that the destruction of the tower of Babel came about because of human vanity. With the increasing use of more obscure and incoherent materials—read "words and propositions"—the building became increasingly unstable: that is, language became increasingly unintelligible. Caillois finds this unintelligible language in what he terms "novelesque literature," a particular type of escapist fiction or babble that he identifies as the ruin of literature. In an editorial for *Lettres Françaises*, Caillois put forward the idea of "une littérature édifiante" (an edifying literature), drawing a parallel between literature and buildings to argue for the construction and cultivation of a literary style.[57] In this timely text, published about a month after D-Day, he points out that everything falls, be it doctrines, walls, or buildings, but society must find a way to defy nature and lift itself up. Style arises, he observes, from this struggle. Edifying literature, for Caillois, has the power to rebuild the city, while the troubling presence of babble represents its destruction. This thinking on literature and babble echoes the dichotomy of elites and masses and replicates its problems. Read in this way, building the city—or society at large—can only be done by the select few.

Back in Europe, Caillois expanded and republished his book on the novel, now titled *Babel: Orgueil, confusion et ruine de la littérature* (Babel: Pride, confusion, and the ruin of literature, Gallimard 1948). The ruins of postwar Paris must have made an impression on him, as he changed the text to argue that a scarcity of monumental architecture is indicative of a society in crisis. In the French edition Caillois laments the lack of buildings, such as churches, palaces, and temples dedicated to the cult of a god or a monarch, which he views as symbols of common greatness and the necessary collective labor of a nation. Caillois's position led to a call for civilization through the construction of guiding works of art—books and buildings that would illuminate society's path. He eventually joined the cultural and educational departments of UNESCO (United Nations Educational, Scientific and Cultural Organization), the group that assigns World Heritage Sites and thus claims to protect monuments as markers of culture.

Echoing Caillois's desire for monuments and Ortega's admonitions on the masses, the editors of *Sur* were interested in shining the spotlight on symbols of common greatness—be they books or buildings—that could guide the growing population and avoid the threat of totalitarianism. This desire for a return to the center, and to an attention to monumental architecture, was echoed in the current plan of Buenos Aires. There the population was housed in the dense grid, split by class between north and south and expanding to the periphery, while the state was represented through a series of monumental buildings in the downtown core to the east. If we turn to Buenos Aires itself, we can see how architects interpreted these conversations over powerful systems of government and the incoming crowds that they were supposed to control with monuments that either celebrated the totalitarian state or revealed its nefarious operations.

OBELISK AND VOID

In 1936 Buenos Aires celebrated the 400th anniversary of its foundation by building a monumental obelisk in the center of the city (FIGURE 2.03). That year, large demolitions carved up Buenos Aires to make space for the masses so they could interact with the newly built state monuments. Reacting to this ruptured landscape, Bonet, upon his arrival in 1938, proposed instead a monumental building to house the masses. While the obelisk was being built in Buenos Aires, French intellectual Georges Bataille wrote about the obelisk in Paris and reflected on ways in which military power uses space to control the disorderly crowd:

> The Place de la Concorde is the space where the death of God must be announced and shouted precisely because the obelisk is its calmest negation. As far as the eye can see, a moving and empty human dust gravitates around it. But nothing

answers so accurately the apparently disordered aspirations of this crowd as the measured and tranquil spaces commanded by its geometric simplicity.[58]

His close collaborator Caillois would arrive in Buenos Aires to find this kind of space and obelisk, which commanded similar ideas of discipline and authority in a public space.

The monumental obelisk responded to and was actually preparing the masses for a larger project that required the demolition of a large swath of downtown to make way for a new avenue, Nueve de Julio (Ninth of July) Avenue. It was named for the date of the country's independence and is still celebrated by Argentinians as one of the widest avenues in the world. The obelisk, imposed by mayor Mariano de Vedia y Mitre without consulting the city council or the national congress, was a controversial monument whose success generated momentum for the avenue.[59] The avenue had first been proposed in 1898 and ratified by Congress in 1912. But its realization stalled through several municipal administrations until 1936, when Mayor de Vedia installed Carlos María Della Paolera, a Paris-trained engineer, as the head of the Dirección del Plan de Urbanización (Department of the Urbanization Plan).[60] The combination of a strong administration eager to make its mark and the fourth centenary of the foundation of the city gave new impetus to the project.

A row of blocks between Pellegrini and Cerritos streets was demolished in order to expand them into this north-south avenue, acknowledging the lack of north-south connections in the city and the divide that had come to characterize its culture and politics. We might describe this operation as an "Haussmannization within the lines"—a different but just as destructive cut through the city. If Georges-Eugène Haussmann cut across the texture of Paris, strategically connecting key sites and monuments, the operation in Buenos Aires cut along the direction of the streets (FIGURE 2.04). In contrast with Paris's sharp triangular lots, remnants of that extreme operation, the operation in Buenos Aires left no trace. The destruction of the city prompted by the construction of the avenue ultimately confirmed the rule of the grid. By 1937 approximately two blocks north and two blocks south of the obelisk had been demolished, and downtown Buenos Aires was left in ruins and debris.[61] Demolitions proceeded slowly, eating away at the center of the city over the years covered by this narrative (to be discussed again in Chapter 4, when it reached the site of Bonet's last housing project in Buenos Aires).

The monumental obelisk stood at the fulcrum of the tension between the grid and its destruction. This tension was captured in an aerial photograph of Buenos Aires credited to Aermap. The image was published in a collection of photographs assembled by Coppola shortly after the obelisk's erection. Coppola had wandered the peripheral neighborhoods of Buenos Aires with Borges in the 1920s and would later return with his wife, photographer Grete Stern. The couple had met in early 1930s Berlin, in the last iteration of the Bauhaus organized by Mies van der Rohe, where she was trained. They married and moved to Buenos Aires in 1935; they would later divorce. Their work was exhibited at an event organized by Ocampo and *Sur*, confirming their acceptance into the tight-knit circle of Argentinian modernists.[62] Ocampo invited key guests to the

FIGURE 2.04.
Demolition of the
Nueve de Julio Avenue:
Old Empire Cinema,
undated, 1930s. AR,
AGN DDF/Consulta
INV: 062-2455.

event: Mayor de Vedia, municipal secretary Atilio Dell'Oro Maini (who had commissioned the obelisk), and obelisk architect Antonio Prebisch.[63]

A few years before, Prebisch had argued in the pages of the journal *Martín Fierro* about the need for a "classicist modernity,"[64] a modern aesthetic of clean lines and white surfaces that hinted at a certain exclusivity and class. The architect and occasional art critic for *Sur* now had the opportunity to design a monument that represented this modernity, but in doing so he linked it to the conservative authorities reshaping the city.[65] The Porteño avant-garde questioned this alliance and the modernity of a classical monument. Prebisch refuted these critiques by arguing that the tectonic modernity of the monument was a natural consequence of modern construction technology: the hollowness of the concrete monument and its stone cladding expressed, rather than simulated, the monument's modernity. Furthermore, Prebisch considered his obelisk design to be a necessary correction to the avenue project, which he related to the problematic expanse of the pampas:

> The streets of Buenos Aires translate some of the spectacle of the pampa. They extend infinitely, without any remarkable detail that stops our gaze. They are, in this sense, streets without personality. The obelisk gives a certain significance to these enormous city works, to the Diagonal and the widened Corrientes Street.[66]

Prebisch reinserts the pampas, as a trope imbuing the streets of Buenos Aires with a desolate sense of infinity, and argues that the obelisk—and by extension the authorities that impose its presence on the city—is a necessary monument. The obelisk marks the center, the void, and prevents it from becoming as desolate as the plains that both surround and metaphorically take over the city. Prebisch's reasoning as the designer of the obelisk ran counter to that of Della Paolera, who designed the avenue and argued for its symbolic charge. In a text published in *Revista de Arquitectura*, this French-trained engineer posited the Nueve de Julio as a way to open up the dense fabric of the city and join the north and south neighborhoods, which had been separated for so long.[67] His logic offers both pragmatic and symbolic arguments for the avenue. Conceived in terms of circulation and monumentality, it would also connect the cultural, political, and economic division between the north and south neighborhoods of the city. Thus the obelisk and the avenue operate in tension with each other. Located in the middle of this axis, four blocks north of Rivadavia Street—where the south begins, per Borges—the obelisk stands guard over the split of the city, pointedly separating these two halves just as the avenue reaches out to unite them.

Recognizing the value of a photographic account of these developments, Coppola convinced de Vedia and Prebisch to fund a book of photographs of

FIGURE 2.05.
Grete Stern, front cover,
Buenos Aires, 1936.
Second edition, 1937.
© copyright The Estate
of Grete Stern, courtesy
Galería Jorge Mara—La
Ruche, Buenos Aires,
Argentina.

the new monument and the city, pictures taken mostly by him and laid out by Stern.[68] The cover of the second edition, which she designed, featured the aforementioned aerial view (FIGURE 2.05). It centers on the obelisk and shows the Buenos Aires downtown grid as it is broken by the diagonal of Avenida Roque Sáenz Peña. The photograph was taken shortly after the obelisk was built (it was inaugurated on May 1936) and shows the long shadow of the tall monument. It also depicts the city blocks that would disappear the following year, when the Avenida Nueve de Julio was inaugurated.[69] The photograph was taken in the short period after the obelisk was built and before the blocks were demolished. The brevity of this moment highlights the pace of urban change in Buenos Aires. Here now, gone tomorrow. Coppola took advantage of this urgency but admittedly regretted it. Some of the images in the book featured buildings yet to be demolished. He was frustrated to realize that looking at the images prompted de Vedia to demolish more structures.[70] This operation was echoed in Stern's cover design, which highlights some blocks and dims others, turning the violence of the demolitions into playful graphic design.

Coppola took advantage of his access to the construction to make a film of this unique moment in Argentinian modernity.[71] In contrast to the elegant white walls of the obelisk and its neoclassical symmetrical design and emplacement in the axis of the avenue, the film reveals the modernity of the monument's construction process. We share a vertical ride upward inside the obelisk's internal elevator. As visitors ascended into the light at the top of the monument, they could survey the seemingly infinite expansion of the city. Construction workers were hard at work below, building the formwork, hammering wooden planks and bending the rebar into repetitive shapes. Coppola's modern eye lingered on the shapes generated by construction materials, the repetitive movements of the workers, the shadows projected by the growing obelisk, and the textures of its various materials. Another film sequence reveals the public's reception. Men stare in silence, raising their hands to their mouths, fascinated by the mass of concrete growing in the middle of the city. We then see the marble plates being stacked and mounted, covering the concrete. By showing us fragments of the seemingly solid monument, Coppola reveals it as a hollow kit of parts, built by the labor of workers rather than by the will of a single ruler—built by the masses. Toward the end, this filmic view returns us to the infinite horizon of the city, visible from the top of the obelisk and growing beyond the human gaze. The final shots reverse this point of view, framing multiple views of the obelisk from the many streets that culminate in its vertical stance, presenting the obelisk as the fulcrum of the tension between center and periphery.

AUSTRAL AND THE PAMPAS

Three years later, in 1939, the same aerial photograph of the obelisk appeared in the first issue of *Austral* (FIGURE 2.06), with a handwritten question scrawled diagonally over it:

> How does one insert into this protoplasm
> the cardiac regime, indispensable
> for the circulation and organization
> of a modern city?[72]

The phrase is a quotation from Le Corbusier's description of Buenos Aires during one of his lectures there in 1929.[73]

FIGURE 2.06A & 2.06B.
Buenos Aires. *Austral* 1
(June 1939): 4–5. CD
BMIN, FADU-UBA.

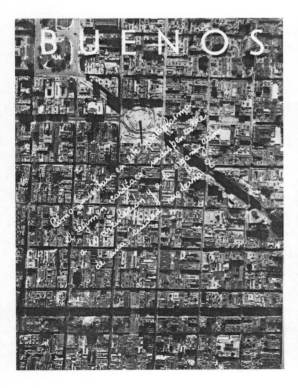

Three photographs by Coppola are featured on the facing page, including views of those tight cubic houses that fascinated Le Corbusier with their unconscious modernism and a street congested with public transportation. An amoeba-like shape floats on top of these images. It frames a transplanted version of Le Corbusier's city diagram and explains his modernist mandate to separate housing and work. This familiar Corbusian narrative is accidentally contradicted by the appearance of the aerial view. By 1939 some of the blocks in the picture no longer existed, having been demolished to make way for Nueve de Julio Avenue.

The architects and members of Austral, who published the homonymous journal, were aware of these disparities. In a letter from Buenos Aires, Kurchan wrote to Ferrari, who was still in Paris: "the NORTH-SOUTH? The only street to scale in Buenos Aires."[74] The architects had integrated the avenue into the Buenos Aires plan that they were designing with Le Corbusier. But while the Swiss architect was still waiting to be hired by the city, the dense grid that he sought to discredit had already been partially demolished. This radical erasure was not executed by modern architects but by a politically motivated conservative mayor, aided by Prebisch. Furthermore, the demolition of the blocks did not mean the destruction of the grid. By selectively eliminating whole blocks, the avenue confirmed rather than negated the rule of the grid. When members of Austral used the same aerial photograph in 1939 to represent the crowded blocks of Buenos Aires, they knew Porteños would recognize it as a symbol of the rapid transformation and improvements being orchestrated by a ruthlessly efficient public administration. Granted, the architects did not have many images to choose from, and the photograph might have been too iconic to ignore. Yet its inclusion in *Austral* points to the contradictions of modern architecture in Argentina, in which a conservative city hall using neoclassical models had superseded Le Corbusier's complaints about the density of the city.

In contrast with this call to demolish the center and clear away the city's dense blocks, in its second issue *Austral* turned to the pampas (FIGURE 2.07). Understanding that the accelerated growth of the city required a regional approach, members of the group focused on what they termed "rural urbanism," to address the problem of increasing migrations from the countryside to Buenos Aires.[75] Years later, Bonet would remember the group's attitude as visionary in predicting what would become a much bigger problem. However, *Austral* 2 made clear that the theme had been prompted by Le Corbusier's projects in the French countryside and the CIAM 5 turn to the countryside. Excerpts from *Des canons, des munitions? Merci! Des logis . . . s. v. p.* (Cannons, munitions? Thank you! housing . . . if you please, 1938) were translated and reprinted in the publication.[76] This line of discourse also had a precedent in Barcelona, where *A.C.* had focused on the need for "recreation for the masses."[77] Peasants had been a strong motif in the Spanish Pavilion of 1937 and in the Paris Exhibition at large. Finally, the emphasis on the countryside in Argentina was developed in tandem with a series of state-sponsored initiatives to study rural housing.[78] *Austral* 2 reinterpreted these European and local discourses by proposing urban industrialization as a solution for rural housing, advocating prefabricated modular housing, and ultimately reclaiming the pampas as a field of action for "rural urbanism" and a "regional plan."[79]

For instance, a section in the same issue linked industrial prefabrication with the infinite expanse of the pampas, calling on industrialists to take charge of the rural housing problem through prefabrication—industry and the countryside would thus be organically linked. Another section included a preliminary design for houses in four zones of the Argentinian countryside, with solar orientation and wind diagrams that identified the climatic specificities of each zone, along with photographs of the landscape, plans, and elevations. This article presented photographs of Argentinians in traditional gaucho setup superimposed in a manner reminiscent of the Matta and Bonet photomontages (FIGURE 2.08). These gauchos, maps, and solar diagrams point to the Argentinian specificity of the project, in contrast to the transplanted Corbusian extracts. The back cover features an image by Le Corbusier, with an industrial worker and a country laborer shaking hands, sealing the deal (FIGURE 2.09). A sign over the foreign architect's drawing reminds us that here it alludes to a national concern: "Toward an Argentinian solution."[80] *Austral* 2 alternated Corbusian and Argentinian images in a conflicting effort to merge them into a unified proposal, but it also hinted at some contradictions ignored by Le Corbusier. The single-family prefabricated or identical detached chalets that the architects espoused would soon take over cities, upending the modern vision of high towers and roaming parks.[81]

These rural projects did not go forward. The movement of the countryside population into the city had a momentum of its own, which could not be reversed. In 1915 the state had created the Comisión Nacional de Casas Baratas (CNCB, National Commission for Low-Cost Housing), an organization

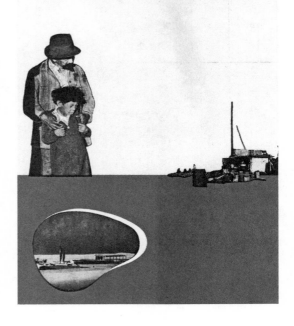

FIGURE 2.07.
Front cover. *Austral 2*
(September 1939). CD
BMIN, FADU-UBA.

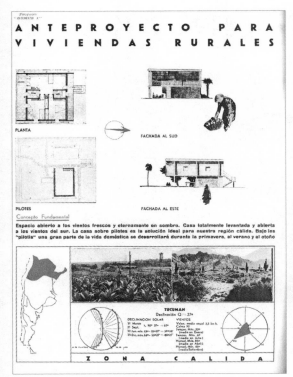

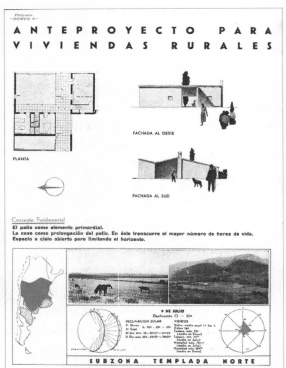

FIGURE 2.08A & 2.08B.
Schematic design for
rural houses. *Austral*
2 (September 1939):
12–13. CD BMIN, FADU-
UBA.

dedicated to solving the housing question exclusively for the capital. Between 1916 and 1944 the CNCB built 972 units in Buenos Aires; its mission was later expanded to operate beyond the city. The CNCB was the result of careful mediation between different entities from progressive groups to land and business owners, but most of its years of operation coincided with a political turn of the state against social housing and in favor of rental and administrative policies.

Despite these policies, the urgent need for housing prompted the state to experiment with different solutions. Single-family housing neighborhoods following the English garden city model were developed both by the state and by private or charity institutions.[82] Requiring larger lots than a dense vertical solution, they were usually located in the periphery of the city. Prebisch himself had been involved with the design of several neighborhoods through the Corporación de Arquitectos Católicos (CAC, Corporation of Catholic Architects). Thus, while participating in the monumental reformulation of the center of Buenos Aires, Prebisch was also active in promoting more traditional single-family housing developments in the periphery. The other typology for social housing was the *casas colectivas* (collective houses), initially large neoclassic buildings, usually four stories high, with multiple apartments per floor surrounding a central patio, which had been built in the city as early as 1917. By 1939 a few *casas colectivas* had been built in modernist style. However, they were designed to fit tightly within the city grid with no space left for lateral setbacks, in the same manner as the modern office buildings being built in the center of Buenos Aires.

In 1943 industrial production surpassed agriculture in the Argentinian economy. By then it was clear that the CNCB could not keep up with the urgent demand for housing and the city's growing population. Congresses and conferences were organized to address this problem, which was increasingly perceived as closely linked to the planning of the city itself. Both logistically and politically, housing the growing population of the city demanded a dramatic solution, on a scale with the urgency and alarm of the discourse on the masses. In other words, rather than small, strategically located, and unobtrusive solutions, the problem strategically called for more dramatic and monumental design strategies that might alleviate the upper classes' perception of this population as a growing threat. Modern architects and their heroic aspirations were ready to take up this call.

The situation was similar to developments taking place in the United States, where the architecture of the 1940s was increasingly taking up the role of urban planning. Architectural historian Andrew Shanken discusses this shift in the object of the architects' attention during the interwar years from "form givers and designers" of buildings to "architect-planners, world-makers, and organizers of vast activities, materials, and geographic regions."[83] Shanken argues that war "generalized and naturalized planning," putting the term in wider circulation. The famous three- and five-year plans of fascist Europe and Soviet communism further increased the stakes of individual acts of planning. Wavering politically between the Axis and the Allies, Argentina was not immune to these fears and anxieties and eventually became immersed in its own planning fever.

Up to that moment, the architects of Austral had been able to procure small jobs through their family and friends, mostly houses and apartment buildings for

FIGURE 2.09. Back cover. *Austral 2* (September 1939). CD BMIN, FADU-UBA.

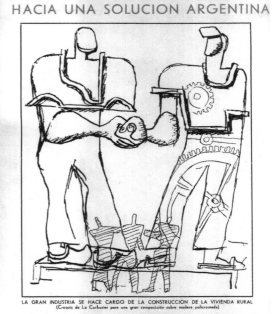

HACIA UNA SOLUCION ARGENTINA

LA GRAN INDUSTRIA SE HACE CARGO DE LA CONSTRUCCION DE LA VIVIENDA RURAL
(Croquis de Le Corbusier para una gran composición sobre madera policromada)

2 AUSTRAL

a comfortable middle class. But these projects were not enough: following Le Corbusier, the members of Austral sought to secure larger commissions that would allow them to operate at an urban scale. In a city already full of modern buildings, they wanted to realize the aspirations of the CIAM and expand the reach of modern architecture to the design of a modern city. The modern solution of a dynamic composition of buildings arranged in a large void shared similarities with the neoclassic composition of the obelisk and the Nueve de Julio, suggesting that different temporalities overlapped in Buenos Aires, where Le Corbusier's ideas seemed to have arrived before Haussmann's. *Austral* featured images from Coppola, the same photographer who documented the obelisk, even though the group belonged to a different generation and was eager for an opportunity to make its mark in the city. As the political situation in Argentina and abroad deteriorated, texts by Caillois, Le Corbusier, and Sert complicated the Argentinian understanding of monumentality by turning it into an architectural strategy meant to rally the masses and counter the increasing dominance of totalitarian governments.

MONUMENTALITY FOR THE MASSES

NATIONALISM AND ARCHITECTURE

The escalating conflict in Europe prompted different waves of immigration and curtailed the circulation of goods to and from some of the most important European trade partners for Argentina. It also affected local politics and the conversations around them. Argentinian intellectuals were careful to examine the rise of fascism abroad and saw it increasingly reflected within their country. However, critiques by the political left were complicated with the signing of the German-Soviet Nonaggression Pact in 1939. Communist intellectuals like Ernesto Giúdici, who had written about the rising threat of Nazi Germany and fascist thought, found themselves tempering their opinions.[84] Reacting to the pact and to the rising power of the United States, Giúdici even stated that "many times, behind this fascist ideology there is a desire of the masses, and because it is from the masses it matters little whether it is fascist or not."[85] In his recent study of Argentinian antifascist documents, historian Andrés Bisso argues that the predominance of fascist thought in the country was a political fabrication arising from the strategies of the Cold War.[86] The intellectuals from *Sur*, in turn, were interested in the discourse of two Europeans stranded in Argentina during the war, Ortega and Caillois. Their thoughts on the masses and totalitarian governments resonated with European and Argentinian politics, and their thoughts on the increasing population of the city resonated with the work of the modern architects who were eager to house these masses, like Bonet.

These discussions were influenced by the politics surrounding World War II and the increasing influence and importance of the United States in the region. The relationship between Argentina and the United States was complicated. Having been an informal economic colony of the United Kingdom for much of the nineteenth century, Argentina was resistant to the growing influence of the United States in South America.[87] Its military connections to Germany made Argentina partial to hedging its bets, in the hopes of either continuing its commercial relationship with the British if the Allies won or establishing stronger ties with Germany in case of an Axis victory. Paradoxically, the United Kingdom favored Argentina's neutrality: it meant their cattle shipments were less likely to be attacked by the Germans.[88] At the same time, an alliance with the geographically distant United States was strategically, economically, and politically inconvenient. In contrast to the American nations in the tropics, Argentina's large plains had little to sell to its northern neighbor, whose staples also happened to be grain and cattle.

These international conflicts complicated the tensions between the city's elite ruling classes and its expanding population. Conservative groups and the ruling class generally sided with the Axis. As the war progressed they preferred to isolate the country from the increasing influence of the Allies, who were supported by the somewhat elitist but liberal avant-garde. Neither of these alternatives was especially convincing to more radical Communist and anarchist groups or ultimately to the larger population, which saw these disputes as distant from their own interests. Throughout the 1930s Argentina had transitioned from one conservative candidate to another, who were all voted into office in fraudulent and corrupt elections. This Infamous Decade ended when local elections were upended by the international conflict. Although outgoing president Ramón Castillo leaned toward the politics of the Axis, he chose a successor with exceptionally poor popular and political support who also had openly admitted to Allied sympathies.[89] In the midst of this transition, the bombing of Pearl Harbor in 1941 prompted the Pan-American Conference of Foreign Heads of State in Rio de Janeiro in January 1942. The United States put forward a vote asking all the countries in the Western Hemisphere to break with the Axis, a motion resisted by Chile and Argentina. The bombing also generated immediate support from *Sur*, which dedicated a special issue to the Allied cause, framing the attack on Pearl Harbor as an attack to the American continent at large.

The pressure to side with the Allies was met with ambivalence by the Argentinian army. The conservative factions that had ruled Argentina favored the rule of landowning, powerful elites over popular democracy, making the democratic ideals preached by the United States unpopular. Castillo's prospective candidate, also unpopular, received the grudging support of intellectuals partial to the United Nations, who saw the organization as a way out of the conflict. But the elections never took place. On June 4, 1943, the military took control of the country, in a coup d'état known as the "Revolution of '43."[90] During this confusing period, three generals rapidly succeeded each other in the presidency. Under additional pressure from the United States, the regime eventually broke its ties to the Axis in 1944. This concession led to the ascendance of Gen. Edelmiro Farrell—who represented a more extreme authoritarian faction—and the rise of his assistant, Juan Perón, a young army colonel just returning from training in Mussolini's Italy. Argentinian historian Tulio Halperin Donghi describes Farrell's politics as not so much fascist as akin to those of Vichy France.[91] Farrell's views were authoritarian, conservative, and on the extreme right of the political spectrum, focused on a return to traditional forms of culture and religion and the construction of a nationalist agenda and outspokenly hostile to outside influences.

This regime's posture of extreme political isolation and hostility toward anything foreign prompted different reactions from Argentina's main architecture journals, *Nuestra Arquitectura* and *Revista de Arquitectura*. In the early 1940s *Nuestra Arquitectura* discontinued its publication of a varied roster of international and local modern architects and started focusing instead almost exclusively on Argentinian traditional houses (although it kept advocating for the construction of social housing by the state, a progressive position that might be shared by a paternalist regime). This editorial policy continued until 1944, when Argentina finally sided with the Allies. At this point, the journal returned to its prior openness toward foreign architects and modern architecture.

The architectural repercussions of both local and international political conflicts were even clearer in *Revista de Arquitectura*, whose more eclectic editorial choices, from Italian neorationalism to modern local architecture, also took a sharp turn after the military coup. In contrast to *Nuestra Arquitectura*'s careful elision of modern architecture during the conflict, *Revista de Arquitectura*'s editorials clearly and forcefully expressed the journal's—and by extension the Sociedad Central de Arquitectos'—political support of the nationalist, isolationist position of the new regime. The journal put itself at the service of the state. In an editorial in July 1943, directly after the military takeover, it critiqued the former government's public works administration, which it claimed was encumbered with corruption and inflated budgets, and made the following call:

The current Executive Power, which in words and deeds has demonstrated itself to be animated by a true fervor for public works, which does not have the ties and political compromises that lately have ruined everything, and which does not lack either the trust of the Nation or the patriotic collaboration of its technical and professional organisms, and among which we have the pleasure of including ourselves, is the one called to put order in this serious problem. And everything forces us to think that it will.[92]

In an article penned by the journal's committee on May 1944, *Revista de Arquitectura* called on the state to hire the "most capable professionals," who should work for public projects promoted by the state instead of focusing on private practice.[93] In a later editorial the journal even protested against excessive "internationalism" and threatened that "anyone who does not feel that he is really an Argentine and an architect, and flaunts these two titles by habit, out of convenience or without knowing why, will not be able to do anything that exalts Argentina or architecture."[94] Given the extreme nationalism of this political posture, who would determine the final image of Argentinian architecture? With unintended irony, the Sociedad Central de Arquitectos considered the eclectic reproductions of French Beaux Arts buildings to be the ultimate paradigm of Argentinian architecture, equating classical with national and modern with foreign. Echoing similar developments in the United States, conservative architects thought modern architecture was "not Argentinian."[95]

While *Nuestra Arquitectura* timidly retreated from modernism and *Revista de Arquitectura* completely allied itself with the state, a new journal, *Tecné*, was launched in August 1942 by editors Pedro Conrado Sonderéguer and Simón Ungar.[96] Partially sponsored by Austral, it positioned itself in defense of modern architecture.[97] The journal, whose full name was *Technique—Architecture—Urbanism*, listed familiar names as its "sponsors and collaborators," including Le Corbusier, Victor Bourgeois, Alfred Roth, Edgar Kaufmann, and Richard Neutra. *Tecné* promoted Austral's efforts by publishing the work and essays of group members and similarly combined a focus on art and architecture with technical data and research on materials. Its openness to international figures put it in clear opposition to the increasingly hermetic nationalism of the new regime.

Le Corbusier's influence was particularly strong in the first issue of *Tecné*, the cover of which was designed by Bonet and featured Le Corbusier's 1929 sketch for Buenos Aires. Bonet had not been involved in that project, but it now clearly centered his understanding of the Swiss architect's relationship to Argentina. The first article is a translation of his essay "Le lyrisme des temps nouveaux et l'urbanisme" (The lyricism of the new times and urbanism—our architects would have been reminded of their master's Pavillon des Temps

Nouveaux). A quotation from the first issue of Le Corbusier's journal *Plans* is featured as an epigram for the journal's introduction.[98] While the conspicuous quotation, images, and text positioned *Tecné* as responding to Le Corbusier, the editors incorporated their own critical position—something that Austral had not been able to do with its own journal. They describe their intention as the promotion of intellectual discourse between architects across the American continent and *Tecné* as an instrument to further architectural production. Only a few months after the bombing of Pearl Harbor, the use of the word "America" had a deliberate political meaning: to emphasize the common American bond in circles partial to the Allies, in an outpouring of hemispheric solidarity with the United States. We can read between the lines the more pragmatic intentions of this stance, which implies a political position against the hermetic nationalism of Argentina's conservative state.

"THE LYRICISM OF NEW TIMES" AND MONUMENTALITY

Le Corbusier's call to rally the emotional life of the masses in "Le lyrisme des temps nouveaux et l'urbanisme" was first published in Paris in 1939 and translated and published in Buenos Aires in 1942. His exhortations were bracketed by the great shock experienced throughout the American continent by the attack on Pearl Harbor and the takeover of Argentina by a military dictatorship two years later, in 1943. Only a few months after ascending to power, this volatile regime received a proposal from Austral for a monumental housing project in the neighborhood of Casa Amarilla in Barrio Sur, by Bonet and his team. Discussions on monumentality at this time link the architects Giedion and Sert, who had just settled in the United States, to this text by Le Corbusier as well as to previously discussed texts by Caillois and Bataille. These discussions on monumentality and the emotional and symbolic role of architecture taking place near the end of the war laid the discursive ground for Casa Amarilla.

Le Corbusier's article gives us important insights into the specifics of the discourse of Argentinian architecture in the early 1940s and how it related to conversations going on in Paris and New York in the context of the war. "Le lyrisme des temps nouveaux et l'urbanisme" was first published in the French journal *Le Point* in April 1939.[99] Ferrari's wife, Silvia, translated it into Spanish: it appeared in *Tecné* 1 with several images, including a photograph of Le Corbusier, signed and dedicated to Kurchan, reminding readers of his close ties to Austral.[100] Le Corbusier sent the text, written on the brink of World War II, to Argentina in 1941 while he was living under Vichy rule in occupied France. He was eager to finally get the commission for the Buenos Aires plan.

Speaking against the excessive use of rationalism, Le Corbusier extols the virtues of lyricism (the architect's expression for emotion) to activate the masses and the strength of poetry in architecture, echoing prior appeals to emotion, most notably in *Vers une architecture* (1923). But in the newer text we can sense the looming presence of the upcoming war: architecture and urbanism take on ominous overtones as Le Corbusier hints at large-scale transformations in land occupation:

> I think an immense mutation is at work, that there are imminent migrations, that cities will be made and unmade, in a word that the occupation of the land will be the topic of [our] work, once again. Era of movements, of displacements, of transformations. Architecture and urbanism will testify to all this.[101]

Le Corbusier seems mesmerized by the transformations going on before his eyes, and his foresight is excellent. By the time this was published in Argentina, large populations had indeed shifted, migrated, or been exterminated, cities had been destroyed, and large urban projects were being planned. The world was feeling the effects of the war, yet Le Corbusier's focus is the emotional charge that architecture and urbanism can contribute to this shaken, mutable world: "What remains from human enterprise is not that which serves a purpose but that which affects us."[102] He mentions as examples his schematic projects for Argentina and Brazil in 1929 and his project for Algiers in 1935. The links between nature and humankind, he concludes, will restore a poetic order after "the revolution of the machine" has overcrowded cities and emptied the countryside.[103] His words position architecture as capable of bringing forth a new civilization. Through its lyricism, architecture can activate the masses and "raise societies." To Le Corbusier, authorities are incapable of action on their own:

> *The authority chained to the daily explosive events of these transition times has not been able yet to understand the immense amplitude of this mutation* and thus is not prepared for these new tasks. These new tasks are the ones that carry human happiness.[104]

Le Corbusier concludes that it is the architect who must guide both the state and the masses in this transition. The essay resonates with Austral's program and with Casa Amarilla, the project that it would soon embark upon. Le Corbusier called for architecture to be the medium to convey the emotional life of the masses and deliver them from the cataclysm of war. Bonet had considered surrealism for its humanizing potential, but now his master called for monumentality as the only way to mediate between collective emotions and political struggle.

These two interrelated arguments—that architecture should appeal to the people's emotions and that architects are the ones who should act as mediators—were echoed in the so-called monumentality debate, a series of texts written in New York by close associates of Le Corbusier—Giedion, Léger, and Sert. In 1943 they were asked by the American Abstract Artists (AAA) group to contribute to an upcoming publication and penned a collaborative manifesto titled "Nine Points on Monumentality."[105] The manifesto can be read as a call to modern architecture when the idea of the heroic modern architect as the sole planner of a utopian future needed to shift to heed to the greater agency and power of large populations and the states that controlled them. While historian Joan Ockman considers this text to be a response to Lewis Mumford, I argue that it was Le Corbusier's writings on lyricism that helped Giedion, Léger, and Sert transform the idea of monumentality into a collective event closer to Caillois and Bataille's theory of the festival.[106] They do so by tasking architects, planners, and artists to collaborate in the design of spaces that would host these celebrations: civic centers, monumental ensembles, and other venues for public spectacles.

Their manifesto begins by stressing the importance of monuments as links between past and future, as bearers of culture in which the collective force of the people is translated into symbols. The authors then speak of the imminent economic changes brought on by the war and the people's need for "monumentality, joy, pride, and excitement."[107] It is in this emphasis on the capacity of monumentality to satisfy an emotional need that the text is closest to Le Corbusier's lyricism. Sert likely knew about this essay, as he was in Paris when it was written.[108]

The following year Sert and Giedion published their original independent essays for AAA in an anthology edited by Paul Zucker, titled *New Architecture and City Planning: On a Symposium*.[109] Giedion's contribution, "The Need for a New Monumentality," is most related to the contents of their manifesto. It also echoes several arguments in Le Corbusier's essay. Giedion begins the essay with an epigram: "Motto: Emotional training is necessary today. For whom? First of all for those who govern and administer the people."[110]

Echoing Le Corbusier, Giedion calls for architects to help the authorities understand the emotional needs of the people, arguing that those who govern and administer lack the capacity to understand the people's needs for public monuments and buildings. He similarly emphasizes placing emotion over function: "[The people] want their buildings to be more than a functional fulfillment. They seek the expression of their aspirations for monumentality, for joy and excitement."[111] Monuments, for him, satisfy the need "to create symbols" and act as "things that remind."[112] Artists are to collaborate in this enterprise through the incorporation of great works of public art, although states usually lack the foresight to hire them. Picasso's *Guernica*, exhibited in Sert's Pavilion of the Spanish Republic of 1937, is cited as a rare example of an artist being given the opportunity to contribute to "the emotional life of the community." City planners are to create the great civic spaces "to instill the public with the old love for festivals," such as the 1937 Paris Exhibition and the 1939 New York World's Fair.[113] Despite Giedion's careful negotiation, we cannot help but note the similarity of his description of these spectacles to the events that Albert Speer orchestrated for Nazi Germany. The text is full of allusions to the politics and actors of the 1937 Paris exhibition, including the standoff between the Soviet and German monumental pavilions and the tragedy narrated by the Spanish pavilion. But the essay seems determined to extract these events, and monumentality itself, from their association with totalitarian governments and associate them with the rising power of democracy in the United States.

One moment hints at the darker side of monumentality: Giedion cites Picasso's *Monument en bois* (1930) as foreshadowing "the horror of war." The tiny human figure in the corner of this painting is key in understanding the monumental scale given to the large figure that dominates the composition. It has unfortunately been cropped out of all printed reproductions of the essay except in the original publication. The painting foreshadows terrors that Giedion finds "verified by later events," but Picasso's presence in the essay also recalls his *Guernica* and the very real events it depicted. After going through an era of blood and horror, painting likewise will foreshadow a new period, a rebirth out of the horror of war.[114] The small reminder of the dark side of such *terribilità* has echoes of the overwhelming feelings provoked by the Kantian sublime. The impotence of spectators when confronted with forces beyond their control is here reframed into a bipolarity: confronted with the enormous scale of spectacle, the crowd either succumbs into joy and happiness or recoils in terror.

Sert's contribution to this publication, titled "The Human Scale in City Planning," does not call for the drama and emotional strife of monumental scale. It argues instead for the emotional life of the collective as a bulwark against suburban growth. The condensation and compactness of cities, with their dense, walkable centers and civic common spaces, are the panacea against horizontal sprawl. It is in this sense that monumental architecture must be employed "to satisfy an elementary human need."[115] However, Sert is also negotiating the vast scale of his proposals and their proximity to the work of totalitarian governments, whose technical achievements (Hitler's road system and Mussolini's reclamation of the Pontine Marshes) have been misapplied, "put at the service of military ambitions of conquest and aggression or of personal megalomaniac propaganda."[116] Though he is careful to clarify his opposition to these regimes, Sert cannot help but admire their technical accomplishments, particularly when faced with the growing sprawl of the US suburbs supported by the Federal Highway Act (also, ironically, inspired by Hitler's highways).[117] The same year he wrote this, Sert started lecturing and working in several cities in South America with his partner Paul Lester Wiener, under the auspices of their firm Town Planning and Associates (TPA). He applied these thoughts on monumentality and civic centers to their projects in Brazil, Peru, and Colombia, moving fluidly between these countries and their office in New York.[118] We have every reason to think that news of his heavily advertised presence reached his old employee Bonet in Buenos Aires.

In these texts on monumentality, architecture's role in negotiating among the elements of monumentality, the emotional conquest of the masses, and the role of the state are dubious. The architects conceive of themselves as guides for the state, leading regimes through the murky waters of the "emotional life" of the masses. Le Corbusier's lyricism text offers an additional argument to justify this position. Writing in 1939, he was not far geographically or thematically from the Collège de Sociologie discussions by Caillois and Bataille in Paris. Le Corbusier's call for monuments to be symbols of the emotional life of the community and Giedion's claim that festivals were needed to create a feeling of collectivity resemble their ideas on the festival as a necessary release of energy for large societies. Yet these arguments, even if outspokenly elaborated to counter totalitarian systems, were contaminated by the fascist tendencies that they aimed to resist. I propose that these ideas, discussed so adamantly in Paris, were transplanted into the Americas through the work of Caillois, Giedion, and Sert. But while Caillois came to reject the idea of a cathartic festival in favor of monuments as civilizing agents, in New York the discourse on the "New Monumentality" merged festival and monumentality. Furthermore, Caillois's critique of democracy situated monuments—parallel to his elevation of the elites—as shining beacons that would guide the masses. In contrast, Giedion, Léger, and Sert, writing in the United States, addressed a society based on democracy and middle-class values. These European migrants both in Argentina and in the United States sought to distance themselves from the horrors of war being perpetrated by totalitarian governments in Europe,[119] but their writings betray some ambivalence and admiration for their strategies to impress and control populations. The rise of the Argentinian military dictatorship in 1943 added particular urgency to this discourse. It gave Bonet the opportunity to embody the new regime in Casa Amarilla, his own monumental project.

CASA AMARILLA (1943)

Casa Amarilla was a Bonet-led housing project that responded to the challenges posed by Le Corbusier's lyricism essay and offered an alternative to the
monumentality debate. It was meant to house precisely those masses that had
moved into Buenos Aires and caused so much anxiety to its elites, but it problematically proposed to do so by monumentalizing the masses in an image that
spoke the language of the dictatorial regime that ruled over them. The project's
convoluted origin helps us understand some of its paradoxical contradictions,
starting with Bonet, who was a foreigner hired to lead a project that addressed
an intensely nationalist regime.

On July 29, 1943, Austral member architect Amancio Williams convened
a meeting to inform the group that the military government installed in June
had designated a special commission to study the housing problem.[120] The
commission was led by Raúl Lissarrague, president of the Sociedad Central
de Arquitectos, and was given a thirty-day term to prepare a report advis-
ing the state on possible solutions. With the work of the commission lagging,
Lissarrague delegated the task to two teams, one of them to be led by Williams
and a team of his choice.[121] Williams, an ambitious architect whose reputation
was growing, reached out to Austral. After much discussion, the members of
the group decided to present their ideas to Lissarrague and, through him, to
the new regime, in the form of a study of the city's problems.[122] Meeting notes
suggest that Austral heeded Le Corbusier's advice and hoped that the project
would influence and educate the Argentinian military regime on the housing
question. The main founders of Austral did not attend, although Bonet's name
and influence are mentioned. With the promise of an official audience but no
official commission, the architects transferred the leadership of the team from
Williams to Bonet, who eventually was credited with the design of the project,
although we can trace some of its language and design traits to Williams.[123]

Casa Amarilla was designed at a frantic pace. In under a month the team
produced a small pamphlet titled "Study of the Contemporary Problems for
the Organization of Integral Housing in the Argentinean Republic," which
included a short analysis of housing in Argentina and a proposal for a housing
project sited in Casa Amarilla, an empty lot just south of downtown Buenos
Aires. The text and project were said to be the work of OVRA, alluding to the
acronym of its long title in Spanish (Organización de la Vivienda Integral
en la República Argentina) but also a play on the word *obra*, meaning built
work. OVRA was led by wealthy businessman Ernesto Santamarina as president (and likely sponsor).[124] Bonet served as general secretary, along with a

team of specialists in law, economics, and social services, and five architects, including Williams.[125] The project was never realized, but the pamphlet was circulated within Buenos Aires.[126] It was Bonet who kept the drawings and documentation of the project and in later years attributed the formation of OVRA and the design of Casa Amarilla exclusively to himself.[127] However, the project was the result of many different voices: a closer look reveals how these voices represented different points of view, echoing the Porteño avant-garde's ambiguous relationship with both the city's growing crowds and the state that ruled over them.

Casa Amarilla was the first housing project designed for Buenos Aires following the CIAM tenets. Earlier social housing in Argentina had been designed as fairly unassuming buildings fit into the urban grid and single-family units laid out uneventfully into the periphery. The avant-garde language of the group Sur had projected the large crowds of Buenos Aires to these spaces of banal repetition. In Casa Amarilla, however, social housing and the masses it was designed to contain were elevated to a monumental scale through a sculptural form that was literally lifted above its surroundings.

This grand gesture proved challenging in the midst of a totalitarian regime during World War II, and OVRA's text seems consciously to omit this situation. The study opens by stating that the group is "outside any political idea and every ideological preconception," thus avoiding a declaration of partisanship toward the militantly isolationist goals of the regime. The following statements, however, suggest an eagerness for the universal values and transnational alliances that the regime opposed. The group hoped that Argentina, aware of Europe's "cities tormented by war" and "a world of towns in flames and ruins," would lead the way toward new universal models and new forms of human coexistence. Argentina's former allies were at war in Europe at that time. The country had been abandoned by the Pan-American Union after the disagreement in the Rio de Janeiro conference, and its nationalist military government was openly antagonistic to outside influences. By encouraging universal models and the resolution of international conflict, OVRA's statement positioned the group members in support of the United Nations and the Allies, which would likely limit their prospects of playing a role in the regime's housing plans. Furthermore, the text supported a balance of individual and collective needs and, more tellingly, called for "urban rights": the right of the population to access public space in the city.[128] In contrast to Ortega, who feared the revolt of the masses, the architects were eager to provide housing for the working class near the city center, taking advantage of the connection to the south promised by the slow expansion of the Nueve de Julio Avenue. The idea of collective need and a population's right to the city was progressive in the context of the conservative state. We can detect the voice of Bonet here, who in later years made similar appeals to the need to develop housing projects in the center of the city.

OVRA's text combines Corbusian motifs with the group's read of Argentina's landscape and culture—the pampas and the growing *arrabales*, the small houses on the edges of the city—as well as with the more generic and international concepts of the suburb. The architects warn that urban growth must be controlled with rational and humane means: otherwise humankind "degenerates and perishes." Images of crowded *conventillos* (tenements) are followed by an aerial view of the suburbs, presented as "a new barrier" between the people of the city and the countryside. The suburbs extend indefinitely, prolonging workers' commutes and decreasing the quality of their lives. Too frequently there is a constant slippage of terms between pampas and *arrabal*. One particular passage describes the accelerated expansion of the Argentinian city as "extending out of control, flat, and sad."[129] The architects' argument is often contradictory, in one instance conflating CIAM arguments on the status of European cities with the situation of Buenos Aires: "The inhabitants of the large *arrabales* have not encountered the countryside they dreamed of, because of the loss of the great open spaces."[130] Yet the *arrabales* were populated by people coming to the city from the pampas. Thus OVRA is paradoxically arguing that the rural migrations populating the suburbs had come to the city in search of the great open spaces of the countryside. Rather than take the city to the countryside as OVRA suggests the suburbs tried to do, the group proposes inserting nature into the center of the city. Rejecting the flat and sprawling ground cover of small single-family houses, the group embraces the CIAM prescription of modern towers rising from a sea of green, illustrated with friendly children's parks and images of cozy families enjoying the outdoor spaces.

Having made their critical analysis of the city, the architects move on to a list of "Basic Ideas for the New Integral Housing," which includes the need for sunlight and nature combined with collective services and high density achieved through tall towers. The text is here laying the ground to justify the project's modern layout. All of Casa Amarilla's ground surface was dedicated to a large park. However, this should not be mistaken for the traditional Corbusian lawn. The architects proposed a green expanse incorporating the specific qualities of the Argentinian imaginary, the pampas.

In the introduction OVRA clarifies that the study and proposed project should not be considered a utopian enterprise. While the boldness of the proposal, accompanied by only a few photographs and photomontages, gives the impression of a mere schematic design, Bonet and his team worked on detailed drawings of the project, including plans, sections, and elevations, carefully designing the housing units, and calculated the population that they would serve. The complex was designed for a density of 700 inhabitants per hectare, in contrast with the 130 inhabitants per hectare density found in Buenos Aires neighborhoods. The bold, high-impact images were thus backed up by a fairly developed architectural scheme. Its layout and representation, and its intended and suggested messages, require further analysis.

A GRID IN THE MIDDLE OF THE PAMPAS

Casa Amarilla was sited on a 25-hectare, roughly triangular lot south of downtown, at the meeting of three different grids. The site forms a wedge between the large Lezama Park (undermining their argument for more green spaces) and La Bombonera, a brand-new iconic soccer stadium in the working-class Italian neighborhood of La Boca, built in 1938.[131] The site itself had no grid. It had been used as a maneuvering yard for the regional train and at some point housed a trolley station. OVRA's proposal completely cleared the ground for a large-scale park, containing a series of buildings elevated on large *pilotis* in typical Corbusian fashion.

The architects introduced a new grid in an elegant exercise of formal composition (FIGURE 2.10). A thin network of pedestrian pathways crisscrosses through the cleared landscape. These paths project traces of the neighboring grids onto the site, outlining a central plaza that contains a single square block. Surrounded by a church and a few community buildings, this block

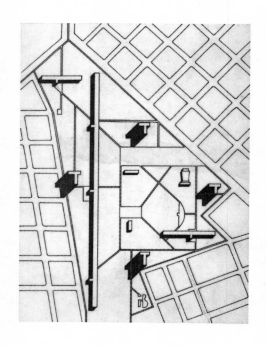

seems like a vestige of the blocks founded by the Spanish conquistadors: the original block, where a plaza surrounded by the main institutions marked the beginning of a new city. A long, thin band of housing, labeled Bloc H, cuts across the extent of the site, seemingly ignoring all the various angles of the surrounding grids.[132] Bloc H is the longest structure in their design and acts as the main grounding object around which all the other components are ordered. Perpendicular to it, two shorter bands seem to push outward against the boundaries of the tight site. These three thin bands of housing are each only fifteen stories high and contrast with the four T-shaped towers that are roughly triple that height. The rotating thrust of the low horizontal bars is pinned down by the tall vertical towers. While following the CIAM tenets, with this dynamic composition OVRA went beyond Le Corbusier's more static

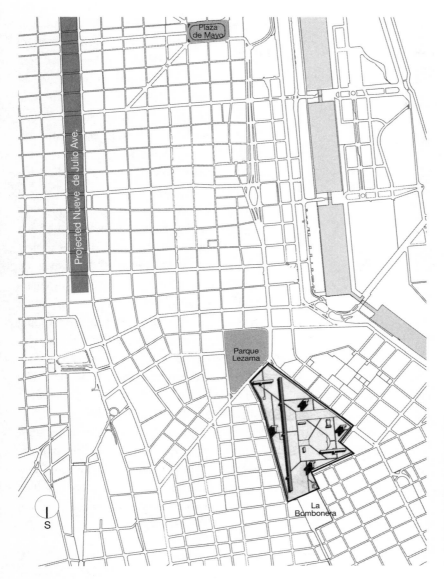

FIGURE 2.11.
Site plan highlighting
relationship between
Nueve de Julio Avenue
and Casa Amarilla over
plan of Buenos Aires.
Site plan from FABC,
© copyright AHCOAC
(OVRA). Montage by
Linda Lee under the
direction of the author.

urban compositions such as the League of Nations project (1927) and the lay-out for St. Dié (1945). In contrast, Casa Amarilla's rotating thrust and tight fit resolve the irregular shape of the site as part of the composition.[133]

If we insert the site plan into a plan of Buenos Aires, additional formal relationships become clear. Casa Amarilla's main axis is a response to the city's new axis, created with the carving of Nueve de Julio Avenue (FIGURE 2.11). This solid/void relationship—the solidity of Bloc H resonating with the void of the avenue—highlights the similarity between the vertical elements found in the

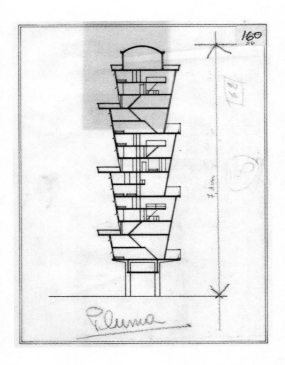

FIGURE 2.12.
Section for Bloc H. OVRA,
Casa Amarilla (1943).
FABC, © copyright
AHCOAC (OVRA).

two locations. The obelisk in the avenue resonates in Bonet and team's four T-shaped towers
that pin down Casa Amarilla's horizontal bars.
The relationship of the project to the avenue
is not accidental. The lot corresponds to one
of the sites that Le Corbusier called a "Housing Neighborhood," which he assigned in his
plan for Buenos Aires in 1938. Little remains
of this preliminary project, where housing
blocks were arranged in Le Corbusier's zigzag
pattern (corresponding to his *à redent* building type). Only the bold intersection of two
lines in a dynamic acute angle in that project
points to the implied presence of the Nueve de
Julio. In Le Corbusier, Ferrari, and Kurchan's
drawing, a line extends beyond the site, cutting
through the whole of the building and recalling
the strong axis of the avenue. In a similar way,
OVRA presented an implicit correspondence
between the proposed housing block and the avenue, connecting the public
space of the Nueve de Julio with the private space that was supposed to house
the masses who would inhabit these two modern interventions.

Bloc H was undoubtedly the most important element of the composition,
so the architects gave it the most detailed treatment. In plans and sections not
included in the original publication but stored in Bonet's archive and published later in a monographic compilation of his projects, the section of Bloc
H reveals a complex articulation of circulation strategies within each housing
unit (FIGURE 2.12). Each (five-story tall) arrangement is repeated three times:

- The street units, one-story apartments accessed by an outdoor "street"
  or corridor and stairs leading up to floors above and below the apartment (FIGURE 2.13).
- The upper units, two-story apartments with a double-height living
  space accessed by going one floor up (FIGURE 2.14).
- The lower units, two-story apartments with a double-height living
  space and a balcony toward the opposite façade, accessed by going
  down one floor (FIGURE 2.15).

In the final design, one side of the long hovering volume has three continuous corridors or "street" floors. The other side has three long rows of balconies corresponding to the lower apartments, one floor below the street floors.

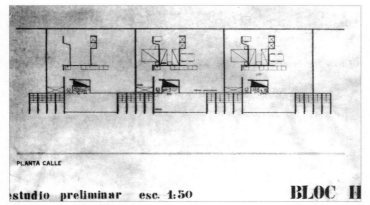

PLANTA CALLE

estudio preliminar esc. 1:50

BLOC H

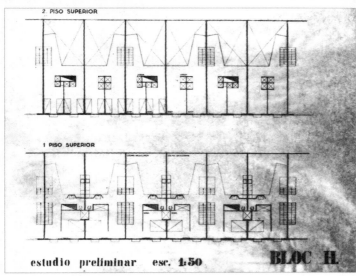

2. PISO SUPERIOR

1 PISO SUPERIOR

estudio preliminar esc. 1:50

BLOC H.

FIGURE 2.13.
Street unit floor plan.
OVRA, Casa Amarilla
(1943). FABC, ©
copyright AHCOAC
(OVRA).

FIGURE 2.14.
Upper unit floor plan.
OVRA, Casa Amarilla
(1943). FABC, ©
copyright AHCOAC
(OVRA).

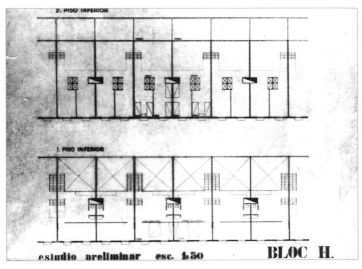

2. PISO INFERIOR

1. PISO INFERIOR

estudio preliminar esc. 1:50

BLOC H.

FIGURE 2.15.
Lower unit floor plan.
OVRA, Casa Amarilla
(1943). FABC, ©
copyright AHCOAC
(OVRA).

THE MACHINE IN THE PAMPAS 117

FIGURE 2.16.
Photograph of model,
OVRA, Casa Amarilla
(1943). FABC, ©
copyright AHCOAC
(OVRA).

The Corbusian garden roof is here partially covered by a long barrel vault reminiscent of a Catalan vault, a favorite of Bonet's but here extruded to a completely different scale. The double-height living space is a common modern layout seen in Moisei Ginzburg's Narkomfin Building built in Moscow in 1930 (a well-known example for Bonet, published in *A.C.* and visited by Matta) and also seen in Le Corbusier's Ville Radieuse, proposed in 1930 as well. Casa Amarilla differs from these examples, however, in that it pushes the corridors to the outside. These "floating streets" recall the corridors of the GATCPAC's only social housing project in Barcelona, Casa Bloc, which were similarly named: "streets in the air." The mild winters of Buenos Aires, unlike Moscow or Paris, easily allow for these outdoor circulation spaces. Revisiting the project years later, Williams described these streets as "wide sidewalks," suggesting that these urban elements had been successfully made part of the building.[134] Additional vertical circulation is provided by stair towers adjacent to the building, which, according to Williams, were meant to be mechanical escalators. The architects worked on different iterations of the section, each increasingly sculptural.[135] In the final design the façades are angled over each public corridor on one side or over the private balcony on the other, seen clearly in the section. The corridors and balconies cantilever slightly, creating stark shadow lines on the façade, resulting in a more sculptural object where the parts fit into each other like a puzzle. The "floating streets" run along the façade of an architectural object, in the end forming a grid of their own, which has shifted from the city streets to these large-scaled architectural objects. Bloc H absorbs the city's fabric and re-creates it in its own composition: the grid becomes part of the building, transforming it into an analog of the city.

The site's landscape, as it is represented in one of the four photomontages produced by the architects and the site model, shows us that Casa Amarilla is no more than a microcosm of Buenos Aires—a grid in the middle of the pampas. The first images are different views of a large model of the project, showing the surrounding site, which includes the park and soccer stadium (FIGURES 2.01, 2.16). They inadvertently highlight the radical change of scale between the city and the project—in a photograph shot from above, we can see the outline of soccer fields in the longitudinal space to the east of Bloc H. Most strikingly, in these images nature is represented as wilderness, a wiry brush of uncontrolled growth very different from Le Corbusier's manicured lawns. The fourth photomontage provides us with a more ambiguous image of the "nature" over which the project is supposed to float (FIGURE 2.17). The architects fabricated a large-scaled model of the lower part of Bloc H and placed on it what appear to be twigs as stand-ins for trees, with a photographic background of a field of trunks. We see very little of the architecture, only the requisite *pilotis*. Photographs of two men and two women are superimposed on this image: they look like stranded urbanites strolling in this forest of trunks and *pilotis*. There is nothing Corbusian about these green spaces: his pristine parks are closer to the French landscape tradition in their ordered

FIGURE 2.17.
Photomontage. OVRA,
Casa Amarilla (1943).
FABC, © AHCOAC
(OVRA).

geometry and rationality. In fact, what we see here is closer to Sarmiento's "flat and hairy" pampas.

Bonet was familiar with photomontage, as we know from his work with Matta, but this particular composition was a common modern trope. Ginzburg had used it eight years earlier in a photomontage of the Narkomfin, published in *A.C.* 17.[136] The angle and framing of the two images are quite similar, as well as the trees and human figures in the foreground, the housing block elevated on *pilotis*, and the suggestion of nature slipping below.[137] A similar photomontage was included in the publication of Le Corbusier's lyricism essay in *Le Point*, with a caption indicating that the composition is "an interpretation" of housing quarters by a young architect from Anvers. The image includes some Corbusian themes, such as young gymnasts and a building raised on *pilotis* in the middle of a wooded park.[138] All of these images repeat familiar modern tropes, and it is useful to consider them side by side as we unpack the image constructed by OVRA.

Bonet was further connected to the technique of photomontage through his collaboration with Horacio Coppola, whose photographs were also used in the OVRA publication. Though Coppola himself never experimented with photomontage, preferring candid captions of urban life and formal compositions of light and shadow, his wife, Grete Stern, did. After training in the last days of the Berlin Bauhaus, Stern briefly teamed up with Ellen Auerbach to form ringl + pit, an advertising studio that specialized in photomontage. Once in Buenos Aires, Stern worked with Coppola before divorcing him in 1943, the year Casa Amarilla was published. I speculate that Stern, who was interested in psychoanalysis and later collaborated extensively with Bonet (as discussed in chapter 3), could have been involved in the enigmatic last photomontage for Casa Amarilla. Certain qualities of Casa Amarilla also recall Amancio Williams's contemporaneous project for an auditorium, which was illustrated with a similar photomontage, in which Williams uses a photograph of a park in Belgrano, a neighborhood north of Buenos Aires. It features several small children running toward the auditorium, a rather strange object that looks like it has just landed in an idyllic landscape. Nature in Williams's image is friendly and welcoming—it is the architectural object that looks foreign.[139]

In the enigmatic last photomontage for Casa Amarilla (FIGURE 2.17), long, horizontal megastructures float as strange objects amid an overgrown, almost hostile nature populated by stranded urbanites. Contrary to Ginzburg's pointing men or Williams's running children, the figures take on a slightly subversive attitude. They are positioned at odds with the conventions of architectural representation, where they usually mark scale and depth of field. Here all the images are collapsed into a tight middle ground. A young woman, the only figure dressed in light tones, dominates the center of the image: she holds onto her hat as a gust of wind blows her skirt close to her legs. Bathed in light, she walks purposefully yet alone in the middle of this constructed forest. A man in dark clothing stares back at us from the right edge of the frame. An older woman standing slightly behind him clutches her purse. Lurking behind one of the monumental columns is a figure shrouded in shadow despite the light that falls on that side of the column. Both he and the older woman seem to be looking at the figure in the light dress, creating a visual triangle. The image contradicts the narrative of family togetherness that had dominated OVRA's text. Casa Amarilla, it seems, was meant to be inhabited by isolated, unruly urban strangers.

The hostile, barbaric wilderness that they inhabit is in conflict with the proposal as described in the text, which purports to want to bring nature to the city as a pleasant park. The nature depicted in the photomontage seems closer to the wild and unruly character of the Argentinian pampas. According to Beatriz Penny, an architect who participated in the architecture class trip to Europe with Kurchan and Ferrari: "The 'lawns' in Europe are pretty, made up of well-cared for little gardens. Here [in Argentina] nature is something more than pretty."[140]

In Casa Amarilla the "pretty" European lawn has been made Argentinian: following Sarmiento, both the landscape and the masses that will live within it are wild, savage, and barbaric. However, these are not the pampas, which are traditionally represented with sparse vegetation and almost no trees. Instead the dark, tall trees in the image are characteristic of the tall trees that line the streets of Buenos Aires. Perhaps these are reinterpreted urban pampas, seen through the eyes of a foreigner: Bonet had often admired these Porteño trees, as noted by Zalba.[141] In the photomontage Bonet ended up synthesizing different instances of the Argentinian landscape, bringing together the city, its wandering strangers, the barbaric connotation of the pampas, and the tall Porteño trees. The wild nature of the pampas, conflated with the city's tall trees and the migrating crowds of which the Argentinian avant-garde had been so wary, is inserted in the middle of the city.

A SURREALIST LANDSCAPE

We can trace Bonet's use of photomontage to his collaboration with Roberto Matta on the Maison Jaoul project at Le Corbusier's office and Matta's early collages from the same period. In these works, Matta seems fascinated by the dark mysterious qualities of nature, a dark, untamed environment that seemingly contaminated and deformed formerly normative architectural elements. Bonet had mobilized these forces in the Artists' Ateliers in the playful assemblage of movable parts, to be explored through the senses of touch, sight, and smell. In Casa Amarilla there is no longer a sense of play, as the eerie images reemerge. The visual representations resemble Matta's depictions of nature as an unhomely environment. This threatening environment in the early 1940s, with a menacing dictatorship similar to the regimes that Bonet had escaped from in Spain, may have painted a different Argentina for him. Now rational architecture mutates—through the tilted planes, changes in scale, and formal composition—into a giant object. A machine as strange to the city as the wilderness that receives it emerges out of Bonet's mind. Only the Buenos Aires trees remain, recontextualized in this strange new terrain. Architecture itself is now transformed into a surrealist object, a monumental armature framed by wild, untamed nature.

This alternate interpretation of architecture as surrealist object can be expanded with some help from Dalí's paranoid-critical method, a surrealist tactic aimed at activating paranoia in order to elucidate the irrational notions of the world and make them visible to others. In 1930 Dalí had declared the potential of paranoia to "systematize confusion" and "discredit the world of reality," using materials and objects of the exterior world.[142] Because paranoid activity always utilizes recognizable and controllable materials, "the reality of the exterior world serves as illustration and proof and is put in the service of the reality of our spirit."[143] Consequently, the paranoid process results in a double image: the representation of an object and, thanks to the cunning and violence of paranoid thought, the representation of a completely different object, a haunting image. Thus the paranoid mechanism is the key to the origin of simulacra. Accepting simulacra as instances where reality attempts to imitate appearances leads to the "desire for ideal things." This occurs in the dream world of modern architecture, whose buildings constitute "the true realizations of solidified desire, where the most violent and cruel automatism painfully betrays the hate for reality and the desire for refuge in an ideal world, in the manner of one who is passing through a childhood neurosis."[144] Thus, for Dalí, modern architecture's images sought to hide in the illusion of an ideal world. In contrast, surrealist images increasingly represented only demoralization and confusion, in an effort to contribute to the ruin of reality and in the service of the crisis of conscience that is the revolution.

Building on Dalí's thoughts on the paranoid, Breton argued that a surrealist object would be invested with the power to make the irrational world visible:

> It is a question of speculating ardently on that property of uninterrupted transformation of any object on which the paranoiac activity seizes, in other words, the

ultra-confusional activity which takes its source in the obsessive idea. This unin-
terrupted transformation permits the paranoiac to regard the very images of the
external world as unstable and transitory, if not as suspect, and it is, disturbingly,
in his power to impose the reality of his impression on others.[145]

Historian Maurice Nadeau further describes the paranoid-critical method as
"any alienated object" extricated from its habitual context that makes visible
"the desires of the unconscious, of the dream."[146] The surrealists believed that
these objects might then be launched into the world, awakening unconscious
desires and making us aware of our lacks.

While Dalí argued for the liberating potential of the paranoid-critical
method, he had also critiqued Bataille's observations on architecture as confusing simulacra with the violence of reality.[147] Indeed, Bataille had proposed
an alternate model following his expulsion from the surrealist movement in
1929. In a series of dictionary entries in his journal *Documents*, he embraces
formless, sordid, and discarded people, objects, and buildings, highlighting
their relationship to power in an alienated world. For instance, he examines
how the traditional authority of the state or the church asserts its power to
silence the multitudes and concludes that architecture is the very expression of
societies. But in contrast to Caillois's faith in churches and other monuments
as celebratory results of collective effort, for Bataille these buildings reveal
society as an oppressive system. He describes museums and skyscrapers as
instances of the spatialization of power and violence and compares slaughterhouses to temples as sites of prayer and murder in which the power of myth is
revealed by the flowing of blood. In another entry he reflects on space as both
an abstract, rational extension and conversely, as a concrete, preintellectual
site that is irrational and antispiritual. In his entry on architecture Bataille clarifies this duality by arguing that the "mathematical order" imposed to stones
reveals itself as the violent action of power, exposing the dark forces at work in
the seemingly rational display of order. It is precisely this excessive rationality
that reveals the oppressive traits of power.[148]

Reading Dalí, we can think of OVRA's proposal for Casa Amarilla as an
envisioned surrealist object that makes the irrational world visible. It does this
by introducing an alternative gridded site with unprecedented building types
at the juncture of a chaotic gridded urbanity whose conspicuous realization
on the landscape was a testament to the city's disorder. But it is ultimately
the scale that is truly jarring and prompts us to read the buildings as surrealist objects. Furthermore, Bataille's work complicates this reading by proposing that this irrational world is not the dream world of modern architecture
but actually the site of state power and violence. Bataille's work suggests that

monumental architectural projects such as Casa Amarilla embody the dark forces behind the rational order of the state.

Bonet, attuned to Dalí's work, would have noted any mention of modern architecture by Dalí, but as a modern architect he would have resisted conceding that "the modern style" was an idealized state and would have rejected Bataille's theory in favor of a beneficent state.[149] The shift from the object to the building to the city is, from a design point of view, only a change in scale. Could buildings function as surrealist objects, awakening and liberating our unconscious as we are immersed in their environments? Furthermore, could situating architecture as an object that liberates people's unconscious channel Le Corbusier's proposal for an architecture of lyricism and poetry that activates the emotional life of the collective? Might architecture function as a surrealist object, following Dalí's paranoid-critical method? Le Corbusier's lyricism and Dalí's surrealism intersect in Casa Amarilla, a project whose disruptive, revolutionary character might be understood as a double operation executed by Bonet. He inserted a wilderness into the dense texture of Buenos Aires, and within this wilderness, he installed a monumental project meant to house the masses.

While Nueve de Julio Avenue was akin to a Haussmannian project—idealized, controlled, and controlling—Casa Amarilla returned the open space to its original, archaic anxiety, producing the sublime image of the pampas. The masses coming from the pampas are housed within this marked void in a monumental, sculptural grid. Many of these operations were prefigured in *Austral*'s first cover, with the Picasso sculpture rising above a horizontal line made up of a row of men; a square, the origin of the grid, overlaid in the foreground; and a small, machinelike object, its orthogonal composition recalling Casa Amarilla (FIGURE 1.13). If the Buenos Aires avant-garde had wondered whether the city was defined by the growing masses of the periphery or the monumental construction of the center, Casa Amarilla seems to have responded by collapsing these two possibilities, turning the very center into a space for the masses. The project announces a moment of arrival, a need for the masses to be seen, as Ortega feared. They are not tucked away in small units on the periphery or pushed aside, per the Sociedad Central de Arquitectos' pronouncement, for their lack of "Argentinianness." As a migrant himself, who had come to Argentina with the express intention of building, Bonet would have had little patience with a system in which architecture could only be designed by and for locals.

However, we cannot forget that the project was meant to serve a regime that advanced these nationalist ideals. In this context, Casa Amarilla echoes Caillois's longing for a monumental architecture that would symbolize the collective work of the nation, a new Argentina, wished into existence through a new monumentality. Linking the sublime qualities of the Argentinian landscape with the new population, the project proposed a new Porteño who united the archaic wilderness of the pampas with the modernity of the city. But it also points to Caillois's description of the totalitarian regime as a rigid machine, which dismisses pluralism in order to unify and organize all structures into a singular totality. Casa Amarilla is an architectural monument meant to house the Argentinian masses, but it best represents the totalitarian regime that rules them.

By inserting housing as a large sculptural project in the middle of the city, Casa Amarilla reclaimed monumentality for the masses. But in doing so it problematically collapsed the migratory bodies that the project was meant to house and the totalitarian qualities of the state that it was meant to serve. Its monumental scale and aggressive ground clearing responded to Le Corbusier's call to lift societies through emotional excess. The team complied, perhaps unaware of Le Corbusier's own political ambiguities and his repeated appeals to totalitarian leaders. Such emotional manipulation replicates the strategies of totalitarian states, making the project an even more accurate representation of the totalitarian regimes that the intellectuals of Sur had feared. Just as grandiose excess (lyricism or monumentality) is meant to prompt uniform reactions from a crowd, rather than house the disordered masses, in this case the project snaps them into a repetitive, singular order. Like Borges's library of Babel, Casa Amarilla reminds us that the singularity of "the Order" is the sign of absolute power.[150] Past violences are implicit in this operation: by staging the intrusion of modernity into the pampas, Casa Amarilla also points to the violence of the Argentinian state. This violence began with the nineteenth century wars against Argentina's Indigenous population and continued in the military coup d'état of 1943. Following Sarmiento's call for civilization over barbarism, here the architectural object was to operate as a colonial apparatus, ordering and controlling its population to produce disciplined citizens.[151] Just as historian Leo Marx titled his canonical book on United States pastoral visions of modernity *The Machine in the Garden*, forgetting the colonial violence exerted by this machine, Casa Amarilla works as a similar machine illustrating the violence exerted over the Argentinian pampas and the masses that they embodied.[152]

In *The Critique of Judgement*, Kant described the sublime as a feeling both mathematical and dynamic.[153] This duality is helpful in reassembling Casa Amarilla's representations of infinity, might, and strangeness. The mathematical sublime recalls the confrontation with the infinite, a magnitude that can only be apprehended in the abstract realm of ideas. The dynamically sublime is conjured in the confrontation with nature as might, a dominion superior to human resistance. The sublime provokes awe: the viewer is overwhelmed by the impossibility of resisting its pull and can only experience it at a safe distance. This distance "gives us courage to measure ourselves against the apparent almightiness of nature."[154] These two definitions come together in Casa Amarilla. From the endless repetition of Babel's library cells or houses and city blocks to the approximated expanse of the pampas, the mathematically sublime is the city itself, infinitely extending toward the edges and ultimately becoming part of the pampas beyond. Inserted into this infinite expanse, the housing project floats above it as the dynamically sublime analog of the city, an overscaled machine under which human beings can only wander in isolation, a fitting representation of Caillois's conception of the totalitarian state. It is an organized world, tight and closed, with no dead zones. Both the revolving blocks of Casa Amarilla and the infinite expanse they float over—the machine and the pampas—are sublime effects of the regime for which they were created.

A MONUMENT TO CONTROL

On January 15, 1944, the strongest earthquake recorded in Argentina's history destroyed the city of San Juan, in the northwest edge of the country. The urgency of the reconstruction eliminated any prospects of Casa Amarilla being considered by the state. By the end of the month, Bonet had been named a member of the Comisión de Urbanismo para la Reconstrucción de San Juan (Urbanism Committee for the Reconstruction of San Juan). OVRA's plans were tabled in favor of the more urgent needs of reconstructing the distant city.[155] Bonet was quick to accept these posts, which promised access to the urban scale that he had been so eager to operate on, yet he left little trace in them. They seem to have lacked the urgency of a grand narrative responding to the operations of a large state. Years later, Bonet blamed a young military officer who served as minister of national labor for profiting from this tragedy by creating "an immense demagogy" in San Juan that blocked all attempts at developing an urban plan.[156] This officer was Lt. Col. Juan Perón, who was rapidly rising in prominence in the regime.[157] He had served as a military observer in Europe and studied the different variants of European government, including Mussolini's fascism and Hitler's Nazi Germany, summing up his conclusions in a publication titled *Apuntes de historia militar* (Notes on military history, 1933). If Caillois had come to see the masses as an uncontrollable threat, for Perón the masses were a resource to be harnessed. He believed that he could use army techniques to organize people, by applying his interests in mass psychology and late nineteenth-century German military theory.

Perón worked his way through existing labor organizations and gained the support of the working class through his skilled management of labor disputes. He was placed in charge of the Department of Labor, until then considered an insignificant post, and quickly transformed it into the Secretariat of Work and Social Prevention, placing preexisting entities that managed and promoted social housing rental, promotion, and administration under its supervision.[158] His growing popularity and support for better wages created animosity from the conservative regime he served. He was forced to resign and then arrested, leading to the iconic event described at the beginning of this book. Large crowds, many organized by the unions, moved into the city, from the southern edges, and occupied the voids in its center, Nueve de Julio Avenue and the Plaza de Mayo, in front of the Presidential Palace—as described in the introduction (FIGURE 0.01). These ceremonial spaces, meant for the celebration of the state, were taken over by crowds demanding Perón's liberation. He was later elected president of Argentina by the same crowds, transforming the conservative state into one governed by populist rule and confirming the power and potential of the crowds that both the liberal avant-garde and the conservative state had so feared (FIGURE 2.18).

Casa Amarilla remains an enigmatic project: was it meant to influence the military regime or was it a counterproposal to its madness? The project articulates a different take on Le Corbusier's call for lyricism in architecture.

FIGURE 2.18.
Peronist crowds fill the Nueve de Julio Avenue, with obelisk in the background, August 22, 1951. AR, AGN DDF/ Consulta INV: 2042-197237.

I have argued that the New Monumentality debate in the United States was in part a response to this less-known essay by Le Corbusier. Further, we have seen how the positioning of the role of the architect as a guide to the state in interpreting the emotional life of the masses was taken up by Giedion, Léger, and Sert as an appeal to democracy.

A different response to Le Corbusier's call was made in Buenos Aires, where Bonet now had to deal with a military dictatorship that resembled the European regimes he had fled. The ambivalent claims of OVRA, appealing to American unity while offering its service to this regime, can thus be understood as a response to Le Corbusier's description of unprepared states that need to be trained to deal with the emotional needs of their people. If the European migrants in New York interpreted Le Corbusier's appeal to the emotions of the masses through a grander scale of civic monuments and spectacles, Bonet and his colleagues gave this scale to housing in Buenos Aires by elevating the masses themselves into a monument. But ultimately this monument reflected the controlling characteristics of the regime it was designed under. Perón's ascent made Le Corbusier's discourse irrelevant. The new type of state that he represented was more attuned to the emotional needs of the masses than were our architects. His entry into Argentina's politics required a change of strategy for Bonet.

mire...

ESTO será SU BUENOS AIRES

- tránsito rápido para el vehículo y segura para el peatón.
- vivienda cómoda, independiente, moderna y saludable.
- ambiente íntimo, con luz, aire y sol a raudales.
- esparcimiento al pie de la manzana vertical.

Son imágenes del film documental LA CIUDAD FRENTE AL RIO que puede Vd. ver en esta exposición.
Realizado por el Estudio del Plan de Buenos Aires, de la Municipalidad, muestra cómo será la ciudad futura iniciada en el BARRIO BAJO BELGRANO.
Barrio nuevo y distinto, construido conforme a nuestras necesidades e idiosincrasia, formado por 20 "manzanas verticales", con vivienda para 2.300 personas por unidad. 50.000 vecinos habitarán un barrio obra de la correcta aplicación de las normas del Urbanismo moderno y de la cooperación de la iniciativa privada.
50.000 personas alojadas en 8.000 casas propias, independientes, íntimas, que forman ese nuevo BARRIO BAJO BELGRANO, dotado de un completo Centro Cívico, compuesto de ramblas de negocios, clubes, escuelas, colegios, iglesias y servicios sanitarios.

ASI ES EL BARRIO QUE NACE EN EL BAJO BELGRANO

ES A VD. COMO PORTEÑO A QUIEN SE DIRIGE ESTE FOLLETO

Los problemas encarados en ellos son SUS problemas
La solución planteada en ellos será SU solución

SU SOLUCION Y LA DE TODOS

Vea el film y después medite sobre lo que ha visto. DIVULGUELO!
Con la comprensión, la colaboración y el apoyo moral de todos, mediante un Plan Urbanístico, lógico y humano, Buenos Aires volverá a ser "La Ciudad frente al Río".
En ella vivirán, rodeados de verde, aire y sol, los porteños, una vida feliz en una ciudad feliz.

Coopere con la obra emprendida por la Municipalidad por intermedio del Estudio del Plan de Buenos Aires.

Todos los informes o consultas con referencia a desarrollo de los trabajos, su financiación, propiedad de las unidades por convenio colectivo, etc., etc., serán contestado por el

epba
ESTUDIO DEL PLAN
DE BUENOS AIRES

POSADAS 1609 · TEL. 48-9891-9892

1749 : 13.000 HABITANTES VIVIAN SOBRE 158 MANZANAS

3ª FUNDACION de BUENOS AIRES

1949 : 500.000 HABITANTES SE AMONTONAN SOBRE 150 MANZANAS

piénselo bien

ESTE es SU BUENOS AIRES

- una ciudad sitiada por miles de chimeneas que arrojan millones de metros cúbicos de humo dirigido directamente contra los pulmones de los porteños.
- una ciudad asaltada por centenares de máquinas que la estrujan al despojarla de su verde y sus árboles, que es lo mismo que arrebatarle su respiración.
- una ciudad invadida por decenas de millares de vehículos, indiferentes al peatón obligado a cederles continuamente el paso a los amos de la calle.
- una ciudad conquistada por millones de manos que levantan edificios que son pantallas para su sol y su luz.

Así es su Buenos Aires. Ese Buenos Aires donde los niños viven en corredores que parecen catacumbas; juegan en baldíos insalubres, y duermen, hacinados, en celdillas que son refugios más que viviendas.

ESE ES EL BUENOS AIRES DE hoy

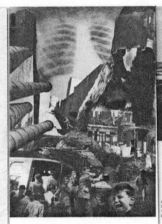

PLANTA GENERAL DE LA ZONA DE VIVIENDA DEL BAJO BELGRANO.

LA CIUDAD VUELVE A ASOMARSE A SU RIO OLVIDADO

Nace por iniciativa de la Municipalidad de la Ciudad de Buenos Aires en los terrenos del Bajo Belgrano.

chapter three

THE PERONIST UNCONSCIOUS

A promotional brochure designed by Grete Stern introduces us to Bajo Belgrano, the next modern housing project designed by Jorge Ferrari and Antonio Bonet in 1948–1949 (FIGURE 3.01). The brochure, which was part of a carefully orchestrated promotional campaign, brings together disparate images in support of the project's narrative. These include views of modernist landscapes, historical references to the city of Buenos Aires, a photomontage of chaotic images meant to describe its current condition, and a nostalgic rural landscape with the Río de La Plata in the background. The images were meant to illustrate that the city's chaotic condition could be countered with what I will describe as a pastoral modernity. Bajo Belgrano was sponsored by the Buenos Aires local government under the auspices of populist president Juan Perón, in the context of his media-savvy presidency. It was meant to spearhead a broader set of initiatives led by the Estudio del Plan de Buenos Aires (EPBA, Study for the Plan of Buenos Aires), a municipal entity that was studying the possible implementation of Le Corbusier's plan for Buenos Aires.

These images for a new and modern capital city were part of Perón's efforts to construct a new Argentina, so the project was bolstered by the regime's elaborate propaganda system. Perón's tactics emulated Mussolini's savvy use of mass media, but Argentina mobilized media toward a more ambiguous political message, combining the promise of the new with the comforting presence of the past. Breaking with both the conservative elites that preceded him and the revolutionary leftist groups that associated him with fascism, Perón allied himself directly with *el pueblo* (the people), who had been an object of fear and contempt for politicians and intellectuals alike. In contrast, Perón skillfully transformed the masses into a source of power, mounting a state apparatus that appealed to their urges and desires and thereby ending any hope for a liberatory project of surrealism and producing instead its other

FIGURE 3.01A & 3.01B. (opposite) Bajo Belgrano promotional brochure, front and back, Grete Stern for EPBA (1949). © copyright The Estate of Grete Stern, courtesy Galería Jorge Mara—La Ruche, Buenos Aires, Argentina.

project: propaganda—or public relations as it had come to be known in the United States.

Casa Amarilla, with Bonet's guidance, was intended to address the masses as beings who required containment and control by the totalitarian state. In Bajo Belgrano the team instead followed Perón's tactics and appealed to the desires of the masses. This was more than a housing project—it was a public relations strategy in which modern architecture followed Peronism's skillful use of visual cues and tropes. Some of these tropes were mobilized through the modernist aesthetics of artists such as Tomás Maldonado, leader of a new generation of avant-garde groups, and Stern, who produced photo-montages of women's dreams for an advice column. Their work was used to present Bajo Belgrano to different audiences: in a large exhibition in Buenos Aires addressed to the general public and visiting foreign diplomats and to an international audience of architects at CIAM 7 in Bergamo, Italy, in 1949. The brochures, exhibitions, and a film produced by the EPBA to promote Bajo Belgrano demonstrate that these Peronist strategies and avant-garde tactics were in synch. Under the guise of modernism, the project ultimately conveyed the state's nostalgic appeal to a mythical past. The architects used the state and its message to justify their own elusive dream for a modern city.

INVENTING ARGENTINA

A MYTHICAL PAST FOR A NEW ARGENTINA

> The dictatorship abominated (pretended to abominate) capitalism but copied its methods, as in Russia, and dictated names and slogans to the people, with the tenacity used by businesses to impose razor blades, cigarettes, or washing machines.
>
> JORGE LUIS BORGES[1]

Requiring grand plans and a technocratic outlook of self-produced modernity, Peronism capitalized on and fostered the popularity of its leader and fabricated around him an image of nostalgia for a fictitious, idealized past. The paradox of this message was reflected in its cultural production that pervaded the nation. Perón was elected in 1946 thanks to a strategic but temporary coalition of disparate forces, with the overall support of the working-class neighborhoods of Barrio Sur, the southern part of Buenos Aires.[2] Once in office, however, he was left without the support of a unified party structure and consolidated his followers into a party of his own, the Partido Justicialista (PJ, Social Justice

Party).[3] This was a period of fast and abrupt change for Argentina. Merging the pattern of European fascism with the incipient developmentalist ideas of the postwar moment, planning and plans dominated Peronism and were key in laying out the image of a new country, a new Argentina.[4] This was a period of invention guided by a vision of internal progress and self-produced nationalist modernity. Perón wasted no time in implementing it.

Perón instituted new labor laws benefiting the working class and the unions that had supported him and invested in social services such as hospitals, schools, and public housing.[5] He nationalized railways and public utilities, giving millions of people access to running water and sewage systems. He built new roads and bridges and instituted social benefits, including retirement, health, and social assistance. Perón also restored diplomatic relations with the Soviet Union and found an ally in Franco's Spain, which shared Argentina's ambiguous neutrality and ambivalence about the growing power of the United States. But for the most part Argentina was detached from the political realignments taking place around the world in the first years after the war. The country turned inward and focused on the massive social changes orchestrated by its charismatic president, which required strong political support. While prior Argentinian regimes had depended on military might and the strength of capital, Perón harnessed the power of the population itself.

To foster a close relationship between himself and the Argentinian masses, however, Perón emulated some of the strategies of European fascism, which he had witnessed in Mussolini's Italy during his time as an attaché there. At the same time, he was critical of Mussolini and eager to assert an independent political position through a fairly heterogeneous set of politics.[6] He had toppled the traditional elites but had been trained by the profascist group of the Argentinian army. He eschewed more progressive Communist and anarchist factions and favored the traditional family unit but also enacted women's suffrage. And although he used nationalist rhetoric, Perón distanced himself from fascism's racialization, never choosing to target specific cultural or ethnic groups during his presidency.[7] Capitalizing on Argentina's large urban populations and their long history of disenfranchisement, Perón transformed Ortega's mass-man into *el pueblo* and described himself as their "Conductor."[8]

The Peronist masses came to be both dismissed and embraced as the *descamisados* (the shirtless) or *cabecitas negras* (little black heads). The racist perception of this population continued, with his opposition disparaging, stereotyping, and racializing his followers.[9] Perón celebrated the mixed (*mestizo*) heritage of the inhabitants of the growing shantytowns, known as *villas miseria*, turning their countryside past into the marker of Argentinian nationality.[10] He embraced prior recuperations of the gaucho and the pampas, tropes associated with his sympathizers,[11] although this celebration overemphasized the influence of Spain and dismissed Indigenous and African legacies. Following fascist guidelines, these cultural tropes appeared in propaganda campaigns used to promote an invented, mythical past for the new Argentina. The growth of mass media and popular culture facilitated the connection between Perón and his constituents, with printed material, posters and films, and ritual celebrations all orchestrated to create Peronist citizens. The totalizing aspects of this systemic propaganda gradually took over the public and private life of most Argentinians.

The state's increasing power over all aspects of its citizens' lives did put Perón at odds with cosmopolitan intellectual groups that had experienced the repression and extreme nationalism of the 1943 dictatorship.[12] Borges's sister Norah and mother, Leonor Acevedo Suárez, as well as Victoria Ocampo were all arrested for protesting against Perón. In a much-mythologized incident, after the election Borges was "promoted" from his post as a local librarian to "inspector of eggs." He immediately quit and became a figure of the opposition, ultimately gathering commissions and prestige. To antifascist groups like Sur, Perón's sympathies with Italian fascism were a threat. Some of these groups were part of a more recent wave of Italian immigrants escaping from Mussolini's policies in the 1930s. They included an important Jewish community that maintained links to Europe.[13] The mutual distrust between these groups and the state led the government to increase its control of all cultural output, eventually leading to academic censure and repression.[14] Public university professors who opposed the regime were fired.[15] Independent institutions that resisted the regime were also targeted, in particular the Colegio Libre de Estudios Superiores (CLES, Free College of Higher Education), an academic institution established in 1930 that offered university professors and professionals a series of free advanced classes in fields that had escaped the attention of university departments.[16] The new regime's academic censure prompted the CLES to hire university professors fired by Perón, and it became a focus of intellectual opposition. Its staff included art critics Jorge Romero Brest and Julio E. Payró, both affiliated with the group Sur,[17] as well as important Argentinian intellectuals, including historian Tulio Halperin Donghi and sociologist Gino Germani.[18]

The increasing control of all cultural production under Perón, however, was more focused on content than on form. For the most part, the visual aesthetic of Peronism celebrated the kitschy, figurative, symbolic, and narrative potential of the image, an aesthetic far from the abstraction promoted by avant-garde groups. However, the regime's cultural production was heterogeneous: it also experimented with modern art and architecture. Minister of education

Oscar Ivanissevich spoke strongly against modern art, but Argentinian historians have come to understand his speeches as isolated instances within the regime's more ambivalent attitude toward aesthetics.[19] In her analysis of the Argentinian avant-garde's relationship to politics, art historian Andrea Giunta has argued that by the early 1950s abstract art had been mobilized in support of Peronism. Abstract artists were included in official Peronist exhibitions within Argentina and, notably, represented the country at the 1953 São Paulo Biennial.[20] At the same time, these artists were introduced in the exhibition literature by Jorge Romero Brest, who opposed the regime and had been fired at the start of Perón's tenure.[21] These collaborations hint at a complicated network of alliances in which opposing politics were sometimes superseded by aesthetic preferences or perhaps simply by the desire to exhibit.

The Peronist regime's foremost contribution to the imaginary of the country was the construction of its political symbolism through an elaborate series of rituals and mass celebrations.[22] Starting with the election of Perón, ritualistic celebrations of May Day and October 17 had been used to create a narrative for Perón as leader of the people. In his study of the cultural tropes of Peronism, Mariano Ben Plotkin explains how the regime rooted these celebrations in a fictitious past, blurring their origins and shifting their focus from the people to their leader.[23] May Day was no longer a workers' celebration: it was now a celebration of Perón as leader of the workers. Similarly, October 17, later colloquially known as San Perón, was transformed from the day when the workers demanded the liberation of Perón to a day when they thanked Perón for his leadership. Starting in 1948, these dates were turned into quasi-religious celebrations culminating at the Plaza de Mayo (FIGURE 3.02). The cult of Perón and his wife, Eva "Evita" Duarte de Perón, became a political religion, will-ingly appropriating and displacing the symbols and rituals of Catholicism and ultimately conflating the nation and its leader.[24] By turning the Peróns into objects of adoration, Peronism responded to the population's desire for stability and safety after years of turmoil and the need for inclusion after a regime that only fostered the nation's elites.

We can understand the way these events operated by returning to Caillois, who had advocated for similar events from a different

FIGURE 3.02.
Loyalty Day celebration at the Plaza de Mayo, Casa Rosada, with portraits of Juan and Eva Perón, October 17, 1953. AR, AGN DDF/Consulta INV: 1660-207048.

point of view: "These huge gatherings are eminently favorable to the birth and contagion of an intense excitement spent in cries and gestures, inciting an unchecked abandonment to the most reckless impulses." Caillois called for society's renewal through the figure of the festival and the expenditure of excess energy as a pantomime of "the destruction of the universe, in order to assure its periodic restoration."[25]

By the time Perón ascended to power, Caillois had returned to Europe, but throughout the war he had argued for the renewal of societies through festivals and rituals as necessary events of excess, waste, and destruction. After the war, Caillois lamented the consequences of these expenditures, finding similarities between festival and war: "The war had shown us the inanity of the attempts of the College of Sociology. The dark forces that we had dreamed of unleashing had liberated themselves, but the consequences were not those that we had anticipated."[26]

The new Peronist state also believed in the powerful effects of such events, but while Caillois meant the ritualistic celebrations to be a means of liberating the crowds, Peronism sought to seduce them into the cult of the leader. The expenditure of energy here was meant to lull the crowd into the assurance of good governance and the comfort of participation within it.

These ritual celebrations were accompanied by a massive output of promotional materials. Throughout Perón's first two terms as president, the country was inundated with pamphlets, leaflets, posters, journals, books, photography, radio, and film, presided over by the Subsecretaría de Información, Prensa y Propaganda (SIPP, Department of Information, Press, and Propaganda), which operated from 1946 through 1955.[27] These images featured the main actors of the Peronist imaginary: the leader and his people. The Porteños featured in these images were rural or urban workers—perhaps single but expected to marry soon and become part of a traditional, close-knit family unit, as the visual discourse of Peronism encouraged. They included women for the first time: Perón had implemented women's suffrage in 1949, three years after his election, changing the composition of the electorate.[28] The transformation of women into active citizens meant that they were also a target audience for the Peronist message of progress and upward mobility, albeit within gendered roles. Women were critical in the continuing construction of the nation, all thanks to the generosity of its leaders and role models: Juan and Eva Perón, the ultimate Argentinians.

The Peróns' images were ceaselessly reproduced. Giunta has examined the work of French painter Numa Ayrinhac, who from 1948 until his death in 1951 served as their "official painter," producing more than twenty portraits of them.[29] According to Giunta, Ayrinhac created Eva Perón's portraits using multiple photographs (the hands from one, the face from another, this background, and that dress)—another form of photomontage, no less. The contradiction between the use of such often incidental modern tactics and their deliberately conservative strategy was characteristic of the Peronist visual vocabulary. The Peróns' paintings eventually became reproductions themselves. They were mechanically reproduced on posters and brochures, postage stamps, and schoolbooks. Art, divested of the revolutionary impulse of the European avant-garde and redressed with the comforting message of Peronism, thus returned to daily use.[30] Perón's clever use of modern media, his general faith in technology, and his ability to understand and channel the irrational desires and urges of his constituents were his aids in the invention of a new Argentina.

Perón was not the only one intent on using images to reinvent the nation. In 1944 a new generation of artists came together under the neologism *invencionismo* (inventionism).[31] As members of the Partido Comunista Argentino (PCA, Communist Argentinian Party) and part of the intellectual circles of Buenos Aires, the *invencionistas* were opposed to Perón. But their discourses shared some common tactics and objectives, and some of the *invencionistas* eventually collaborated with projects affiliated with the state.[32] Rejecting the more romantic and realist strands that they saw as dominating the Porteño literature of the first decades of the twentieth century, the *invencionistas* instead proposed that pure creation, opposed to any attempt at representation, should guide any artistic work. Embracing Marxist politics, they rejected the nostalgia of past art movements and argued for a moment of renewed creation, influenced by the techno-utopianism of Swiss artist Max Bill, an increasingly important presence in the region, and a more ludic sense of art as event. Eventually the *invencionistas* split into two groups: Asociación Arte Concreto Invención (AACI, Association of Concrete Invention Art), and Madí. AACI appealed to science and technology, arguing for the invention of concrete objects that "participate in the daily life of men, that help in establishing direct relationships with the things we want to modify."[33] The group was led by brothers Edgar (Maldonado) Bayley and Tomás Maldonado.[34] The members of Madí were interested in actions, events, and the mythification of their own work.[35] It was led by Gyula Kosice, and its signature image was famously photomontaged by their close friend Grete Stern (FIGURE 3.03).[36] Together, AACI's aspirations to create direct connections between art and daily life and Madí's interest in art as event were not far from the tactics of Peronist propaganda.

Plotkin concludes that Peronism "presented itself simultaneously as a complete and revolutionary rupture with the past and as a conservative force preserving the most traditional values."[37] This paradoxical combination provided common ground between Peronism and the *invencionistas*. Both were

eager to frame science and technology as markers of modernity and ostensibly addressed their projects to the working class through staged events. But while these tactics were no more than a utopian dream for the *invencionistas*, for Perón they were the way to win over the masses and thereby invent a new Argentina.

PSYCHOANALYSIS WILL HELP YOU

Peronism and *invencionismo*'s shared tactics can be partially explained by the context in which they emerged, amid the rise in prominence of psychoanalysis in Argentina as a specialized discipline and in popular culture, where it pervaded the image production taking place in the city, from political propaganda to art. The promotion of Bajo Belgrano, with images by photographer and graphic designer Grete Stern, also contributed to this visual language. We can better understand the significance of this language by looking at her other job, because her two occupations shared several traits and influenced each other. While working for the Estudio del Plan de Buenos Aires (EPBA, Studio of the Plan of Buenos Aires), Stern was also playing an understated but key role in developing a new identity for Porteñas with the popular female advice column that she illustrated with photomontages. Let us briefly turn to her contribution to the visual identity of the city. We encountered Stern earlier as the Bauhaus-trained designer of the Buenos Aires city hall photography book produced in 1936 by her then husband, Horacio Coppola. In 1948 she joined the EPBA team but supplemented her income with this second job as a periodical illustrator, which allowed her to introduce alternative types of images that soon inundated the country. She began working for *Idilio* (Idyll), launched in October 1948 as "a young and feminine magazine."[38] She produced a series of photomontages that accompanied an advice column titled "Psychoanalysis Will Help You," which appeared in the magazine's opening pages.

The advice column was part of the rise of psychoanalysis in Argentina as a specialized discipline and its growing role in popular culture, largely influenced by the translation and circulation of Freud's texts and the proliferation of newspaper advice columns.[39] As mentioned in chapter 1, the Asociación Psicoanalítica Argentina (APA) was founded in 1942 with the intent of turning the specialty into a properly recognized discipline and further advanced the dissemination of the field through courses for the general public.[40] The group included Ferrari's brother Guillermo Ferrari and Spanish doctor Ángel Garma, a close friend of Bonet. Furthermore, in contrast to the contentious relationship between surrealism and psychoanalysis in Europe, in Argentina psychoanalysts eagerly mingled and collaborated with artists including surrealists and the *invencionistas*.[41] This context produced Stern's photomontages, which brought together her training at the Bauhaus, her contact with the Porteño avant-garde, and her status as a newly divorced woman in a populist profamily regime eager to court the female vote. In his research on the rise of psychoanalysis in Argentina, historian Hugo Vezzetti speculates that the epistolary format of the advice column allowed for a new form of individual expression within the anonymous masses, transcending Ortega's flattening characterization. But while the individual was allowed some expression in this framework, the reading of a patient's dreams and neurosis was subjected to a translation process, with the premise that the expert held the key to their meaning, and then offered to the public with the assumption that particular situations could be extrapolated as lessons for the masses. Stern occupied an intermediary role in this process and within this network. She illustrated the advice laid out by the specialists for their readers with increasing agency and prominence.[42]

Idilio's advice column was penned by Dr. Richard Rest, the collective pseudonym of Gino Germani and Enrique Butelman, neither of them psychoanalysts.[43] The conspicuous title and English name gave them the authority of the expert.[44] Germani and Butelman taught at the Universidad de Buenos Aires (UBA) and were part of the faculty expelled by the Perón regime. They became Dr. Rest out of their need for a job. The existence of this character was thus a direct consequence of Perón's feuds with Porteño intellectuals. Germani was an Italian sociologist interested in the relationship between processes of modernization and urbanization and the mobility between social classes.[45] He was part of the CLES and the extended network of intellectuals opposed to Perón. In a study published by the Sociology Institute of the Universidad de Buenos Aires in 1942, Germani analyzed the Buenos Aires middle classes in terms of their composition according to employment, living conditions, and social mobility.[46] Based on the comparison of a series of city censuses, he determined that the percentage of people who could be described as middle class in the city had increased vastly in a relatively short period. Such an upward movement, he concluded, should have vast consequences not only in the class structure of the city but in all aspects of social life. The political tension of these pronouncements can be read between the lines—the Peronist masses were constructed by the more established Porteño society as newcomers without social mobility, so their rise to middle class comfort had political connotations of Peronist success. While he researched the Argentinian desire for upward mobility as a sociologist, Germani got specific insights into the dreams of the Porteñas through his undercover role. He was in the end a romantic and life advice columnist masquerading as a psychoanalyst, although he never cited these extracurricular sources in his scholarly writing.

While Germani analyzed the dreams of the Peronist masses, Butelman, the other half of "Dr. Rest," built on the insights gathered by the dream analysis to write advice and recommendations for the letter writers, usually pontificating to the audience as well. Butelman was an Argentine publisher and psychologist who had studied under Carl Jung in Switzerland.[47] The dual Dr. Rest gave the following instructions to readers as the subtitle of the column: "We want to help you know yourself, fortify your soul, solve your problems, respond to your doubts, overcome your complexes, and get ahead." Dr. Rest advised: "Psychoanalysis provides us with the road to know ourselves, to discover those complexes that, hidden in the depths of our soul, are the true cause of our unhappiness."[48] A long list of questions followed, asking for intimate details from the readers' lives: their oldest childhood memories; their concerns over work, friendships, and other people's opinions; the frequency of their dreams; and, finally, a detailed description of their most memorable or recent dream.

The letters to Dr. Rest were never published, only his responses, thus erasing the women's voices. Rest/Germani would first explain the significance of the dream and its images, then Rest/Butelman would note the reader's obsessions and displaced neurosis, gently admonishing her and suggesting new behaviors. The advice was usually meant to guide women toward relative self-assurance and independence as they strove to secure true love and a happy marriage along the Peronist models—an ironic turn, given Germani's political opposition to the popular president.

In contrast to the combined answers from both halves of Dr. Rest, the graphic component of the column was produced by Stern, who synthesized it all after getting instructions from Germani and reading the original letter.[49] She described her role:

> Germani would give me the text of the dream, a true copy, in most cases, of one of the many letters addressed to Editorial Abril asking for interpretation. Sometimes, before starting my work, Germani and I would talk about the interpretation. Usually Germani would have specific requirements related to the layout: it should be horizontal or vertical, or with a darker foreground than the background, or it

should represent unquiet shapes. Other times he pointed out that a figure should appear doing one thing or another, or insisted that I should use elements like flowers or animals.[50]

Yet there was a certain latitude for interpretation. As art historian Luis Priamo has noted, in several cases Stern inserted into the photomontage images unrelated to Germani's interpretation, complicating and sometimes contesting his advice.[51] A fisherman's net, for instance, turns Germani's description of an ideal mate into someone about to trap the dreamer. Stern's lightness and humor in depicting the dreams, which are not found in Dr. Rest's gendered, paternalistic advice, similarly strike a subversive note (FIGURE 3.04). She had a similar dynamic with the architectural experts that she was simultaneously working for, Ferrari and Bonet.

FIGURE 3.04.
Grete Stern, *Dreams of Persecutions*, in "Psychoanalysis Will Help You," *Idilio* (April 5, 1949). © copyright The Estate of Grete Stern, courtesy Galería Jorge Mara—La Ruche, Buenos Aires, Argentina.

From 1948 through 1951 Stern illustrated the desires, fears, jealousies, and doubts of the Argentinian woman in photomontages that sketch an image of the new Porteña: a partially fictional creature, like the protagonist depicted in the oil-based montages of Eva Perón. Were these anxieties real or just encouraged by the relentless visuals of *Idilio*, constantly instructing its readers about their needs for romance, beauty, and general fulfillment? Stern seems to be telling us that these fears are not altogether real. The mock horror depicted in her images prompts us to be skeptical of these supposed threats. Stern's images, usually staged photographs of her daughter or her housekeeper and friend Etelvina del Carmen Alaniz (known as Cacho), have an overacted, cheeky quality. They mix body parts and characters—the hands of a friend with the face of another, inserted into a different setting. The composite nature, the stiff acting, and the predominance of the woman as protagonist link the montages to the innumerable Peronist advertisements, brochures, and posters. They reproduce the images of Juan and Eva Perón and the happy Argentinian workers they served, though these lacked the self-awareness and humor of Stern's work. The combination of body parts and characters can also be compared to Ayrinhac's approach in his spliced-together portraits of Eva Perón, their role model. Fragmented assemblages of Eva Perón's multiple bodies betrayed the expression of the individual. This new Porteña was a montage of individual fears and dreams, turned, through the magic of the camera and paintbrush, into the objective correlative of Buenos Aires's collective unconscious—a Peronist unconscious.

In his canonical essay on technological reproducibility, Walter Benjamin associated the insights provided by the camera with those of psychoanalysis: "It is through the camera that we first discover the optical unconscious, just as we discover the instinctual unconscious through psychoanalysis."[52] Benjamin ponders the ability of the camera to capture details that escape our eyes: shapes, patterns, and blurs that exist but escape our senses, a world of physical reality beyond our capacity to perceive it. Through photography and film, Benjamin conjectured, this world is rendered visible: the intricate patterns traced in the air by a running horse, the delicate veins in the petals of a flower, a gaze that was not directed to us. These aspects of reality are not only comparable to the workings of the unconscious mind, captured by the processes of psychoanalysis, but often linked to it. The deformations and transformations captured by film reproduce the world of psychoses, hallucinations, and dreams. The camera allows this individual experience to be "appropriated by the collective perception of the audience."[53] Thus the camera not only reveals a world beyond the senses but also transforms the private apprehension of this world into a collective experience. This translation of the private interior life of the individual through the lens of the camera was enacted in Buenos Aires in the pages of popular magazines and women's journals, thanks to the city's psychoanalytic fever.

A few months after Stern stopped producing images for "Psychoanalysis Will Help You," Perón decided to capitalize on many letters that he had received during his first term. In December 1951, one month after being reelected, he asked Argentines to write to him with suggestions for his second presidential term. The extensive state-sponsored letter-writing campaign was titled "Perón Wants to Know What the People Want."[54] The results were meant to help structure Perón's upcoming Second Five-Year Plan, a roadmap for his second presidential term. Just as the Porteñas had been asked to write to Dr. Rest about their dreams, the Argentine people were asked to write to Perón about theirs. The difference was Perón's promise to transform their dreams into plans: planning, architectural and otherwise, was the government's version of Dr. Rest's column: images of planning projects took over Stern's photomontages in her work for the EPBA.

Perón's propaganda images, like Stern's photomontages, mined the inner irrational desires of their audience. In doing so they had something in common with Breton's surrealist objects, although they had different purposes. In 1947 Argentinian surrealists Aldo Pellegrini and Elías Piterbarg visited Breton in Paris. Upon their return to Argentina, they published their encounter in a new journal titled *CICLO* (Cycle).[55] They also published a short text by Breton in which he cites Malcolm de Chazal to make an interesting parallel between mass media and the operation of surrealist objects: "Every object is a radio-telegraphic micro-transmitter of shortwaves that issues variable waves according to the facets of its shapes."[56]

By then, surrealist artists in Argentina had turned to commercial venues. In one case they were organized to design the storefronts for the British department store Harrods in downtown Buenos Aires, recalling Dalí's storefront in New York.[57] Disappointed by surrealism both abroad and in Argentina, Pellegrini and Piterbarg turned to Maldonado and the *invencionistas*, whom they viewed as having the revolutionary potential that surrealism had lost. As we will see, Maldonado's and Stern's work ultimately informed the aesthetics of Peronism's incursion into modern architecture, but in doing so they returned to the irrational by a different path. By participating in Perón's propaganda machine, they joined in the production of objects designed to address the inner desires of the Argentinian population and keep them happy and docile. Upending the surrealist dream, art objects were turned into propaganda objects, which, like a radio, emitted variable waves reaching out to the society that surrounded it. In late 1940s Argentina, many objects emitted these waves, but most of them transmitted in the frequency of Peronism.

BAJO BELGRANO (1949)

PERONISM AND MODERN ARCHITECTURE

While Peronism had an ambivalent relationship with art, the regime was very aware of the importance of its buildings and wanted them to display the labor of the state's work on behalf of its citizens.[58] To this end, the regime used style as a lexicon to convey specific messages. Government institutions and offices hoped to project power and authority through the language of Italian fascist architecture. Hospitals and similar institutions communicated efficacy and modernity with an austere, functionalist aesthetic. The state's paternalist care for its people was transmitted in housing through chalet houses and tiled roofs that pointed to a vague Spanish past (paralleling Perón's increasing closeness to Franco). The regime was also open to modern experiments. While various examples of Peronist kitsch and modernity have received scholarly attention, the regime's involvement with the discourses of modern art and architecture bears further analysis. Housing for the poorest segment of the population had become an increasingly urgent matter in Buenos Aires, with both *Nuestra Arquitectura* and *Revista de Arquitectura* dedicating editorials to it.[59] The state, dealing with a rapidly growing population in need of housing, turned to modern architecture. Its celebration of reason, function, and standardized solutions that could be repeated ad infinitum was appealing. But while Perón was interested in industrialization and in modernizing the state, his pseudo-religious tactics, his paternalism, and his complicated attitude toward the past contradicted modernity's basic tenets. Housing the Peronist masses required a delicate balance.

The first Peronist housing plans followed the general layout of those of the military regime that had preceded them, though they were less regimented. These projects were carried out by the Ministerio de Obras Públicas (MOP, Ministry of Public Works).[60] On October 17, 1949 (Loyalty Day), the president inaugurated the eponymous Barrio Presidente Perón (President Perón Neighborhood), situated on the western edge of Buenos Aires, bordering General Paz Avenue. Echoing a garden city, a typology that had received close attention in Argentinian architecture journals, Barrio Presidente Perón included a church, a school, a civic center, some retail establishments, a community garage, a post office, and 427 housing units, mostly single-family houses, with some combined duplexes and two large collective houses similar to the ones built in early twentieth-century Buenos Aires.[61] The barrio resembled contemporaneous US suburbs, with an additional wash of a rural imaginary (FIGURE 3.05). As the regime consolidated its position, it was emboldened to redraw its image as a more progressive, technologically advanced, modern state. It produced several modern housing blocks between 1948 and 1954, most notably the 17 de Octubre neighborhood.[62] However, these modern blocks followed a tighter, more regular layout that emphasized pragmatic efficiency over modernist discourse.

One atypical, unbuilt modern project does help clarify the circumstances that brought Peronism and modern architecture together. Itala Fulvia Villa, one of Austral's first members and a friend of Bonet, Kurchan, and Ferrari, designed Urbanización del Bajo Flores with Horacio Nazar, prior to Perón's administration. Villa had gone on the Argentinian postgraduation tour to Europe with Ferrari and Kurchan and was familiar with modern urban planning, although in Austral meetings she was usually assigned uninspiring tasks such as serving as group treasurer.[63] Bajo Flores was a relatively unpopulated neighborhood that in 1946 found itself strategically near the projected road for the new airport, a Peronist project southwest of the city.[64] Villa and Nazar's housing project had won the first prize in the VIth National Salon of Architecture in 1945, prior to Perón's presidency.

FIGURE 3.05.
Barrio Presidente Perón, residential area. *RdA* 365 (February 1952): 26. CD BMIN, FADU-UBA.

Taking advantage of the low density of the neighborhood, the architects proposed a series of parallel housing blocks over a green park as well as a more traditional sector with single-family housing arranged in a grid. They designed the layouts for seven different apartment types to accommodate different family compositions, proposed the use of fibrocement (back then a relatively novel construction material), and designed a system of independent laundry units grouped on the roof of the ten-story buildings. They also redesigned the rail infrastructure and created a train station within the site, a grand and modern move. Villa and Nazar paid careful attention to the daily routines of a dwelling, to spaces that might accommodate the traditionally female tasks of doing laundry and caring for children, and to recreational activities, in particular soccer, as weekly events that could create big disruptions in transportation if resources were not available in the neighborhood. This project is important as one of a few projects led by a female architect at this time in Latin America, contemporaneous with Lina Bo Bardi's work in Brazil. Another woman participated in this project: Stern did the graphic design layout for the project boards.[65] She later joined the team composed to design and promote Bajo Belgrano.

If built, Bajo Flores would have been the largest-scale built project by a woman in the Americas, in one of its largest capital cities. Ostensibly due to the complexity of the required expropriations, the city government let the project fade into oblivion. It is more likely that it was inconvenient both to Peronism and to Austral. As a plan designed for the prior regime it could not be presented as a Peronist product, and its use of the grid went against the Corbusian tenets that Austral's leadership had advocated. However, the general configuration of the slabs, the location of the site outside the center of the city but within its limits, and the aesthetic of Stern's project presentation make Bajo Flores an important precedent for Bajo Belgrano, the plan that would finally reawaken Le Corbusier's dream of modernizing Buenos Aires.[66] The failures of Bajo Flores highlight the political advantages of embracing a new plan. While it was circumscribed within a neighborhood, Bajo Belgrano, sanctioned by its association with Le Corbusier, was projected as part of a plan for the whole city. As we shall see, however, in the end the neighborhood proposal became the main focus of the architects' work. This larger scale meshed with Perón's discourse of planning and the grand scale of his ambitions. Ultimately, Bajo Belgrano was the right plan for this moment in Argentinian history because it suited the ambition of two powerful men, Le Corbusier and Perón. It also served the aspirations of two men who had worked under the former and now came to serve the latter: Bonet and Ferrari.

Upon ascending to power in 1946, Perón named Guillermo Borda as secretary of public works and urbanism of the Buenos Aires local government. Borda was a childhood friend of Ferrari and admired his talent. By the end of the year Ferrari had been named director of the Estudio del Plan de Buenos Aires (EPBA), a completely new entity outside the city's planning structure, created with the sole purpose of promoting Le Corbusier's plan for Buenos Aires. The plan was first sketched out during Le Corbusier's visit to the city in 1929 and revisited when Ferrari and Kurchan knocked on the architect's door in Paris. In 1947 Ferrari and Kurchan had published the plan in a local journal, renewing interest in the discourse of planning the city.[67] This coincided with Perón's increased interest in the model of the five-year plan. The day after writing the first draft of the decree forming the EPBA and handing it over to Borda, Ferrari wrote to Bonet, who had spent the first years of Perón's presidency working on the design and construction of Punta Ballena, an ambitious beach resort in Uruguay.[68] Ferrari attached a copy of the draft decree, requesting comments, and told Bonet that he had asked Borda officially to invite him to join the project. Bonet disentangled himself from his obligations in Uruguay, by then complicated by a difficult team and stressed resources, and moved back to Argentina with the challenge of designing a Porteño modernity responding to the strategies of Peronism.

The renewed interest in his Buenos Aires plan intrigued Le Corbusier. He had visited Bogotá in June 1947, so his official commission for a master plan for that city, in collaboration with Sert and Wiener's firm, Town Planning and Associates (TPA), was in his mind. Wiener had acted as Le Corbusier's assistant for his New York affairs related to the United Nations commission. Following the Bogotá commission Wiener made a rushed, two-day trip to Buenos Aires on August 2, in order to get in touch with the Argentinian factions of the CIAM and invite them to join the first postwar congress, to take place in September in Bridgwater, England.[69] This trip conveniently prompted a reunion between Ferrari and Le Corbusier, bringing Le Corbusier's dream of planning Buenos Aires closer than ever.

Soon after being designated director of the EPBA, Ferrari attended CIAM 6 in England, where he met with Le Corbusier and rekindled his old mentor's desire to plan Buenos Aires. Perón's own planning interests, his radical invention of a new Argentina, and the EPBA's abundant funds and the freedom it was given made anything seem possible. In a letter to Sert in April 1948, an optimistic Ferrari boasts: "The Municipality has given this problem the importance it deserves: we have abundant funds and liberty from the technical point of view."[70] But as the project progressed, the increased nationalism of the state made hiring a foreign architect a political impossibility. A Peronist plan had to be made by Argentinians like Ferrari (with Bonet in the sidelines). A famous, expensive European architect known for his close association with Argentinian elites such as Ocampo would have detracted from Perón's nationalist discourse. Moreover, Borda argued that the plan had substantially changed in strategy and scope since Le Corbusier's involvement. Despite Ferrari's good intentions, Borda would not authorize him to invite Le Corbusier to participate and only conceded him a nominal role in which he would sanction the plan after it was finished. The Argentinian architects soon found themselves in a messy relationship with Le Corbusier, interested in his involvement but ultimately aware that the political climate made it impossible. At the same time, Le Corbusier pitted the EPBA against Sert and Wiener's TPA working in Colombia, using each one alternatively to provoke the other one.[71] Ultimately both teams were increasingly interested in establishing a mark of their own and were aware of how far their mentor's expertise was from the realities on the ground. They knew enough to be cautious about the advantages provided by their association with him.

The Buenos Aires Plan was generously funded, but its careful organizational structure was superseded by the protagonist roles of Ferrari and Bonet. The EPBA was initially organized around a careful structure of separate departments with their respective heads (Planning, Analysis, Housing Units, and others) and three lead advisors: Bonet, fellow Austral member Jorge Vivanco, and Miguel C. Roca, all working under Ferrari as director.[72] A few months later, the EPBA was effectively being led by Ferrari and Bonet.[73] We learn about the actual working structure of the EPBA through a letter to Ferrari from a disgruntled employee, Chilean architect Enrique Gebhard.[74] According to Gebhard, the plan was directed by Ferrari and Bonet "and particularly by the latter, who most of the time, without being in full knowledge of the development of the EPBA's problems because of his long absences from the country, his arbitrariness, [and] his narcissism, gives orders and counterorders, with the resulting consequences in the normal advancement of the works."[75] Gebhard complained that the planning department had been dissolved, and the EPBA had stopped focusing on the broader scale of the region and the country. He pointed out how several consultants were brought in only to be dismissed, wasting time and resources.

Gebhard's comments point to a contradiction in the organization of the EPBA. It advertised itself as a typically Peronist series of departments and subdivided hierarchical structures, but in practice it operated horizontally as a series of teams, with Ferrari and Bonet overseeing everything, curtailing the authority of the different department leaders.[76] This appearance of hierarchical division, in practice overruled by a single authority, was not far from the management methods of Perón himself, for whom a complicated structure presented the appearance of organization, only to be superseded by the commands of the authorities at the top. Given the nationalist agenda of the regime, the appearance of a hierarchical structure had the additional advantage of masking Bonet's authority, which had to remain secondary, at least on paper—he was not Argentinian.

There was truth in Gebhard's complaints about the lack of a regional perspective. Indeed the energies of the group members had moved away from the city plan and become focused on the representation and promotion of Bajo Belgrano, which they saw as a necessary gateway into their long-term goal of planning the city. The housing project was sited in a 54-acre lot facing the Río La Plata, northwest of Buenos Aires (FIGURES 0.02, 3.06).[77] Overall, EPBA's design for Bajo Belgrano was conceptualized in the spirit of Le Corbusier's initial plans for the city, but on a more modest scale and applied to a less glamorous and less central area of the city. The housing project was far away from the downtown area, the main focus of Le Corbusier's plan as depicted in his famous drawing of the city. It was also far from the class tensions between the northern and southern neighborhoods. The project was meant to house a total of 50,000 people, dispersed across a large park. The main design element was the vertical block or "monoblock," a building 200 meters long, 18 meters wide, and 50 meters tall that would house 500 apartment units. Twenty-one of these monoblocks were to be distributed evenly throughout the site, all oriented along the same roughly north-south axis. Although the standard section varied, the corridors were located on every third floor, running down the middle of the block. They served a typical modern apartment with a double-height common space as well as several variations of single-floor apartments. This was a return to a more conventional configuration after the intricate section of Casa Amarilla, with its floating outdoor streets, balconies, and interlocking units.

Bonet was not involved in the initial design of the block: hence the differences. He instead focused his attention on the presentation and promotion of the project. The housing team, led by Kurchan, researched several modern apartment types, including housing blocks by Le Corbusier, Gropius, Brazilian architects Lucio Costa and Oscar Niemeyer, and Dutch architects Willem van Tijen, Hugh Maaskant, Johannes Andreas Brinkman, and Leendert Cornelis van der Vlugt. They also considered Ferrari and Kurchan's own Los Eucaliptos apartments built in 1941–1943. They made comparative charts with dimensions and materials and considered costs and relative construction time. Despite or perhaps because of this research, and the particular attention placed on Le Corbusier, the resulting section of Bajo Belgrano resembled a Unité

d'Habitation apartment (Marseille, 1947–1952), and lacked the interlocking section and other innovations of Casa Amarilla.

During the design phase, the architect's efforts were focused on the larger programmatic requirements of the site and its prospective population, with specific departments within the EPBA devoted to the history of the city, urban analysis, transportation, environment and recreation, ordinances, and the promotion of the project. However, very few of these exhaustive numerical data, solar charts, and research on architectural typologies were published at the time. It was not until 1953, when the full extent of the plan for Bajo Belgrano was published in a special issue of *Revista de Arquitectura*, that this research was made widely available.[78] By then the plan had been canceled. As the architects prepared for a large exhibition, the promotion of the plan overpowered all other aspects of the work, distracting Ferrari and Bonet's attention and prompting them to neglect their own design.

FIGURE 3.06.
EPBA, Bajo Belgrano, site plan (1949). JFHA, courtesy FLL, Harvard University, GSD.

Bajo Belgrano was more than a housing project—it was part of the Peronist propaganda system and as such a vehicle to deliver Perón's message. It was conceived in that way from the start. The need to promote it was mentioned at the very first committee meeting of the EPBA in February 1948, and a department was created within the EPBA with the sole purpose of promoting Bajo Belgrano.[79] Italian architect Ernesto Rogers, stopping in Buenos Aires on his way to Tucumán to visit Vivanco's architecture school, the Instituto de Arquitectura y Urbanismo (IAU, Institute of Architecture and Urbanism), met with Ferrari and agreed to direct the Departamento de Difusión y Educación Urbana (DDEU, Department of Promotion and Urban Education), although as we will see his role was minor. Rogers also participated in *invencionista* exhibitions and publications organized in 1948, linking this group and Bajo Belgrano.[80] The DDEU followed the model of the SIPP, Perón's propaganda department, and produced printed material and media advertisements for the EPBA.

The Argentinian economy had experienced a period of high growth, but it was now slowing down. With presidential elections scheduled for 1951, two years away, and housing still a key demand from the working-class population of Perón supporters, the state could not afford to launch an unpopular plan. The DDEU felt the pressure. One complication was that the Bajo Belgrano lot was not a tabula rasa. A property dispute was being sorted out, and buildings of various types had been erected, including precarious wooden shacks with zinc roofs that were occasionally flooded by the river. The city tried to resolve the legal issues of ownership, ordering evictions, but the current residents started to protest, disrupting the populist narrative of the project. A Peronist project could not be seen as opposing the disenfranchised, Perón's main constituents. The architects followed the local controversy carefully, collecting various newspaper clippings about the dispute.[81] They decided that public support for their project could be gained only if they educated the public about the virtues of modern urbanism. The DDEU was given the following mandate:

> The current principles of urbanism and architecture, and the works realized on the basis of those principles, are practically unknown to the public. From this lack of knowledge arise the doubt and the reaction to the propositions of urbanism. That is why it is necessary to put the environment in contact with the elements managed herein through clear and dynamic systems. This is the function of this department, which utilizes to this end a wide range of media (publications in newspapers and magazines, brochures, and documentary films, special publications, expositions, etc.).[82]

Rogers led the DDEU, which was staffed by a team of graphic artists, including Stern, who was in charge of photography and graphic layouts, and Italian-born *Sur* art critic and artist Attilio Rossi. But Rogers thought of himself as a consultant, present only periodically to dispense advice. His key contribution was recommending the hiring of Italian filmmaker Enrico Gras to direct a promotional film of the project. The DDEU soon focused exclusively on producing this film and designing a large exhibition to promote Bajo Belgrano and the EPBA, including a complete set of printed materials. Gras took charge of an expanded DDEU in August 1949, reporting directly to Ferrari and Bonet. He separated the department into two teams: one dedicated to film production and organization, and the other to the group's "distribution, publicity, control, and cultural exploitation."[83] This second team was made up of four members, including Rossi and Stern.[84] Gras proposed a temporary third team that would prepare the models and drawings needed for the film. Ferrari overrode this proposal in Gras's memo, scribbling over it that the design team would take care of this task, further conflating design and promotion, architecture and propaganda. Needless to say, a grand production was anticipated by all.

The consensus around a promotional film owed much to Perón's own use of this modern medium, including his increased state supervision of the film industry.[85] Eva Perón, a former radio and film actress, probably influenced the president's interest. The Peronist state created favorable economic, legal, and administrative conditions to support the private film industry in the production of films that promoted its message, usually resulting in comedies or light dramas.[86] Between 1946 and 1955 over 400 films were produced in support of the state, which was represented and legitimized through the use of characters and narrative. Perón's training in Italy would have familiarized him with Mussolini's use of cinema through L'Unione Cinematografica Educativa (LUCE, Educational Film Union), a supposedly public institute owned by Il Duce and mobilized for state propaganda.[87] Gras, who described his work as surrealist, had worked for LUCE in collaboration with his partner Luciano Emmer, producing the scenography, montage, and music for a series of propaganda shorts for the Mussolini regime.[88] The Peronist cinematographic industry was therefore engaged in a modernist project directed by an Italian filmmaker with links to both fascism and surrealism. Traces of both can be found in the promotional film that Gras created for Bajo Belgrano.

A traveling exhibition promoting the project was going to be showcased first at Galerías Pacífico, a large conglomerate of shopping arcades with an exhibition space, and later at the "Urbanism Exhibition" held in connection with the IV Congreso Histórico Municipal Interamericano (IVth Inter-American Historical Municipal Congress), a large event that was going to take place in

Buenos Aires in late 1949. It received extensive local coverage, particularly from *Revista de Arquitectura*, which had warned against the Argentinian architects' use of excessive internationalism during the last regime. While Perón shaped his regime as a cult of his own personality, he engaged the nationalist rhetoric of the prior regime. At the same time, he was eager to present his state as a modern and efficient machine. *Revista de Arquitectura*'s editorial in support of Bajo Belgrano highlights the careful negotiation that the architects had to undertake in its presentation and promotion. It was, after all, a modern plan at the service of the Peronist state with roots in Le Corbusier's office in Paris. These negotiations occurred amid the work that the architects were doing to prepare for a similar presentation at CIAM 7, taking place in July 1949 in Bergamo, Italy. The proximity between the exhibition in Buenos Aires and this meeting meant that the promotional material and film would be presented at both venues: Perón's message would be taken all the way to the CIAM. Bonet was selected to present this Argentinian material in Italy, in a memorable trip that marked his first return to Europe (I will return to this trip).

In September Ferrari wrote to Bonet requesting his return.[89] After spending time in Italy at CIAM 7, he was vacationing in Barcelona. The team was hastily preparing for the inter-American exhibition. With only twenty days left, Ferrari asked Bonet to return to help in the preparation and perhaps prepare a presentation on his experience at the CIAM. Upon his return, Bonet continued his supervision of all the departments, with special focus on the DDEU and efforts to increase the publicity for and distribution of the film. A long memo addressed to him, probably written by Ferrari to bring him up to date after his two-month absence, ostensibly directs his attention to the DDEU's tasks.[90] Here we learn the architects were not happy with the film's distribution and wanted to increase the showings in Buenos Aires, target better theaters, and expand distribution to the United States and Europe.[91] The memo requests that English copies be made to send to Edgar Kaufmann, director of the Industrial Design Department at the Museum of Modern Art in New York.[92] Copies would also go to the Argentinian Embassy in New York: clearly Ferrari and Bonet hoped to expose the project to an international audience.

This flurry of activity was suddenly cut short in November, when government official Borda and Mayor Emilio Siri, previous loyal supporters, quit their posts. The new mayor, Juan Virgilio Debenedetti, terminated the activities of the EPBA as soon as he was in office and shifted the focus of his administration to short-term objectives like road repair and the reorganization of the city hospitals. The exhibition closed in November 19: by the end of the month the plan was canceled, the EPBA was shut down, and its personnel were transferred to the Public Works Division. The new mayor justified this abrupt closing by arguing that the EPBA's spending was excessive and its role was redundant with the technical team of the city.[93] The EPBA's premature closure brought this brief alliance between Peronism and avant-garde aesthetics to an end. Through the exhibition and film, this alliance conveyed the Peronist message of nationalist nostalgia for a fictional past through a modernist housing project.

PASTORAL MODERNITY

DAPHNE AND EVA

Promoting Bajo Belgrano at the Urbanism Exhibition for the IV Congreso Histórico Municipal Interamericano required crafting an international message that fit into the realm of Pan-American unifying discourse that dated back to the late nineteenth century.[94] On October 12, 1949, delegates from different cities of the American continent came together to celebrate the supposed European discovery of the Americas. The date revealed the contradictory attitudes toward Europe. While much of the language used to present the congress dismissed Europe as old and outdated, in favor of the new and modern nations of the Americas, this very newness came precisely at a cost: dismissing the region's Indigenous civilizations.[95] The overall discourse was inflected with conservative moral and religious values that were linked back to Spain. The conference program included a study of so-called primitive communities, a history of local institutions, and a history, firmly beginning in 1492, of the development of urbanism and art, from the Spanish conquest to the present. It also provided an overview of the social and judicial organization of different Argentinian city halls and of "the architecture of today and tomorrow."[96] While the exhibitions focused on Argentina, the congress's outspoken aim was to strengthen the ties between the cities of the Americas. These contradictions were resolved in the inaugural speech of minister of foreign relations and religion Hipólito J. Paz, which suggested a different objective: the desire to cast Perón's influence from the nation across the Western Hemisphere.[97] This desire for international projection helps unpack the exhibitions held in parallel with this congress, which were meant to reaffirm Perón's cultural success, both to this select international audience and to the local public.

The exhibitions were up for a month and received widespread attention from the Porteño public, their main audience. Their mix of antiquity and modernity produced a cultural alternative for the masses that bypassed Perón's anti-intellectual stance. For instance, the City Hall Central Library mounted a display of antique maps and books published and edited in Buenos Aires in the eighteenth and nineteenth centuries, together with collections of the first newspapers printed in the city. Photographs of the exhibition show the books piled on top of each other in glass cases, sometimes with their pages artistically folded tantalizingly to conceal and reveal their contents, conveying that they represent specimens of antiquity and nothing more. The library elided the state's broken relationship with the country's writers and intellectuals and treated books as objects to be observed but not read.

Another exhibition presented popular art as an "eloquent demonstration of the artistic work of the citizen masses."[98] The conspicuous absence of Argentinian artists, who showed their work at the 34th Fine Arts Salon instead, again sent a clear message of the state's priorities. The same message was repeated in an exhibition of prints by national and foreign artists. Through this carefully curated content, the congress avoided presenting established artists and their work, preferring instead to showcase reproducible prints that anyone could purchase. This choice made an implicit statement against the elitist discourse that had characterized the Argentinian avant-garde. While these attacks sometimes veered into an attack on knowledge itself, as with the book displays, in many instances the exhibition's populist goals evidenced a subtle understanding of the advantages of presenting an aesthetic alternative to the avant-garde.

The event culminated with an exhibition that presented state housing projects, framed by maternal feminine figures. Depicted through modernist aesthetics, they suggested a similarly nurturing modern state. Itala Villa Flores and her project were absent from this display. The exhibit was titled "Exhibition of Urbanism, City Hall Public Works, Housing, and Flowers," and its climax was Bajo Belgrano and its promotional film.[99] The housing exhibition was a large affair with gravitas, with presentations made by several state institutions and contributions from important modern artists and architects. An affiliated series of lectures on the history of the cities of the Americas was later reproduced in *Revista de Arquitectura*, complicating the European bias of the congress with lectures on Inka and Aztec cities. The journal also included views of the exhibition.[100] A local newspaper described its contents:

> The exhibition included an interesting collection of plates, aerial photographs, photographic compositions, and models, which detailed the technical and economic-financial studies by the department. In different "stands" visitors were shown works of cartography and aerial photography and the evolution of the city from different points of view.[101]

The highly technical demonstration of modern progress, a common practice of world's fairs and expositions of the twentieth century, also harkened back to Mussolini's Italian Aeronautical Exhibition in Milan in 1934.[102] This was a benchmark of exhibition design and a well-known moment in which modernist aesthetics were used to advance fascist politics.[103] This link between Italian modernity and fascism was familiar in Buenos Aires, where curator and critic Pietro Maria Bardi had exhibited Italian modern architecture in 1933 to encourage Italo-Argentinian support for Mussolini.[104] Like the Milan exhibition, the Buenos Aires exhibition used aesthetic means to advertise technological advancements that it had not quite achieved yet.

The exhibition took place in the venue of La Sociedad Rural Argentina (known locally as La Rural, the Argentine Rural Society), an association of landowners and cattle breeders in the northern neighborhood of Palermo. This space associated with privilege and wealth hosted the populist affair, revealing that Porteño society and Peronist politics were not altogether separate. Inside, the sequence began in the main hallway, which was dominated by a large, centrally placed, suspended staircase leading to a second floor. This tubular structure coiled around an 8-meter high sculpture by Miguel Nevot and Antonio Devoto representing a strange tree, whose branches appear to simultaneously embrace, restrain, and merge into the figure of a woman gazing peacefully into the distance. Was she the mythological Daphne, the forest nymph who was transformed into a tree as she fled Apollo? In the 1930s Daphne was rediscovered by surrealists when Dalí included her image in his novel and in an installation.[105] The legacy of Daphne's image, which architectural historian Spyros Papapetros has explored, includes the manner in which the multiple interpretations of the myth have inspired architecture.[106] This elucidates what it meant for a figure of Daphne to welcome visitors to a Perón-sponsored vision of modern Buenos Aires. While her body was often used to display traces of desire and violence or presented as a hybrid of the human and vegetal, in the Argentine exhibition Daphne is supported by nature. The tree snakes around her legs and torso, lifting her up in an intimate, organic embrace. Erasing the violent sexuality of the original Greek myth, and its surrealist reinterpretations, Nevot and Devoto transform her into symbol of the serene coexistence of the human, mineral, and vegetal worlds, domesticated and deprived of the surrealist affinity for rupture and shock. The metallic staircase snaking around the sculpture suggests a harmonious relationship between nature and technology. This domesticated surrealist muse brought order to the central hall and the exhibition spaces accessed through it.[107] The highlight of these rooms was the space shared by the Dirección Municipal de Vivienda (City Hall Housing Department) and the EPBA's display for Bajo Belgrano.

Upon entering the Housing Department exhibition, the visitor was confronted with a large mural by Tomás Maldonado (FIGURE 3.07) that clearly pointed to the Peronist narrative of Eva guarding the people. Its angled lines and shapes cross the frame diagonally, creating a space for two photographs. The first shows a woman and child viewed from above, with their bodies foreshortened. The second is the profile of a woman surrounded by a circle of light, presumably the sun referenced by the text on the top (sadly, the rest of the text is unreadable). It is an atypical mural for Maldonado, an abstract *invencionista* artist who had spoken strongly against figurative representation and symbolism and would go on to lead the Ulm School of Design in Germany. It was an atypical mural for Peronism as well, as the regime veered toward variants of social realism for its representations of Eva, usually described as unintended expressions of kitsch and camp.

This rare intersection of Peronism and modernism has been overlooked in aesthetic analysis of this period. Examined through the lens of the Peronist imaginary, the mother and child are being guarded and contained by the main female figure, haloed by the sun, portraying an Eva-like image. Lines and shapes radiate from the female profile and extend toward the mother and child. Maldonado, who had repeatedly argued against an imposed government aesthetic, had reached a compromise. The human bodies included in the composition were photographed "architecturally": orthogonal views in plan (the mother and child) and elevation (the woman's profile), a strategy that both abstracts them and fixes them in place. In contrast, the lines and shapes that float freely between them insinuate movement and play. While this tendency toward abstraction is explained by Maldonado's *invencionismo*, in terms of symbolism the mural follows the Peronist narrative, with Eva guarding a

FIGURE 3.07.
Tomás Maldonado, mural at the Architecture and Urbanism Exhibition. *RdA* (November 1949): 302. CD BMIN, FADU-UBA.

happy family. This maternal image harkened back to the nonaggressive femininity of Daphne and welcomed the visitors into the state's housing exhibition. Between a domesticated Daphne and a domesticator Eva, the stage was set for the merging of Peronist politics and a Corbusian modernism.

The architects working for the EPBA took advantage of the building height and organized their boards and objects as a double-height display, with a Corbusian ramp offering multiple views of the exhibited objects and setting up the promenade. Floating in the middle of this space, a skeletal cubic structure was used to suspend photomontages of Bajo Belgrano (FIGURE 3.08). Thick bands crossed the structure, anchoring it to the hall and creating a large three-dimensional composition. The resulting effect is reminiscent of the Gold Medal Hall of the Italian Aeronautical Exhibition noted earlier. One of these photomontages portrays the city's return to the river, a Corbusian vision. A large model of Bajo Belgrano was set directly on the floor. The surrounding panels discreetly displayed relevant information. At the end of the promenade, the ramp took the visitors up to a vantage point where they could observe the model from above (FIGURE 3.09). The ramp ended at a small cinema showing Gras's promotional film, which according to *Revista de Arquitectura* was one of the most popular attractions in the whole exhibition.[108]

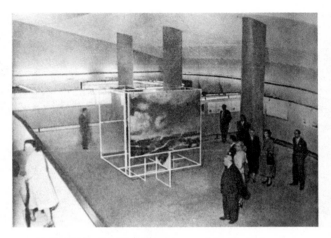

FIGURE 3.08.
EPBA stand, *RdA* (November 1949): 303. CD BMIN, FADU-UBA.

FIGURE 3.09.
Access ramp to cinema and observation post of the Bajo Belgrano model, *RdA* (November 1949): 303. CD BMIN, FADU-UBA.

THE CITY IN FRONT OF THE RIVER (1949)

In the narrated short appropriately titled *La ciudad frente al río* (The city in front of the river) camera movements, rotation, cropping, and the montage of images and sound are used to convey a diseased city under attack from pollution, traffic, and excess building. The message was that the city needed to be rebuilt into a vision that can be described as a pastoral modernity. Gras's film is loosely structured in three parts.[109] The first and longest sequence introduces the city, describing how rapid vertical growth had congested the colonial grid, blocking access to sunlight and to the river. The tone has echoes of sickness

and war. The city is a sick patient and must be cured: she (in Spanish the city is female, *la ciudad*) is explicitly "under siege." Like Breton's conflation between Nadja and Paris, the film presents the city as a woman who needs to be cared for or—perhaps better—controlled. If Benjamin had read Nadja as an exponent of the masses, here urban growth stands in for the disorder that they have wrought.

With a combination of cinematic and classical music, a male narrator describes the ills facing residents of late 1940s Buenos Aires. With urgency, he describes a city that is overcrowded because of urban planning mistakes, imprisoned by the constraints of the grid, and under attack from construction noise. The Porteños' lungs are being "bombarded" with dust, bacteria, and impurities from excess traffic, construction, and factory smoke.[110] Gras rotates factory chimneys to resemble cannons and inserts the image and sound of a street drill to echo a machine gun aimed at innocent children running in a park (FIGURE 3.10). Amid this attack, the narrator assures that "the block resists as the last bulwark," a hint at the virtues of the new "vertical block" proposed by Bajo Belgrano.

Gras introduces the modern architects next: men dressed in white lab coats who examine the city grid with a large magnifying glass (FIGURE 3.11). The narrator informs us that these specialists can cure the city's ills—their status as supposed scientists is a reminder of other attempts at expertise: Dr. Richard Rest and the designers of Bajo Belgrano, who displayed scientific knowledge through schoolbooks. The next sequence shows the master hand of the architect propping up and moving the city's blocks, transforming the tight grid into modern housing blocks and uncovering "the green of the pampa that sleeps under the cement" (FIGURE 3.12). Lined up into tightly ordered rows, the new housing blocks have a menacing military air, perhaps unintentional, reminding the viewer of Perón's military roots and of the totalitarian environment of his rule. The emphasis is not on the blocks but on the space that lies beneath them: the pampa. There is a positive psychological result in seeing the green below exposed to the sunlight. By connecting these green spaces to the pampas, the architects give their modern project a wash of Peronist nationalism in the form of pastoral nostalgia. If Casa Amarilla had inadvertently presented the pampas as populated by unruly and menacing strangers, Bajo Belgrano expressly framed them as a return to a mythical rural past.

FIGURE 3.11.
Architects examine the city. EPBA, *La ciudad frente al río* (1949). JFHA, courtesy FLL, Harvard University, GSD.

FIGURE 3.12.
Architect's hand assembling the city. EPBA, *La ciudad frente al río* (1949). JFHA, courtesy FLL, Harvard University, GSD.

The film's last section shows a montage of built projects, reassembled into a dreamlike city set in the not-so-distant future. The architect's disembodied hand returns, pointing with a pencil to the different buildings set in a model of the project, emulating the well-known photograph of Le Corbusier's hand over the Ville Radieuse. Images combine perspectival renderings of generic modern buildings with shots of people strolling and moving around the space. Views of Ferrari, Bonet, and Kurchan's other projects are cleverly inserted into this new landscape, with their contexts erased. Ferrari and Kurchan's Los Eucaliptos apartment building, which the locals might recognize, is in real life squeezed into the city's tight urban fabric. But here it is tightly cropped to erase neighboring buildings and presented as a sample façade of Bajo Belgrano. In another sequence pedestrian bridges within the Uruguayan forest from Bonet's project in

Punta Ballena are used as a stand-in for Bajo Belgrano's green expanse. The specificities of these architectural projects are irrelevant to this image of pastoral modernity. The narrator reassures the audience that these apartments will be owned by their inhabitants and that they will be "authentic intimate spaces, where family life will develop with dignity." In other words, no matter how radical the images might look, this modern project is meant to house the most traditional of societies. The final sequence reinforces the idea of modernity as a return to nature—the sun, the river, and the pampas, explicitly specified by the narrator—by showing a photomontage of the gleaming river and a sunflower turning toward the sun in the final frames, overlaid with the logo of the EPBA.

The conflation of Corbusian and Peronist tropes was executed brilliantly by Gras, who conveys the contrast between urban chaos and pastoral dream through both form and content. In the first segment, the sound is set up in jarring juxtaposition to images. We hear what sounds like the outburst of a machine gun over views of playing children, only to discover in the next image that it is the sound of a street drill. Inanimate objects take on uncanny qualities as they move before our eyes. In his early career in Italy, Gras had experimented with cartoons, working with artist Luciano Emmer to produce what they termed "a series of experiments in surrealist film, attempting to develop a poetic documentary form."[111] He was fond of creating the illusion of movement by either panning past inanimate objects or framing them animated by wind, water, or other forces. These techniques are present in the first segment of the film, where he uses the camera to create the illusion of moving objects by adjusting the frame, circling around them, or juxtaposing images to suggest their impending collision. A different kind of animation takes place in the next segment, where the playful hand of the godlike male architect moves and shapes the city. In the last section of the film, Gras uses fixed viewpoints and slow pans to portray the tranquil vistas of the dream modern city, reinforcing the message of a return to nature. Here he combines segments of strolling citizens with architectural renderings, lending a fictitious air to the new Buenos Aires. The music adds a pompous official note, using different fragments of the first movement of Ludwig van Beethoven's Symphony No. 9 and Bagatelle No. 25, "Für Elise." As the shock of the first segment transitions into the more idyllic views of the project, the melancholic Beethoven pieces reinforce the pastoral fantasy.

The range of film techniques, from fast-paced montage in the first sequence to slow pans in the last one, as well as the brooding music reinforce the idea of an implicit return: from the urban chaos of the present to a fictitious, tranquil past, echoing the Peronist message. The revolutionary thrust of modern architecture is manipulated to present a moment of constructed nostalgia that endowed the pampas with new connotations. The pastoral quality places Bajo Belgrano at the nexus of the pampas and the river. Philosopher Marshall Berman has discussed what he calls a techno-pastoral or pastoral modernism to point to variants of modernism deprived of criticality and dissonance, closer to a naive celebration of its cultural traits over a critical analysis of the processes that produce them.[112] Imagining the compromised modernity of Peronist cultural production as a pastoral modernity, through Berman's concept, allows us to tease out the paradoxical nature of modern architecture under Perón: specifically, Peronism's celebration of the state's narrative, its use of nationalist tropes like the pampa, and its appeal to traditional values of family and private property, access to green and sunny land being an imperative.[113]

"A HAPPY LIFE IN A HAPPY CITY"

Grete Stern's graphics for the film reinforced the narrative of pastoral modernity. As part of her work for the EPBA, she designed the logo and printed material for Bajo Belgrano, including a brochure used to reinforce the message of the film (FIGURE 3.01). The brochure reinforces the promotional logic of the project under the narrative of Peronism. Bajo Belgrano—as we are told on the cover—will be a third foundation of Buenos Aires (the city was famously founded twice). In *La ciudad frente al río*, the brochure promises, Porteños will live *una vida feliz en una ciudad feliz* (a happy life in a happy city). The brochure echoes the film's script. The text and images describe the current Buenos Aires as a city under siege, to be rescued by modern architecture. Using images from the film, Stern's photomontage depicts the city as a jumble of menacing chimneys discharging smoke against an X-ray of presumably Porteño lungs, vehicles overtaking the streets, tall buildings blocking the sunlight, and children crying. To remedy these ills, the project proposes a return to Buenos Aires's forgotten river with a romantic view of that landscape, complete with horses and a large tree looming over the water. This is the largest image in the brochure, yet it includes no buildings. Instead, it brings together the pampas and the Río La Plata. The brochure also advertises the future Buenos Aires, describing the details of Bajo Belgrano with images from the film. Finally, the reader is instructed to see the film, digest it, and divulge its message. The cover's promise of happiness is a reminder of the logic of propaganda: that contented citizens are passive and docile citizens.

Yet certain images in the film and the brochure run counter to the call for happiness and compliance. Stern often recycled and borrowed images, sometimes using images from her ex-husband, Coppola. It is no surprise that in a later "dream" illustration for *Idilio* we find some images that look like the threatening chimneys portrayed in the film.[114] They could be stills from the film, pointing to the conflation between these contemporaneous works. But the factory chimney is a loaded image. Bataille had described it in his critical dictionary as a fear-inspiring memory of early childhood indicative of rage and inner unrest. It is through a child's eyes that we can truly see these associations, while the technician reads the factory as a prosaic indicator of labor. Bataille concludes:

> That is why, when placing it in a dictionary, it is more logical to call upon the little boy, the terrified witness of the birth of that image of the immense and sinister convulsions in which this whole life will unfold, rather than the technician, who is necessarily blind.[115]

Gras and Stern's filmic and graphic narratives parallel Bataille's juxtaposition of children and technicians—perhaps a coincidence, or left over from our architects' surrealist interests and the association of children with an evocation of the irrational and the masses' emotional life. The correspondence in the archive points to Bonet and Ferrari's strong involvement in the film and brochure content. The recurring slippage between Porteños and children ultimately suggests that the Porteños *are* the children in the film, an infantilized public that must be treated and tended by the architect-technicians, affirming the dynamic of authoritarian control at play.

At the same time, a careful reading of the children's actions throughout the film points to a subtle, perhaps even subversive role in their actions. In the first segment they are innocent victims, threatened by the violence

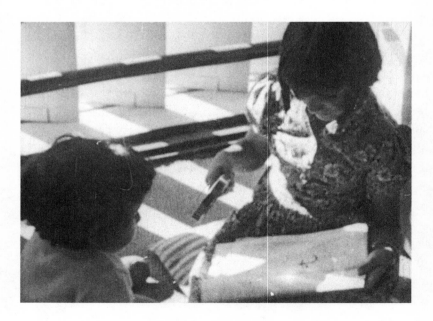

FIGURE 3.13.
Children burning the city plan. EPBA, *La ciudad frente al río* (1949). JFHA, courtesy FLL, Harvard University, GSD.

MODERNITY FOR THE MASSES

Del Buenos Aires de hoy. Bajo de Flores.

Del Buenos Aires de mañana. Bajo de Flores. Es tarea del urbanista el lograr en la ciudad misma y en gran escala la recuperación del medio físico que se ilustra aquí mediante la simple supresión en la fotografía de una parte de la realidad actual.

FIGURE 3.14.
Urbanism Exhibition catalog. FABC, © copyright AHCOAC (EPBA).

of polluting factories and chaotic traffic. But as the city is "cured" by the architect-scientists with their antiseptic white coats and large magnifying glasses—they need the magnifying glasses to "see"—the children take over their tools with troublesome intentions. A quick take on the final segment shows the pivoting louvers of Bonet's Artists' Ateliers, presented as a modern interior of Bajo Belgrano. The viewer is inside the building's curved corner: the entire production is now turned into a filmic photomontage and a promotional medium for the architects. Sitting on the floor by the louvers, in an eerie twist, a girl uses a magnifying glass to capture the sun and burn what looks like the plan of an orthogonal city grid (FIGURE 3.13). The energy of the sun, which throughout this idyllic vision has been built up as a benefit, is suddenly transformed into an agent of destruction through the actions of a child. Are the children destroying the dense old grid of the city? Or are they reminders of the untamed, irrational forces of the masses that persist even after all order is established? Is their potential to destroy the rationality of the world? The children's role in the film strikes a disquieting note, hinting that the public for these projects requires care and council from the state but also careful supervision and control.

The Urbanism Exhibition catalog, also designed by Stern, introduces the EPBA team and its aims with two paired image spreads. The first one is a photograph of a littered landscape, contrasted in the facing page with the same image with the garbage cropped out (FIGURE 3.14). The urbanists' task, explains the caption, is to recuperate the landscape in the same way that it has been recuperated by cropping the photograph—out of sight, out of mind. The second spread contrasts an image of different textures superimposed on a pile of garbage with what looks like a slum in the blurry background, with the clean layout promised for Bajo Belgrano. The caption says that these images represent the present and future of the city: the existing slums of the past blurry and out of focus and the crisp view of the future's promised land, with Bajo Belgrano as solution. Stern could have just taken a picture of the slums. Instead, the emphasis on the garbage in the foreground leaves the actual slum construction in the blurry background. Is that a shack in the background or not? Is the chain-link fence an element in the composition or a piece of trash? We are not sure. We only know that eliminating these problems—the garbage, the pollution, the evasive lover or the personal insecurities—ensures upward mobility. The takeaway message of the propaganda for Bajo Belgrano (and the sentimental advice column) is that the scientific or technical methods are there to help us. If romantic felicity can be attained by the readers of Dr. Rest, a happy city can be attained by the Porteños.

The promise of happiness was in keeping with Peronist strategies. Argentinians were asked to tolerate a hard-working present with the promise of happiness in a not-too distant future. This also reminds us of the readers of *Idilio*, advised by the experts to perform certain tasks to erase their traumas and improve their mental health. The journal and the film have parallel elements: the expert as authority, an infantilized public in need of guidance, and the outcome as an illusory utopia. Like Dr. Richard Rest, the architects of the EPBA felt compelled to instruct members of their public on the conditions they needed for happiness and upward mobility. *Idilio* advised members of the female public to master their insecurities and negotiate their self-worth while still playing traditional gender roles. In Bajo Belgrano the Porteño public—increasingly a politicized female population—was similarly instructed to discover just how disordered and polluted the city was and advised about its cure. With the incorporation of the female vote, the Peronist voting masses had become increasingly female. Stern was part of the production of their new female Peronist image. Perhaps this is how Stern thought about her work for the EPBA. As in her dreams for *Idilio*, here she was receiving instructions from the experts, the architects, to contrast the besieged city of pollution and noise with the dreamlike modern, happy city. In all these cases, the authority of experts—the architects, the fake psychoanalysts, the instructions of the Peronist state—lured the public into specific behaviors in exchange for the promise of future happiness. We do not know if these images were deliberately subversive or accidentally inserted as surrealist remnants, traces of the various interests that Ferrari, Bonet, Stern, and Gras had in this movement. But they certainly push back against the Peronist tropes pervasive in the film and affiliated propaganda.

RETURN OF THE MOTHER

The public's reaction provided by the notes left in the exhibition's guest book reveals a cautionary reception. Many visitors felt compelled to write down their opinion of the images and objects that they had just viewed. Most of these notes ignore the role of the architects and directly praise Perón for Bajo Belgrano. One boasts about the "Argentina of the Future, which I believe will make future generations proud."[116] There is a constant conflation of the project, the city, and the country, turning the construction of a new neighborhood into the building of a new Argentina. Many opinions echo the language of the film and the pamphlets: the return to the river, the pampa underneath, and the monoblock as panacea. A few saw the plan as a step backward. One particularly revealing note praises the work but cautions against the use of the apartment block: "The monoblock is the perfect realization of individualism without personalism, creator of the mass-man, of the culture by delivery, of directed and controlled opinion. As an emergency solution, it is logical; the problem is that this case will set a precedent."[117]

The note goes on to say that the problem is the loss of property ownership, which is the basis of society. The use of the term *personalismo* (personalism) points both to a philosophical school centered on the uniqueness of human beings and—increasingly at this moment in Latin America—to a political current focused on the cult of the leader. The writer combines the cult of the personalist leader with Ortega's definition of the mass-man, suggesting that these characters create each other. The phrasing is ambiguous, seeming to extricate the monoblock from the Peronist cult of personality (it creates individuals) while accusing it of creating mass-men by the same token, because of the difficulties of land ownership in vertical solutions. The difficult job of negotiating public and private interests, exemplified in the project, was exacerbated by the contradictions between Perón's populist rhetoric and his appeal to property ownership as an assertion of individuality and independent thinking.

While many of these appeals to ownership can be read as a coded reminder of Perón's opposition to communism, these contradictions also recall Frankfurt School philosophers Max Horkheimer and Theodor Adorno's critique of the false individualism promoted by consumer society in their canonical treatise *Dialectic of Enlightenment* (1944).[118] Populations in North and South America were similarly coerced into desired behaviors in the 1940s,

whether propelled to consumerism by capitalist advertisements or persuaded into good citizenship by Peronist propaganda.

Before the closing of the EPBA mentioned above, Bajo Belgrano was trumped by a more overt vision of the state caring for its citizens: the Ciudad Infantil (Children's City), a miniature city with buildings scaled down to host orphaned children sponsored by Eva Perón (FIGURE 3.15).[119] Anahí Ballent describes how this project operated as a "machine for learning" that produced new Peronist citizens.[120] Modern architecture could not compete with this alluring vision dressed in the language of kitsch. In the context of Perón's promotion of the image of the traditional family, the First Lady was a married woman without children and thus incomplete in terms of the female roles promoted by the state. But she strategically cultivated her image as a motherly figure to the nation. Years later, Ferrari stated that Bajo Belgrano came to an end because it overlapped with the projects of the Fundación Eva Perón (FEP, Eva Perón Foundation), the institutional arm of her social work.[121] But the overlap of these projects was a reality before the closing of the EPBA on November 1949.

Eva Perón inaugurated the Ciudad Infantil on July 14, 1949, in the block enclosed by Echeverría, Húsares, Juramento, and Dragones streets.[122] The Ciudad Estudiantil (Student City), a similar project also sponsored by the FEP but addressed to students, was inaugurated in 1951. These two so-called cities were located inside the limits projected for Bajo Belgrano, but they had been completely ignored by the EPBA (FIGURE 3.16).[123] It seems inconceivable that the architects were not aware of them, as one was already being built as they were exhibiting their plans. In a later publication of their research in 1953, we see that the EPBA architects carefully mapped the site. The block where the Ciudad Infantil was located was designated for recreational use in the site analysis and excluded from a map summarizing land values, together with other lots that would not have to be expropriated.[124] Incidentally, the same piece includes photographs of the site, in all likelihood taken by Stern, who was in charge of photography at the EPBA. The images depict women going about their daily lives, hinting at subtle ways in which Stern might have resisted the architects' efforts at erasing the site. This site analysis, published later but done prior to the project, suggests that the architects were aware of the site and the neighborhood. The two "cities" could have been incorporated into the design of Bajo Belgrano, but that would have meant compromising modern architecture's clean lines and taking Eva Perón's kitschy, children-sized buildings all the way to the CIAM.

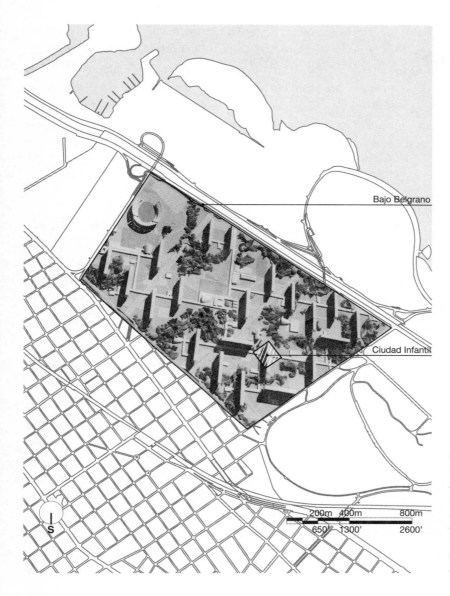

FIGURE 3.16.
Bajo Belgrano in Buenos Aires, with location of Eva Perón's Ciudad Infantil. Site plan from JFHA, courtesy FLL, Harvard University, GSD. Montage by Linda Lee under the direction of the author.

In 1951 Perón's SIPP made a promotional film at the Ciudad Infantil appropriately titled *Soñemos* (Let Us Dream). The twenty-minute film directed by Luis César Amadori follows the introduction of a blonde girl, reminiscent of Eva, into the Peronist city of children and her development as a Peronist citizen. Appropriately, all the other children have dark hair, as *cabecitas negras*. While in the Ciudad Infantil modernity was put aside in favor of a caricaturesque fantasy closer to the aesthetics of Walt Disney World, *Soñemos* reveals that the true intent of the city of children is the formation of future Peronists.

The authoritarian surrealism of this fantasy urbanism—built only a few years after Dalí's frustrated collaboration with Walt Disney—escaped our architects and prompted the end of their project.[125] The architects' film, mediated by Gras's direction, used children as symbols of the untamed and irrational and personified the city as a mentally ill woman. In a complicated turn, it was architecture meant to discipline children, built under the leadership of a powerful woman, that determined the end of the architects' modern dream.

LET US DREAM

> And so begins a new and limpid child's dream under the roof of the City of Children, the wonderful city populated by little inhabitants that dream day and night, with their eyes closed and with their eyes open. This city is reminiscent of a fairy tale, but it is nevertheless a tender reality thanks to Eva Perón, the extraordinary woman who does not sleep so that the children of the nation can dream and in order to accomplish the intimate longing of General Perón: the Argentines are a little happier watching their children dream.
>
> *Soñemos*[126]

The parting words for *Soñemos* equate happiness with a permanent state of dreaming. Ultimately this is the message behind all of these cities. Although it was never built, Bajo Belgrano's legacy is a unique body of work produced by avant-garde artists and architects working in alliance with the nostalgia and populism that characterized what we might call the Peronist unconscious. The film, brochures, and exhibition, strategically mounted to promote this housing project, demonstrate how the EPBA readily appropriated the tropes and messages of Peronism and found a way to convey them through modern means. Furthermore, Bonet and Ferrari's increasing concern with the promotion and public reception of the project decreased their involvement in the architectural design of the project itself. They mobilized Stern's modernist aesthetics as well as Gras's surrealist and fascist experiences to advance a message of modernism at the service of Peronism.

As Perón's opponent Borges surmised, Peronism's methods closely approximated those of capitalism's consumer society—the word *propaganda* in Spanish, after all, is used for both political advertisement and marketing. Perón built a formidable propaganda platform through the promotion of images of him and his wife and engineered a difficult task: the invention of a new country. He was perhaps the greatest *invencionista* of all: he invented a new Argentina, a space where the Porteños could forget the embarrassments of the Infamous Decade and the short-lived revolution of 1943. Peronist textbooks for schoolchildren strategically erased unpleasant histories, and a similar strategy can be detected in broader Peronist narratives. In his very own constructed visual aesthetic Perón was everything the *invencionistas* rejected. His aesthetic language celebrated the kitschy, figurative, symbolic, and narrative potential of the image. At the same time, his tactics were resolutely modern. The voice of the expert and the promise of utopia were compressed into concrete, wave-emanating objects that were infinitely reproduced through mass media. In the end, these projects shared similar tactics. Whether kitsch objects, political propaganda, women's journals, or modern architecture, these works all sought to reach forward in order to conjure up the past and give concrete shape to an elusive dream.

The dreams of *Idilio*, the imagined city of Bajo Belgrano, the Ciudad Infantil, and the utopian Argentina invented by Perón all embody the common collective dreams of the Peronist unconscious. In Freud's stratification of the bourgeois mind, the unconscious corresponds to repressed thoughts that the individual actively suppresses, which are revealed through symptoms such as dreams, free associations, or verbal slips. The unconscious thus belonged to the private realm of the individual and was revealed to her through the disclosure and analysis of these symptoms. Both the advice column "Psychoanalysis Will Help You" and the film *La ciudad frente al río* overtly applied a simplified version of this under-standing of the unconscious. While the advice column mined its readers' dreams for these associations and advised them on proper behavior, the film mapped the unconscious of Buenos Aires onto the chaos of city life and posited a pastoral modernity as the cure. A nostalgic return to the past was masked by a veneer of modernity—an invitation to sleep, perchance to dream.

Beyond the possible embodiment of the Freudian unconscious in these works, we can glean additional insights into their status as cultural products by thinking about them and their reception as collective products. Carl Jung's definition of the collective unconscious aids in unpacking these works:

> The collective unconscious—so far as we can say anything about it at all—appears to consist of mythological motifs or primordial images, for which reason the myths of all nations are its real exponents. In fact, the whole of mythology could be taken as a sort of projection of the collective unconscious. . . . We can there-fore study the collective unconscious in two ways, either in mythology or in the analysis of the individual.[127]

In contrast to other examples of surrealist art, Stern's dream images for *Idilio* and Gras's filmic vision of a new Buenos Aires were meant to be reproduced, in both form and content. Furthermore, although the dreams were prompted by an individual's letter, they were always framed as a type; note the titles: "Dreams of Anguish" or "Dreams of Floating." Here the individual's isolated experience is turned into a collective dream, shared by many of the journal's readers, and used as a means to establish a lexicon of common symbols and corresponding desires, anxieties, and prescriptive behaviors. Similarly, the implicit message of the film, orchestrated by Bonet and Ferrari, was that all Porteños should dream of living in Bajo Belgrano. These works were directed at an audience that was produced to participate in the production of this collective unconscious. We must also add a political context to the collective nature of this unconscious.

In arguing for the political interpretation of literary texts, Fredric Jameson claims that these texts are interpreted through "sedimented reading habits and categories developed by those inherited interpretive traditions."[128] In examining these texts, images, or architectural projects, we can engage in what Jameson calls ideological analysis—an analysis of the ideology that produces texts or images and within which they are enmeshed (here following Louis Althusser). Such analysis informs what Jameson terms the political unconscious. I have turned to this politically informed collective unconscious in my reading of Gras's film and Stern's photomontages. By the late 1940s Porteños had been exposed to Peronist mythology and had learned to negotiate it—like the unruly children referenced in the film or Stern's ironically resistant women. These projects all shared similar "mythological motifs or primordial images," to use Jung's words, that pervaded the nation. From romantic bliss in a happy marriage to pastoral nostalgia through modern architecture, these images tell us that happiness for these unruly children could only be found through slumber. While some of their aesthetics presumably originated in their authors' European origins, they were produced in the context of Perón's pervasive propaganda machine. Stern's attempts at subverting Dr. Rest's advice and Gras's portrayal of unruly children destroying the plan of the city only hint at these artists' awareness of the totalizing vision that they were helping to build.

The role of the architects in the production of this content points to their anxiety to please the Peronist state. The audience they addressed, both this state and its masses, was adept at reading, assimilating, and decoding Peronist mythology as it was being invented. This was an audience composed of the growing middle class, of which Germani was so skeptical, which participated in the massive ritual celebrations of Perón-as-nation. Either rebellious or compliant, the children in these different films and projects stand in for these masses, who were instructed to dream "day and night, with their eyes closed and with their eyes open." These projects reveal a different kind of Peronist unconscious, a collectively produced social myth tuned to the frequency of Peronism. By closing their eyes to this unconscious, Bonet and Ferrari allowed it to overcome their modern dreams.

While preparing material on Bajo Belgrano to be exhibited in Buenos Aires, the architects of the EPBA had to prepare for an earlier presentation for CIAM 7, to be held from July 22 to 31, 1949, in Bergamo, Italy.[129] These events had different audiences and required different strategies. While the Buenos Aires exhibitions followed the Perón propaganda script, with printed materials and a film, the CIAM material required the use of the *grille*, a gridded layout of graphic information, a requirement of Le Corbusier. However, the film was finished in time for Bergamo, hinting at the architects' desire to display it at the congress. Thus, even though *La ciudad frente al río* was directed by an Italian surrealist with fascist training and produced specifically for an Argentinian audience, it was also displayed at the CIAM. Since Ferrari was busy managing the EPBA, Bonet was delegated to represent the group and present the project. His first return to Europe thus entailed presenting a pastoral modern project framed by Peronist tropes to this elite audience, which included his two former employers: Sert and Le Corbusier.

Beyond his role as one of the architects of the plan that Le Corbusier had tried to secure, Bonet was presenting a design that was not really his. Kurchan had been in charge of the Bajo Belgrano housing unit. This placed him in an awkward position, particularly as the project was poorly received:

> Our project, in general, was not understood. L.C., I think, understood but remained quiet. I think we were right in 90% of our approach to the problem. Sert didn't want to accept completely the idea of the neighborhood as unit, but I think it was a bit because of hurt pride. L.C. was completely in agreement in that there is nothing more than the "housing unit of 'grandeur conforme'" as he calls it, and the neighborhood. Only we should keep in sight that a bloc for him is not the same as for us. In the end, his bloc is almost a neighborhood unit and to me that is where his mistake is. An Italian, Gardela [*sic*], made us a very important critique we should consider. MAX BILL in the public assembly spoke about the lack of scale in speaking about our project, but I think he was confused because of the perspective.[130]

The critique of the project revolved around the definition of the neighborhood unit and its scale within a broader urban project, prompting Bonet to reconsider the neighborhood scale, which was missing from the project's grandiose evocation of the pampas. There is no mention of the Peronist framing given to the modern project or how these contradictory appeals of a pastoral modernism might have played out at the CIAM.

Disappointed with the project's reception and the congress in general, Bonet participated in an "Auto-critique," a collective text penned by a group led by Italian Enrico Peressutti.[131] The group members accused fellow participants of being poorly prepared and denounced the congress as badly organized.[132] With so much time allotted for recreational activities, they warned, the CIAM risked losing its working character and becoming merely a social gathering. They proposed the formation of a permanent working commission with increased participation from its geographically broadening bases.[133] The protest was drowned out by the multiple critiques and amendments read at the end of the congress, but it suggests the frustration of a younger generation at the lack of opportunities for further involvement in the congress. This critique might also be applied to the EPBA, where Ferrari and Bonet had made themselves into a supervising clique disconnected both from the design of the project and from the input of other architects. Perhaps this detail did not escape Bonet: additional correspondence from the trip hints at his thoughts of returning to a more active role as an architectural designer.

After Bergamo, Bonet visited Marseille and slept in Le Corbusier's Unité d'Habitation. The experience prompted some doubts about the design of Bajo Belgrano, specifically the large scale of the "bloc" and the need for a double height:

> I was in Marseille and slept in the show unit. In spite of everything, there we can find all the genius of L.C. It is a very dangerous experience but it marks an epoch in modern architecture. After Marseille, I'm convinced that the "City Hall Housing Division" alone should not do the bloc. In our initial scheme there was 80% truth. I am really worried about the bloc that is set to be built. When I think that in Marseille there is forty years of accumulated experience and still at this moment they are experimenting with materials because they haven't found what they are looking for. And in Buenos Aires a bloc was designed with all the details in three months!!! This might repeat the sad experience of the "l'Armeé de Salud" [sic] the problems of a building like that cannot be reduced to "trying" to make a metal kitchen! The size of the bloc will be huge and could be a disaster for all of us. Plastically it will be low and tight. The duplex without a double height makes no sense.[134]

The trip to Europe and this stay-over reawakened Bonet as a designer. In Bajo Belgrano he had been distracted by broader organizational and promotional matters, so the design of an actual building had not been a priority for him. In correspondence between Sert and Ferrari, the architects described their opinions as the "technical point of view,"[135] emphasizing their status as postwar technocrats who based their knowledge on the accumulation of data. Gone was their prewar enthusiasm about surrealist art or even architecture.

In returning to Europe and reencountering Le Corbusier, some of the enthusiasm of Bonet's youth was returning, but it was now specifically redirected toward his new home, Argentina.

In CIAM 7 Bonet started reconsidering some principles of modern urban design and rethinking traditional elements, such as neighborhoods and plazas. Other reactions that he encountered gave him some insights about the differences between European and American perspectives. Years later, he remembered:

> Everybody was surprised by the size of the green spaces we were proposing. We were applying the theories of the CIAM but viewed from America, and of course, to the Europeans it was a surprise to see the size of the green spaces, and in a certain way they were right. They did not have the environment of a city. I think it is valuable as a lesson.[136]

Still thinking about the expansive green spaces of Bajo Belgrano, he considered the virtues of well-defined plazas such as San Marco in Venice, mentioning this in his letter to Ferrari and Kurchan, written shortly after the congress ended:

> I have been to Venice. It is the ultimate lesson of Urbanism. I think I learned a lot. The Plaza San Marco, fantastic! We have arrived to something good in the center of our neighborhood. My opinion is that we should continue the study of this center of the neighborhood, which is very well thought out, and propose the construction of one of each in every neighborhood according to the plan, even if we keep the existing houses.[137]

Bonet would remember the importance of the plaza in his next project. There is no mention in the letter of the vast changes that Europe had gone through in the years of his absence, no mention of the devastations of war or Spain's prolonged Franco dictatorship. Instead, he is surprised by his own perception: it is he who has changed, not Europe. The view of Europe "from America" presented a different continent: "Even though I expected it in part, I did not think it would be so curious, the vision of Europe 'from America.' I mean everything: the architects, their projects, the cities, the countries, the people."[138]

At the end of the letter, Bonet rallies both himself and his friends about their future potential: "I have a lot of trust in our group and in general in South America. I think the line of Austral was good. Evolution will come on its own. If we know how to do things, I think our horizon is magnificent."[139] He came back from Europe transformed, at least in his eyes, into an Argentinian, ready to leave his old mentors behind and participate in the construction of a new Argentina.

However, for many of his Argentinian colleagues, Bonet would always be a foreigner. In a letter that Kurchan, the third original member of Austral, wrote to Ferrari, from Madrid, he placates his old friend about the difficulties of assembling the EPBA team, warning him against the problem of European architects, particularly ones trained in Europe: "The European professional has a sum of solved problems that are not rooted in his soul but in his intellect, one single direction in his will, a lack of plasticity to confront new and unknown problems that in his almost completely full head remain without answer."[140] Kurchan is speaking about several architects about whom Ferrari has complained, including Bonet and his "Catalan defects." He argues that American (that is, Argentinian) professionals, in contrast, are agile and flexible in confronting multiple problems.

In another letter to Ferrari from about the same time, former Austral member Jorge Vivanco also considers Bonet an outsider:

> I think we should send something "against" the CIAM. Against the Rogers, Bonets, Serts, Wieners, etc. The CIAM of the group of Corbu, Gropius, etc., was one thing—but these people, this exhibition grille, etc., are the same as Amancio, with his "merit ladder in the modern movement"—today for you, tomorrow for me. Another Academy.[141]

A subtle additional distinction is made here: Europeans of the first generation of modernism, such as Le Corbusier and Gropius, are acceptable. It is the second generation, "the Rogers, Bonets, Serts, Wieners, etc.," whom they consider opportunists, turning the noble aims of the CIAM into a merit system. It so happens that these are also the European architects operating from America (North and South), thus encroaching into the territory of the South American architects.[142] Notably, Vivanco groups Williams—a member of the conservative Argentinian upper class who never left Argentina—with Sert and Bonet, hinting at the conflation of class and nationality. It is their elitist, merit-based system that is ruining the modern movement in his estimation.

CIAM 7 was not considered a success. It highlighted the difficult relationship between "foreign" and "local" architects, European and American. These relationships were often tense. South American architects often welcomed their colleagues' expertise and status but were not always willing to give up potential projects. European architects such as Sert were more interested in doing business than in sharing knowledge, credit, and commissions. With the majority of his work in Argentina, and his roots in Europe, Bonet was caught in the middle of this tension. South America had allowed him to establish a successful practice, but after the war older hierarchies were returning. At the same time, CIAM 7 marked a generational divide. The repeated references in the architects' correspondence to their scientific expertise, the best specialists, the hiring of consultants, and the excessive time for leisure in the congress point to a different conception of the role of the architect in the postwar era. The younger generation had turned to technical expertise.

Liernur outlines this shift from avant-garde to expertise, arguing that the war prompted some CIAM leaders to retreat into "art" and plastic creation but the years after the conflict led them to seek out the appearance of technological expertise.[143] This turn was prompted in part by the technological advances and planning emphasis produced by World War II, as argued by Jean Louis Cohen.[144] In the United States these developments would lead to the rise of large corporate offices, in what Henry-Russell Hitchcock described as the architecture of bureaucracy.[145] Eric Mumford notes that this turn was awkward for the older generation of CIAM members, most of whom had not achieved posts in city planning.[146]

The EPBA similarly projected the image of the architect as expert, but viewed through the lens of the Peronist unconscious. Ferrari and Bonet distanced themselves from Le Corbusier and, with the support and leadership of the Peronist regime, turned their actions to propaganda. Their generous funding allowed them to dedicate a great deal of effort to the collection and analysis of data or at least the appearance of data. It would seem as if this large flow of numbers, lists, diagrams, and charts helped present them to the regime as hard-working specialists—technicians in white lab coats, per the film—with access to a higher knowledge, in opposition to the prewar model of the mysteriously inspired artist. While hard numbers and diagrams were architectural tools that could be wielded as "proof" of expertise, they also meant that the design of space was no longer the main métier of the architect. The loss of Peronist support revealed the architects' fragility and their failure to command an expertise that might secure them the continued trust of the state.

When Bonet wrote from Paris, the future was indeed magnificent. He and his friends were finally at work on the modern plan of their dreams. A month later everything came to a halt. With the insights gained from Bajo Belgrano, the discussions with old colleagues and new allies at Bergamo, and his tour of postwar Europe, Bonet was ready to tackle a large urban project. The opportunity to do so, however, did not come until seven years later—and for the very regime that ousted Perón.

chapter four

ETERNAL RETURNS

On June 16, 1955, thirty aircraft from the Argentinian air force and navy bombarded the presidential palace, known as the Casa Rosada, and the Plaza de Mayo (just in front of it) during a popular demonstration in support of Perón. This resulted in 308 identified casualties and an indeterminate number of victims who were never tallied or properly identified. The symbolism was not lost on the nation—the massacre took place in the same space as the iconic occupation of the plaza in 1945, which Perón had commemorated as Loyalty Day. In bombarding this space of ritual celebration, the military violently replaced the images of happy crowds celebrating Perón with images of dead bodies. These shocking images circulated in newspapers and journals around the country. After additional months of attacks and instability, Perón was forced to quit his post and leave the country, fleeing to Paraguay and settling in Spain in 1960. He was replaced by the perpetrators of this violence.[1]

One year after this tragedy, Bonet was completing the design of another housing project, Barrio Sur, sited in San Telmo and named after the southern half of the city—the traditionally populist, working-class sector that had housed the majority of Perón's supporters.[2] Barrio Sur included not one but six plazas, all on a scale similar to the iconic Plaza de Mayo, just north of the project (one is shown in FIGURE 4.01). Despite the similarities in scale, they look nothing like the Plaza de Mayo. Nor are there any unruly crowds dipping their feet in a fountain—only window shoppers strolling past the many stores that dominate, with their foreign logos highlighting the project's allegiances. If Bajo Belgrano was designed as part of Perón's propaganda system, Barrio Sur was made for advertisements.

A large isolated tree is the only landscape in this otherwise empty square, while a lone skyscraper reminds us of the modern project of which it is a part. As in the case of Casa Amarilla, the views that illustrate Barrio Sur show very

FIGURE 4.01. (*opposite*) Photomontage. Bonet, Barrio Sur (1956). FABC, © copyright AHCOAC (Bonet).

little of the architectural project and reveal their ideology through the close-up renderings of the spaces that the project would produce. The image's ambiguity was a strategy later mined by Bonet when he used the project to reintroduce himself to Spain in the early 1960s. This would be a complicated return. Bonet arrived back in Spain in the context of Franco's turn to the United States and the so-called Spanish Miracle. His return also meant a return to the Mediterranean aesthetic as a trope for modern architecture, now recontextualized by Spain's venture into the enterprise of tourism. These returns point to a transformation of modern architecture's definition of housing, from human right to market commodity.

REPLACING PERÓN

ANOTHER REVOLUTION

After enjoying the widespread support of the military, church, and labor unions in his first term, Perón faced increased opposition soon after his second election in 1952. His downturn in popularity also followed Eva Perón's death of cancer at thirty-three, a traumatic event for the country. Economic troubles, confrontations with the Catholic church, and harsh treatment of opposition voices created a complicated alliance against Perón, composed of a range of opposing groups, from the radical and socialist parties to the military, the church, and other conservative associations. In 1955 various civilian and military sectors united under the name of the Revolución Libertadora (Liberating Revolution) and ended Perón's rule. The group's name recalled the "Revolution of '43," the military coup d'état of the prior decade, giving the events a strange familiarity.

In 1943 writer Jorge Luis Borges had published a newspaper article explaining Friedrich Nietzsche's notion of eternal recurrence: "the men that now populate the world will be reborn in other cycles, they will repeat the same acts and pronounce the same words; we will live (and have lived) an infinite number of times."[3] Borges's reading of Nietzsche takes us back to the "unlimited and cyclical" nature of his library of Babel. Speculating that the repetitive cells that populate the library emulate the grid of the city and Ortega's description of the mass-man, we might also consider that the rule of chance that governs the library points to the chaos of the Infamous Decade that resulted in Perón's rise. Reading Borges's interpretation of Nietzsche, we can also read the infinite and periodic nature of the library as an allegory for the latter's formulation of history as unending and cyclical. There is no path through the library, no beginning and no end, only infinite, random, and chaotic repetition of uniform books. Considering the possibility of an eternally recurring world, Nietzsche wondered whether a life experienced to the fullest could withstand the burden of such repetition.[4] Eternal recurrence here would be the heaviest burden, an unbearable punishment that might perhaps crush us.

Given the repetitive military coups of 1930, 1943, and 1955 (as well as 1976) the idea of repetition had a particular urgency in a country held hostage by its own military. In 1955 this repetition took the form of tragedy. The military uprising of that year, organized by the Argentine navy and air force, bombarded several strategic sites in Buenos Aires, including the Casa Rosada and the Plaza de Mayo, causing hundreds of deaths in an attempt to kill Perón and overthrow his government (FIGURE 4.02). In militaristic language, the film *La ciudad frente al río* had described the city as bombarded by chimney fumes: an actual bombardment had now happened. The military also orchestrated attacks in smaller cities. With the country immersed in civil war, Perón eventually capitulated. The new government had to reckon with a difficult task: establishing its authority after ousting a president who still enjoyed a large popular following. Gen. Eduardo Lonardi Doucet assumed the de facto presidency, but his conciliatory tone prompted distrust from the military, who

FIGURE 4.02.
Casa Rosada after the bombardment of the Plaza de Mayo, June 16, 1955. AR, AGN DDF/Consulta INV: 350208.

replaced him after only two months with Gen. Pedro Eugenio Aramburu.[5] Balancing the need to maintain a unified front in the first months of the new regime, the coalition of disparate political forces at the head of the state focused on countering the cult of personality created by Juan and Eva Perón.

The state sought first to discredit Perón and then to erase all traces of him. Not only were the Peróns viciously attacked in the press, but their names and images were expunged from the public realm and the public record. A law officially dissolved the Peronist party and declared it illegal.[6] It was soon followed by a law prohibiting any public reference to Perón, including mention of his name, his wife's name, his political party, and any phrases, slogans, or music that evoked him or his presidency.[7] Perón's speeches could not be quoted; nor could his image, symbols, or any visual reference to his person be used. The breach of these laws was punishable by prison, disqualification from public posts, and permanent closure in the case of a business or collective group. Perhaps the most radical erasure of all was the sequestering of Eva Perón's remains, which were secretly transported to Italy. This erasure was echoed in the built environment with the demolition of the Unzué Palace, which had been used as the presidential residence since the 1930s and where Eva Perón had famously lived and tragically died. The building was targeted as a possible place of pilgrimage but was demolished in 1958 after a strong campaign in the press.[8]

The new regime sought to change the built environment and its perception. Following a broad smear campaign, the state also sought to discredit Perón's efforts in the area of housing. The growth of informal settlements or slums, known in Argentina as *villas miseria* (misery villas), was interpreted as a sign of this failure to provide social housing. The reality was more complicated. By the time Perón was ousted, he had built several housing projects: first, single-family neotraditional chalets and later more modern apartment blocks. He had allowed substantial amounts of energy and capital to go into the development and promotion of the EPBA and Bajo Belgrano, which was promoted and received as a Peronist project even though it was funded by the Buenos Aires City Hall. In fact, the real problem for the new administration was the ubiquity of Peronist references in the built landscape. He was everywhere. Its first gesture was to obliterate his name from the many buildings and projects named after him and his wife, including important dates in the Perón calendar.

The housing problem, however, was urgent—the state needed to address the growing slums. About a month after Perón was ousted, Gen. Lonardi, serving as de facto president, created the Comisión Nacional de la Vivienda (CNV, National Housing Commission), which effectively replaced the prior Comisión Nacional de Casas Baratas (CNCB, National Commission for Low-Cost Housing—see chapter 2). Lonardi hoped to create an "integral plan" to deal with the country's housing emergency. The CNV had several architects among its members, including Bonet (representing the Sociedad Central de Arquitectos), Walter Hylton Scott (editor of *Nuestra Arquitectura*), and Hilario Zalba (former Austral member). Bonet's presence in the commission underlines the advantages of his low-profile role in the EPBA. Ferrari was absent, perhaps disqualified because of his formative role in the Peronist plan.[9] In his recounting of the multiple state commissions and private groups that attempted to tackle the housing question under the Revolución Libertadora, historian Jorge Liernur highlights the role of Luis Migone, an engineer rather than a politician or architect, who was appointed to lead the CNV. He notes that Migone focused on facts over politics and outspokenly attributed the housing deficit to problems in the construction industry.[10] Liernur's close reading of the CNV reports reveals that other members of the commission did not follow Migone's lead, choosing instead to present contradictory and often uninformed opinions that usually blamed Perón's tenure for the housing crisis. They stereotyped the slums as insalubrious and their inhabitants (known as *villeros*) as sexually promiscuous and partial to drinking. Whether deliberately or not, these self-righteous assessments meshed with the new regime's characterizations of Perón, extending his supposedly immoral behavior to his followers, the *cabecitas negras*.

In the end the CNV was unable to put together the "integral plan" that Lonardi envisioned. It did not help that Lonardi's tenure in office only lasted two months. Several other state-funded and private groups attempted to tackle the housing question, but they generated too many reports and too few results for the regime's purposes—the housing projects that were built were either too small or took too long. In order to demolish Perón's legacy effectively, a grand, theatrical gesture was needed: a large urban project that would solve the housing problem and, more importantly, contain the Peronist masses, now ubiquitous in the city because of the growth of the slums. Perhaps by virtue of their absorption into the project, they might be transformed into citizens of the new regime.

"A PHARAONIC WORK"

To contrast itself to the image it had constructed of Perón, the new regime sought to present itself as modern and technologically efficient, but it needed to balance this with an appeal to conservative politics. This political mandate was echoed in the architectural production and discourse of the nation, also inflected by architects' attention to international work that displayed attributes of modernity and technological advancement through its large scale and structural prowess. As pointed out by historian Federico Deambrosis, the popularity of architects like Italian Pier Luigi Nervi and Brazilian Oscar Niemeyer in Argentinian architecture journals was reflected in the ambitious projects of Argentine architects Amancio Williams and Eduardo Catalano—many unbuilt but nonetheless significant to the local imaginary.[11] In 1951 former *invencionista* Tomás Maldonado started editing a new journal, *Nueva Visión* (New Vision, 1951–1957) dedicated to promoting the ideals of concrete art (with several features on the work of former *invencionistas*), graphic design, music, poetry, and architecture and the built environment, with a particular emphasis on large-scale structures. The journal's first issue featured an article on Bonet's architecture, with special focus on a project that he worked on in Le Corbusier's office with a structurally daring solution, the Water Pavilion for Liège, Belgium (1938–1939).[12] Throughout its run, the journal combined the work of Argentinian and Brazilian artists and architects with the work of Europeans relocated to the United States, such as Mies van der Rohe, Xanti Schawinsky, Alexander Dorner, and Richard Neutra. These editorial choices suggested a link between a technocratic approach to modernity and the work of the European diaspora on the Atlantic side of the larger countries in North and South America.

But Bonet's built work up to this point did not include the large-scale projects that the moment called for. Throughout his involvement with groups like Austral, OVRA, and the EPBA, his individual built work had mostly consisted of houses in and around Buenos Aires. In the late 1940s, before Bajo Belgrano, he had built Punta Ballena (1945–1948), a resort in Uruguay that included a hotel and a few vacation homes, including his own. In the early 1950s he engaged in projects like Casa Oks (1953–1956), a turn from the playful surrealist attempts of the Artists' Atelier to a colder, more rational Miesian aesthetic. After the closing of the EPBA, Bonet turned to publishing. In 1955 he started co-editing *Mirador: Panorama de la Civilización Industrial* (Lookout: Panorama of industrial civilization, 1955–1961), a journal focused on industrial design, with the industrialist Carlos Levin. In 1952 Levin commissioned a few projects from Bonet, including a large campus for his textile factory, Textil Oeste SA (TOSA), which included three large blocks to house factory workers. We see here a design solution similar to what he proposed for Casa Amarilla and Bajo Belgrano, with blocks laid out as solids over a green void. The TOSA factory, which advanced far into the design development stage before the commission fell through, suggests that Bonet was still invested in the same urban design paradigms he had been using throughout his career. He proposed a similar solution for an urban plan contest for the small city of Necochea-Quequén (1953), for which he won first place. None of these larger projects panned out, however, leaving this ambitious architect without building credentials at the urban scale.

Bonet's problems would soon be solved by Manuel Rawson, the president of the Banco Hipotecario Nacional (BHN, National Mortgage Bank), who replaced the CNV housing plans with a proposal for the construction of a new neighborhood south of the center of the city. Liernur describes Rawson as an "inconspicuous figure with important links to powerful sectors." He was a personal friend and cousin of the new president and had been a trusted counselor of Arturo Rawson, who preceded Perón.[13] These links might explain similarities between the aims of the new project and those stated in OVRA's report. The most direct link, however, was Bonet, the architect who led both projects. Bonet believed that he might have inspired the project: he remembered lecturing at the School of Philosophy in Buenos Aires: "I insisted on the need to remodel atrophied but central neighborhoods, instead of continuing to extend the city toward the infinite."[14] The lecture prompted a call from Rawson, leading to a series of conversations where "the idea came up to remodel the most important of these neighborhoods, the so-called Barrio Sur."[15] Not only was Bonet able to secure the commission, but he would also determine the location in the traditional old neighborhood of San Telmo.

San Telmo is only a fragment of what is understood to be Barrio Sur, which is roughly the southern half the city, but it is still a considerable site, totaling 200 hectares (500 acres). This had been the neighborhood of the working class and more politically revolutionary groups in the 1920s and later the home of a large part of the *cabecitas negras* that had supported Perón. The carving out of the north-south axis of the Nueve de Julio had not changed the local understanding of the city as fragmented into two opposing halves. While a project in San Telmo had the appearance of addressing the Peronist constituency, in reality it was addressing members of the middle class, which was moving or had already relocated to an ever-growing suburban periphery. Bonet's proposal explicitly proposed to bring them closer to their workplaces.[16] The project was meant to displace the working class in favor of a wealthier middle class, who would become the new inhabitants of Barrio Sur.

The newly installed regime of Gen. Pedro Aramburu, who succeeded Lonardi, commissioned the project directly to Bonet. The difference from prior commissions was not lost on him—presenting the project at a later conference, he wrote in his notes: "In this case, the responsibility was exclusively mine, and accordingly the new approach was not disputed."[17] The last phrase is crossed out in his notes, hinting at Bonet's reluctance to admit prior tensions in his professional collaborations. He took on Barrio Sur with great energy, putting together a team of about twenty employees, including architects, draftspeople, model makers, and other specialists.[18] Some team members were recruited from the Porteño avant-garde, including *invencionista* artist

Antonio Hlito, who was put in charge of the graphic layouts. The team worked on a complete set of architectural and urban plans, a large site model, and an extensive folder detailing an introduction to and justification for the project, ordinances, a budget, and a draft of the law that would make these actions possible. Architect Justo Solsona, a draftsman on the project, remembers it as "a pharaonic work," housed in offices that took over one full floor in the Automóvil Club Argentino, a large modern building on Libertadores Avenue.[19] The contract was signed in February 1956, and a large documentation folder with the finished project was turned in at the end of December that year, giving us an idea of the team's frantic pace.[20] The resources and energy allocated to Barrio Sur are emblematic of different political and architectural projects coming together with ease. The state was eager to erase all traces of Perón from the built landscape, and Bonet was eager finally to complete an urban design project of his own. These political and urban design projects in Barrio Sur were the fruit of a new economic strategy: state intervention clearing the ground for private investment.

OUT WITH THE OLD: DEMOLISHING SAN TELMO

Bonet provided his own narrative for the project in the general introduction included in the documentation folder. This text provides us with key insights not only into the architectural project but also into the project of land extraction and private development carried within it and the ways in which they intersected. Bonet argues that San Telmo's tenements and slums require state intervention in order to clear the ground for private investment. Sketching out an abbreviated history of the city, he describes San Telmo as a formerly wealthy neighborhood that had been long occupied by tenements and slums with "appalling living conditions." The neighborhood, he tells us, "retains nothing of its former colonial appearance, because an examination of its buildings does not show them to keep the characteristics of the time." Having laid out an argument for demolition, Bonet mentions a few of the buildings that he considers salvageable and concludes by praising the logic of the grid, the block, and the street as valuable urban planning tools that allowed the first settlers of the city to grow and "occupy space, an inherent purpose of any human settlement that establishes itself in a primarily hostile medium that must be gradually dominated."[21] This depiction of a "primarily hostile medium" resonates ominously at the end of a section dedicated to the current situation of San Telmo and reminds us of Gras's film. The text concludes that San Telmo must be demolished and that salvaging a reinterpreted grid is a rational way to honor the merits of Argentina's colonial past while looking toward a modern future.

In the next section Bonet goes through earlier urban solutions, highlighting the difficulties of the old city ordinance and the density of the *medianeras*: the narrow vertical shafts that provide ventilation between apartments lined up one behind the other in the city's deep lots (described in chapter 1). He also dismisses his own prior attempts at urban planning, dramatically crossing them out in an illustration, including a modified layout of TOSA, mentioned earlier.[22] He describes these projects as monotonous, oblivious of the human scale, and difficult to finance because of their low densities. This last justification is clearly strategic and meant to strengthen the argument for Barrio Sur. This development, according to Bonet's argument, was dependent on private investment and would work because of its high population target.[23] The project's narrative expects all new development to be managed by private enterprise, with the possible exception of a few housing projects by the state to house the population displaced by the expropriations or the option to house them elsewhere with preferential treatment facilitated by the BHN. Ultimately the displaced population—the *cabecitas negras*—is considered insignificant in comparison to the incoming population: its absorption into the new development is taken for granted.

The multiple references to private investment and dense population in the introduction come together in the ordinance of the project. This, Bonet argues, provides the necessary density for the project to be financially successful. The ordinance also specifies a few buildings that would be exempt from expropriation (and therefore demolition). After surveying the site, he concluded that only two groups of buildings merited conservation: those of "historic, artistic, and religious value" and those of "economic value, which because of their location can be integrated in the project without affecting the ordinance." The first group included seven churches, the writers' association, and a theater. The second group included ten apartment buildings. Thus, with the exception of these nineteen buildings, the rest of the neighborhood would be gradually cleared and eventually replaced by private development. The extremely detailed ordinance and plans that follow this section offer a marked contrast to the sparse explanation of how this expropriation would take place. This process is summarily laid aside by stating that the exact order of expropriation and demolitions would be determined "at the right moment, according to the circumstances," so that the new sectors would be built without affecting the normal activity of the city.[24]

This rather breezy attitude toward demolition was perhaps inspired by a very familiar project on the western edge of the site: Nueve de Julio Avenue, which in similar pharaonic fashion had continued demolishing blocks north and south of the obelisk and by 1956 had reached all the way to the northern edge of the projected site for Barrio Sur. The Nueve de Julio was the logical counterpart and ally of Bonet's design. He knew it would be wise to push it forward by incorporating the blocks to be demolished and continue the grand avenue's extension along the lot's western edge. This would continue the slow, inexorable progress of the monumental linear void along the city. The Nueve de Julio ultimately became part of Barrio Sur, continuing Haussmannian work that dated back to 1936. In looking back at this project, and at Austral's earlier condemnation of the grid, we can gauge the distance that Bonet had traveled in his understanding of the city in general and Buenos Aires in particular. Back then, the architects of Austral had commended the avenue and argued with Corbusian fervor for the destruction of the grid that suffocated the city. Now Bonet argued for a reinterpretation of the old city grid, whose large scale, he claimed, responded to the increased demands of traffic and population.

The arguments for the project denounced San Telmo's old and decrepit buildings with a language similar to that used by the regime to call for the erasure of Perón's traces in the built environment. The documentation folder also included a series of photographs of San Telmo, illustrating the deteriorated condition of the old neighborhood, a tactic similar to that used in the case of Casa Amarilla. However, in contrast to the human pathos openly displayed in that project's publicity materials, in San Telmo the photographer avoided capturing human figures and instead focused on the architectural patterns of the zone—courtyard spaces and stark volumes—paradoxically hinting at the similarity between the courtyard at the architectural scale and the plaza at the urban scale, a feature of the final project. This extensive documentation of the courtyards of San Telmo hints at a contradiction embodied by Barrio Sur. While it was meant to do away with the image of age and decrepitude associated with Perón and represent a new, modern technocratic state, the architectural approach implied a return to older urban forms, like the grid and the plaza. Architecture thus emulated the operation of the state, which also sought to mask its conservatism under a modern technocratic guise. Ultimately the design of Barrio Sur ignored these contradictions to promote the objective of the regime that sponsored it: to replace Perón's housing legacy with a (supposedly) bigger and better project.

BARRIO SUR, 1956

A SUSPENDED SUPERSTRUCTURE

How does one balance the state's conservative politics with modern aspirations? How does one incorporate the grid and the plaza into the modern urban design paradigm? And who is the ideal inhabitant of this new urban realm? These were the architectural and political challenges for Barrio Sur. Bonet's approach was to combine a careful reading of Buenos Aires's urban typologies, his observations of Venice, and, possibly, postwar CIAM discourse on the urban core. This required bringing various typologies and case studies together in an effort to understand how the city would produce a new civic realm.

Bonet organized Barrio Sur by subdividing the neighborhood into six sectors and combining three main building typologies to create an urban fabric (FIGURE 4.03). This "megagrid," overlaid over the existing grid, resulted in a system of large avenues for fast transit, with intersections every 500 meters. Each sector was composed of an area of approximately 16 hectares meant to house a population of about 75,000 people, for a total population of 450,000. The sectors followed a similar pattern, with civic centers in the middle, surrounded by housing, and retail on the periphery, lining the edges and creating continuity

FIGURE 4.03.
Site plan. Bonet, Barrio Sur (1956). North is oriented to the right. FABC, © copyright AHCOAC (Bonet).

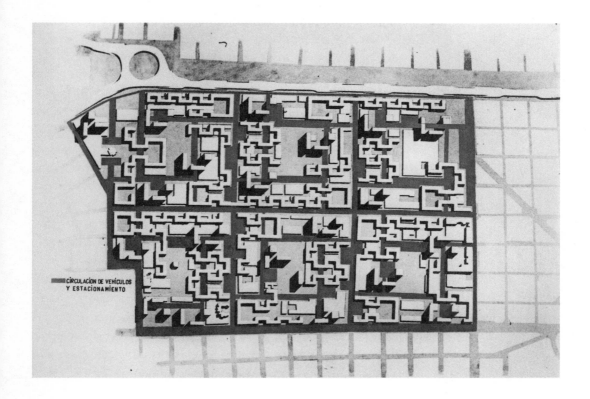

CIRCULACIÓN DE VEHÍCULOS Y ESTACIONAMIENTO

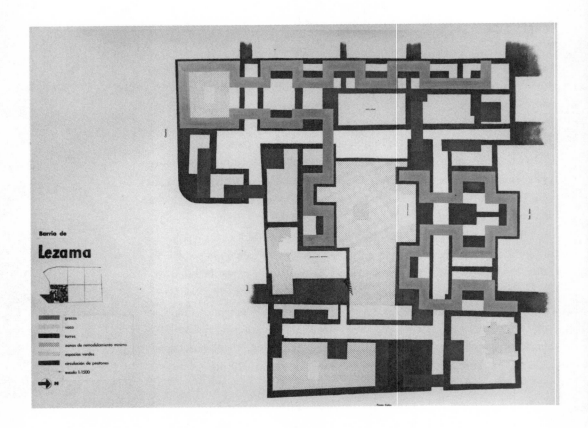

Barrio de

Lezama

grecas
vaca
torres
zonas de remodelamiento mínimo
espacios verdes
circulación de peatones
escala 1:1500

N

FIGURE 4.04.
Lezama sector plan.
Bonet, Barrio Sur (1956).
FABC, © copyright
AHCOAC (Bonet).

with the adjoining sectors (FIGURE 4.04). Thus, while the edges of each sector have a larger, car-driven scale, the center is dedicated to pedestrian use. This variation in scale is achieved through the arrangement of three building types: *vacas* (cows, alluding to this Argentinian staple, 6 meters or two stories high), *grecas* (frets or friezes, 30 meters or eleven stories), and *torres* (towers, 100 meters or thirty-five stories).

Bonet interpreted these three poetic scales as corresponding to the city of Buenos Aires, its trees, and its sense of space. According to the project's description:

> The first [type] proposes contact with the life of the city, with its intensity and noise; the second, which is the usual [height] in current apartment houses, establishes a relative independence, maintaining the relationship with the ground through the presence of the trees, developed freely in the new green spaces; the third one signifies almost complete isolation, the perception of practically pure space, within which the urban landscape is no more than a point of reference and value.[25]

Most likely inspired by Le Corbusier's tripartite goals for the Ville Radieuse, in Barrio Sur these scales referred to the specifics of Buenos Aires, supporting some urban typologies and rejecting others. The scale of the "city" responded to the sidewalk cafes and shopping gallerias—commercial corridors similar to the Paris Arcades, which give the city an active pedestrian life at ground level, while still allowing for apartment housing above. The scale of the trees, determining the height of the *grecas*, responded to existing apartment buildings and their relationship to the long rows of tall trees that lined the city's streets, which had made such a big impression on Bonet.[26] They form corridors so thick and lush that the city's streetlamps are dangled from cables in the middle of the road so that the corridors will not be completely blocked. The city's wide avenues and large open parks are the consequence of its dense fabric, the product of a building ordinance that requires no lateral setbacks. This ordinance is what yields the *medianera*—the tall narrow, lateral patio discussed in chapter 1. The roaming cows of this revised vision of pastoral modernity no longer aimed to comfort through nostalgia, as in Bajo Belgrano. While the *vacas* and *grecas* reinterpret specific qualities of the city, the *torres* go against the local type in order to connect its inhabitants with "pure space," with an isolation that hints at the tropes of solitude and infinite sublime associated with the pampas (FIGURE 4.05).

Finally, taking advantage of the site's slope, a design move clearly hinted at in the introduction to the project, Bonet separated car traffic, pedestrians, and parking, creating a three-dimensional grid. Car traffic was situated in a half basement, 4 meters underground, which would be level toward the river; the ground level was for pedestrians; and parking was elevated 5 meters above ground. These different levels were meant to create a "suspended superstructure" for pedestrians that would become "the true and new urban land."[27] A working section drawing representing the layers included an image of the Vasari corridor in Florence, hinting that the modern project is a reinterpretation of the past (FIGURE 4.06). Despite this reference, the inspiration was more likely Nueve de Julio Avenue, which had a parking basement that included a growing underground world of passages and shops connecting it to the city subway. In 1949 a commercial gallery was built on the north passage under the obelisk. Although it was not opened until 1959, it probably suggested the benefits of a parking level with commerce for Barrio Sur (a section in the project description was dedicated to the avenue). Through these different urban types and layers, Bonet created a rhythmic pattern that he described as "the urban fabric of the project"—in complete opposition to the green void that had been the significant ground plan, the datum of his prior projects. Barrio

Sur collapsed housing, commercial, and civic uses into a multilayered, mixed-use project that had its roots in the city of Buenos Aires.

Although, as we have seen, Bonet had started reconsidering the scale of the neighborhood and the plaza when he visited Venice after CIAM 7, his attention to Buenos Aires's urban condition might have been prompted, paradoxically, by his former mentors, Le Corbusier and Sert. The *greca* buildings follow Le Corbusier's buildings *à redent*: that is, medium-height buildings laid out in a zigzag pattern but here modified with the added Porteño typology of the *galería* (a shopping arcade). The tight, matlike arrangements with an open center resemble Sert and Wiener's plan for the small town of Chimbote in Peru, with its reformulation of the plaza.[28] Sert had become an advocate for the plaza and the patio and described this urban formation as a scaling of the patio into different types of community spaces.[29] We might also note the similarity between the building ordinances of cities in Peru and Argentina, both of which have no lateral setbacks, thus creating a dense continuous

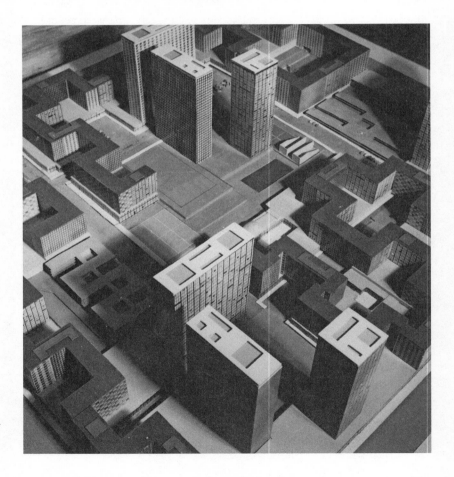

FIGURE 4.05.
Photograph of model.
Bonet, Barrio Sur (1956).
FABC, © copyright
AHCOAC (Bonet).

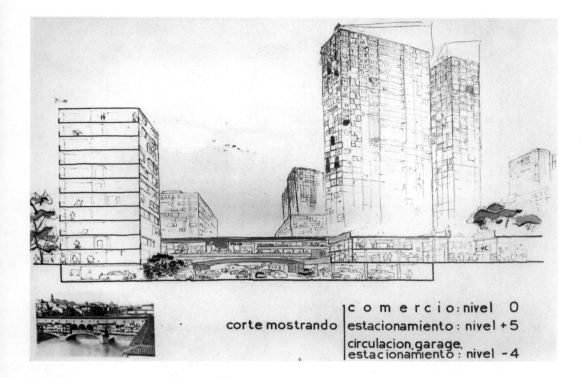

corte mostrando

c o m e r c i o : nivel   0
estacionamiento : nivel + 5
circulacion garage,
estacionamiento : nivel - 4

urban façade along the streets. Both Sert's "mat buildings" and Bonet's *grecas* are skillful responses to local conditions, which create the need for some open space within the lot. But the similarities end here. Chimbote was quite different from the intense urban density that Bonet was proposing for Buenos Aires. Rather than the "flattened" one- to two-story mat suggested by the Chimbote drawings, Barrio Sur proposed a three-dimensional city grid. This strategy was also very different from Lucio Costa's *supercuadra*s in Brasilia, designed at about the same time, which are grouped around a retail axis that articulates neighborhood life close to but separate from the housing blocks. Despite their differences, Bonet's, Sert's, and Costa's projects all shared a grand scale and a grand ambition, which was also shared by the regimes that sponsored them.

REPRESENTING THE PLAZAS

Barrio Sur was presented very differently from Bonet's other work. There is an emphasis on diagrams and multiple plans of the several levels of each sector. For TOSA, only a few years before, Bonet had produced a few photomontages, black-and-white compositions with strategic elements highlighted in bright colors. But the only rendered views of Barrio Sur were a few black-and-white hand-drawn perspectives showing how the *vacas*, *grecas*, and *torres* would

FIGURE 4.06.
Unpublished section sketch. Bonet, Barrio Sur (1956). FABC, © copyright AHCOAC (Bonet).

come together in a reinterpretation of the Buenos Aires urban experience. A lot of energy was dedicated to building a large model that was extensively photographed (FIGURES 4.05, 4.10). The elegant black-and-white pictures enhance the regularity and repetitiveness of the project, abstracting and blurring overlapping forms. Consistently shot from above, these photographs give us a bird's-eye view of the large project. In order to illustrate the pedestrian point of view, the team focused on depicting the central plazas through perspectival drawings (FIGURES 4.07, 4.08) and only one photomontage (FIGURE 4.01). These images hold the key to the project.

The single photomontage seems deliberately produced to highlight the strategic presence of private enterprise in the project. Here the conspicuous store advertisements overwhelm the plaza with careful reproduction of foreign brands and their logos, hinting at the kind of investment that the project hoped to attract. A few photographs of human figures have been collaged into the drawing. In the foreground a smiling young woman mounts her bicycle. Behind her, a man in a suit walks toward us. Various other figures fill in the shaded spaces of the commercial galleries, assuring the success of the project's retail spaces. Finally, although each center plaza of Barrio Sur is supposed to contain a large park, the different perspectives show barren plazas with limited green space. One of the drawings shows a bigger park, with some leafless trees in the background (FIGURE 4.07). One child holds onto its mother, while another one leans against a shaded pillar. These are not the stranded urbanites of Casa Amarilla but compliant citizen/consumers.

The project's description explains the reasons behind this turn away from nature:

> In the center of each 16 ha. sector there is a great space of this type [an outdoor space], and its location and dimensions do not justify using it exclusively as a park. The parks of the city, Palermo is a clear example, are places with very scarce intensity of life. They do not receive true and daily use except by older people and children.[30]

Bonet goes on to say that green spaces are costly to maintain for City Hall and create "an evident injustice" because the majority of the city's inhabitants cannot use them. All these inconveniences would disappear, Bonet argues, if the spaces were ceded to "the clubs that are part of each sector" for the installation of their outdoor facilities, particularly sports facilities. These clubs would be in charge of their administration and maintenance. Although it is neither mentioned nor drawn in the various perspectives or in the plans, this description of clubs and sports activities makes the intended use of these spaces clear. The city's immense soccer following is organized through a series of neighborhood

FIGURE 4.07. (*top left*) View of plaza. Bonet, Barrio Sur (1956). FABC, © copyright AHCOAC (Bonet).

FIGURE 4.08. (*bottom left*) View of plaza. Bonet, Barrio Sur (1956). FABC, © copyright AHCOAC (Bonet).

soccer clubs. The design of the neighborhoods transformed these traditional associations into "social and sports centers" that would be assigned the administration of these central spaces, in a rather cavalier privatization of the control over public space, peremptorily shifting "older people and children" aside for the benefit of the young men who usually dominate these associations. The confined pampas came with a membership fee.

However, as mentioned above, none of the plans and perspectives of the project show these spaces being used for sports activities. In contrast with earlier projects by Bonet, they include only confined green space. Barrio Sur has no soccer matches, although some of the model photographs show tennis courts, hinting at a different, wealthier public. No children run or mischievously play, as in Bajo Belgrano. The much-celebrated green of the pampa, discovered under the cement of the city, is now gone. The spaces are depicted as barren plazas, where citizens stroll in a polite, civilized manner. Bonet's projects had consistently featured the use of green spaces in different but important ways. The inner garden at the Artists' Ateliers forcefully pushed toward the outside through the bulging curves of the project, the wild landscape under Casa Amarilla alluded to the wilderness of the pampas and its unruly inhabitants migrating into the city, and the pastoral modernity of Bajo Belgrano embraced these inhabitants in a nostalgic return to the pampas. These tropes that Bonet had previously mobilized in his projects have been eradicated in Barrio Sur. All that remains is a barren enclosed expanse with a single tree, perhaps a more accurate description of the pampas than in any of the prior projects. This modern plaza is deserted.

What led to this radical erasure? In *The Heart of the City: Towards the Humanisation of Urban Life* (1952), Sert's architectural obsession with the patio is scaled up and transformed into a meditation on the importance of urban cores and a return to older urban typologies, such as the Piazza San Marco in Venice.[31] Bonet did not attend CIAM 8, "The Heart of the City," held in England in 1951, but in his first return to Europe he had also praised San Marco. It is likely that he saw the book when he participated in the MOMA exhibition of Latin American architecture in 1955 and would have followed CIAM activities. The dominant presence of the plaza in Barrio Sur, its attention to older urban patterns, and the eradication of the "wild" parks and green spaces suggest Bonet's awareness of the international discourse taking place overseas, but his own thoughts on urban design in the context of Argentina were also evolving.

Both in the congress and in the book, Sert introduced the idea of the core or heart with a long quotation from *Revolt of the Masses* concerning massman. In the extract cited by Sert, Ortega focuses on public squares and plazas

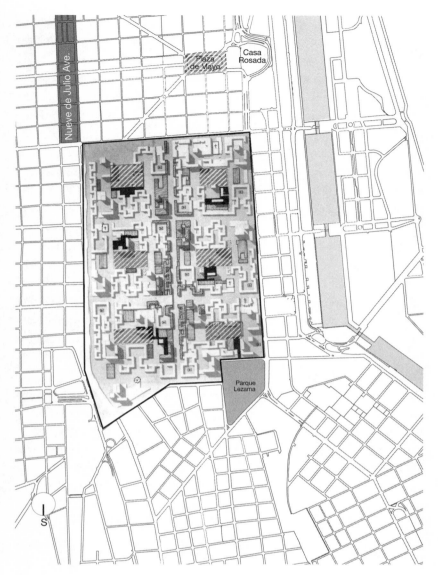

FIGURE 4.09.
Plazas at Barrio Sur and Plaza de Mayo, Buenos Aires. Site plan from FABC, © copyright AHCOAC (Bonet). Montage by Linda Lee under the direction of the author.

as civilizing, enclosed outdoor spaces that bring citizens together, in contrast to the fields where people roam without the ability to confer with each other. Ortega proposes these civilizing spaces as a remedy for the increasing dominance of the masses, composed of people who think of themselves only as part of a crowd.

The architecture and the politics of *Barrio Sur* came together in this idea of the plaza, and the pampas receded. Ortega was popular in anti-Peronist circles in Argentina, which saw the labor unions that had supported Perón as a threat like the masses. Bonet reinterpreted Ortega and Sert's ideas by placing a plaza at the heart of each sector in Barrio Sur. He writes that these are the places in which "social life will develop."[32] The plazas of Barrio Sur are the civilizing spaces that will create new, well-behaved urban citizens. In the aftermath of the 1955 coup d'état, modernity for the masses was a matter of discipline. The idea of the public square as a civilizing space would have resonated with the regime.

Among the many large plazas and green parks of Buenos Aires, however, one plaza stands out—the Plaza de Mayo, tragically bombarded in 1955, only one year before the design of Barrio Sur. If we locate the project within the Buenos Aires grid, we can see how the six proposed plazas repeat the approximate scale and proportion of this significant plaza, witness to so many events and located just north of Barrio Sur (FIGURE 4.09). In his attempt to create new spaces for Buenos Aires, Bonet reproduced its most historic plaza and thereby inadvertently called up a memory that the regime was most eager to erase. To argue for the civilizing action of the plaza as an urban device was a painful reminder of the plaza that had been bombarded by the same forces promoting this project.

A NEW CIVIC REALM

Barrio Sur was not for the masses. The lists and charts of spaces, numbers, and areas (carefully denoted in the project description) as well as its civilizing intent addressed an audience composed of the bureaucrats of the BHN and the private financial institutions that it hoped to impress. As stated in the folder documentation, the target population was the middle classes moving away from the city, complicating its traffic problems and, implicitly, abandoning it to the less desirable masses.[33] By purchasing housing in Barrio Sur, middle class Porteños would become customers of the project with its shops and arcades as well as well-behaved tax-paying citizens replacing the population of the South. Perhaps this would even "protect" the Plaza de Mayo and the Casa Rosada from further Peronist occupation.

The project's message was amplified in journals partial to the regime, most tellingly *Leoplán*, a periodical ostensibly about general culture meant to encourage personal improvement through reading. A conspicuous heliport featured in the model may have prompted the journal to create its own rendering of Barrio Sur, with a helicopter in the foreground announcing the project's modernity.[34] In this issue Barrio Sur shares space with an article on President Aramburu, portrayed as a solitary fisherman and an accessible yet introspective leader, prone to action rather than to speech.[35] This situated him as the antithesis of the image that the regime had constructed for Perón. Similarly, the promotion of Barrio Sur was also the reverse of Bajo Belgrano, although Bonet had been involved in crafting the narrative of both projects. If Bajo Belgrano aspired to a pastoral modernism, Barrio Sur was now presented as a radical technocratic urban landscape that erased the past in favor of the clean, antiseptic, and melancholic future.

A combination of factors prevented the realization of Barrio Sur. A team of architects led by Luis Morea highlighted the unnecessarily high densities, which they denounced as financially motivated to maximize gain for construction companies and the project's architects.[36] An opposing political party went as far as assigning a commission to study the plan, publishing a piece in *NA*.[37] This article savvily pointed out the existence of free land for which other projects had already been designed, Casa Amarilla and Bajo Belgrano. Although Bonet's name is not mentioned, it is clear that the article is referring to him. Most important, San Telmo residents protested their complete exclusion from the process and the project's excessive demolitions and expropriations, which would have resulted in increased costs.[38] Ironically, the residents, probably prompted by informed architects, noted that the project was not in agreement with the EPBA plan started in Le Corbusier's office, which Bonet had worked on through his involvement in Bajo Belgrano. In August 1957 the government halted all work on Barrio Sur.

We might argue that the biggest strike against the plan was its own conflicted identity. Its civilizing mission clashed with recent events in Argentina, and the focus on the plaza made matters worse. Perhaps the state's insistence on erasing Perón was based on its anxiety to erase the memory of the violence that it had committed against its own citizens—perhaps it was not, after all, a matter of erasing Perón but of erasing the massacre. Echoes of this violence in the planned demolitions and expropriations of Barrio Sur likely resonated in the opposition to it. Bonet's reading of both old and modern urban types had creatively reassembled the city into a series of interconnected yet self-sufficient neighborhoods. A plaza at the center of each neighborhood was meant to articulate these various types into a coherent, civilizing whole. Yet these civilizing aspirations were, in the end, too entangled with the regime's politics: the voids that Bonet proposed resembled the site of necropolitics. Public spaces and plazas certainly have the ability to promote civic discourse and social interaction. But the plaza had acquired a different meaning in Buenos Aires after the events of the Revolución Libertadora.[39]

Between the echoes of the tragedy of 1955 and the discussions on the civilizing effect of its plazas, another aspect of the project was left undiscussed. Barrio Sur was a return to the infinitely repetitive grid of Buenos Aires that Borges had so precisely described in the configuration of his library. This grid remained as a testament to Bonet's maturing urban sensibilities, which lost the shock and serendipity that he had mastered in the Artists' Ateliers. In many ways the plan's repetitive modules, multiple levels, and compounded layers of complexity echo the structure of Borges's library, which condemns its occupants to wandering infinitely among its identical cells, encountering the same books, the same stories, and the same political revolutions again and again. Bonet re-created this space in Barrio Sur through the large grid of six sectors, repetitive use of building types, and enclosed plazas. Would the almost but not quite identical plazas of Barrio Sur provide the same confusion as the library's cells, in which books repeat themselves in almost but not quite identical fashion, with an altered page or sentence or building corner, betraying small differences? In his early projects Bonet had argued against the dense, overwhelming, repetitive grid of Buenos Aires. Twenty years later he reproduced it on an even grander scale.

If we think of the project in a broader political context, Barrio Sur was doomed from the start: weakened by President Aramburu's tenuous hold on office and the decision to call for democratic elections, while maintaining the prohibition of the Peronist party. This period of military rule was technically ended when Arturo Frondizi was democratically elected with the support of Perón (still in exile) in 1958. Frondizi, who embraced a developmentalist agenda focused on foreign investment, was deposed by a military coup in 1962. This was followed by additional military confrontations and takeovers in 1963, 1966–1973 (a military regime that called itself the "Revolución Argentina"), and 1976–1983 (alternatively known as the "National Reorganization process" and the "Dirty War" because of its extreme violence). These increasingly violent regimes embraced a conservative political agenda and extreme privatization, taking the solution to the housing problem out of the hands of the state and into private projects. This alliance between necropolitical military dictatorships and the rise of neoliberalism extended across South America. This suggests that the biggest problem with Barrio Sur ultimately was that it embodied a political contradiction. No matter how much it claimed to open space for private enterprise, the state investment required by mass expropriations and demolitions no longer made sense in a state machinery turning increasingly toward privatization. Bonet's grid was a way of stabilizing this commission, the largest that he was ever to receive in the Americas.

A telling coincidence closes the story of Barrio Sur. Borges's beloved neighborhood library of San Telmo, the original Library of Babel, was to be demolished, to be replaced by a new national library that would be the heart of one of the sectors.[40] Eventually the plan for a new library found its ideal site in the lot of the demolished Unzué Palace, Perón's former residence. This new monument was meant to symbolize the new Argentina, an intellectual, learned society distant from Perón's popular kitsch. Borges, previously fired from his post at the small San Telmo library, was named director of the national library. He nominally supervised an architecture contest for the design of the new building, which would include a School of Librarians, an institution to educate new generations in the tradition of the consecrated writer. The plan was to install Borges, the diffident intellectual, as Perón's replacement and as the model for the new Argentinian.[41]

THE LATIN CITY

ARCHITECTURE AS PUBLIC RELATIONS

Bonet and his team anxiously worked on ordinances, work phases, and finance mechanisms, hoping to get the project approved. Photographs of a government visit to the project's offices show Bonet (center) nervously clutching his hands in front of the large model (FIGURE 4.10). He tilts forward as he looks at one of the group of government functionaries, perhaps waiting for a response. Other functionaries surrounding them look either at the model or at the more important representative in the room. He does not look back, instead staring

FIGURE 4.10
Bonet (center) presenting Barrio Sur to unknown government officials. FABC, AHCOAC (photographer unknown).

FIGURE 4.11.
Bonet (left) presenting Barrio Sur to President Pedro Eugenio Aramburu (second from right). FABC, AHCOAC (photographer unknown).

at the model, hesitating, his mouth slightly open. President Aramburu, also confronted with this exhaustive work when he visited the offices (FIGURE 4.11), told the press as he left the presentation: "I think we have exploited this Catalan."[42] What Aramburu did not understand was that the work was addressed not only to him but to an audience on the other side of the Atlantic. The presentation panels, visible in the photographs of the visit, suggest a different audience.[43] Together with the multiple descriptions of the project translated to English and French, they suggest that Bonet was planning to present Barrio Sur at the next CIAM, projecting himself onto the international scene. But it was too late. The CIAM that would potentially have hosted Barrio Sur took place in 1959, when Team X determined the dissolution of the congress. The auto-critique that Bonet had joined back in 1949 ironically culminated with the termination of the congress just in time to preempt the presentation of his own project.

Nevertheless, Barrio Sur, with its return to the grid, became the vehicle for Bonet's return to Spain. In the 1950s Bonet had started promoting himself and his work in different venues outside Argentina. In 1952 he published the Artists' Ateliers in *Acrópole*, a Brazilian architecture journal (1938–1971).[44] In this piece Bonet figures as the main architect, with Abel López Chas and Ricardo Vera Barros as collaborators. There is no date for the project, perhaps to hide the

MODERNITY FOR THE MASSES

fact that it was built in 1939 and was being featured among Brazilian buildings from the early 1950s. It must have been disappointing for Bonet that he did not have a large-scale project to show alongside the abundant architectural production that Brazil had mustered in the last few decades. He later acknowledged his frustration and blamed his lack of built work on Argentina's politics, comparing it to neighboring Brazil:

> This series of political failures has been distancing Argentina from its advanced position in Latin America, leaving space for other countries such as Mexico and Brazil, especially Brazil, whose political stability, both in the democratic regime and during the dictatorship, has been notable. The construction of Brasilia has been possible precisely because of this, and it has been, although it might seem paradoxical, in one of the most democratic periods of the country.[45]

Indeed, the "pharaonic" scale of Barrio Sur is less surprising if we compare it with the construction of Brasilia, also started in 1956. With the benefit of hindsight, Bonet compares Argentina's political instability to the leadership of Juscelino Kubitschek in Brazil, which he credits with the building of Brasilia. Such a paradoxical analysis completely disregards the longer stability of the Perón regime in Argentina as well as the political chaos that erupted in Brazil after Kubitschek. While Brazil had decided to embrace modern architecture, through Oscar Niemeyer's work, as the language of the state, the Argentinian state experimented with modernity but never fully embraced it. This choice was not arbitrary. It reflected the tendency of centralized states strategically to adopt particular formal languages to promote specific economic systems. After the failure of Barrio Sur, it was clear to Bonet that neither the populist fervor of Perón nor the liberal politics of the right-wing military were conducive to his modern ambitions.

Starting in 1955, the year the Revolución Libertadora took over Argentina, Bonet began promoting his work through a series of international exhibitions. In 1955 he was featured in Henry-Russell Hitchcock's "Latin American Architecture since 1945" exhibition at MOMA. In 1957 he exhibited at the Triennale di Milano, and the following year he exhibited in Brussels and Moscow. In the meantime he kept working on a few more private commissions, including several apartment buildings in Mar del Plata, Argentina, and a house in the outskirts of Barcelona (1958). In the late 1950s he published in international journals, including a feature on Barrio Sur in his own journal, *Mirador* 2 (1957), as well as the Brazilian journals *Módulo* (1957) and *Habitat* (1958), the Spanish journals *Revista Nacional de Arquitectura* (1956) and *Cuadernos de Arquitectura* (1959), and the German journal *Bauen und Wohnen* (1958). Barrio Sur's extensive documentation gave him ample material to draw on, providing an important source of images and material for Bonet's international promotion of himself and his work. This international circulation of images of his work increased as Argentina sunk deeper into political and economic crisis. Bonet did not stop looking for work and opportunities elsewhere.

Attentive to Sert's career, Bonet would have seen the benefit that his former employer gained from the public promotion of his unbuilt plans. Through his firm TPA, Sert had designed a series of unbuilt city plans throughout South America and the Caribbean. His strong promotion of these plans in architectural journals greatly strengthened his credentials to become president of the CIAM (1947–1956), and later dean at the Harvard Graduate School of Design (1953–1969). Many of these plans had been funded by the frazzled economies of South American countries going through political and economic crises and increasingly being taken over by dictatorial regimes, which underscores the distance between Sert's image and his politics, an important lesson for Bonet.[46]

RETURN TO THE MEDITERRANEAN

This active search for international attention culminated in 1960, when Bonet returned to his native Barcelona with a one-man exhibition at the Museo de Arte Contemporáneo, a prior iteration of a contemporary art museum not to be confused with the current Museu d'Art Contemporani de Barcelona (MACBA, Museum of Contemporary Art of Barcelona). It was jointly sponsored by Barcelona City Hall and the Consulate General of Argentina in Spain—that is to say, Bonet's native city and his adopted country.[47] This exhibition officially reintroduced Bonet as an architect to his homeland, reframed by his work in Argentina and Uruguay. The catalog presented Bonet's projects in Argentina and Uruguay with essays written by art historian Alexandre Cirici-Pellicer and by architect and urban planner Oriol Bohigas, who was also one of the exhibition organizers. These writers were affiliated with the art and architecture sections for *Serra d'Or* (Golden Saw), the journal for the Guild of Our Lady of Montserrat. The journal and its writers were associated with the more liberal side of the Catholic church, one of the few possible avenues left to resist the ongoing dictatorship.[48] These essays help us understand the Spain that Bonet was returning to and the role that he and Barrio Sur might have within it.

Cirici-Pellicer's essay presents Bonet as the product of a Mediterranean sensibility and a modern pedigree. The former is invoked with images of his work in the Uruguayan resort of Punta Ballena (1945–1948), but the description does not correspond with the project. The author conjures nonexistent interior patios for houses in this resort, as markers of Bonet's "Mediterranean-ness." Bonet's modern pedigree is showcased through his association with Sert and Le Corbusier and his interest in modularity and industrial reproduction. However, this affinity is illustrated by two recent private commissions that were not intended for reproduction: Casa Oks (Buenos Aires, 1953–1956) and a rendering of the chapel in Soca, Uruguay (1960), a project still in the planning stages at that point.[49] Although Bonet had expressed some interest in automatization and industrial production, the text reads more like wishful thinking than actual description. In the end, the essay conjures a mirage, ultimately revealing the author's desire to view Bonet as both Mediterranean and modern, rather than locating these traits in his work.

Bohigas's essay presents Barrio Sur as the new Latin city, pushing back against what he calls the modern model of towers in a park as a conservative and degenerate Nordic model (in this context meaning northern European and particularly English and German, as opposed to Latin). This model, he argues, has destroyed the concept of the street, creating dehumanizing neighborhoods of isolated blocks that go against the social nature of the "gregarious Mediterranean man." In contrast, the Latin city—"our city"—is presented as a complex, living organism, full of noisy people bumping into each other.[50] For Bohigas, this is Bonet's achievement in Barrio Sur. He has returned to the Latin city centered around the street and the plaza. He concludes by connecting the project to the urbanism of Ildefonso Cerdá, the Catalan urban planner responsible for the Barcelona grid, and thereby deems it a Catalan project. In an undated conference in Barcelona, Bonet appropriates Bohigas's own interpretation of his work:

> The idea is to rethink the "Latin city" with the human being as protagonist, pedestrian streets and porticoed little plazas for the development of retail, separate from vehicular circulation; semiautonomous communities with a maximum of 15 minutes of pedestrian travel, and cultural and recreational services near housing; autonomous civic esplanades and green spaces for each neighborhood, the center of each one's life, and enough subterranean parking to liberate the city.[51]

Nothing in this description contradicts the project, but there is a vast difference between the "pedestrian streets and porticoed little plazas" presented in Spain and the bold "suspended superstructure" that was to become "the true and new urban land" in Argentina.[52] The vision of Barrio Sur that Bonet had offered to Buenos Aires, with its radical erasure of the city, cold grand-scale plazas, and conspicuous heliport, was presented in Argentinian publications as a sign of modernity and an erasure of the old. In Spain it was presented as a recovery of a Spanish past.

Following this line of argumentation, Spanish journals like *Mundo Hispánico* described the original San Telmo neighborhood as unequivocally

Spanish, a place "where they threw out the English with stones . . . with Spanish courage."[53] The journalist argues that San Telmo's urgent need for "rejuvenation"—not erasure—was made possible by the virtues of the Spanish grid, which allowed the plan to evolve in stages. The journalist concludes that the design of Barrio Sur is a "Mediterranean fantasy (Bonet is from Barcelona) adjusted to the rigor of numbers and technique."[54] As the project crossed the Atlantic it acquired "Latin" sensibilities never noted before. The press and critics praised its connections to the Mediterranean past, with small streets (the pedestrian paths) and quaint plazas, turning the whole neighborhood into a representation of Spain itself. But in addition to the convenience of "turning the project Spanish" for the sake of a Spanish public, there are political motivations. To understand them, and the circumstances of Bonet's return, we must return to Spain under Franco and to Argentina under Perón.

HISPANIDAD AND LATINIDAD

After the Civil War, Spain was left with a collapsed economy and deteriorated armed forces and was in no position to participate in World War II.[55] Although Franco never officially sided with the Axis, he leaned toward their cause and provided some logistical support. As the Allies advanced, Franco strategically turned toward them, ushering in a period of cautious neutrality. Economically weak, politically isolated, and devastated by a series of droughts, Spain found its strongest ally in another cautiously neutral country—Perón's Argentina.[56] Perón shipped grain and meat and provided diplomatic support in international meetings, helping reintegrate Spain into larger political forums. The reasons for this alliance were complicated. Perón was a populist president opposed to conservative Argentinian factions closer to the Franco regime. His choice may have been pragmatic rather than ideological. The countries shared an ambiguous neutrality, and both resisted the growing power of the United States, which had actively opposed Perón's election. In a polarized world, Franco's Spain and Peron's Argentina benefited from a mutual alliance. To explain and bolster this alliance, Franco and Perón favored a discourse of *hispanidad*, a Spain-centered term that pointed back to a benign image of their colonial past and that justified Argentina's assistance to Spain as restitution.[57]

We can find a clear instance of how this discourse was deployed in the cultural life of the country in the speeches that opened the IV Congreso Histórico Municipal Interamericano (IVth Inter-American Historical Municipal Congress), the international event that prompted the exhibitions that included the promotion of Bajo Belgrano and the EPBA (discussed in chapter 3). With its focus on America (the continent), this event had reframed Spain as the country responsible for "the marvelous mission of discovery."[58] The congress was inaugurated on October 12, a symbolic date marking a movement to celebrate this day as the Día de la Hispanidad (Hispanicness Day).[59] The official inaugural speech was delivered by intellectual and Peronist sympathizer Dr. Roberto Tamagno.[60] His speech centered on the significance of the date of Christopher Columbus's arrival to highlight the continent as a site of renewal and growth, with all its potential promise and risk, as opposed to what he described as the nostalgic, outdated cities of Europe. This cautious embrace of the future was framed as rooted in the past, through the privileged position of Spain as mother country—carefully extracted from the otherwise negative vision of Europe—and of the Catholic church as its main guide. In this context, the modernity prescribed by the exhibition was tempered with spiritual values, recognizing the memories of an implicitly Spanish past, to project a future development that avoided the perils of "a chaos of cement," one of the phrases from Gras's film *La ciudad frente al río*.

This mixture of conservative politics wrapped in the promise of the new was consistent with Perón's discourse. In fact, Tamagno's triangulation of a hard-working America, an outdated Europe, and the savior figure of Spain could easily be replaced by the Argentinian people (America), the abusive older landowning classes (Europe), and Saint Evita (the savior figure), the mainstays of Perón's speeches. Thus the speech replicated the Peronist formula and applied it to Argentina's international politics. It also set the stage for a more outspokenly political speech by the minister of foreign relationships and worship, the official title of Dr. Hipólito Paz, who positioned Argentina within the international landscape as a noninterventionist country led by the progressive, successful policies of Perón. Paz reframed the American continent's destiny as a synthesizer of cultures and values. America, here implicitly led by Argentina/Perón, would thus be charged with a quasi-religious mission to lead the world.[61] Paz's words capture the optimism and ambition of the Perón regime and its eagerness to project the success of his tenure on an international scale.

Alas, Argentina's economic prosperity came to a halt. By the late 1940s the economic growth that Perón had achieved in his first years in office started to stagnate, bolstering his political opposition. The aid shipments to Spain stopped in 1949. In turn, Spain's staunch anti-Communist stance brought the regime closer to the United States, easing the way for a new political alliance. The 1953 Pact of Madrid ended Spain's neutrality, allowing the United States to build and use air and naval bases in Spanish territory during the Korean War.[62] In exchange, Spain benefited from economic assistance, significant credit, and capital investments.[63] Despite his initial sympathy toward the Axis, Franco had successfully maneuvered into a political alliance with the United States without making any significant political changes.

As Spain turned to the United States, Perón turned away from Spain and took advantage of Argentina's large Italian population to secure financial assistance from Italy.[64] These shifts were reflected in a shift of terms, from *hispanidad* to *latinidad*. In turning to Italy, Perón bolstered the idea of *latinidad*, underlining Latin America and the Mediterranean's shared heritage, brought together in an egalitarian relationship of friendship. However, this Mediterranean turn did not last long. When Perón was ousted in 1955, the new regime brought Argentina closer to the new Franco model (a conservative dictatorship interested in creating economic alliances with the United States) and focused on accelerated technocratic development combined with conservative policies. Somewhat ironically, Perón wandered in exile throughout Latin America after his removal, eventually finding a home in Madrid under the reluctant protection of Franco.

These political and economic links between Spain and Argentina lead us back to the new Spain that Bonet had returned to in 1960, where the term *latinidad* was wielded as an invocation of Mediterranean heritage in opposition to Franco, joining a long Catalonian tradition of resistance to Spain. It is in this context that we should read the introduction of Bonet as the representative of the Latin, Mediterranean city. Indeed, although never politically militant, Bonet had sympathized with the republic. But his politics were rooted in the ideas of Francisco Giner de los Ríos and José Ortega y Gasset—the so-called Third Spain, politically opposed to Franco but not actively resisting him.[65] Bonet was welcomed back into these circles of cautious, pragmatic opposition.[66] Barrio Sur had been used in Argentina to try to erase Perón as outdated, old, and corrupt, to be replaced by the "the true and new urban land" and the slick modernity of the military regime that ousted him.[67] Upon crossing the Atlantic, it was transformed into a project of *latinidad*, as part of a shy, cautious resistance, nostalgic for revolution but not actively participating in it.

Bonet aspired to mobilize this *latinidad* as his brand, the latest component of his urban design toolbox. He had the gumption to go after the Barcelona urban plan, based on his unbuilt work in Argentina and his tenure in Sert's office during his collaboration with Le Corbusier for the Plan Macià.[68] But this did not pan out. The turn toward the United States in the late 1950s was translated into new economic policies. Franco's economic consultants (known as the technocrats) belonged to the Opus Dei, an extremely conservative group within the Catholic church opposed to the liberal humanism of *Serra d'Or*. These consultants promoted foreign investment, careful industrialization, and attention to tourism, leading to a reactivation of the Spanish economy known as the Spanish Miracle (1959–1974). Bonet's architecture followed, by turning to the realm of tourism. Most of his commissions soon consisted of small resort communities on the Mediterranean coast of Spain, single-family houses or small apartment complexes that had little in common with the CIAM discourse that he had promoted.[69] Their small scale, tranquil landscape, and characteristic whiteness look back with nostalgia to the Mediterranean houses that Torres Clavé had heralded as the roots of modern architecture.

Barrio Sur was a convenient public-relations tool for Bonet as he rebranded himself back in Spain. But as a conveyor of advertisements, with plazas full of foreign goods and strolling consumers, the sudden loss of nature as a key element is ironic. Shifting from the sculptural monumentality of Casa Amarilla, floating over an indeterminate wilderness, and the repetitive blocks of Bajo Belgrano gliding over a nostalgic version of the pampas, Barrio Sur's plazas are the antithesis of nature. These civilized plazas followed a logic supposedly inspired by European cities, even though they were really a product of American *and* European urban typologies. San Telmo's courtyard spaces and the Buenos Aires colonial grid predate Ildefonso Cerdá's project for the Barcelona *ensanche*, a gridded expansion that echoes the success of the grid applied in the Americas. At the same time, Barrio Sur's enormous scale and multiple levels effectively organized into a gigantic megastructure were a product of the technocratically ambitious moment that Argentina was going through in both its politics and its architecture.

The discourse surrounding Barrio Sur and its development from Argentina to Spain reflects larger shifts in the discourse of modern architecture. Before the war, Spanish modernity had invoked the Mediterranean as origin, as seen in *A.C.*, the journal of the GATCPAC. After the war, *latinidad* acquired additional political connotations, opposing Franco's discourse of *hispanidad* with less nationalist, more regional egalitarian ideas. In architecture, this pointed to a nostalgia for quaint plazas and small streets, for gregarious Mediterranean people and a lost past that might perhaps erase the Franco years. In Bonet's case, this anxiety resolved itself in a final transformation: from the CIAM aspiration to house the masses to the postwar world of the resort. With the small, white, quiet, and unobtrusive beach houses that Bonet designed toward the end of his career, his modern architecture returned to the Mediterranean. But we can never return. Nostalgia is an anxiety tied to time as much as to place. Bonet's journey back to Spain points to the broader transformation of modern architecture's understanding of itself, from an active agent of change to the passive subject of capital.

"EL ÚLTIMO INDIANO"

Volver
Con la frente marchita
Las nieves del tiempo
Platearon mi sien

Sentir
Que es un soplo la vida
Que veinte años no es nada
Que febril la mirada
Errante en las sombras
Te busca y te nombra

ALFREDO LE PERA[70]

We all know the foreigner who survives with a tearful face turned toward the lost homeland. Melancholy lover of a vanished space, he cannot, in fact, get over his having abandoned a period of time. The lost paradise is a mirage of the past he will never be able to recover.

JULIA KRISTEVA[71]

Bonet's final return to Spain was at the same time impulsive, disorganized, slow, and reluctant. Upon his return in 1959 he opened an architectural studio, first in Barcelona and then in Madrid, with work continuing back in Buenos Aires. He left several cherished valuables behind. His correspondence from those years is full of letters to his assistants back in Argentina, asking them to send forgotten furniture or artwork to Spain. But his Argentinian assistants found him increasingly hard to reach, yet unable to relinquish control of ongoing projects. During this time he built several apartment buildings in Mar del Plata, an Argentinian resort town. The buildings demonstrate an increased urban awareness. He reinterprets the Argentinian gallery, an interior corridor space with shops on the sides related to the Parisian arcades, and uses it to connect the ground floor to the busy urban life of the sidewalk. He combines Barrio Sur's different building types—the height and housing component of the *torres*, the galleries of the *grecas*—and shows the possibilities of some of the components of his unbuilt urban plans. He finally closed his Argentinian office in 1965, leaving all pending matters in the hands of his assistant, architect Marta Inés Allio.

Bonet's last years in Spain were haunted by nostalgia. In his work in Argentina he had often returned to the shapes of the Mediterranean: the Catalan vaults of his youth, the fantastic shapes of Gaudí, and the allusions to

European plazas. When he returned to Spain, he kept remembering Argentina. His last visit to Buenos Aires was in 1987. His friend and colleague Carlos Coire remembered the visit:

> Such was his enthusiasm for the city that he made us value many things that we considered obvious because of their quotidian aspect and, without realizing, had forgotten to appreciate. I had the impression of Bonet as a child that had never left his country and observed with surprised eyes everything that was new and agreeable, although he was very aware of what was happening to us and remembered with precision the political events from 1939 to 1962.[72]

Although other Argentinian architects had used Bonet's status as a foreigner to justify feelings of distance toward him, in the end it was this very condition that allowed him to see the city differently. Coire's memories of Bonet were shared as part of an event organized in Buenos Aires to honor Bonet's memory, shortly after his death in Barcelona in 1989. He was warmly remembered.

Thinking about Bonet's return to Barcelona, historian Fernando Álvarez Prozorovich, also Bonet's biographer, organizer of his archive, and architect in charge of preserving some of his buildings in Barcelona, summed up his return to Spain with these words: "I think Bonet was the last *indiano* [*el último indiano*]."[73] The word *indiano* was used in Spain to refer to returning Spanish adventurers who had traveled to the New World in search of wealth. While many of them did not succeed there, those who did would return to Spain to enjoy their good fortune. As the purveyor of purchased rather than inherited signifiers of wealth (acquired through looting the New World), the *indiano* was enmeshed in a discourse that conflated class and race. His racial and class status was constructed by his geographic trajectory. These men became known for the eclectic and sometimes ostentatious ornamentation of the houses that they built with their newly acquired fortunes at the end of the nineteenth century and in the first decade of the twentieth century. The *casas de indianos* became known for a distinctive marker.[74] A palm, an exotic sign of the new world, would proudly announce their status.[75] The gesture was purely symbolic— many of these travelers lived in regions of South America where these trees are not particularly prevalent.

The Spanish Civil War prompted a new generation of travelers, including several architects.[76] Álvarez also notes that Bonet was the youngest of those who migrated to Argentina—others had arrived with an already substantial career in Spain. Following the philosopher Julia Kristeva's line of thinking, Bonet's nostalgia for Argentina was probably not so much a nostalgia for a place but for a time: the moment when everything seemed possible, when he sat on the terrace roof of the Artists' Ateliers and could look ambitiously at the bustling urban landscape of Buenos Aires. It was also, perhaps, a nostalgia for the future that never was, for the projects that he did not build, and the heroic architect that he aspired to be but never became. Perhaps it was this nostalgia for a time that prompted the *indianos* to plant a palm tree, in remembrance and celebration of their period in the Americas—embracing rather than denying their temporal Americanized status. Back in Barcelona, Bonet designed his last home: a modern apartment building. He used the basement as an architectural studio and the penthouse as his home (FIGURE 4.12). This arrangement, similar to his penthouse in the Artists' Ateliers, must have reminded him of his penthouse in Buenos Aires. In front of this building, he planted a palm tree.[77]

FIGURE 4.12. (*opposite*) Palm tree in front of Bonet's Pedralbes I (1972), his last residence in Barcelona. Author's photo 2012.

MODERNITY FOR THE MASSES

CONCLUSION

But the town-planning projects, which are supposed to perpetuate individuals as autonomous units in hygienic small apartments, subjugate them only more completely to their adversary, the total power of capital. Just as the occupants of city centers are uniformly summoned there for purposes of work and leisure, as producers and consumers, so the living cells crystallize into homogenous, well-organized complexes.

MAX HORKHEIMER AND THEODOR W. ADORNO,
Dialectic of Enlightenment: Philosophical Fragments

It is not that the solution of the housing question simultaneously solves the social question, but that only by the solution of the social question, that is, by the abolition of the capitalist mode of production, is the solution of the housing question made possible.

FRIEDRICH ENGELS, *The Housing Question* (1872)

In their canonical work of critical theory, *Dialectic of Enlightenment* (1944), Theodor Adorno and Max Horkheimer argue that the Enlightenment's rational construction of the world through instrumental reason aspired to liberate humanity from the uncertainties of myth but ultimately resulted in unreflective, compulsive, and mindless oppression—a more pervasive type of myth that carries over to the present.[1] The sense of unfreedom that they describe connects fascism and capitalism as ideologies that ultimately aim to control their populations: we can find it in fascism's repetitive rituals and resistance to all forms of "otherness" and in capitalism's consumer society and its illusion of independent thinking. In the projects examined here, the burgeoning population of Buenos Aires is the subject of this dialectic. The masses are both the prospective inhabitants of the projects that Bonet aspired to build, and the potentially revolutionary subjects in need of control by the states he aimed to please. These various regimes' attempts to manage their populations are revealed by these projects, from the simultaneous celebration and containment

213

of the masses in Casa Amarilla to the seduction of the *cabecitas negras* through the pastoral modernism of Bajo Belgrano and the displacement of San Telmo residents in favor of a consumer middle class in Barrio Sur, where the attempt to "civilize" the population masked the regime's barbaric actions in the Plaza de Mayo.

Thinking through the changing role of the population as this "other" reveals its ongoing presence in the discourse of modern architecture. We find it in Le Corbusier's lyricism and his embrace of ritualistic collective celebration, as well as in modern architects' aspirations to house the masses by serving the states that rule over them. While surrealism mined the aleatory images of the unconscious for their potential to incite revolution, Bonet and his colleagues found that they could also be used to persuade, control, and discipline populations. The monumentality of Casa Amarilla attempted to embody lyricism while serving a military dictatorship—contradictory aims that reveal a compromised architecture community, struggling to position itself as an avant-garde while collaborating with the state so that it might build.

The rise of psychoanalysis in Argentina expanded the exploration of the interior life of the mind—not of the individual artist but that of the masses—to politics, propaganda, and public relations.[2] This influence was externalized in the media strategies of Perón and his strategic appeal to his constituents. The work of Gras, a participant in both fascist and surrealist traditions, most strikingly demonstrates the complications that arise from combining these opposing movements. While the surrealists had sought to propel their art into the future and exert revolutionary change, Peronism relied on wielding nostalgia, a much more effective tool in appealing to *el pueblo*. As it turns out, a mythical past was a more tempting proposition than the uncertainty of revolution—a revolution that Perón, from his point of view, had already staged and that now needed to be reenacted periodically. Countering Perón's mythification of the country, the regime that toppled him attempted to eradicate all traces of what it viewed as the irrational forces that had taken over Argentina. In doing so, Aramburu turned the cult of rationality into yet another myth—one that ultimately served Bonet's interests.

In this narrative I have followed two interrelated phenomena: the spatial politics of the city's monumental center and growing periphery and the construction of a collective unconscious to stand in for the masses in order to control them. Buenos Aires's spatial politics—its iconic plaza, its relationship with the pampas, and its north/south division—inform the political nuances of Bonet's housing project designs, their location within the city, their solid/void relationships, and the role that "nature" plays in them. As the solids in these compositions, the buildings are meant to contain the masses and their private lives. But it is the voids that the modern architects chose to highlight: they came to stand in for these projects' public presence in the city and to describe the desired behavior of the masses by alluding to the city's avenues and plazas. While the solids are part of the background of many compositions, it is the voids, the plazas and landscapes, that are foregrounded to dominate the narrative. Private spaces are rarely depicted.[3] The tacit assumption about housing suggested by these projects and their representations is that the private space of the home ought not to be shown. The projects come to be represented by their public spaces, whose scale can more properly emulate the large ambitions of the architects and the states that funded them.

In the Artists' Ateliers the role of the void is still tentative—it is a reinterpretation of the patio typology, required because of the lack of lateral setbacks. Through the patio, the Ateliers participate in a particular type of dense, tightly knit urban living; the space also becomes a place of social encounter for the building's inhabitants, though these social relations are not the architects' focus. Rather, they are interested in the building's presence as it faces the street, an advertisement of their work in the city. In the solid/void relationship of Casa Amarilla and Nueve de Julio Avenue, the act of demolishing a linear path through the southern neighborhood is reciprocated by returning this space to the masses in the housing block—the building as symbolic gesture filling the void of the north-south avenue.

But it is the representation of the void underneath these blocks that illustrates how the architects understand the populations that they are meant to house. They are depicted as dark and unruly strangers inhabiting a menacing wilderness. In Bajo Belgrano the modern landscape is described as the pampa underneath the cement, but this pampa has been turned into a pastoral modernity far away from the center of the city—an antiseptic representation cleansed of any danger by expert architects posing as pseudo-scientists. Finally this antiseptic quality is presented as civic virtue in Barrio Sur, a project meant to demolish San Telmo and displace its inhabitants. This project's inversion of the modern paradigm of solid/void turns the plazas into loaded voids, tragically connected with the Plaza de Mayo only a year after the massacre.

The formal, aesthetic, and representational manifestations of Bonet's interest in "a true collective psychology" reveal his personal reading of the masses, first as a recently arrived foreigner and later as an "Argentinian" who comes to view Europe "from America."[4] The playful objects in the Artists' Ateliers echo the artworks at the Spanish Pavilion and his work with Matta on the Jaoul House. This appeal to the senses eventually expands to the building itself. In Casa Amarilla these become surreal objects inserted into the fabric of the city. In Bajo Belgrano the city is the subject of psychoanalysis: its congestion and disorder are portrayed as equally dangerous and violent as the devastation of war. Finally, in Barrio Sur the very disorder and chaos that threatened the earlier projects are eradicated: its multiple scales and building types attempt to re-create the qualities of a prior, mythical, and orderly city. As it turns out, this city means to control and "civilize" its citizens by turning them into consumers. Bonet and his colleagues aspired to understand the masses, but instead their projects reveal their own fears and anxieties about them and the ways in which the state might alternatively contain, celebrate, or control them.

The language of these three unbuilt housing projects points back, in turn, to the regimes that they served. Casa Amarilla attempted to elevate the masses and insert them in the center of the city but ultimately embodied the fears of the Porteño avant-garde, anxious about the waves of migrants coming into the city, and of the military dictatorship that took control of these crowds. Bajo Belgrano's dreamy photomontages and surrealist film were meant to appeal to the irrational emotions of the masses, emulating Perón's populist discourse and propaganda machine. Barrio Sur's language of absolute facts and numbers echoed the authoritative military regime of Aramburu and the Revolución Libertadora. Its desolate plazas meant as civilizing agents ultimately recalled the regime's ruthless violence.

These projects' politics are shaped by formal means, pointing to the complicity between architectural design and power. The public's resistance to these projects, and their ultimate failure, calls attention to the ways in which other agents participated in this political conversation. The occupation of the plaza to liberate Perón as well as various protests against prospective removals and demolitions and written critiques in the exhibition guest book or published in various journals attest to an active public eager to participate in these processes despite the authoritarian regimes that governed them.

While Casa Amarilla, Bajo Belgrano, and Barrio Sur were all meant to be publicly funded, the states that sponsored them aimed to serve different publics. The "Revolución del '43" military dictatorship sought to house the masses coming into Buenos Aires, prompted by vague fears of their revolutionary potential. These anxieties were mobilized through a project that elevated and monumentalized the masses while at the same time isolating and dominating them. The revolutionary promise of the people gave rise to Peronism, which sought to house and recruit its constituents using more paternalist and seductive means. The project turned fascism on its head by embracing the former "other"—the *cabecitas negras* that had been so distrusted and rejected by prior regimes. In Bajo Belgrano the architectural project recedes behind its promotion: the film and exhibition reveal the project's aims and politics and the changing role of the architects immersed in these tasks. In contrast,

Bonet abandons any notion of housing the masses in Barrio Sur, displacing Porteños from the South—Perón's sympathizers—and addressing the project to the middle classes fleeing to the suburbs. The promotional potential of Barrio Sur is embraced by Bonet, who turns it into a public-relations vehicle for his return to Spain and, problematically, to Franco, bringing him full circle geographically as well as revealing the similarities between the Revolución Libertadora and Franco's Spanish Miracle. While they addressed different populations, these regimes' shared insistence on the sanctity of home ownership—a consequence of their opposition to communism—points to the ways in which their different views of the people came together in the production of a compliant labor force. It is striking to note that Bonet's plazas are populated by isolated individuals. As Hannah Arendt has theorized, isolation is a precondition to totalitarianism, which is opposed by the power of acting together. Arendt concludes that "isolated men are powerless by definition."[5]

Beyond the political traces of different regimes present in these projects and the audiences they served, their promotional strategies reveal the architect's transformation from aspiring but compromised avant-garde artist to managerial bureaucrat and finally to public-relations expert. Several architecture historians have written about the rising role of media and advertising in modern architecture, from the savvy promotional expertise of Le Corbusier and Frank Lloyd Wright to the rise of the technocrat after World War II and the transition in the late 1960s and 1970s to paper architecture and the language of exhibitions.[6] Bonet's trajectory reveals the continuity in these processes and their intensification: from the Corbusian tactics of his early projects, including journal publications and the use of avant-garde techniques of representation, to the strange marriage of surrealism and fascism in Gras's film, to Bonet's active courting of exhibitions and publications, culminating in the remobilization of Barrio Sur in Spain as an example of *latinidad*. The modern architectural project goes from media to marketing, shifting registers from an eagerness to build to an overt will to promote—a rule of the image that has only accelerated in recent years.

The dialectic of the Enlightenment reveals how all of these projects—whether idealizing the masses through surrealist operations, persuading them with propaganda, or civilizing them to become good consumers—operate in the register of myth. Ultimately, Bonet embraced the seeming technocratic rationality of the Revolución Libertadora, turning a blind eye to the regime's violence. Barrio Sur is a project that demonstrates an obstinate blindness, the refusal to see the bodies strewn in the Plaza de Mayo, the images that had filled the newspapers only a year before. Under the pretense of rationality, our modern architect asserted himself as a blind believer of an even bigger myth:

capitalism. As Franco's Spain refashioned itself into the market economy of the Spanish Miracle, we have a final ideological transformation into neoliberalism, a logic that, by dominating built environments and landscapes, also dominates the discourse and production of architecture, transforming housing from a right into a commodity.

In the late twentieth century South American populations stubbornly claimed their right to the city against increasingly necropolitical states. The collusion between these states and the neoliberalist policies dictated by the Washington Consensus sheds new light on the modern architecture project, its failures, and its potential futures.[7] The rise of neoliberalism capitalized on these failures, prompting states to turn away from modern architecture's dream of collective housing and toward increasing privatization. At the start of the twenty-first century housing solutions in South America have been reduced to credit systems for purchasing privately developed single-family units in projects that leave both the state and the architect out of the process and reduce the built environment to a series of decisions based on maximum short-term profit, involving longer distances, less collective services, and ultimately more isolated environments. To reject this model involves rethinking modern architecture's problematic complicities with totalitarian states and the possibility of alternative solutions that reject these politics: new projects in which populations are no longer "othered" or fetishized as a rationale for design but rather engaged as co-participants in new answers to the housing question.

ACKNOWLEDGMENTS

This book started as my doctoral dissertation. Heartfelt thanks are due to my wonderful committee at the Massachusetts Institute of Technology (MIT): Mark Jarzombek, Arindam Dutta, and Robin Greeley. Their voices are also the voices of the History, Theory and Criticism of Architecture and Art program, which will always be my scholarly home. At the same time, this research was possible thanks to the work of several generations of South American historians. First, I owe an enormous debt to Fernando Álvarez Prozorovich, Bonet's biographer and the organizer of his archive. Fernando generously met with me for long conversations in Barcelona and personally guided me through Bonet's works in the city. I learned of his passing as I wrote these notes. I hope that my thanks reach him somehow. I am indebted to the personal generosity and insights of Paula Bertúa, Gonzalo Fuzs, Adrián Gorelik, Jorge Francisco Liernur, Jorge Nudelman, Luis Priamo, Ingrid Quintana, and Graciela Silvestri. I also want to acknowledge my debt to the work of historians Andrea Giunta, Anahí Ballent, Mariano Ben Plotkin, Beatriz Sarlo, and Tulio Halperin Donghi. This book is written in English, but I hope to speak, like them and with them, from the South. In doing so, this book participates in conversations and efforts started by Luis Castañeda, Fabiola López-Durán, Fernando Luiz Lara, Luis Carranza, and others. I thank these historians for their friendship and guidance.

Archivists are the backbone of this project. Thanks to Inés Zalduendo at Loeb Special Collections, Harvard University; Montse Viu, Andreu Carrascal i Simon, and Núria Masnou, at Arxiu Històric, Col·legi d'Arquitectes de Catalunya, Barcelona; Isabelle Godineau at Fondation Le Corbusier in Paris; Fabienne Gelin and Martine Chosson of the Médiathèque Valery-Larbaud in Vichy; and Ana María Miyno at the Biblioteca Nacional de la República Argentina. Juan Mandelbaum, director of a documentary on Grete Stern, generously shared his insights with me. Yamil Kairuz opened the doors to the Artists' Ateliers. I was privileged to be able to meet several relatives of the various actors involved in this story. Carlos Peralta Ramos generously allowed me to access the Grete Stern Archive while it was still in formation. Silvia and

221

Giselda Batlle shared the archive of their father, Juan Batlle Planas, and their memories and welcomed me into their home along with Giselda's husband, Roly Schere. Claudio Williams opened the archive of his father, Amancio, and arranged an interview with his mother, Delfina Gálvez de Williams. Betina, Graciela, and Selva Ferreres, the daughters of Gabriel Ferreres—a Catalan architect who worked with Bonet in Punta Ballena and remained in the area—shared their memories of their father and the construction of Punta Ballena with me. Although that chapter of Bonet's career did not make it into this book, it informed my overall understanding of his work.

This project received financial and institutional support from MIT, the Society of Architectural Historians (SAH), and the University of Michigan. Early extracts from this project were presented at the Buell Symposium, Museo Reina Sofía, SAH, the Museum of Modern Art (MOMA), the European Architectural History Network (EAHN), and the College Art Association (CAA). The conversations generated in these venues were of great help. My thanks go to the panel organizers and respondents. The communities convened around the Global Architectural History Teaching Collaborative (GAHTC), Systems and the South (S+S), and the Feminist Art and Architecture Collaborative (FAAC) provided me with intellectual discussion and solidarity—thanks particularly to Martina Tanga, Tessa Paneth-Pollak, and Olga Touloumi for being co-conspirators and accomplices. The folks at Detroit Resists taught me that there are always other Souths. The conversations from the Decolonizing Pedagogies Workshop (DPW) and the Settler Colonial City Project (SCCP) opened up new dimensions in this project. The South-South conversation promoted by Nuestro Norte es el Sur, a project in collaboration with Fernando Luis Martínez Nespral, has renewed my determination to write from the South. Despite working in the North, I still hope to be able to take this conceptual and political position.

At MIT, Anne Deveau and Kate Brearley unfailingly rooted for me: it meant more than they will ever know. Marilyn Levine at the MIT Writing Center provided dissertation writing therapy. At the University of Michigan, Jeff Craft's unfailing support has helped me negotiate the institution's labyrinths and challenges. Lisa Bessette's sharp eye helped me cut and reshape the final manuscript; Linda Lee assembled the maps; Stephanie Triplett produced the index. At the University of Texas Press, thanks to series editors Felipe Correa and Bruno Carvalho for supporting the project from the start, to Sarah McGavick for her help with images, and to Robert Kimzey and Kathy Lewis for their editorial work. Thanks especially to Robert Devens for his constant support, clarity, and straightforward approach and to Robert Alexander González, Luis Carranza, and Jennifer Josten for their generous insights on the text.

This book was completed within the wonderful intellectual community that has supported me at the University of Michigan. Thanks to my students: their engagement with this material was key in helping me firm up these concepts. Matt Biro, Elizabeth Sears, and Christiane Gruber (my chairs at History of Art) and Cristina Moreiras-Menor and Gareth Williams (at Romance Languages and Literatures) provided an environment of unwavering support. Jonathan Massey at Taubman has cheered me on throughout. Conversations with Nilo Couret, Paulina Alberto, and Dan Nemser gave me new insights into the project. I greatly benefited from the Michigan tradition of a manuscript workshop, and a day of conversation about this work with Barry Bergdoll, Eduardo Elena, and colleagues from History of Art, Romance Languages and Literatures, and Taubman. Heartfelt thanks to Alex Potts for seeing the argument when I thought I had lost it and for helping me bring it to the fore, and to Rebecca Zurier for careful feedback and constant support. Thanks to Andrew Herscher; the multiple projects in which we have collaborated have enriched this book in many ways. Thanks for the long and strong friendships of Laura Román, Valentina Brevi, Rebecca Uchill, Niko Vicario, Kelly Presutti, Dubravka Sekulić, Ateya Khorakiwala, Alla Vronskaya, Quilian Riano, Irina Chernyakova, Anooradha Iyer Siddiqi, Sophie Hochhäusl, Ann Lui, María Arquero de Alarcón, Kira Thurman, Joy Knoblauch, and Jennifer Nelson.

Gracias a mi hermano Agustín, por estar siempre ahí.

Este libro está dedicado, con mucho amor y gratitud, a mi padre Agustín y a mi madre Mercedes.

ABBREVIATIONS

ASSOCIATIONS, INSTITUTIONS, AND POLITICAL PARTIES

AAA	American Abstract Artists
AACI	Asociación Arte Concreto Invención
ADAGP	Société des Auteurs dans les Arts Graphiques et Plastiques
ADLAN	Amics de l'Art Nou
APA	Asociación Psicoanalítica Argentina
AR	Argentina
ARS	Artists Rights Society
BHN	Banco Hipotecario Nacional
CAC	Corporación de Arquitectos Católicos
CIAM	Congrès Internationaux d'Architecture Moderne
CIRPAC	Comité International pour la Résolution des Problèmes de l'Architecture Contemporaine
CLES	Colegio Libre de Estudios Superiores
CNCB	Comisión Nacional de Casas Baratas
CNT	Confederación Nacional de Trabajo
CNV	Comisión Nacional de la Vivienda
COAC	Col·legi d'Arquitectes de Catalunya
DDEU	Departamento de Difusión y Educación Urbana
DDF	Departamento de Documentos Fotográficos
DGBA	Dirección General de Bellas Artes
EPBA	Estudio del Plan de Buenos Aires
ERC	Esquerra Republicana de Catalunya
ESA	Escuela Superior de Arquitectura
ETSAB	Escola Tècnica Superior d'Arquitectura de Barcelona
FADU-UBA	Facultad de Arquitectura—Universidad de Buenos Aires
FEP	Fundación Eva Perón
FORJA	Fuerza de Orientación Radical de la Joven Argentina
GAMA	Grupo de Artistas Modernos Argentinos
GATCPAC	Grup d'Artistes i Tècnics Catalans per al Progrés de l'Arquitectura Contemporània
GATEPAC	Grupo de Artistas y Técnicos Españoles para el Progreso de la Arquitectura Contemporánea
GEPAC	Grupo de Estudios de los Problemas de la Arquitectura Contemporánea
IAU	Instituto de Arquitectura y Urbanismo

ICA	Instituto Cinematográfico Argentino
ILE	Institución Libre de Enseñanza
LUCE	L'Unione Cinematografica Educativa
MACBA	Museu d'Art Contemporani de Barcelona
MNBA	Museo Nacional de Bellas Artes
MoMA	Museum of Modern Art
MOP	Ministerio de Obras Públicas
OAS	Organization of American States
OVRA	Organización de la Vivienda Integral en la República Argentina
PCA	Partido Comunista Argentino
PJ	Partido Justicialista
PSC	Partido de los Socialistas de Cataluña
PSOE	Partido Socialista Obrero Español
PSUC	Partit Socialista Unificat de Catalunya
SADE	Sociedad Argentina de Escritores
SCA	Sociedad Central de Arquitectos
SIPP	Subsecretaría de Información, Prensa y Propaganda
TOSA	Textil Oeste SA
TPA	Town Planning and Associates
UBA	Universidad de Buenos Aires
UCR	Unión Cívica Radical
UNESCO	United Nations Educational, Scientific and Cultural Organization

ARCHIVES

AAAB	Association Atelier André Breton, Paris, France
AGN	Archivo General de la Nación, Departamento de Documentos Fotográficos, Buenos Aires, Argentina
AGS	Archivo Grete Stern, Buenos Aires, Argentina
AHCOAC	Arxiu Històric, Col·legi d'Arquitectes de Catalunya
AW	Archivo Williams, Buenos Aires, Argentina
BC	Biblioteca de Catalunya, Barcelona, Spain
BNRA	Biblioteca Nacional de la República Argentina, Buenos Aires, Argentina
CC	Casal de Catalunya, Buenos Aires, Argentina
CD BMIN	Centro de Documentación, Biblioteca "Prof. Arq. Manuel Ignacio Net," Buenos Aires, Argentina
CeDInCI	Centro de Documentación e Investigación de la Cultura de Izquierdas en Argentina, Buenos Aires, Argentina
FABC	Fons Antoni Bonet i Castellana, Arxiu Històric, Col·legi d'Arquitectes de Catalunya, Barcelona, Spain
FADU-UBA	Facultad de Arquitectura, Diseño y Urbanismo, Universidad de Buenos Aires, Buenos Aires, Argentina
FE	Fundación Espigas, Buenos Aires, Argentina
FLC	Fondation Le Corbusier, Paris, France
FLL	Frances Loeb Library, Harvard University, GSD, Cambridge, MA
FRC	Fonds Roger Caillois, Médiathèque Valery-Larbaud, Vichy, France
GSD	Graduate School of Design, Harvard University, Cambridge, MA

ICAA	International Center for the Arts of the Americas at the Museum of Fine Arts, Houston, TX
JFHA	Jorge Ferrari Hardoy Archive, FLL, Harvard University GSD, Cambridge, MA
JLSC	Josep Lluís Sert Collection, FLL, Harvard GSD, Cambridge, MA
MNBA	Museo Nacional de Bellas Artes, Buenos Aires, Argentina
SCA	Sociedad Central de Arquitectos, Buenos Aires, Argentina
VOP	Victoria Ocampo Papers, Houghton Library, Harvard University, Cambridge, MA

JOURNALS

A.C.: Documentos de Actividad Contemporánea (Barcelona, 1931–1937)

Acéphale (Paris, 1936–1939)

Acrópole (São Paulo, 1938–1971)

L'Amic de les Arts (Barcelona, 1926–1929)

Arturo (Buenos Aires, 1944)

CICLO (Buenos Aires, 1948–1949)

Documents: Doctrines, Archéologie, Beaux-Arts, Ethnographie, Variétés (Paris, 1929–1930)

Lettres Françaises: Cahiers Trimestriels de Littérature Française, Édités par les Soins de la Revue "Sur" avec la Collaboration des Écrivains Français Résidant en France et à l'Étranger (Buenos Aires, 1941–1947)

Minotaure (Paris, 1933–1939)

Mirador (Buenos Aires, 1956–1961)

Nuestra Arquitectura (Buenos Aires, 1929–1986)

Nueva Visión (Buenos Aires, 1951–1957)

Revista de Arquitectura (Buenos Aires, 1915–)

Revista de Occidente (Madrid, 1923–)

Summa (Buenos Aires, 1963–1992)

Sur (Buenos Aires, 1931–1992)

Tecné (Buenos Aires, 1942–1944)

NOTES

INTRODUCTION

1 Spanish speakers both in Spain and in its former colonies in the Americas use two last names, which correspond to the first part of their father's and mother's last names. This extended last name is used only for official documents and is reduced to the paternal last name for daily use. Hence it is correct to refer to Jorge Ferrari Hardoy as Ferrari (not Ferrari Hardoy) if not using compound last names for all actors. In the case of Catalan names, I have followed their owners' lead in translating them to Spanish for use outside Catalonia: Antoni Bonet i Castellana becomes Antonio Bonet, and Josep Lluís Sert i López becomes José Luis Sert.

2 Antonio Bonet, Jorge Ferrari, and Juan Kurchan, "Voluntad y acción," *Austral* 1 (June 1939): 3.

3 Domingo Faustino Sarmiento, *Facundo* (1845) (Buenos Aires: Librería La Facultad, de J. Roldán, 1921).

4 Paulina L. Alberto and Eduardo Elena, eds., "Introduction: The Shades of the Nation," in *Rethinking Race in Modern Argentina: The Shades of the Nation* (New York: Cambridge University Press, 2015), 1–22.

5 José Ortega y Gasset, *La rebelión de las masas* (Madrid: Revista de Occidente, 1929); and Le Corbusier, "Le lyrisme des temps nouveaux et l'urbanisme," *Le Point: Revue Artistique et Littéraire* 20 (1939): entire issue.

6 Ryan Grauer, "Moderating Diffusion: Military Bureaucratic Politics and the Implementation of German Doctrine in South America, 1885–1914," *World Politics* 67, no. 2 (May 4, 2015): 268–312.

7 Public housing was a particular interest of the CIAM. Eric Mumford, *The CIAM Discourse on Urbanism, 1928–1960* (Cambridge, MA: MIT Press, 2000).

8 Branden W. Joseph, *Beyond the Dream Syndicate: Tony Conrad and the Arts after Cage (A "Minor" History)* (New York: Zone Books, 2008), 49.

9 For the first survey of Bonet's work, see Ernesto Katzenstein, Gustravo Natanson, and Hugo Schvartzman, *Antonio Bonet: Arquitectura y urbanismo en el Río de la Plata y España* (Buenos Aires: Espacio Editora, 1984). Architecture historian Fernando Álvarez Prozorovich has published a monograph on Bonet as well as several essays on specific works in Barcelona. His approach is biographical and comprehensive. See Antoni Bonet Castellana and Fernando Álvarez, *Antonio Bonet Castellana*, Clásicos Del Diseño (Barcelona: Santa y Cole, 1999); and Antoni Bonet Castellana, Fernando Álvarez, and Jordi Roig, *Antoni Bonet Castellana, 1913–1989* (Barcelona: Col·legi d'Arquitectes de Catalunya, 1996). Álvarez is also the organizer of Bonet's archive

in the Historic Archive at the Col·legi d'Arquitectes de Catalunya (COAC, College of Architects of Catalunya) in Barcelona. Architecture historian Jorge Nudelman has published on the work of Bonet and other Le Corbusier disciplines in Uruguay, with particular focus on his work in Punta Ballena. His doctoral dissertation is an important contribution to Uruguayan connections with Le Corbusier's studio. Gonzalo Fuzs wrote a doctoral dissertation on Austral: "Austral 1938–1944: Lo individual y lo colectivo" (Universitat Politècnica de Catalunya, 2012). Recent research by Helena Bender and Paolo Giardiello also centers on Bonet and his architectural projects. Ingrid Quintana Guerrero's recent survey of Latin American collaborators in Le Corbusier's studio includes references to Bonet and Matta's work there. Bonet's work has been recovered in the broader context of the history of modern architecture in Latin America through Luis Carranza and Fernando Lara's important survey, *Modern Architecture in Latin America: Art, Technology, and Utopia* (Austin: University of Texas Press, 2015).

10 Jorge Francisco Liernur with Pablo Pschepiurca, *La red Austral: Obras y proyectos de Le Corbusier y sus discípulos en la Argentina (1924–1965)* (Bernal: Universidad Nacional de Quilmes, 2008).

11 Henry-Russell Hitchcock and the Museum of Modern Art (MOMA), *Latin American Architecture since 1945* (New York: Museum of Modern Art, 1955); and Francisco Bullrich, *New Directions in Latin American Architecture* (New York: George Braziller, 1969). More recently the Museum of Modern Art (MOMA) followed up on Hitchcock's exhibition with the excellent *Latin America in Construction: Architecture 1955–1980*, curated by Barry Bergdoll, Jorge Francisco Liernur, and Carlos Comas. This book expands on their contribution by turning to unbuilt projects and focusing on the period that preceded these developments.

12 Andrew Michael Shanken, *194X: Architecture, Planning, and Consumer Culture on the American Home Front* (Minneapolis: University of Minnesota Press, 2009); Jean-Louis Cohen, *Architecture in Uniform: Designing and Building for the Second World War* (Montréal: Canadian Centre for Architecture, Hazan, distributed by Yale University Press, 2011); Lucia Allais, *Designs of Destruction: The Making of Monuments in the Twentieth Century* (Chicago: University of Chicago Press, 2018).

13 Anahí Ballent and Jorge Francisco Liernur, *La casa y la multitud: Vivienda, política y cultura en la Argentina moderna* (Buenos Aires: Fondo de Cultura Económica, 2014); Anahí Ballent, *Las huellas de la política: Vivienda, ciudad, Peronismo en Buenos Aires, 1943–1955* (Bernal: Universidad Nacional de Quilmes, 2005); and Ramón Gutiérrez, ed., *La habitación popular Bonaerense, 1943–1955: Aprendiendo en la historia* (Buenos Aires: CEDODAL, 2011).

14 Beatriz Colomina, *Privacy and Publicity: Modern Architecture as Mass Media* (Cambridge, MA: MIT Press, 1994).

15 Adrián Gorelik, *La grilla y el parque: Espacio público y cultura urbana en Buenos Aires, 1887–1936* (Buenos Aires: Universidad Nacional de Quilmes, 1998); Graciela Silvestri, *El lugar común: Una historia de las figuras de paisaje en el Río de la Plata*, ed. Juan Suriano (Buenos Aires: Edhasa, 2011); and Graciela Silvestri, *Ars pública: Ensayos de crítica e historia de la arquitectura, la ciudad y el paisaje* (Buenos Aires: Nobuko, 2011).

16 John King, *Sur: A Study of the Argentine Literary Journal and Its Role in the Development of a Culture, 1931–1970* (Cambridge: Cambridge University Press, 1986); Beatriz Sarlo, *Una modernidad periférica: Buenos Aires, 1920 y 1930* (Buenos Aires: Ediciones Nueva Visión, 1988); Beatriz Sarlo and John King, *Jorge Luis Borges: A Writer on the*

Edge (London: Verso, 1993); Dennis Hollier, *The College of Sociology (1937–39)* (Minneapolis: University of Minnesota Press, 1988).

17 Claudine Frank has edited a comprehensive anthology of the writings of Caillois: Roger Caillois, *The Edge of Surrealism: A Roger Caillois Reader* (Durham, NC: Duke University Press Books, 2003).

18 Thomas Mical, *Surrealism and Architecture* (London: Routledge, 2005); Anthony Vidler, *The Architectural Uncanny: Essays in the Modern Unhomely* (Cambridge, MA: MIT Press, 1992); and Neil Spiller, *Architecture and Surrealism*, 1st ed. (New York: Thames and Hudson, 2016).

CHAPTER ONE: A WANDERING SHIP

1 The GATEPAC was created in October 1930 in Zaragoza, Spain. It was meant to have three subgroups: Grupo Centro, corresponding to Madrid, Grupo Norte for Biscay and Guipuzcoa, and Grupo Este for Barcelona, known as GATEPAC (GE). César Antonio Molina, "Introduction," in Josep M. Rovira i Gimeno et al., *A.C.: La revista del GATEPAC, 1931–1937: 28 de octubre de 2008–5 de enero de 2009* (Madrid: Museo Nacional Centro de Arte Reina Sofía, 2008).

2 Catalonia is located on the Mediterranean coast of Spain bordering southern France and derives much of its identity from these connections. Catalan, the language of the region, is a Latin language with links to both Spanish and French. A fundamental part of Catalonian culture, the language is also a political marker that distances the region from the rest of Spain. To speak Catalan instead of Spanish is a political act that implies pride in the region and its culture and support for its autonomy.

3 For more on ADLAN, see *Cuadernos de Arquitectura* 79 (1970); Enrique Granell, "ADLAN," *A.C.: La revista del GATEPAC*, 115–127; and Jaime Brihuega, *Manifiestos, proclamas, panfletos y textos doctrinales (las vanguardias artísticas en España, 1910–1931)* (Madrid: Ediciones Cátedra, 1979), 331–333.

4 "Torres Clavé era un personaje extraordinario. Era un hombre muy espontáneo, muy apasionado, un ser humano excepcional. Como arq. era menos creador que Sert, pero le era indispensable. Congeniaban estupendamente. Torres Clavé era la persona que trabajaba duro, un obrero de la arq.; Sert era la persona que estaba para dar ideas. Con la guerra nombran a Torres Clavé presidente de la Sociedad de Arquitectos de Barcelona y de la revista. A último momento se le ocurre ir al frente. Allí murió. Fue por un exceso de apasionamiento." "Entrevista Arq. Antonio Bonet," Folder C1305/168/1.2, 1, FABC.

5 Ortega, speech at a dinner for Madrid intellectuals visiting Barcelona on March 23, 1930, recounted in Ramón Pérez de Ayala, *Escritos políticos* (Madrid: Alianza Editorial, 1967).

6 Ortega y Gasset, "La deshumanización del arte" (1925), in Ortega y Gasset, *Velazquez, Goya and the Dehumanization of Art* (New York: W.W. Norton, 1972), 67.

7 Fernando Álvarez, "Bonet notes per a una biografía," in *Antonio Bonet Castellana, 1913–1989*, ed. Fernando Álvarez and Jordi Roig (Barcelona: COAC 1996), 9.

8 The ILE was inspired by the philosophy of German Romantic Karl Christian Friedrich Krause. Luis Araquistáin, "El krausismo en España," *Cuadernos del Congreso por la Libertad de la Cultura* 44 (Paris, September–October 1960): 3–12 (http://www.filosofia.org/hem/dep/clc/n44p003.htm).

9 *A.C.* 6 (1932): 30.

10 "La arquitectura popular mediterránea," *A.C.* 18 (1935): 15.

11 See Dalí, "De la beauté terrifiante et comestible de l'architecture 'modern' style."

12 These events took place in the GATCPAC offices, the Syra gallery, or Sert's own attic. Many of the ADLAN events were one-night installations. Granell, "ADLAN," 116. According to Cesáreo Rodríguez Aguilera, larger, more inclusive exhibitions were met with public indifference and often rejection, both from more traditional circles and sometimes from modern art supporters who rejected ADLAN's work as already outdated: "Los amigos del arte nuevo," *Quaderns d'Arquitectura i Urbanisme* 79 (1970): 5–18. In his article Granell agrees that by the 1930s ADLAN's proposal could not really be qualified as avant-gardist. Members of ADLAN also distributed the surrealist journal *Minotaure*, starting with issue 3–4, which included a piece by Dalí on Gaudí (December 1933).

13 Torres Clavé, Fons GATCPAC, Arxiu Històric, COAC. Reproduced in Granell, "ADLAN," 119.

14 See Robin Greeley's thorough reading of Ortega and Dalí, in the context of the Generación del '27, and her analysis of Dalí's polemic use of Nazi imaginary in "Dalí, Fascism, and the 'Ruin of Surrealism,'" in Robin Greeley, *Surrealism and the Spanish Civil War* (New Haven, CT: Yale University Press, 2006), 51–89.

15 "¡Cuidado también con el falso aspecto de modernidad!—tristes caricaturas de la apariencia más superficial de la plástica cubista. El cubismo es un producto de época, y se parece a ésta, pero no tiene nada que ver con su influencia decorativista, anecdótica y pintoresca que haya podido tener en los espíritus superficiales y esnobs." Salvador Dalí, "Poesía de l'útil standarditzat," *L'Amic de les Arts* 23 (Sitges, March 31, 1928): 176–177. Reproduced and translated to Spanish as "Poesía de lo útil estandarizado," in *A.C.: La Revista del GATEPAC*: 46–47.

16 Dalí, "Poesía de lo útil estandarizado," 47. By denouncing the *objet-types* as fetishes, Dalí shares common ground with a later text by German philosopher Theodor Adorno, who also distrusted modern architecture's fetish for the *objet-type* and the stylized but often deceptive appearance of functionalism. Adorno read Adolf Loos's rejection of ornament as a rejection of erotic symbolism, highlighting how surrealists "made much use of such unreflected expressions." Theodor Adorno, "Functionalism Today" (1965), in *Rethinking Architecture*, ed. Neil Leach (London: Routledge, 1997), 9.

17 Adolf Loos, "Ornament and Crime" (1908), in *Programs and Manifestoes on 20th-Century Architecture*, ed. Ulrich Conrads (Cambridge, MA: MIT Press, 2002), 19–24.

18 "Exposición permanente que el 'grupo este' del G.A.T.E.P.A.C. ha inaugurado en Barcelona," *A.C.* 2 (1931): 13–17.

19 Adorno would also highlight this contradiction in which "the fittingness of the means becomes an end in itself," presenting the appearance of the worker while catering to the bourgeoisie. "The handworker mentality begins to produce the opposite effect from its original intention, when it was used to fight the silk smoking jacket and the beret." Adorno, "Functionalism Today," 13.

20 "CIAM: Charter of Athens: Tenets" (1933), in *Programs and Manifestoes on 20th-Century Architecture*, ed. Conrads, 139.

21 Le Corbusier published the charter in 1943. See CIAM, "Charter of Athens: Tenets" (1933), in *Programs and Manifestoes on 20th-Century Architecture*, 137–145.

22 In 1932 the GATCPAC organized a meeting of the Comité International pour la Résolution des Problèmes de l'Architecture Contemporaine (CIRPAC, International Committee for the Resolution of the Problems of Contemporary Architecture) in Barcelona. See "La ciudad funcional," *A.C.* 5 (1932): 17. At the same time, Le Corbusier was working on the urban plan for Algiers. For a detailed history of these events, see Josep

M. Rovira i Gimeno, "Barcelona, the Macià Plan and the CIAMs," in *José Luis Sert: 1901–1983* (Milan: Electa Architecture, 2003), 46–91.

23 The units of Casa Bloc were arranged following the double-height layout of Le Corbusier's Pavillon de l'Esprit Nouveau (Paris, 1924) and Moisei Ginzburg's Narkomfin (Moscow, 1930), both projects familiar to the Catalan architects. But the project differed from these modern examples by offering alternatives, with additional bedrooms instead of the double height, and by moving the corridors to the outside, taking advantage of the mild Spanish weather. *A.C.* included a spread on the Narkomfin in a 1935 issue: "Urbanismo y Arquitectura en la U.R.S.S.," *A.C.* 17 (1935): 30.

24 A letter on January 18, 1934, from a Mussolini representative thanks Le Corbusier for sending him his book, *Croisade, ou le crépuscule des académies* (Crusade, or the twilight of the academies), C3-3-94-001, FLC. For a discussion on Le Corbusier and Mussolini, see Simone Brott, "Architecture et Révolution: Le Corbusier and the Fascist Revolution," *Thresholds* 41: REVOLUTION! (Spring 2013): 146–157. Le Corbusier scholars Jean Louis Cohen and Mary McLeod have extensively discussed his politics.

25 Antonio Bonet, transcript of undated interview, Folder C1305/168/1.2, 1, FABC.

26 Antonio Bonet, transcript of undated interview. Folder C1305/168/1.2, 1, FABC. The start of the war dates Bonet's graduation to around July 2, 1936; according to Danilo Udovicki-Selb, Le Corbusier left for Brazil on July 6, 1936. Danilo Udovicki-Selb, "The Elusive Faces of Modernity: The Invention of the 1937 Paris Exhibition and the Temps Nouveaux Pavilion" (PhD diss., MIT, 1995), 309.

27 It was Le Corbusier's second visit to South America, after his trip to Argentina, Uruguay, and Brazil in 1929. This time he spent most of his time in Rio de Janeiro, consulting on the design of the Ministry of Health and Education and lecturing on modern urban design. Elizabeth Harris, "Le Corbusier and the Headquarters of the Brazilian Ministry of Education and Health, 1936–1945" (PhD diss., University of Chicago, 1984), appendix G.

28 Sert was caught off guard and had to safeguard his family's house before also leaving for Paris. Torres Clavé joined Sert and the organizing committee of the CIAM, the CIRPAC, in a meeting in La Sarraz, Switzerland, in September 1936 and then returned to Barcelona to become director of the architecture school (the Escola Tècnica Superior d'Arquitectura de Barcelona, ETSAB). Mumford, *The CIAM Discourse on Urbanism*, 105.

29 According to Sert's account, he joined the design of the pavilion in December 1936. Folder B11-C, JLSC. In his book on Sert, Josep Rovira goes through the controversy of the appropriation of the commission, which seems to have been given first to Lacasa: Rovira, *José Luis Sert*, 236–238. Luis Lacasa Navarro was from the northern town of Ribadesella and did his architecture studies in the Madrid ESA. After the war he was one of three architects penalized by the Colegio de Arquitectos de Madrid with the removal of his right to practice the discipline (1942). He moved to Moscow, where he lived until his death in 1966.

30 Bonet remembered and defined his position as "collaborating architect" (*arquitecto colaborador*)—a title that he used selectively and later denied to his own employees when asked about their role in his projects. Bonet, Letter to Lala Méndez Mosquera, dated September 17, 1976, Fons Bonet, Folder 1305/168/1, COAC. See also Antonio Bonet, "El CIAM i l'estança a Paris" (1947), *Quaderns* 174 (July–August–September 1987): 54.

31 For a history of the pavilion and its art works, see Catherine Blanton Freedberg, *The Spanish Pavilion at the Paris World's Fair*, Outstanding Dissertations in the Fine Arts

(New York: Garland, 1986), especially chapters 4 and 5, 283–470. The artists' involvement has been recounted by Josefina Alix, "From War to Magic: The Spanish Pavilion,
Paris 1937," in William H. Robinson, Jordi Falgàs, Carmen Belen Lord, Robert Hughes,
Josefina Aix Trueba, et al., *Barcelona and Modernity: Picasso, Gaudí, Miró, Dalí*
(Cleveland: Cleveland Museum of Art in association with Yale University Press, 2006),
450–457. On *Guernica*, see "The Body as a Political Metaphor: Picasso and the Perfor-
mance of Guernica," in Greeley, *Surrealism and the Spanish Civil War*, 147–187.

32 Ludwig Mies van der Rohe, who was in Paris in the summer of 1937 and would have
been able to visit the pavilion, would reinterpret it in his Museum for a Small City
Project, Interior Perspective (1941–1943). In his photomontage, *Guernica* takes pre-
cedence over two background views of nature (trees and water), while two Aristide
Maillol sculptures aid in creating a foreground and background. Mies was in Paris to
discuss a commission, possibly in July 1937. See Franz Schulze and Mies van der Rohe
Archive, *Mies van Der Rohe: A Critical Biography* (Chicago: University of Chicago
Press, 1985), 209.

33 "El objetivo del pabellón era de exponer al mundo la situación del país en guerra,
informarles sobre las verdaderas condiciones y la heroica lucha de un pueblo defen-
diendo sus derechos. Con objeto de contrarrestar los muchos falsos rumores que la
prensa entonces circulaba." Sert, "La victoria del Guernica," Folder D15, JLSC.

34 Folder B11, JLSC.

35 Renau was a militant Communist and had helped the cause of the republic by designing propaganda posters. At the time of the pavilion he was director general of fine arts
but was commissioned by the government to oversee the pavilion. He chose to work
alongside the painters and workers that he was meant to supervise. Freedberg, *The
Spanish Pavilion at the Paris World's Fair*, 131. For more on Renau, see Valeriano Bozal,
El realismo plástico en España de 1900 a 1936 (Madrid: Península, 1967), 139–143.

36 Greeley, *Surrealism and the Spanish Civil War*, 40–41.

37 The small, circular Polish pavilion was in between the Spanish and Germany pavilions.
Famously, the Soviet Union pavilion confronted the Germany pavilion across the
fountain.

38 Although many pavilions in the fair used large photomontaged murals, the Spanish
Pavilion seems to have been the only one that changed them periodically. Photographs of the setup show different variants. For an expanded examination of the use of
photomontaged murals in the fair, see Romy Golan, "Photomurals Real and Painted,"
in *Muralnomad: The Paradox of Wall Painting, Europe 1927–1957* (New Haven, CT: Yale
University Press, 2009).

39 Sánchez was soon to become Luis Lacasa's brother-in-law. The sculpture was
destroyed on dismounting the pavilion. It has now been reconstructed in front of
Museo Santa Sofía, Madrid, where *Guernica* is now on view.

40 The Spanish Republic had originally sent a large marble fountain with the same title
for the pavilion, but its classicist aesthetics did not fit the modern pavilion. Sert commissioned Calder, living in Paris at the time and part of ADLAN's circle, to produce a
new work. See Freedberg, *The Spanish Pavilion at the Paris World's Fair*, chapter 6, for
the story of the fountain. Bonet also remembers the story in his homage to Sert. Bonet,
"Josep Lluís Sert, el Gatepac y el C.I.A.M.," Folder c1305/168/12, FABC.

41 The three-hour bombing of several civilian targets destroyed the small town and
shocked the world with its images of human carnage. Picasso's large painting, depict-

ing the horror and suffering of this moment, came to represent the pain and suffering of the Spanish people.

42 Years later, Bonet was called upon to reinstall the Calder fountain in the Fundació Joan Miró, a building also designed by Sert in Barcelona (1975). Bonet conveyed this anecdote to Fernando Álvarez. Álvarez, in conversation with author, June 18, 2012.

43 Bonet, undated notes for an interview with Clarín (Buenos Aires) in Folder c1305/168/1, 2, FABC.

44 Sert remembers: "We decided to eliminate a metal column to give it the visual space which its monumental scale demanded. At six o'clock in the morning on the eve of the inauguration, after hanging a supporting structure from a girder of the roof, the pillar was taken away and the deflection turned out to be minimal. We breathed a sigh of relief after the critical moment had passed!" Folder D15, JLSC.

45 Rovira, *José Luis Sert*, 240.

46 The bases of these sculptures were all built by the architects and are part of their budget. Folder B11-C, JLSC.

47 Photographs in Sert's archive give us partial views into this space. Folder B11-E, JLSC.

48 See Greeley, "Nationalism, Civil War, and Painting: Joan Miró and Political Agency in the Pictorial Realm," in *Surrealism and the Spanish Civil War*.

49 Of course, this was an illusion: the mural was painted around the handrail and beam, once the building was up, but the general impression was that the building components were being punched into the work.

50 The first floor contained more straightforward government propaganda in the form of illustrations and photomontage depicting different government projects. Visitors exited this exhibition and the building via a large outdoor stair on the front façade.

51 The two pavilions shared some team members, including Miró and Sert. The pavilion was detailed in a publication one year later: Le Corbusier and Pierre Jeanneret, *Des canons, des munitions? Merci! Des logis … s.v.p. … Pavillon des temps nouveaux* (Boulogne: Éditions de l'Architecture d'Aujourd'hui, 1938); Danilo Udovicki-Selb, "Le Corbusier and the Paris Exhibition of 1937: The Temps Nouveaux Pavilion," *Journal of the Society of Architectural Historians* 56, no. 1 (March 1, 1997): 42–63; Udovicki-Selb, "The Elusive Faces of Modernity"; Ivan Rumenov Shumkov and Pep Quetglas, "Architecture and Revolution: Pavillon des Temps Nouveaux by Le Corbusier and Pierre Jeanneret at the International Exposition of 1937 in Paris" (Universitat Politècnica de Catalunya and Departament de Projectes Arquitectònics, 2009); Flora Samuel, *Le Corbusier and the Architectural Promenade* (Basel: Birkhäuser, 2010).

52 Roberto Matta, "Auto-Elasto-Infra Biografía," in *Roberto Sebastián Matta* (Buenos Aires: Der Brücke, 1990), unpaginated. Another biography says that he worked in the studio from 1935 to 1937. Roberto Sebastián Matta Echaurren and Eduardo Carrasco, *Conversaciones con Matta* (Santiago, Chile: Ediciones Universidad Diego Portales, 2011); Roberto Sebastián Matta Echaurren and Germana Ferrari, *Entretiens Morphologiques: Notebook No 1, 1936–1944* (London: Sistan, 1987), 14–15.

53 Matta, "Auto-Elasto-Infra Biografía," 109.

54 Sert remembers how the team would meet with the artists: "Veíamos a Picasso casi cada noche en el Café de Flore en Saint Germain des Près [the next segment is crossed out in the original]. Venía con Dora Maar su amiga, y nos reuníamos con José Bergamín, Juan Larrea, Paul Éluard, Tristan Tzara, Aragón, Joan Miró, Christian Zervos (redactor de Cahiers d'Art) Giacometti y otros, durante aquellos meses de construcción del pabellón. Más tarde hacia el final de las obras el equipo de Pabellón se reunía

también en Montparnasse en 'Le Select' Jose [*sic*] Renau, Bergamin, Luis Lacasa, Larrea, Max Aub, Alonso, Gori Muñoz" (We saw Picasso almost every night in the Café de Flore in Saint Germain des Près [the next segment is crossed out in the original]. He came with his friend Dora Maar and we would get together with José Bergamín, Juan Larrea, Paul Eluard, Tristan Tzara, Aragón, Joan Miró, Christian Zervos (writer at Cahiers d'Art), Giacometti and others, during those months of the construction of the pavilion. Later toward the end of the works the pavilion team also got together in Montparnasse in 'Le Select' Jose [*sic*] Renau, Bergamin, Luis Lacasa, Larrea, Max Aub, Alonso, Gori Muñoz)." Sert, "La victoria del Guernica," Folder D15, JLSC.

55 Matta, "Auto-Elasto-Infra Biografía," 109.

56 "En París veía con frecuencia a los colaboradores del pabellón Español, que eran mas [*sic*] amigos: Picasso, Miró, Calder, Alberto, etc, a Dalí a quien conocí especialmente por sus continuas visitas a la obra del pabellón en cuya obra quería participar. Paralelamente conocí a un joven chileno, teóricamente arquitecto pero en realidad pintor, Roberto Matta Echaurren con quien nos hicimos muy amigos, ya que tanto el como yo estábamos inmersos en cierta manera en el movimiento surrealista, por el que Dalí tanto había luchado en los años precedentes en Barcelona." Bonet, "Austral: Testimonio de Antonio Bonet," Barcelona, September 18, 1981, Folder C1329/228, FABC, 1.

57 Folder Eo, JLSC.

58 André Breton, *Manifestoes of Surrealism* (Ann Arbor: University of Michigan Press, 1972); Maurice Nadeau, *The History of Surrealism* (New York: Macmillan, 1965).

59 "Surrealist Situation of the Object" (1935), in Breton, *Manifestoes of Surrealism*, 263.

60 Breton, "Surrealist Situation of the Object," 263.

61 Karl Marx, *Capital: A Critique of Political Economy* (1867), vol. 1, trans. Ben Fowkes (New York: Penguin, 1990), 165.

62 Walter Benjamin, "Surrealism: The Last Snapshot of the European Intelligentsia" (1929), in Walter Benjamin, *Reflections: Essays, Aphorisms, Autobiographical Writings* (New York: Harcourt Brace Jovanovich, 1978), 210.

63 Benjamin, "Surrealism," 181.

64 André Breton, *Nadja* (Paris: Éditions de la Nouvelle Revue Française, 1928).

65 Walter Benjamin, "Paris, Capital of the Nineteenth Century," in *Reflections: Essays, Aphorisms, Autobiographical Writings* (New York: Harcourt Brace Jovanovich, 1978), 146–162); and Walter Benjamin, *Charles Baudelaire: A Lyric Poet in the Era of High Capitalism* (London: NLB, 1973).

66 Benjamin, "Surrealism," 211.

67 Benjamin, "Surrealism," 215.

68 André Breton, "Surrealist Situation of the Object" (1935), in *Manifestoes of Surrealism*, 260.

69 Breton, "Le message automatique," in *Minotaure* 3–4 (December 12, 1933): 55–65.

70 Ferdinand Cheval, "The Fantastic Palace of Ferdinand Cheval," in *Craft Horizons* 28, no. 1 (1968): 8–15.

71 Dalí, "De la beauté terrifiante et comestible de l'architecture 'modern' style." See also William Jeffett, "Paranoiac Surrealism," in Robinson et al., *Barcelona and Modernity*, 348–353.

72 Dalí, "Le phénomène de le extase," *Minotaure* 3–4 (December 12, 1933): 76.

73 Breton, "Surrealist Situation of the Object," 261.

74 Bonet to Torres Clavé, Paris, February 11, 1938, Folder C1306.168.2, FABC. Bonet also worked on a Water Pavilion for Liège, in Belgium, under the supervision of Pierre

Jeanneret. Bonet, "Testimonio sobre Austral," dated September 18, 1981, in Folder c1329-228 Austral, FABC. Here he remembers doing the Water Pavilion first, although he switches the order of the projects in an undated interview. Folder c1303/168/1.2, FABC. According to the Livre Noir at FLC, the drawings were produced on November 29, 1937. These projects tell us that Bonet definitely worked at Rue des Sèvres between November 1937 and February 1938.

75 Bonet, "Testimonio sobre Austral," dated September 18, 1981, Folder c1329-228 Austral, 2, FABC. According to Bonet, the house was for "Mme. Du Mandrot." "Entrevista al Arq. Bonet," undated, Folder c1305/168/1.2, FABC. This would be Hélène de Mandrot. Le Corbusier built a set of houses for the Jaoul family in 1954–1956, but they correspond to a different site and program.

76 Romy Golan has pointed out that this interest was part of a broader turn in interwar France toward a more "rusticated" and "humanized" modernism, which she theorizes as a response to the growing power of the United States. Romy Golan, *Modernity and Nostalgia: Art and Politics between the Wars* (New Haven, CT: Yale University Press, 1995).

77 The ramp with a circular stair next to it, the ground floor with lower *pilotis* and servant spaces, and the elevated living space are similar to Savoye, but the simple large balcony and general layout have nothing of Poissy's formal complexity. A diagonal wall cuts across the geometry of the living spaces as a nod to the incline in the butterfly roof. The use of wood throughout and the butterfly roof point to Le Corbusier's move away from his purist houses of the 1920s and into more vernacular language.

78 Bonet would continue to use the same tracing paper and colored pencils for initial sketches in Argentina.

79 Bonet, interview, Folder c1305/168/1.2, FABC.

80 *La guerra en civil* (1937) and *Esa guerra desnuda* (August 1937), in Ferrari, *Entretiens morphologiques*, 44–45.

81 Gordon Onslow Ford, "Notes on Matta and Painting (1937–1941)," in Ferrari, *Entretiens morphologiques*, 23.

82 The works were *Scenario no. 1: Succion panique du soleil* (1937), *Scenario no. 2: Pulsions infusoires du soleil* (1937), *Scenario no. 3: Le sperme du temps collé aux déchrirures du jour* (1937), and *Scenario no. 4: Elasticité des intervalles* (1937). Facsimile of the exhibition catalog in Ferrari, *Entretiens Morphologiques*.

83 Roberto Matta, "Mathématique sensible—Architecture du temps," *Minotaure* 11 (Spring 1938): 43. A note at the end of the piece tells us that it was prompted by Breton, adding that he was in Mexico "with Diego Rivera and Trotsky," a small reminder of political revolution.

84 Breton included an anonymous *objet mathématique* in an essay: André Breton, "Crise de l'objet," *Cahiers d'Art* (1936): 21–26.

85 Breton, "Surrealist Situation of the Object," 263.

86 Matta, "Mathématique sensible—Architecture du temps," 43.

87 "Il nous faut des murs comme des draps mouillés qui se déforment et épousent nos peurs psychologiques; des bras pendant parmi des interrupteurs qui jettent une lumière aboyant aux formes et à leurs ombres de couleur susceptibles d'éveiller les gencives elles-mêmes comme des sculptures pour lèvres." Matta, "Mathématique sensible—Architecture du temps," 43.

88 Matta's language suggests the influence of Chilean poet Pablo Neruda, whom he had met in 1936 at his aunt's house in Madrid. Neruda's "Residencia en la tierra" (Residency

on earth): "this great forest respiratory and entwined / with enormous flowers like mouths and teeth / and black roots in the form of fingernails and shoes." Quoted in Valerie Fletcher, *Crosscurrents of Modernism: Four Latin American Pioneers—Diego Rivera, Joaquín Torres-García, Wifredo Lam, Matta* (Washington, DC: Smithsonian Institute, 1992), 237. Neruda's menacing images of nature echo Matta, who admitted in later conversations that "in Latin America I was afraid of nature." Eduardo Carrasco, *Matta: Conversaciones* (Santiago: CENECA, 1987), 13–14, cited in Fletcher (245). This fear, repeatedly portrayed in multiple drawings and paintings, alternated with fascination.

89 Fletcher, *Crosscurrents of Modernism*, 241.

90 Matta, "Mathématique sensible—Architecture du temps," 43.

91 Josefina Alix, *Matta* (Barcelona/Madrid; Museo Nacional Centro de Arte Reina Sofía/ Fundació Caixa Catalunya, 1999), 25.

92 Le Corbusier mentions the journal in his correspondence: letters from November 7 and 24, 1936, in Le Corbusier, *Correspondance: Lettres à la famille 1926–1946* (Paris: FLC, 2013), 546, 548.

93 In the spring of 1938 Matta and his wife, Patricia, left for Switzerland with Gordon Onslow Ford and his partner. Onslow Ford prompted him to paint. Onslow Ford, "Notes on Matta and Painting (1937–1941)," 23.

94 Bonet to Torres Clavé, Paris, February 11, 1938, Folder C1306.168.2, FABC.

95 Unbeknownst to Bonet, Sert was at that time in a dismal situation, requesting payment from the Spanish Republic and being asked in turn to incur further expenses to demolish the Spanish Pavilion and return the site to its prior state. Sert to José Gaos, February 21, 1938, B11C, JLSC.

96 "Crec que estiu bastant preparat per a decidirme a començar la nueva vida d'una manera mes estable i ací a Paris tu ja saps com tot es interí i teòric. Com a arquitecte vull començar a construir i tu ja saps que ací no hi ha res a fer. Per tot això i encara per un seguit més de raons, he decidit anar-m'en a Buenos Aires. Allà tinc familia i amics. I sobretot, allà es construeix. I amb una gran confiança i un gran entusiasme. Tinc ja alguns amics entre arquitects joves com jo d'alla i entusiastes. Crec que farem grans coses. Si mai arribéssim a fer quelcom al sistema del GATCPAC, crec que ho farem millor doncs jo conec totes les coses que no funcionaven a Barna i procuraré evitarles (supon que mes o menys ja sabs de que parle)." Bonet to Torres Clavé, Paris, February 11, 1938, Folder C1306.168.2, FABC.

97 Bonet to Torres Clavé, Paris, February 11, 1938, Folder C1306.168.2, FABC.

98 A document found among Bonet's papers from years later shows listening comprehension of English but no knowledge of writing or spelling. Sert had an English nanny while growing up.

99 A Casal de Catalunya was established in Buenos Aires in 1886 as a space for the Catalan community in the city.

100 "Esto era lo habitual en nuestros encuentros con los republicanos, muy orgullosos de ser rojos aunque algunos fueran apenas rosados." María Rosa Oliver, "España peregrina (Españoles en Buenos Aires)," in *Mi fe es el hombre* (Buenos Aires: C. Lohlé, 1981), 79.

101 In the midst of their European graduation trip, these architects had attended one of Le Corbusier's lectures at the Pavillon des Temps Nouveaux and took it upon themselves to work in his office, starting at the end of October 1937. Liernur quotes Ferrari's narrative on their first meeting with Le Corbusier. Liernur, *La red Austral*, 177, 181–183.

102 Throughout the 1930s Le Corbusier had been immersed in a correspondence with Victoria Ocampo, Enrique Bullrich, and Antonio Vilar in Argentina. Despite their entreaties to visit again, he had refused to travel only to lecture, firmly demanding a commission to return. Le Corbusier to Victoria Ocampo, February 3, 1938, Folder 125, VOP. Liernur explains that Ocampo distanced herself from Le Corbusier because of his closeness to Vichy. Liernur, *La red Austral*, 185–187, and letter to Ferrari, May 27, 1942, JFHA.

103 Fernando Álvarez, "Bonet, notes per a una biografia," in *Antonio Bonet Castellana, 1913–1989*, 10. According to Fuzs, Bonet arrived on April 9, 1938, Kurchan at the start of September, and Ferrari at the end of October. See Fuzs, *Austral 1938–1944*.

104 "Me dío la gran satisfacción de que al llegar en solitario al puerto de Bs.As. en 1938 (entonces no se pasaba el Atlántico en avión), me encontré en el puerto a 3 ó 4 jóvenes arquitectos, esperándome, que eran los que posteriormente iban a formar el 'Grupo Austral.'" Bonet, "Testimonio sobre Austral," dated September 18, 1981, in Folder c1329-228 Austral, FABC, 2. Fuzs found a slightly different version of this story in the same archival folder, in which Bonet details the presence of a great aunt, an uncle, and architects Simón Ungar, Alberto Le Pera, Hilario Zalba, and his wife. See Gonzalo Fuzs, "Austral 1938–1944: Lo individual y lo colectivo" (PhD diss., Universitat Politècnica de Catalunya, 2012), 128.

105 Folder K053, JFHA.

106 "Reportaje: Antonio Bonet, o el espíritu del Movimiento Moderno," in Fuzs, *Austral 1938–1944*, 224.

107 "Ahora BUENOS AIRES! Enorme, febril, sin color, se construye en tal cantidad, que solamente viéndolo se puede creer (pero se construye mal, muy mal, frío, rígido, triste)." This presentation of the city is preceded by a favorable description of the modern architecture being built in Rio de Janeiro, which is contrasted with this desolate description of the building boom in Buenos Aires. Kurchan to Ferrari, October 8, 1938, K053, JFHA.

108 The rail network was installed by England. It included an expansion from 2,500 kilometers of tracks in 1880 to 34,000 kilometers in 1916. See Luis Alberto Romero, *Breve historia contemporánea de la Argentina*, 12th ed. (Buenos Aires: Fondo de Cultura Económica, 2007), 19.

109 Romero, *Breve historia contemporánea de la Argentina*, 18.

110 Including the Safico (Sociedad Anónima Financiera y Comercial) by Swiss engineer Walter Möll (1932–1934); the Comega by Enrique Douillet and Alfredo Joselevich (1933–1934); apartment buildings like the Minner building by Jorge Kalnay (1934); and the Grand Rex Theater, by Alberto Prebisch and Adolfo Moret (1937).

111 See Jorge Francisco Liernur, "Rascacielos de Buenos Aires." *NA* 50, no. 511–512 (1979): 75–88. Liernur notes the visit of German-born New York architect Alfred Zucker to Buenos Aires in 1905 and the observations of Le Corbusier from Avenida Alvear and from Vilar's penthouse apartment in the Palermo neighborhood.

112 I am referring here to office and housing buildings, not related to the war machinery that would take over European architecture. See Cohen, *Architecture in Uniform*.

113 *Nuestra Arquitectura* was published from 1929 to 1986, *Revista de Arquitectura* started publication in 1915 and is still running. For a brief history of these journals, see the corresponding entries in Liernur et al., *Diccionario de arquitectura en la Argentina: Estilos, obras, biografías, instituciones, ciudades* (Buenos Aires: Diario de Arquitectura de Clarín, 2004).

114 *A.C.* shipped 513 issues to Argentina from a total run of 4,881. *A.C.: La Revista del GATEPAC*, 25.

115 For instance, it presented a report on an exhibition of Ludwig Hilberseimer's work in 1933 and published both the plans for the San Isidro horse racetrack stands, with their daring cantilevered slab, and the neoclassical stylings of Marcelo Piacentini's project for a university campus in Rio de Janeiro in 1939.

116 "Yo salía del estudio de Le Corbusier repleto de ideas arquitectónicas racionalistas e imbuido de la mística urbanística de los CIAM y a las que quería incorporar con entusiasmo una esencia surrealista. Yo consideraba que al surrealismo correspondía la tarea de humanizar e individualizar la arquitectura un tanto germánica que estaba emergiendo de los distintos grupos europeos. La realidad cultural, social y política argentina de aquel momento era un reflejo de la situación intensamente conflictiva por la que atravesaba Europa. A través de un gobierno conservador entremezclado de políticos liberales y profascistas, la antigua oligarquía dominante seguía manteniendo el control del país; esta oligarquía culta y afrancesada seguía aferrada a una arquitectura lujosa y académica." Bonet, Conference in Santiago de Compostela, May 17, 1975, Folder 1305/168/2, FABC.

117 Later in life, Bonet took credit for the idea: "My participation in the GATEPAC group and in CIAM international was what led me, when Kurchan and Ferrari convinced me to move to Buenos Aires, to propose to them the formation in Argentina of a group similar to the GATEPAC." "Mi participación en el grupo GATEPAC y CIAM internacional," in Bonet, "Testimonio Austral," Folder c1329/228 Austral, FABC.

118 Members of the avant-garde in these countries would similarly choose the South as their lead: most importantly, Victoria Ocampo's literary journal *Sur* (discussed in chapter 2) and artist Joaquín Torres García's iconic drawing *América invertida* (Inverted America, 1943), based on his statement "our north is the south" (1935). Joaquín Torres García, *Universalismo constructivo* (Madrid: Alianza Editorial, 1942), 213 (quotation)–217.

119 A loose, typewritten cover announces the start of the group's diary. Folder B-4, Austral Archive, Loeb Special Collections. The meeting notes were transcribed. Folder B005, JFHA.

120 See Folder B2, JFHA.

121 Violeta Pouchkine was another colleague and friend but was not part of Austral. See Fuzs, *Austral 1938–1944*, 48–50. Delfina Gálvez de Williams, Amancio Williams's wife and also an architect (b. 1913), remembers that many of these early female architects worked for city hall. Interview with the author, December 5, 2013.

122 This postgraduation trip lasted five months and went through key architectural sites in Italy, France, Germany, Switzerland, and the Czech Republic. The group stayed in the University City in Paris and had the opportunity to talk with Tony Garnier and Gustave Perret. Alfredo Villalonga, "Viaje de los arquitectos argentinos por Europa: Su visita a Francia," *RdA* 206 (Buenos Aires, February 1938): 79, 93. For a detailed account of the trip's motives and travelers, see Fuzs, "El viaje de estudio por Europa," in *Austral 1938–1944*.

123 Villalonga, "Viaje de los arquitectos argentinos por Europa," 79, 93.

124 Bonet, Conference in Santiago de Compostela, May 17, 1975, 6, FABC.

125 Gonzalo Fuzs does a detailed comparison of the statutes of Austral and the GATCPAC: "Austral y GATCPAC Los estatutos gemelos," in *Austral 1938–1944*, 149–158.

126 Folder B002, Austral, JFHA.

127 Folder B002, Austral, JFHA.

128 "Entrevista al arquitecto Jorge Vivanco por el director de la Revista de la SCA, arqui-tecto Carlos Coire" (November 1981), Biblioteca SCA, mimeo. Quoted in Liernur, *La red Austral*, 220.

129 Austral minutes, January 10, 1939, Folder B005, JFHA.

130 See Liernur, *La red austral*, 222–224.

131 "El Pabellón del Grupo debe ser llamativo, fachada renovable cada año. Es necesario amenizar la exposición. Tal vez una Confitería." Austral minutes, November 27, 1939, Folder B008, JFHA.

132 Notes from meeting, December 20, 1938, Folder B005, JFHA. In the notes from meet-ing on March 4, 1939, the cover was delegated to Le Pera. Folder B007, JFHA. Patricia Méndez states that the cover was designed by Grete Stern: *Fotografía de arquitectura moderna: La construcción de su imaginario en las revistas especializadas, 1925–1955* (Buenos Aires: CEDODAL, 2012), 74. This is unlikely, given that Stern's archives hold no record of this important cover.

133 Bonet, Ferrari, and Kurchan, "Voluntad y acción," *Austral* 1 (June 1939): 2–3.

134 Bonet told Jorge Nudelman that the images came from his *A.C.* collection (Nudelman in conversation with author, Montevideo, December 2013).

135 Bonet, Ferrari, and Kurchan, "Voluntad y acción," 3.

136 "La libertad completa que ha permitido a la pintura llegar hasta el surrealismo, denunciando verdades establecidas y planteando problemas psicológicos, no ha sido comprendida por el arquitecto esclavo de su formación." Bonet, Ferrari, and Kurchan, "Voluntad y acción," 2–3 (quotation).

137 *El surrealismo nos hace llegar al fondo de la vida individual. Aprovechando su lección, dejaremos de despreciar al "protagonista" de la casa para realizar la verdadera "machine à habiter."*

Este mismo conocimiento del individuo nos lleva a estudiar los problemas colectivos en función no de una unidad repetida hasta el infinito, sino de una suma de elementos considerados hasta la comprensión, única manera de llegar a la verdadera psicología colectiva. En función de estas consideraciones llegaremos a un nuevo y libre concepto del Standard. La unión entre Urbanismo, Arquitectura, y Arquitectura Interior se completa definitivamente.

— Bonet, Ferrari, and Kurchan, "Voluntad y acción," 3.

138 Marcel Duchamp himself plays a role in the Argentinian surrealist imaginary, having lived in Buenos Aires in 1918–1919. Allegedly, most of his time in the city was spent playing chess.

139 Pichon Rivière later gave a lecture series titled "Psicoanálisis del conde de Lau-tréamont" (Psychoanalysis of the Count of Lautréamont, 1946), further confirming his affinity with surrealism and the Argentinian fascination with Lautréamont.

140 "Bonet, Antonio," in Liernur, *Diccionario de arquitectura en la Argentina*, 94. Garma was a Spanish doctor who trained in Berlin in the 1920s and created links with Argen-tinian psychiatrists then, before arriving in the country in 1938 from France. Jorge Balán, *Profesión e identidad en una sociedad dividida: La medicina y el origen del psi-coanálisis en la Argentina* (Buenos Aires: CEDES, 1988), 20.

141 For a detailed history of psychoanalysis in Argentina, see Balán, *Profesión e identidad en una sociedad dividida*; Mariano Ben Plotkin, *Freud en las pampas: Orígenes y desar-rollo de una cultura psicoanalítica en la Argentina (1910–1983)* (Buenos Aires: Sudamer-icana, 2003); Mariano Ben Plotkin, "The Diffusion of Psychoanalysis in Argentina,"

Latin American Research Review 33, no. 2 (1998): 271–277; and Juan Ramón Beltrán and Hugo Vezzetti, *Freud en Buenos Aires, 1910–1939* (Buenos Aires: Puntosur Editores, 1989).

142 Some of these private writings are archived at JFHA.

143 Bonet, "Testimonio Austral," Folder c1329/228, FABC.

144 Austral, notes from meeting, July 20, 1939, Folder B007, JFHA.

145 "To speak only to speak is the formula for liberation": the architects would have found this Novalis quotation in André Breton and Paul Éluard's *Dictionnaire abrégé du surréalisme*, published along with the International Surrealism Exhibition of 1938.

146 Bonet, Conference at Santiago de Compostela, May 17, 1975, Folder c1305:168:2, FABC.

147 Bonet, "Testimonio sobre Austral," September 18, 1981 in Folder c1329/228, FABC, 1.

148 Copies of the full issue of *NA* 6 were sent to Le Corbusier and Pierre Jeanneret, Eduardo Mallea, and Victoria Ocampo, *Revista "Nosotros,"* Centro Estudiantes de Arquitectura, Centro de Estudiantes de Ingeniería, Sociedad Argentina de Artistas Plásticos, Adolfo Bioy, Nicolás Besio Moreno, Enrique Bullrich, Eduardo Ocantos Acosta (director general of customs), and Julio A. Noble. Copies of only the Austral insert were sent to a longer list, which included members and delegates of the CIAM in Europe and the United States and several surrealists in Paris. Folder B009, JFHA.

149 The acts of the congress show that discussions were more interested in the bureaucratic mechanisms necessary for the construction of popular housing while remaining open to a diversity of architectural solutions, including "collective housing." See Panamerican Union, Division of Labor and Social Affairs, *Resultados del Primer Congreso Panamericano de la Vivienda Popular, celebrado en Buenos Aires del 2 a 7 de octubre de 1939* (Washington, DC: Unión Panamericana, 1950).

150 Bereterbide remained a marginal figure in avant-garde conversations and worked directly with workers' cooperatives. See Juan Molina y Vedia and Rolando Schere, *Fermín Bereterbide: La construcción de lo imposible* (Buenos Aires: Ediciones Colihue, 1997).

151 The minutes also propose several action items including a work schedule, additional work on a proposal for the University City, and finding a radio station willing to broadcast a weekly fifteen-minute program. Austral meeting, November 17, 1939, Folder B008, JFHA.

152 Austral meeting, November 27, 1939, Folder B008, JFHA.

153 "Austral," in Liernur, *Diccionario de arquitectura en la Argentina*, 42.

154 Hilario Zalba, "Homenaje al arquitecto Bonet," *RdA* 145 (January 1990): 12.

155 Letters from Bonet to Ferrari and Kurchan, Folder K053, JFHA.

156 In a site in the intersection of Cangallo and Bartolomé Mitra streets, initially in Corrientes and San Martín, Folder B008, JFHA.

157 There is an image of this project in Álvarez, "Cronología," in *Antoni Bonet Castellana: 1913–1989* (Barcelona: Col·legi d'Arquitectes de Catalunya, 1996), 10. The folder at FABC is empty: the photograph has been lost. The project is dated 1938. In a letter Bonet describes building a "garden-terrace" and a reinforced concrete sculpture of about 2 meters tall. Bonet to Ferrari, undated, Folder K053, JFHA.

158 "Casa Chorizo," in Liernur, *Diccionario de arquitectura en la Argentina*, 29–32.

159 "Casa de Renta," in Liernur, *Diccionario de arquitectura en la Argentina*, 37–40.

160 Liernur expands on the consequences of the evolving ordinance in the vertical growth of the city in Liernur, "Primeros debates modernistas sobre la vivienda en altura en Buenos Aires," in Ballent and Liernur, *La casa y la multitud*, 409–432.

161 Law 13512, sanctioned on October 13, 1948, determined that apartments in a building could belong to different people, superseding the former regimen. Fernando Luis Álvarez de Toledo, "La tipología departamento y la construcción del habitar moderno: Buenos Aires (1930–1960)," *Cuadernos de Vivienda y Urbanismo* 4, no. 8 (July–December 2011): 180–196.

162 "Reglamento general de construcciones," in *Digesto municipal de la ciudad de Buenos Aires* (Buenos Aires: Establecimiento Gráfico "Fermi," 1929).

163 The Cramer Street apartments were designed by Bonet with Ricardo Vera Barros and Abel López Chas between April and October 1938, according to the dates of the drawings (two plans and a perspective). See Folder H 113 d/1/292, FABC.

164 Bonet, undated lecture notes, Folder C1305/168/11/1.1, FABC. By the time Bonet arrived in Buenos Aires, the *Digesto municipal* (building ordinance) had last been updated in 1929 and regulated patios, building heights, and setbacks.

165 Kurchan credits the design fully to Bonet in his letter to Ferrari: "They are doing freer things than the little house of Matta and Bonet, with that I tell you everything. (Of course the ideas in all this are Bonet's, but Vera and López are very hard-working and help him a lot.)" Kurchan to Ferrari, October 8, 1938, Folder K053, JFHA.

166 Chapters 21 and 22 regulate "casas de departamentos" and "casas de inquilinato" (multiple housing units with shared bathrooms). *Digesto municipal* (1929).

167 Bonet quoted in "Edificio Paraguay y Suipacha," in Ernesto Katzenstein, Gustavo Natanson, and Hugo Schvartzman, *Antonio Bonet: Arquitectura y urbanismo en el Río de la Plata y España* (Buenos Aires: Espacio Editora, 1985), 2.

168 Bonet boasts: "I remember that when facing the project, perhaps because of a certain anarchist tendency I have, I did not study the Building Code." He goes on to detail how City Hall called him about the building heights, which were lower than the ones established in the code. At the end of the meeting the city officer told him that the project was so nice that he was going to approve it anyway. "Reportaje: Antonio Bonet, o el espíritu del Movimiento Moderno," *Summa* 188 (Buenos Aires, June 1983): 19–22.

169 The building was presented in the V Triennale di Milano in 1933. Bonet cites it as being from 1934. He cited it years later in a lecture as one of the main examples of modernity, along with a list of more canonical buildings. Bonet, "Nuevas precisiones sobre arquitectura y urbanismo," 20, Folder C1305/168/11, FABC. Gino Pollini and Piero Bottoni are also in the list of recipients of Austral. Folder B009, JFHA.

170 The small building is rumored to have been built with excess material from the Kavanagh.

171 Bonet to Kurchan and Ferrari, June 11, 1938, and Villa to Kurchan and Ferrari, June 17, 1938, Folder K053, JFHA.

172 Jorge Francisco Liernur, in conversation with the author, December 3, 2013.

173 Collective houses were apartment buildings meant to house low-income families and avoid overcrowding; a few were built in the 1920s and 1930s. See "Casa Colectiva" in Liernur, *Diccionario de arquitectura en la Argentina*, 32–35.

174 Chareau was in the list of the first *Austral* journal recipients, with a note saying to send correspondence to him "chez le Docteur d'Alsace" (at the doctor from Alsace's home). Folder B009, JFHA.

175 *A.C.*'s coverage of Sert's office, where Bonet worked, features a conspicuous African statue that shifts to different locations in different views. *A.C.* 8: cover and 30. *A.C.* 17 similarly featured so-called primitive art.

176 The minutes also state these three architects will keep office hours. Minutes from October 3, 1939, meeting, Folder B006, JFHA.

177 Ferrari points his camera toward the saluting crowds, the building, and a woman's behind. He seems curious and unaware of potential dangers. Folder G-111, JFHA.

178 Bonet, Ferrari, and Kurchan, "Voluntad y acción," 3.

CHAPTER TWO: THE MACHINE IN THE PAMPAS

1 The term "Infamous Decade" was coined by historian José Luis Torres in *La década infame* (Buenos Aires: Editorial de Formación "Patria," 1945).

2 Benedict Anderson, *Imagined Communities: Reflections on the Origin and Spread of Nationalism* (London: Verso, 1991). For recent research into Argentina's racialization, see Paulina L. Alberto and Eduardo Elena, eds., *Rethinking Race in Modern Argentina: The Shades of the Nation* (New York: Cambridge University Press, 2015).

3 For an analysis of these different interpretations, see Silvestri, "Fuentes para la pampa modernista," in *El lugar común: Una historia de las figuras de paisaje en el Río de la Plata*, 243–296.

4 "¿Qué impresiones ha de dejar en el habitante de la República Argentina el simple acto de clavar los ojos en el horizonte, i ver . . . no ver nada; porque cuanto mas hunde los ojos en aquel horizonte incierto, vaporoso, indefinido, más se le aleja, más lo fascina, lo confunde, i lo sume en la contemplacion i la duda? ¿Dónde termina aquel mundo que quiere en vano penetrar? No lo sabe! ¿Qué hai mas allá de lo que ve? La soledad, el peligro, el salvaje, la muerte!!!" Sarmiento, *Facundo*, 78 (original nineteenth-century Spanish spelling and punctuation).

5 See Silvestri, "Arquitectura Argentina: Las palabras y las cosas," in *Ars Pública* (Buenos Aires: SCA Nobuko, 2011), 324. Argentinian poet and writer Ezequiel Martínez Estrada made an important contribution to the myth of the pampas, returning to Sarmiento's dichotomy with a more critical, ambiguous, and ultimately pessimistic take on the links between the country's landscape and the nation's character and destiny. See Ezequiel Martínez Estrada, *Radiografía de la pampa* (Buenos Aires: Babel, 1933).

6 Sarmiento, *Facundo*, 78.

7 The "Conquest of the Desert" was a military campaign to take possession of Patagonia, stop the possibility of Chilean expansion, and eradicate the Indigenous population. See David Viñas, Indios, *Ejército y frontera* (Mexico City: Siglo XXI Editores, 1982); Alfred Hasbrouck, "The Conquest of the Desert," *Hispanic American Historical Review* 15, no. 2 (May 1935): 195–228.

8 Many more immigrants moved among several countries, including Argentina, their homelands, and others. Alberto and Elena, *Rethinking Race in Modern Argentina*, 7. Between 1857 and 1958 Argentina received more than 4.5 million immigrants. Almost half of them were Italians, while about a third came from Spain. Gino Germani, "La inmigración masiva y su papel en la modernización del país," in *Política y sociedad en una época de transición, de la sociedad tradicional a la sociedad de masas* (Buenos Aires: Editorial Paidós, 1962).

9 David Marley, "Buenos Aires," in *Historic Cities of the Americas* (Santa Barbara, CA: ABC-CLIO, 2005), 651.

10 The three largest cities (Buenos Aires, Córdoba, and Santa Fe) contained 66,92 percent of the population of the country in 1914. Horacio Vázquez Rial, "Superpoblación y concen-

tración urbana en un país desierto," in *Buenos Aires, la capital de un imperio imaginario*, ed. H. Vázquez Rial (Madrid: Alianza Editorial, 1996), 24.

11 José Hernández, *Martín Fierro* (Buenos Aires: Imprenta de la Pampa, 1872) and *La vuelta de Martín Fierro* (Buenos Aires: Imprenta de la Pampa, 1879).

12 Adrian Gorelik, *La grilla y el parque: Espacio público y cultura urbana en Buenos Aires, 1887–1936* (Buenos Aires: Universidad Nacional de Quilmes, 1998), 13.

13 The plan was published in 1904. Adrian Gorelik, "A Metropolis in the Pampas," in *Cruelty and Utopia*, ed. Jean-François Lejeune (New York: Princeton Architectural Press, 2005), 149.

14 Writing in the 1930s, Leopoldo Marechal sited his novel *Adán Buenosayres* (Buenos Aires: Editorial Sudamericana, 1948) in these neighborhoods.

15 "Buenos Aires è un pezzo di pampa tradotto in città. Questo spiega la sua costruzione per 'quadre.' . . . Ripetendo all'infinito le quadre, si fa una città, senza limiti necessari. . . . Il principio della ripetizione all'infinito, insegnato dalla natura con la Pampa, è stato rispettato scrupolosamente dagli uomini quando hanno avuto da costruire il mondo humano di fronte al mondo naturale." Massimo Bontempelli, *Noi, gli Aria: Interpretazione sudamericane* (1933) (Palermo: Sellerio Editore, 1994), 68–69. Translated in Gorelik, "A Metropolis in the Pampas," 147.

16 Le Corbusier was similarly overwhelmed by the city. He described its late nineteenth-century growth as "an irresistible push, a fever" and declared himself "suffocated" by *le damier maniaque* (the maniacal checkerboard). Le Corbusier, "The Voisin Plan for Paris; Buenos Aires," in *Precisions on the Present State of Architecture and City Planning: With an American Prologue, a Brazilian Corollary Followed by the Temperature of Paris and the Atmosphere of Moscow* (Cambridge, Mass.: MIT Press, 1991), 210–211. His praise for the smaller constructions was part of his avowed appreciation for the "houses of people" as opposed to those designed by architects. Le Corbusier, *Precisions*, 8.

17 Le Corbusier, *Precisions*, 2. The pampas were equally oppressive: "Nothing, no hope, except in oneself alone." Somehow this emptiness was redeemed by the sky, which he implicitly linked to his initial impression from the boat: "it is unlimited, as sparkling by day as by night . . . to tell the truth, all this landscape is one single and straight line: the horizon." Le Corbusier, *Precisions*, 4.

18 Gorelik, "A Metropolis in the Pampas," 155.

19 The economic distribution was partially produced by sickness: the 1871 yellow fever epidemic prompted an exodus of the wealthier families from of San Telmo (south of downtown and also part of Barrio Sur) to Recoleta in Barrio Norte, or northern neighborhood, actually located west of downtown and also including the large middle-income neighborhood of Palermo.

20 "Un mundo más antiguo y más firme." Jorge Luis Borges, "El Sur," first published in *La Nación* (February 8, 1953), second section, 1.

21 Immigrants arriving in the city in the nineteenth century were first compressed into *conventillos* (tenements), old houses in San Telmo (Barrio Sur) subdivided into rooms and rented out to whole families.

22 Boedo Street runs north-south but changes its name north of Rivadavia to Bulmes. Florida runs east-west a few blocks north of Rivadavia.

23 For an analysis of Buenos Aires journals at the start of the century, see John King, *Sur: A Study of the Argentine Literary Journal and Its Role in the Development of a Culture,*

1931–1970 (Cambridge: Cambridge University Press, 1986), especially the section "Magazines in the Cultural Life of Buenos Aires: 1900–30," 13–30.

24 For more on this journal, see Horacio Salas, "El salto a la modernidad," in *Revista Martín Fierro 1924–1927: Edición facsimilar* (Buenos Aires: Fondo Nacional de las Artes, 1995); and King, *Sur*, 22.

25 Florida's manifesto, penned by poet Oliverio Girondo, proposed "a NEW sensibility and a NEW understanding, which, putting us in agreement with ourselves, discover to us unsuspected panoramas and new mediums and forms of expression." "Manifiesto de 'Martín Fierro,'" in Horacio Salas, *Revista Martín Fierro 1924–1927*, xvi (emphasis in the original).

26 "Y estuve entre las casas / miedosas y humilladas / juiciosas cual ovejas en manada, / encarceladas en manzanas / diferentes e iguales / como si fueran todas ellas / recuerdos superpuestos, barajados / de una sola manzana." "Arrabal," *in Fervor de Buenos Aires: Poemas* (Buenos Aires: Imprenta Serrantes, 1923), unpaginated.

27 Felipe Pigna, *Los mitos de la historia argentina 3* (Buenos Aires: Edición Planeta, 2006), 285.

28 In 1936 *provincianos* constituted 16 percent of the population of the city; by 1946 this had risen to 37 percent. By 1960 *provincianos* represented 90 percent of the male working force and 58 percent of the female working force. "Buenos Aires," in Liernur, *Diccionario de arquitectura en la Argentina*, 203.

29 Walter Little dissects these data in relation to these migrations as the source of Peronism, complicating the idea that the migrants were uniformly uneducated, male, and rural: "The Popular Origins of Peronism," in *Argentina in the Twentieth Century*, ed. David Rock (Pittsburgh: University of Pittsburgh Press, 1975), 162–178.

30 "Poseídos de una sed de inmediata conquista siete mil inmigrantes llegaban por semana. Todos tenían que atravesar por un barrio antes de llegar al seno de la ciudad. En esta región se habituaban, para no sufrirlos de golpe, a la edificación poderosa, al clima de la actividad poderosa. También en esta región comenzaba para los miserables, el sometimiento a la ley de la tierra prometida. . . . Los más fuertes entraban después en la ciudad pero los débiles permanecían enquistados en ese barrio, gente que no entraría nunca en el laberinto, pálidos menospreciados de Ariadna." Eduardo Mallea, "Sumersión," *Sur* 2 (1931): 87, 92.

31 Natalia Milanesio, "Peronists and Cabecitas: Stereotypes and Anxieties at the Peak of Social Change," in *The New Cultural History of Peronism: Power and Identity in Mid-Twentieth-Century Argentina*, ed. Matthew B. Karush (Durham, NC: Duke University Press, 2010), 53–84. According to Milanesio, internal migration was related to import substitution industrialization and increased exponentially in the 1940s.

32 Almost half of the migration into Argentina at the turn of the century came from Italy, and about one-third came from Spain. Germani, *Política y sociedad en una época de transición*, 183.

33 "Hubo un momento en que Buenos Aires tenía un carácter definido, es decir una apariencia física perfectamente acordada con su realidad espiritual, sus características no eran como hoy negativas, correspondía admirablemente a su destino, era una ciudad con la belleza de las cosas que son exactamente lo que parecen. El avance inmigratorio no había alterado aún la ordenación jerárquica de su sociedad, ni la fisonomía moral de su pueblo. Hoy, el rumboso parvenu ha extendido, a lo largo de nuestras calles, las más absurdas variedades del disparate arquitectónico." Alberto Prebisch, "Una ciudad de América," *Sur* 2 (1931), 217–218.

34 San Isidro is now a suburb of Buenos Aires. Ocampo famously had architect
    Alejandro Bustillo design her modern house in Palermo, west of downtown Buenos
    Aires, in 1929.

35 "Qué espectáculo desolador: casas, casas pequeñas y grandes, recién construídas y
    profundamente inarmónicas, . . . esta indecible fealdad . . . esta indecorosa mezcla de
    malos gustos distintos, de inculturas que se han arrogado el derecho de expresarse en
    ladrillos." Victoria Ocampo, "Sobre un mal de esta ciudad," *Sur* 14 (1935), 212.

36 Because of territorial disputes with Chile and Brazil in the nineteenth century and
    the German success in the Franco-Prussian War (1870–1871), the Argentinian army
    turned from France to Germany for training and instruction. Officers were routinely
    sent to Germany. Ryan Grauer, "Moderating Diffusion: Military Bureaucratic Politics
    and the Implementation of German Doctrine in South America, 1885–1914," *World
    Politics* 67, no. 2 (May 4, 2015): 268–312.

37 The short story was first published in *El jardín de senderos que se bifurcan* (Buenos
    Aires: Sur, 1941) and later as part of *Ficciones* (Buenos Aires: Sur, 1944).

38 Jorge Luis Borges, "La biblioteca de Babel," in *Ficciones* (Madrid: Alianza, 1985),
    89–100 (quotation). Some English translations change the phrase to "unlimited but
    periodic," I've chosen to translate from the Spanish original. Borges wrote the story
    while working as an assistant in a small branch library. He explains: "My Kafkian
    story 'The Library of Babel' was meant as a nightmare version or magnification of that
    municipal library." Borges, "An Autobiographical Essay," in *Critical Essays on Jorge
    Luis Borges*, ed. Jaime Alazraki (Boston: G.K. Hall, 1987), 45.

39 For Beatriz Sarlo, Borges's library represents a political order that is absolute, ruthless,
    arbitrary, and impenetrable by reason: she reads the library as a description of Argen-
    tinian society. Beatriz Sarlo, *Borges: Un escritor en las orillas* (Buenos Aires: Siglo Vein-
    tiuno Editores, 2015), 148.

40 Jorge Luis Borges, "Assyriennes," *Lettres Françaises* 14 (October 1, 1944): 13–26.

41 In the prologue for "El jardín de los senderos que se bifurcan," Borges later com-
    mented that this story was "not totally innocent of symbolism," which Sarlo interprets
    as an acceptance of its status as politico-philosophical fiction. Sarlo, *Borges: Un escri-
    tor en las orillas*, 154–155.

42 Borges also supported the 1970s military junta but eventually came to be horrified by
    its actions. See Willis Barnstone, *With Borges on an Ordinary Evening in Buenos Aires*
    (Urbana: University of Illinois Press, 1993), 30–31.

43 Gustave Le Bon, *The Crowd, a Study of the Popular Mind* (London: E. Benn, 1896).

44 Oswald Spengler, *The Decline of the West* (New York: Alfred A. Knopf, 1962). Ortega
    translated and published Spengler in his journal, *Revista de Occidente*.

45 Walter Lippmann, *Public Opinion* (New York: Harcourt, Brace and Co., 1922).

46 Sigmund Freud, "Group Psychology and the Analysis of the Ego," in Freud, *The Stan-
    dard Edition of the Complete Psychological Works of Sigmund Freud, Volume XVIII
    (1920–1922), Beyond the Pleasure Principle, Group Psychology and Other Works* (Lon-
    don: Vintage, 2001), 65–144.

47 Freud, "Group Psychology and the Analysis of the Ego," 116.

48 Ortega then resettled in Portugal and made visits to Spain, finally returning in 1948.

49 "La muchedumbre, de pronto, se ha hecho visible, se ha instalado en los lugares pref-
    erentes de la sociedad." Ortega, *Revolt of the Masses*, 13.

50 For data on the composition of these crowds, see Germani, "La inmigración masiva y
    su papel en la modernización del país," in *Política y sociedad en una época de transición*.

51 *Sur*'s second issue included a review of Ortega's book; the author agreed with the need for a peer group to preserve civilization from the advance of mass culture. See Francisco Romero, "Notas al margen de La rebelión de las masas," *Sur* 2 (Fall 1931): 192–205.

52 For the English translation, see "Discussions of Sociological Topics: On 'Defense of the Republic,'" in Caillois, *The Edge of Surrealism*, 214–216. In this transcribed conversation interlocutors request an example of this sort of elite. In response, Ocampo and Caillois agree on the figure of Mahatma Gandhi. Caillois, "En defensa de la república," *Sur* 70: 49–53.

53 Caillois, *The Edge of Surrealism*, 219. See "Debate sobre temas sociológicos," *Sur* 67 (July 1940), 86–104; and "The Nature and Structure of Totalitarian Regimes" in Caillois, *The Edge of Surrealism*, 219–232, originally published as ten separate lectures in various newspapers in Argentina from August to September 1940.

54 Roger Caillois, "The Nature and Structure of Totalitarian Regimes," in *The Edge of Surrealism*, 228. Transcript from Lecture 8, Buenos Aires, September 21, 1940: "The Totalitarian Nation: A Compact and Closed World."

55 Caillois, "Défense de la république," in *Circonstancielles 1940–1945* (Paris: Gallimard, 1980), 23, cited by Frank in Caillois, *The Edge of Surrealism*, 213.

56 *Crisol* (Buenos Aires), September 22, 1940, reprinted in English in Caillois, *The Edge of Surrealism*, 219.

57 Roger Caillois, "Manifeste pour une littérature édifiante," *Lettres Françaises* 13 (July 1, 1944): 1–5.

58 Georges Bataille, "The Obelisk" (1938), in *Visions of Excess: Selected Writings, 1927–1939* (Minneapolis: University of Minnesota Press, 1985), 215; Georges Bataille, *Oeuvres complètes*, vol. 1 (Paris: Gallimard, 1970), 501.

59 For a history of the obelisk, see Jorge Tartarini, "El obelisco," *Summa+* (2004): 127–144.

60 See Gorelik, *La grilla y el parque* for the long history of this project; and Liernur, *Diccionario de arquitectura en la Argentina*, for a summary of Della Paolera's career.

61 Construction started in 1935; the initial phase was inaugurated on July 9, 1937; and the avenue was completed in the 1960s.

62 The couple returned to Buenos Aires in October 1935. Stern left again for London in 1936, where her daughter was born, while pondering whether to return to Argentina or not. She returned the same year and stayed in the country until her death. Luis Priamo and Isaac Fernández Blanco, *Grete Stern: Obra fotográfica en la Argentina* (Buenos Aires: Fondo Nacional de las Artes, 1995). Annemarie Heinrich is another German-born photographer who relocated to Argentina.

63 Alberto Prebisch was trained as an architect in Argentina. After graduating, he traveled to Paris and lived there for two years, from 1922 to 1923. He also traveled to the United States in the early 1930s with a scholarship to study the architecture of museums and concert halls. He was close to Victoria Ocampo's circle and wrote art reviews, initially for *Martín Fierro* and later for *Sur*.

64 "Nuestra época busca realizar ese acuerdo, ese equilibrio, busca un clasicismo, su clasicismo" (Our epoch seeks to realize this agreement, this equilibrium, searches for a classicism, its classicism). Alberto Prebisch, *Martín Fierro* 5–6 (May 15–June 15, 1924), 3.

65 Both Mussolini and Le Corbusier would speak of isolating monuments in similar fashion. See Brott, "Architecture et Révolution."

66 "Las calles de Buenos Aires traducen algo del espectáculo de la pampa. Se prolongan indefinidamente, sin que ningún detalle destacable detenga nuestra mirada. Son, en este sentido, calles sin personalidad. El obelisco da un significado cierto a las enormes

obras ciudadanas que son la Diagonal y la calle Corrientes ensanchada." Alberto Prebisch, in *La Gaceta* (Tucumán), May 1936, cited in Tartarini, "El obelisco," 140.

67 Carlos M. Della Paolera, "La Avenida 9 de Julio," *RdA* 200 (August 1937): 245–351. The avenue cuts perpendicularly across the Avenida de Mayo, a late nineteenth-century project that bisected the grid in half from east to west, starting from the Plaza de Mayo in front of the Presidential Palace and ending in the park in front of the Congress building.

68 Horacio Coppola, Alberto Prebisch, and Ignacio B. Anzoátegui, *Buenos Aires, 1936: Visión fotográfica* (Buenos Aires: Municipalidad, 1936). For a critical history of this book, see Catalina V. Fara, "La construcción de un imaginario de ciudad moderna a través de un fotolibro: Buenos Aires 1936. Visión fotográfica de Horacio Coppola" in *Latin American and Latinx Visual Culture*, vol. 2, no. 1 (2020): 92–100.

69 We know that two blocks north and two blocks south had been demolished by 1937, but these blocks are still shown in the photograph.

70 Horacio Cóppola [*sic*], "Testimonios," *Punto de Vista* 53 (Buenos Aires) (November 1995): 21–25.

71 See Horacio Coppola, Jorge Schwartz, and Alicia Carabias Alvaro, *Horacio Coppola: Fotografía* (Madrid: Fundación Telefónica, 2008). The film is included as a DVD in this publication.

72 *Austral* 1, *NA* (June 1939).

73 "Cómo insertar en este protoplasma el régimen cardíaco indispensable a la circulación y a la organización de una ciudad moderna?" Le Corbusier, "The Voisin Plan for Paris; Buenos Aires," in *Precisions*, 212.

74 Kurchan to Ferrari, September 14, 1938, Folder K053, JFHA (emphasis in original).

75 Bonet, Conference at Santiago de Compostela, Spain, May 17, 1975, Folder C1305/168/2, FABC.

76 "La ferme radieuse" and "Le village coopératif," in Le Corbusier and Jeanneret, *Des canons, des munitions?*, 119–136.

77 The Catalan journal had proposed a series of modular houses that could be assembled and disassembled in various locations: *A.C.* 7 (1932).

78 According to Anahí Ballent, "a contest organized by Banco Nación (1938), one by the Instituto de Colonización de la Provincia de Buenos Aires (1937), the proposals of the Dirección de Tierras y Colonias del Ministerio de Agricultura, and the work of the Consejo Agrario Nacional (created 1939), and the programs of the Banco Hipotecario Nacional." Ballent, *Las huellas de la política*, 62 and footnote 11.

79 *Austral* 2, *NA* (September 1939): 2.

80 The drawing had first been published in Le Corbusier and Jeanneret, *Des Canons, des munitions*, 136, titled "La grande industrie s'empare du bâtiment (Répétition inlassable d'un voeu formulé sans cesse depuis quinze années)" (Big business takes over building [Tireless repetition of a vow made continually for fifteen years]).

81 Isolated prior examples do exist. For an analysis of the discussion prior to 1943, see Elisa Radovanovic, "La vivienda popular anterior al peronismo: Ideas y realizaciones: 1900–1943," in *La habitación popular bonaerense 1943–1955: Aprendiendo en la historia*, ed. Ramón Gutiérrez (Buenos Aires: Cedodal, 2011), 11–22.

82 This movement initiated by Ebenezer Howard in 1898 was meant to incorporate the benefits of the countryside and the city. Howard, *Garden Cities of To-Morrow: A Peaceful Path to Real Reform* (London: Swan Sonnenschein and Co., 1898).

83 Andrew Michael Shanken, *194X: Architecture, Planning, and Consumer Culture on the American Home Front* (Minneapolis: University of Minnesota Press, 2009).

84 Ernesto Giúdici, *Hitler conquista América* (Buenos Aires: Acento, 1938); and Ernesto Giúdici, "El pensamiento fascista en la cultura," *Claridad* 14, no. 290 (June 1935), 65–74.

85 Ernesto Giúdici, *Imperialismo inglés y liberación nacional* (Buenos Aires: Problemas, 1940), cited in Andrés Bisso, *El antifascismo argentino* (Buenos Aires: Editorial Buenos Libros, 2007), 10.

86 Bisso, *El antifascismo argentino*.

87 The Organization of American States (OAS), previously the International Conference of American States or Pan-American Conference, held conferences throughout the early twentieth century. For an architectural history of Pan-Americanism, see Robert Alexander Gonzalez, *Designing Pan-America* (Austin: University of Texas Press, 2011).

88 David Rock, *Argentina 1516–1982: From Spanish Colonization to the Falklands War* (Berkeley: University of California Press, 1985), 246. Such an attack was not a far-fetched threat: at the end of 1939 a German battleship, the *Admiral Graf Spee*, was surrounded by British ships near the La Plata river estuary. Dudley Pope, *The Battle of the River Plate: The Hunt for the German Pocket Battleship Graf Spee* (Ithaca, NY: McBooks Press, 2005).

89 Castillo's chosen successor was Robustiano Patrón Costas. Tulio Halperin Donghi, *Argentina en el callejón* (Montevideo: Arca, 1964).

90 Further internal conflicts were resolved swiftly, sometimes with help from the opposing faction: Cordell Hull was in no mood to negotiate with internal disagreements within a military dictatorship. Halperin, *Argentina en el callejón*, 43.

91 Halperín, *Argentina en el callejón*, 44.

92 "El actual Poder Ejecutivo, que en las palabras y en los hechos viene demostrando hallarse animado de verdadero fervor por la cosa pública, que no tiene las ataduras y los compromisos políticos que, últimamente, todo lo han echado a perder, y al que no le falta ni la confianza total de la Nación, ni la colaboración patriótica de los organismos técnicos y profesionales que la integran y entre los que tenemos el honor de contarnos, es el llamado a poner orden en este serio problema. Y todo nos obliga a pensar, que lo hará." Editorial, *RdA* (July 1943): 254.

93 "Los profesionales más capaces." SCA Committee, "El estado y los arquitectos," *RdA* (May 1944): 181.

94 "Quién no se sienta argentino y arquitecto de veras, quién ostente esos dos títulos por costumbre, por conveniencia o sin saber porqué, no podrá hacer nada que engrandezca a la argentinidad o a la arquitectura." Editorial, *RdA* (April 1944): 137.

95 The United States was also undecided on which style would best represent it: see, for instance, the Chicago Tribune Competition of 1922, in which a neo-Gothic design succeeded over modern entries.

96 Pedro Conrado Sonderéguer has written a summary of this moment: "Proyecto moderno y circunstancias nacionales en la Argentina de 1940: El grupo 'Austral' y la revista *Tecne*," in *America Cahiers du CRICCAL* 4–5 (1990): 431–438. A facsimile edition with a prologue by Juan Mario Molina y Vedia was published in 2015, See Simón Ungar and Pedro Conrado Sonderéguer, *Tecné: Edición facsimilar* (Buenos Aires: Biblioteca Nacional, 2015).

97 Sonderéguer and Ungar had started an architecture group prior to Austral, while Ferrari and Kurchan were in Europe—Ungar had been their partner in a project before their trip. This short-lived group, Grupo de Estudios de los Problemas de la

Arquitectura Contemporánea (GEPAC, Study Group of the Problems of Contemporary Architecture), had been concerned with politics and the architect's loss of agency but was disbanded upon Ferrari and Kurchan's return and the formation of Austral, which Unger promptly joined.

98 "Una revista es un útil: tiene una necesidad, tiene un fin, tiene un plan. Se sitúa en el tiempo y en el espacio" (A journal is a tool: it has a need, it has an end, it has a plan. It situates itself in time and in space). Le Corbusier, *Plans* 1, year 1, quoted in *Tecné* 1.

99 Le Corbusier, "Le lyrisme des temps nouveaux et l'urbanisme," in *Le Point: Revue Artistique et Littéraire* 20 (Colmar: Les Éditions du Point 1939). Throughout 1939 Sonderéguer and Ungar were in direct correspondence with Le Corbusier. In a letter dated December 22, 1941, received in Vichy on March 17, 1942, they thank Le Corbusier for his letter and vouch for the efforts of *Austral* and *Sur* (Victoria Ocampo and Bullrich) to bring Le Corbusier to Argentina. It is likely that the letter they allude to included the essay, dated January 12, 1939, and published in *Tecné* on August 1942 "with the author's permission." Letter from *Tecné* to Le Corbusier, dated December 22, 1941, received March 17, 1942 (handwritten over date), T2-13-90, FLC. Le Corbusier was working on a draft version of the essay through January. A typewritten draft with annotations is available at the FLC, titled "L'urbanisme et le lyrisme des temps nouveaux," B1(15), 270–281 FLC.

100 Ferrari might have suggested that Le Corbusier move to Buenos Aires for an extended period: in his letter Le Corbusier rejects the idea, although "one never knows." Folder E005, JFHA. The article in *Le Point* used a different set of images than the one published in *Tecné*. In *Le Point* Le Corbusier included images from the recent *Des canons* publication (see particularly 74 and 75). In *Tecné* more emphasis was given to projects outside of France.

101 "Pienso que una inmensa mutación se opera, que hay migraciones inminentes, que las ciudades van a hacerse y deshacerse, en una palabra que la ocupación de la tierra será tema de trabajo, todavía una vez más. Era de movimientos, de desplazamientos, de transformaciones. La arquitectura y el urbanismo darán testimonio de todo esto." Le Corbusier, "El lirismo de los tiempos nuevos y el urbanismo," translated by Silvia de Ferrari, *Tecné* 1 (August 1942), no pagination.

102 "Lo que permanece de las empresas humanas no es aquello que sirve, sino aquello que conmueve." Le Corbusier, "El lirismo de los tiempos nuevos y el urbanismo."

103 The essay echoes an earlier debate between the utilitarian, *sachlich* (factual) rhetoric of Hannes Meyer and the humanist formalism of Le Corbusier. Karel Teige had accused Le Corbusier of excessive formalism divorced from function. In his response, Le Corbusier separates beauty from utility and argues for architecture's role in people's happiness. Architecture's function of appealing to people's emotions through its "lyricism" is a thread running through these essays, ten years apart. But while the earlier discussion studiously avoids any reference to politics, the 1939 essay is very aware of the war and keen to appeal to stronger emotions. See George Baird, "Architecture and Politics: A Polemical Dispute, A Critical Introduction to Karel Teige's 'Mundaneum,' 1929; Le Corbusier's 'In Defense of Architecture,' 1933," *Oppositions* 4 (October 1974): 79–108; Kenneth Frampton, "The Humanist v. the Utilitarian Ideal," *Architectural Design* 37, no. 3 (March 1968): 134–136.

104 "*L'autorité enchaînée aux événements explosifs quotidiens de ces temps de transition n'a pas pu encore saisir l'immense ampleur de la mutation*; ainsi n'est-elle pas préparée à ces tâches nouvelles. Ces tâches nouvelles sont les porteuses mêmes du bonheur

humain." Le Corbusier, "Le lyrisme des temps nouveaux et l'urbanisme," 17 (emphasis in the original).

105 Josep Lluís Sert, Fernand Léger, and Sigfried Giedion, "Nine Points on Monumentality," originally written in 1943, first published in English in Giedion, *Architecture You and Me: The Diary of a Development* (Cambridge: Harvard University Press, 1958), 48–51. According to Joan Ockman, the statement was first published in 1956, in the German version of this book.

106 Ockman positions the manifesto as a response to Lewis Mumford's "The Death of the Monument," a section in his book *The Culture of Cities*. Here Mumford associated the monuments of the past with "the eminent and the powerful" and derided them as irrelevant to modern living. Lewis Mumford, "The Death of the Monument," in *The Culture of Cities* (New York: Harcourt, Brace, 1938), 433–440 (quotation on 434). Joan Ockman, "The War Years in America: New York, New Monumentality," in *Sert: Arquitecto en Nueva York* (Barcelona: ACTAR, 1997), 22–47. See also Lewis Mumford, "The New Monumentality," in *The CIAM Discourse on Urbanism*, 150–152; and Sarah Whiting, "Opening Pandora's Box," in "The Jungle in the Clearing: Space, Form and Democracy in America—1940–1949" (PhD diss., Massachusetts Institute of Technology, 2001).

107 Sert, Léger, and Giedion, "Nine Points on Monumentality," 49.

108 An early draft of the essay is dated January 1939, when Sert was still in Paris. See File B1-15-270-001, FLC. Although Sert had left by the time it was published, he corresponded with Le Corbusier from Havana and New York. Copies of *Le Point* containing the essay reached the United States as early as December 1939. Harvard Library owns two copies, dated by their reception stamp at December 1939 and May 1940. Le Corbusier was simultaneously corresponding with Sert and Ferrari.

109 Sigfried Giedion, "The Need for a New Monumentality" and Josep Lluís Sert, "The Human Scale in City Planning," in *New Architecture and City Planning: On a Symposium*, ed. Paul Zucker (New York: Philosophical Library, 1944), 549–568 and 392–412. Léger's essay was published as "Modern Architecture and Color" (1943), in *American Abstract Artists* (New York, Ram Press, 1946), 31–38. Ockman's essay traces all these connections.

110 Giedion, "The Need for a New Monumentality," 549.

111 Giedion, "The Need for a New Monumentality," 552.

112 Giedion mentions Le Corbusier's League of Nations project (1927), also included in Le Corbusier's essay as an example of architectural monumentality. The only built example is the Ministry of Health and Education in Rio de Janeiro (1937–1942), which Giedion views as an announcement of things to come, an example of the possibilities of monumentality to represent states and collectivities. The use of public art in the building would be an ideal example of the integration of art and architecture that he alludes to. Giedion, "The Need for a New Monumentality," 553.

113 Giedion, "The Need for a New Monumentality," 557 (first quotation), 559–561 (second quotation).

114 Giedion, "The Need for a New Monumentality," 561.

115 Sert, "The Human Scale in City Planning," 410.

116 Sert, "The Human Scale in City Planning," 392.

117 Tom Lewis, *Divided Highways: Building the Interstate Highways, Transforming American Life* (New York: Penguin Books, 1999).

118 Sert and Wiener lectured in South America in 1942, 1945, and 1955, financed by the US Department of State. They gave their first series of lectures in Brazil in the winter of 1941–1942, almost at the same time as the Rio Conference of January 1942, and got the Brazilian commission on May 1943, working with the quasi-fascist government of Getúlio Vargas. See Mumford, *The CIAM Discourse on Urbanism*, 151; and Rovira, *José Luis Sert*. Bonet corresponded with Giedion in 1945.

119 The distinction made between migrants and émigrés is an affectation that problematically differentiates European and US migrants from those from other areas of the globe.

120 Notes from Austral meeting, July 29, 1943, Folder B001, JFHA.

121 Raúl Lissarrague to Amancio Williams, July 27, 1943, in Received Correspondence 1943–1947, AW.

122 Williams's original idea was that members of the group should form an internal sub-commission, which would assist Lissarrague and through him expose their ideas on urbanism to the regime. The meeting notes indicate that the main interlocutors in this conversation were Williams and architect Eduardo Sacriste. The discussion was long: the meeting started at 10 P.M. and closed the session at 2:15 A.M. Folder B001, JFHA.

123 The project is listed in Williams's website, run by his son: amanciowilliams.com/archivo/estudio-para-viviendas-en-casa-amarilla (accessed March 29, 2020). The site acknowledges Bonet's leading role in the team.

124 The Santamarina family owned a wealthy *casa consignataria* (an Argentinian entity that manages slaughterhouses and distributes the meat). Santamarina e Hijos SA was founded in 1890 by Spanish migrant Ramón Santamarina (1827–1904). Ernesto Santamarina is listed as the president of OVRA. He maintained a friendly relationship with Bonet: a letter from January 31, 1944, congratulates him for his new position in San Juan. Folder c1306/168/6, FABC.

125 The credits read as follows: "Directive Commission: President, Mr. Ernesto Santamarina; General Secretary, Architect Antonio Bonet; Representatives: Federal District [the city of Buenos Aires], Miss Marta Ezcurra; Province of Buenos Aires; Dr. Alfredo D. Calcagno, Province of Santa Fe, Mr. H. Hernández Larguía. Assistant Commission: Hygiene and Social Services: Prof. Alberto Zwanck; Law, Dr. Pedro Aberastury; Economics: Dr. Nicolás C. Luini. Collaborating Architects: Mr. Amancio Williams, Mr. Hilario A. Zalba, Mr. Eduardo Sacriste, Mr. Ricardo Ribas, Mr. Horacio Caminos." OVRA, FABC.

126 Letters from the journal *España Republicana* dated August 1943 discuss receiving a copy of the pamphlet and ask for further information for an article. Fons Bonet, Letter from *España Republicana* dated August 1943 and signed by Fdo. J.M. Serrano Valerio. Folder c1306/168/6 Biográficas, FABC.

127 Bonet, Letter to Lala Méndez Mosquera, dated September 17, 1976, Folder 1305/168/1, FABC.

128 The statement anticipated Henri Lefebvre's publication by several years: *Le droit à la ville: Suivi de espace et politique* (Paris: Anthropos, 1968).

129 "Entre las gentes de la ciudad y el campo se ha creado una nueva barrera: los suburbios" and "siguen extendiéndose sin control, chatas, tristes." OVRA, *Estudio de los problemas contemporáneos para la Organización de la Vivienda Integral en la República Argentina* (Buenos Aires: Sebastián de Amorrortu e Hijos, [1943]), FABC.

130 "Los habitantes de los grandes arrabales no han encontrado el campo que soñaban, por la pérdida de los grandes espacios libres." OVRA, *Estudio*.

131 La Bombonera is the stadium of Boca Juniors, the more populist of Buenos Aires's two soccer rival teams (the other one being River Plate). Construction started in 1938, and the stadium was opened in 1940: bocajuniors.com.ar/el-club/historia (accessed March 29, 2020).

132 Bonet and the architects of Austral often used the term "bloc" as a phonetic Spanish equivalent for "block," probably following Sert's Casa Bloc.

133 Historian Graciela Silvestri has compared the outward thrust of the project's boundaries to the new language being formulated in the Argentinian art scene, announced in 1945 as Arte Concreto-Invención. These artists became known for dynamic arrangements that gave irregular shape to the frame with their outward thrust. However, instead of the autonomous, internal arrangement of these works, Casa Amarilla's composition directly responds to the axis and geometry of the site and the surrounding city grids. Silvestri, *El lugar común*, 285.

134 Amancio Williams, "Estudio para viviendas en Casa Amarilla. 1942–1943": amanciowilliams.com/15_amarilla.swf?nocaching=63709 (accessed March 29, 2020).

135 The drawings were saved by Bonet and can be found in his archive.

136 "Urbanismo y arquitectura en la U.R.S.S.," *A.C.* 17 (1935), 30. Matta had just visited Moscow before working with Bonet.

137 Historian Jorge Nudelman recalls that Bonet mentioned he took his *A.C.* collection to Argentina. Nudelman, interview with the author, December 12, 2013.

138 Le Corbusier, "Le lyrisme des temps nouveaux et l'urbanisme," p. 11.

139 Williams's tendency toward the grand, sublime gesture—a constant throughout his career—and the utopian character of his projects suggest his possible contribution to Casa Amarilla.

140 Beatriz Penny to Kurchan and Ferrari, May 11, 1938, Folder K053, JFHA.

141 "The trees started to exert a big influence in the life of Antonio when he arrived in Buenos Aires, faced with the enormous variety of magnificent specimens, many for him exotic, which can be admired." Hilario Zalba, "Homenaje al arquitecto Antonio Bonet," *RdA* 145 (January 1990): 10–18.

142 "Je crois qu'est proche le moment où, par un processus de caractère paranoïaque et actif de la pensée, il sera possible (simultanément à l'automatisme et autres états passifs) de systématiser la confusion et de contribuer au discrédit total du monde de la réalité" (I believe the moment is close when, through a process of thought of paranoid and active character, it will be possible [simultaneously with automatism and other passive states] to systematize confusion and to contribute to the total discredit of the world of reality). Salvador Dalí, *La femme visible* (Paris: Éditions Surréalistes, 1930), 11. Dalí distances "automatism and other passive states" from the active role granted by the paranoid-critic method. Paranoia as method would allow the unveiling and disaccreditation of the "exterior world," whose materials and objects it uses. The essay was also published as "The Rotting Donkey" in *Le surréalisme au service de la révolution* 1 (June 1930).

143 "La réalité du monde extérieur sert comme illustration et preuve, et est mise au service de la réalité de notre esprit." Dalí, *La femme visible*, 12.

144 "Des vraies réalisations de désirs solidifiés, où le plus violent et cruel automatisme trahit douloureusement la haine de la réalité et le besoin de refuge dans un monde idéal, à la manière de ce qui se passe dans une névrose d'enfance." Dalí, *La femme visible*, 19. As discussed in chapter 1, Dalí also wrote about modern architecture in *Minotaure*, three years later.

145 Breton, cited in Maurice Nadeau, *The History of Surrealism*, 184.

146 Nadeau, *The History of Surrealism*, 185.

147 Dalí argued that Bataille attempts to rejuvenate his materialist ideas by relying freely on modern psychology: *La femme visible*, 17.

148 Bataille: "Architecture," *Documents* 2 (March 15, 1929), 117; "Abattoir," *Documents* 6 (December 15, 1929), 329; and "Espace," *Documents* 1 (1930), 41. Compiled in Georges Bataille, *Encyclopaedia acephalica: Comprising the Critical Dictionary and Related Texts*, ed. Robert Lebel and Isabelle Waldberg (London: Atlas Press, 1995).

149 Salvador Dalí, "De la beauté terrifiante et comestible de l'architecture 'modern' style," *Minotaure* 3–4 (December 12, 1933): 69.

150 Jorge Luis Borges, "La biblioteca de Babel," in *Ficciones* (Madrid: Alianza, 1985), 100.

151 See Gilles Deleuze and Félix Guattari on the war machine: *A Thousand Plateaus: Capitalism and Schizophrenia* (London: Bloomsbury, 2001), 351.

152 Leo Marx, *The Machine in the Garden: Technology and the Pastoral Ideal in America* (New York: Oxford University Press, 1964).

153 Immanuel Kant, §24–28, *The Critique of Judgement*, trans. J. H. Bernard (London: MacMillan, 1914), 105–129.

154 Kant, *The Critique of Judgement*, 125.

155 Continuing this short period of state appointments, Bonet later joined the Public Works Department for the Municipality of Vicente López, an area adjacent to the northern edge of Buenos Aires.

156 Bonet, Conference at Santiago de Compostela, Spain, May 17, 1975, 10, Folder c1305/168/2, FABC.

157 For more on Perón's work in San Juan, see Mark Alan Healey, *The Ruins of the New Argentina: Peronism and the Remaking of San Juan after the 1944 Earthquake* (Durham, NC: Duke University Press, 2011).

158 These included the Rental Commission, the National Commission for Low-Cost Housing, and the recently created Consulting Commission for Popular Housing. Ballent, *Las huellas de la política*, 63–64.

CHAPTER THREE: THE PERONIST UNCONSCIOUS

1 "La dictadura abominó (simuló abominar) del capitalismo, pero copió sus métodos, como en Rusia, y dictó nombres y consignas al pueblo, con la tenacidad que usan las empresas para imponer navajas, cigarrillos, o máquinas de lavar." Jorge Luis Borges, "L'Illusion comique," *Sur* 237 (1955): 9.

2 Perón ran as the representative of the short-lived Partido Laborista (Labor Party) with the support of various factions.

3 Initially called the Partido Peronista (Peronist Party), it was later renamed the Partido Justicialista. The party defined itself through its focus on social justice, economic independence, and political sovereignty (known as the "three flags"). In other words, the party was structured around a combination of the populist drive that had elected Perón, the economic pragmatism required by postwar circumstances, and traces of the nationalist roots of the regime that had trained him. He served two consecutive periods until 1955.

4 Ana María Rigotti has written on the confluence between the Peronist planning state and urban planning: "Todos hablan del plan," in *Las invenciones del urbanismo*

en Argentina (1900–1960) (PhD diss., Universidad Nacional de Rosario, 2005). See Eduardo Elena, "What the People Want: State Planning and Political Participation in Peronist Argentina, 1946–1955," *Journal of Latin American Studies* 37, no. 1 (February 2005): 81–108; and Eduardo Elena, *Dignifying Argentina: Peronism, Citizenship, and Mass Consumption* (Pittsburgh: University of Pittsburgh Press, 2011).

5 For a history of Perón's relationship with the working class, see Daniel James, *Resistance and Integration: Peronism and the Argentine Working Class, 1946–1976* (Cambridge: Cambridge University Press, 1988).

6 See Jason Stanley, *How Fascism Works: The Politics of Us and Them* (New York: Random House, 2018); and Stanley G. Payne, *Fascism: Comparison and Definition* (Madison: University of Wisconsin Press, 1987).

7 This combination of tradition and reform came to characterize Latin American populism.

8 Juan Domingo Perón, *Conducción política* (Buenos Aires: Escuela Superior Peronista, 1951), 240, cited in Elena, "What the People Want," 88.

9 See Natalia Milanesio, "Peronists and Cabecitas: Stereotypes and Anxieties at the Peak of Social Change," in *The New Cultural History of Peronism: Power and Identity in Mid-Twentieth Century Argentina*, ed. Matthew B. Karush and Oscar Chamosa (Durham, NC: Duke University Press, 2010), 53–84. According to Milanesio, internal migration was related to import substitution industrialization and increased exponentially in the 1940s.

10 For the racial politics of Peronism, see Oscar Chamosa, "Criollo and Peronist: The Argentina Folklore Movement during the First Peronism, 1945–1955," in *The New Cultural History of Peronism*. See also Ezequiel Adamovsky, "Race and Class through the Visual Culture of Peronism"; and Eduardo Elena, "Argentina in Black and White: Race, Peronism, and the Color of Politics, 1940s to the Present," in Alberto and Elena, *Rethinking Race in Modern Argentina*.

11 Chamosa, "Criollo and Peronist," in *The New Cultural History of Peronism*, 114.

12 Perón's relationship with Argentinian intellectual circles was complicated and has elicited several studies. See Flavia Fiorucci, *Intelectuales y peronismo: 1945–1955* (Buenos Aires: Biblos, 2011); Jorge Nallim, *Transformations and Crisis of Liberalism in Argentina, 1930–1955* (Pittsburgh: University of Pittsburgh Press, 2012); Marcela García Sebastiani, *Los antiperonistas en la Argentina peronista: Radicales y socialistas en la política Argentina entre 1943 y 1951* (Buenos Aires: Prometeo Libros, 2005); Marcela García Sebastiani, ed., *Fascismo i antifascismo: Peronismo y antiperonismo: Conflictos políticos e ideológicos en la Argentina (1930–1955)* (Madrid/Frankfurt am Main: Iberoamericana/Vervuert, 2006).

13 Perón resisted the anti-Semitic elements left over from the prior regime. Ricardo Pasolini discusses the case of Jewish Italian immigrants escaping Mussolini's anti-Semitic policies, noting their continued links to Italy as well as the additional presence of Italian fascists in Argentina: "'La internacional del espíritu': La cultura antifascista y las redes de solidaridad intelectual en la Argentina de los años treinta," in *Fascismo i antifascismo*, ed. Marcela García Sebastiani (Madrid: Iberoamericana, 2006).

14 García Sebastiani, *Fascismo i antifascismo*, 10.

15 Federico Neiburg cites a study claiming that 1,250 professors were dismissed from the University of Buenos Aires: 825 quit and 423 were expelled. "Élites sociales y élites intelectuales. El Colegio Libre de Estudios Superiores (1930–1961)," in *Los intelectuales y la invención del peronismo* (Buenos Aires: Alianza, 1998), 166.

16 For more on the CLES, see Neiburg, "Élites sociales y élites intelectuales. El Colegio Libre de Estudios Superiores," 137–182. This description comes from the founding act, quoted on 142. The CLES was funded by publications, a donation system for its members, and the sponsorship of powerful financial institutions, including famed industrialist Torcuato di Tella, whose son was a noted sociologist, and Manuel Miranda, Perón's first minister of finance. See also Pasolini, "La internacional del espíritu."

17 Neiburg, "Élites sociales y élites intelectuales. El Colegio Libre de Estudios Superiores."

18 The Buenos Aires chapter was closed by the regime in 1952, but an expanded network remained in more distant areas of the country where Peronism had less strength.

19 Ivanissevich was trained as a surgeon, and his speeches were full of surgical metaphors on how modern art was sick and must be extirpated. He firmly opposed all tendencies of modern art as sick, repugnant, and amoral in speeches inaugurating national art exhibitions. See "Inauguró el Dr. Ivanissevich el XXXVIII Salón Nacional de Artes Plásticas: Positivos valores del arte nacional congrega la importante muestra," *Guía Quincenal de la Actividad Intelectual y Artística Argentina* (Buenos Aires) 2, no. 29 (October 1948): 4–11, ICAA 824379; and "Inauguróse ayer el XXXIX Salón de Artes Plásticas," *La Nación* (September 22, 1949), ICAA 824394.

20 Andrea Giunta, "El arte moderno en los márgenes del Peronismo," in *Avant-garde, Internationalism, and Politics: Argentine Art in the Sixties* (Durham, NC: Duke University Press, 2007).

21 The artists were the concretes Lidy Prati, Tomás Maldonado, Alfredo Hlito, Enio Iommi, and Claudio Girola, by then associated as Grupo de Artistas Modernos Argentinos (GAMA, Group of Modern Argentinian Artists), and independent artists Miguel Ocampo, Antonio Fernández Muro, Sarah Grilo, Clorindo Testa, and Rafael Onetto. Jorge Romero Brest distinguishes between the two groups in his introduction, describing the concretes as related to formal geometry and the second group as guided by individual sensibility and organic rhythms: "Um grupo de jovens pintores e escultores argentinos," in *Grupo de Artistas Modernos Argentinos* (Rio de Janeiro: Museu de Arte Moderna do Rio de Janeiro, 1953), ICAA 743236.

22 These were initiated by Oscar Ivanissevich. Mariano Ben Plotkin, *Mañana Es San Perón: A Cultural History of Perón's Argentina* (Wilmington, DE: Scholarly Resources, 2003).

23 Plotkin, *Mañana Es San Perón.*

24 October 17 became known as "San Perón"; in 1951, with Eva Perón gravely ill, it was transformed into "Santa Evita." Plotkin, *Mañana Es San Perón*, 79–80. In 1952, after her death, it was transformed into a memorial for Eva Perón.

25 "The festival was the creation of the imagination. It was facsimile, dance, and play. It pantomimed the destruction of the universe, in order to assure its periodic restoration." Roger Caillois, *Man and the Sacred* (Glencoe, IL: Free Press of Glencoe, 1959), 180 (a chapter added after the war). Georges Bataille, Caillois's partner at the College de Sociologie, reformulated these ideas through the concept of the "accursed share," an excess energy that must be spent either in luxurious spending such as spectacles or monuments or in catastrophic outpourings, such as war or sacrifice. Georges Bataille, *The Accursed Share* (New York: Zone Books, 1989), originally published in France as *La part maudite* (Paris: Les Éditions de Minuit, 1949).

26 "La guerre nous avait montré l'inanité de la tentative de Collège de Sociologie. Les forces noires que nous avions rêvé de déclencher s'étaient libérées toutes seules, leurs

conséquences n'étaient pas celles que nous avions attendues." Roger Caillois, "Entretien avec Roger Caillois," *La Quinzaine Littéraire* 97 (June 16, 1970): 8.

27 In turn, the SIPP managed five departments: the Department of Public Spectacles (in charge of film), the Department of Diffusion, the Department of Publicity, the Department of the Press, and the Department of Radio. These departments managed the propaganda production of the ministries and various entities, including Fundación Eva Perón. For a detailed analysis of the aesthetics of the Peronist propaganda, see Gabriel H. Rosa, "La propaganda gráfica peronista (46–55): Subjetivación y conflicto a través de una propuesta estética": uba.academia.edu/gabrielrosa (accessed April 3, 2020).

28 Although the famous photograph of the crowds dipping their feet in the fountain in front of the presidential palace depicted mostly male bodies, a few women can be seen in the background (**FIGURE 0.01**).

29 Andrea Giunta, "Eva Perón: Imágenes y público," VII *Jornadas de Teoría e Historia de las Artes: Arte y Recepción* (1997): 177–184.

30 Complicating this circulation of texts and images was the underlying shift of political and economic power from Europe to the United States at the end of the war, highlighting the rising dominance of the United States in both aesthetics and politics. The shift was resented by the more politically militant leftist groups of the Argentinian avant-garde. In contrast, the intellectuals of Sur, opposed to fascism and to Perón, were more open to the United States. This power realignment had consequences in the way these different groups positioned their stance on art's engagement with or autonomy from politics.

31 The *invencionistas* first proclaimed their movement by producing *Arturo*, a journal launched in the southern summer of 1944 (that is, the start of the calendar year). Although only one issue of the journal was published, it was the starting point of a new avant-garde impetus in the city, combining aesthetics, literature, and philosophy. The strong influence of two older artists loomed over the group and over modern art in Buenos Aires in general: Uruguayan artist Joaquín Torres-García (and his combination of cosmic mysticism and abstract aesthetics) and Chilean modern poet Vicente Huidobro, self-declared founder of Chilean *creacionismo* and part of the Mandrágora surrealist movement in Chile (1938). Both artists were featured in *Arturo*.

32 The intersection between modern art and Peronism has been largely unexplored. An exception is the doctoral dissertation of Ana Jorgelina Pozzi-Harris, which discusses the work of the *invencionistas* and their overlaps and collaborations with Peronism: "Marginal Disruptions: Concrete and Madí Art in Argentina, 1940–1955" (PhD diss., University of Texas at Austin, 2007).

33 Edgar Bayley, *Invención—Arte Concreto—Invención*, Archivo Gyula Kosice, Folder 1, FE. In this 1946 pamphlet with statements by the AACI, Maldonado's insistence on linking the group to the European avant-gardes was the origin of the "concretist" component of the name, connecting it to the circle of Max Bill.

34 The AACI included Alfredo Hlito (1923–1993); Edgar Maldonado Bayley (1919–1990), whose poems and writings have been compiled in Spanish in Edgar Bayley, *Edgar Bayley: Obras*, ed. Julia Saltzmann and Daniel Freidemberg (Buenos Aires: Grijalbo Mondadori, 1999); his brother, Tomás Maldonado (1922–2018); and his brother's wife, Lidy Prati (1922–2008). Brothers Claudio Girola and Enio Iommi were also part of the group.

35 Gabriel Pérez Barreiro, "Buenos Aires: Rompiendo el marco," in *The Geometry of Hope: Latin American Abstract Art from the Patricia Phelps de Cisneros Collection*, ed. Pérez Barreiro (Austin: Blanton Museum of Art, 2006).

36 Madí was led by Ferdinand Fallik "Gyula Kosice" (1924–2016); his wife, Diyi Laañ (1927–2007); Carlos María "Rhod" Rodfuss (1920–1969); and Arden Quin, born Carmelo Heriberto Alves Oyarzun (1913–2010). For more on Arden Quin's work, see Agnès de Maistre and Carmelo Arden Quin, *Carmelo Arden Quin* (Recco, Italy: Demaistre, 1996). The women's role in Madí has been long forgotten but was recently researched by Carla Bertone. Her interviews with Diyi Laañ and Lidy Prati are available in *Revista Ramona* 62 (July 2006).

37 Plotkin, *Mañana Es San Perón*, 197.

38 The magazine in general tended to prompt imaginary narratives: romantic stories were conveyed through photographs and drawings in comic-book format, giving them an increased fictional quality, fluidly interspersing reality and fiction.

39 Hugo Vezzetti has traced the history of psychoanalysis and its popularization in Argentina: Beltrán, Juan Ramón, and Hugo Vezzetti, *Freud en Buenos Aires, 1910–1939* (Buenos Aires: Puntosur Editores, 1989); and Hugo Vezzetti, "Las promesas del psicoanálisis en la cultura de las masas," in *Historia de la vida privada en la Argentina*, ed. Fernando Devoto and Marta Madero (Madrid / Buenos Aires: Taurus, 1999); Mariano Ben Plotkin, Germán Leopoldo García, Hugo Vezzetti, and Jorge Balán, "The Diffusion of Psychoanalysis in Argentina," *Latin American Research Review* 33, no. 2 (1998): 271–277; Mariano Ben Plotkin, "Freud, Politics, and the Porteños: The Reception of Psychoanalysis in Buenos Aires, 1910–1943," *Hispanic American Historical Review* 77, no. 1 (1997): 45; Plotkin, *Freud en las pampas*. One of the earlier studies on this topic is Jorge Balán, *Profesión e identidad en una sociedad dividida: La medicina y el origen del psicoanálisis en la Argentina* (Buenos Aires: CEDES, 1988).

40 The group granted professional credentials to recognize psychoanalysts, but its courses were open to the public, with some preference (under Enrique Pichon Rivière's guidance), to medical doctors trained in psychiatry. See Plotkin, *Freud in the Pampas*; and Balán, *Profesión e identidad en una sociedad dividida*, 20.

41 For instance, Swiss psychiatrist Enrique Pichon Rivière developed a special unit in the Hospicio de las Mercedes, a mental health asylum in Buenos Aires (now Borda Hospital) that specialized in the treatment of teenaged patients. In conjunction with a team of colleagues, Pichon Rivière enlisted the cooperation of artists, including self-denominated surrealist Juan Batlle Planas and Grete Stern, just arrived from Europe with her husband, Horacio Coppola. Victoria Azurduy, "Pichon Rivière," *El Intérprete* 2, no. 7 (October 2007): 9. Pichon Rivière also hosted the first Madí exhibition in 1945; the second one was held the same year at Grete Stern's house. Paula Bertúa, *La cámara en el umbral de lo sensible: Grete Stern y la revista Idilio, 1948–1951* (Buenos Aires: Editorial Biblos, 2012), 82.

42 By 1949 the layout had changed, leaving only Stern's images, Dr. Rest's questionnaire, and the description of the dream on the first page, while analysis and advice were relegated to the last pages. Stern's images seem to have captured her audience's attention, overshadowing Dr. Rest's opinions. Stern began signing her name to the photomontages, which were initially anonymous. The gesture points to her increased pride and confidence in the value of the work.

43 Butelman revealed the real identities of Dr. Rest when he spoke candidly about the column as an amusing anecdote years later. In contrast, Germani never discussed

or admitted to writing it. He eventually left Argentina for the United States, where he taught at Harvard University while writing and editing books on modernity and urbanization.

44 Argentina was dependent on England through most of the nineteenth and early twentieth century, which was akin to economic colonialism.

45 I have cited Germani's research on the population of Argentina, but he now joins the text as an active participant. He emigrated to Argentina in 1934 (escaping fascism) and studied philosophy in Buenos Aires, although he was more interested in sociology. See Mariano Ben Plotkin, "Tell Me Your Dreams: Psychoanalysis and Popular Culture in Buenos Aires, 1930–1950," *Americas* 55, no. 4 (April 1999): 601–629.

46 Gino Germani, "La clase media en la ciudad de Buenos Aires: Estudio preliminar," *Desarrollo Económico* 21, no. (April 1, 1981): 109–27. First published in *Boletín del Instituto de Sociología* 1 (1942).

47 Plotkin, "Tell Me Your Dreams," 621. Butelman played an important role in the introduction of psychoanalysis to Argentina through his publishing house, Paidós. Vezzetti, "Las promesas del psicoanálisis en la cultura de masas," 173–197. Butelman and Germani edited a book series for this editorial, titled "Library of Social Psychology and Sociology."

48 Richard Rest, "El psicoanálisis te ayudará," *Idilio* 1, year 1 (October 26, 1948): 2.

49 Grete Stern, Luis Priamo, and Hugo Vezzetti, *Sueños: Fotomontajes de Grete Stern: Serie completa* (Buenos Aires: Ediciones Fundación CEPPA, Centro de Estudios de Políticas Públicas Aplicadas, 2003); Bertúa, *La cámara en el umbral de lo sensible*.

50 Grete Stern, "Apuntes sobre fotomontaje," read at Foto Club Argentino (September 1967), later published in *Fotomundo* 310 (Buenos Aires, February 1994).

51 Priamo notes that Stern's retitling of the images for exhibition and her refashioning of some of them further demonstrate how she came to embrace her role and her work for *Idilio*: she specifically pointed out how important titles are to a photomontage. Priamo, *Sueños*.

52 Walter Benjamin, "The Work of Art in the Age of Its Technological Reproducibility [First Version]," *Grey Room* 39 (Spring 2010): 30.

53 Benjamin, "The Work of Art in the Age of Its Technological Reproducibility," 31.

54 Elena, "State Planning and Political Participation in Peronist Argentina"; Elena, *Dignifying Argentina*.

55 The text is dated October 3, 1947, and translated by Aldo Pellegrini. André Breton, "Jacques Hérold," *CICLO* 1 (November–December 1948): 53–56.

56 Malcolm de Chazal quoted by André Breton in "Jacques Hérold," *CICLO* 1 (November December 1948): 55.

57 The program started in 1949 and lasted until 1964. It included artists Juan Batlle Planas, Raquel Forner, Héctor Basaldúa, Horacio Butler, and Lino Spilimbergo. The project recalled Salvador Dalí's storefront windows for New York department store Bonwit Teller in 1936, in the context of Alfred Barr's exhibition at MOMA, and again in 1939.

58 Anahí Ballent has written a thorough study of architecture sponsored by the Perón regime: *Las huellas de la política*. See also Anahí Ballent, "Unforgettable Kitsch: Images around Eva Perón," in *The New Cultural History of Peronism*, 143–170; and Anahí Ballent, "Faces of Modernity in the Architecture of the Peronist State, 1943–1955," *Fascism* 7, no. 1 (May 5, 2018): 80–108.

59 "El problema de la vivienda popular," *NA* 225 (April 1948): 113; "Cara a cara con el problema de la Vivienda Popular," *RdA* (May 1949): 108.

60 The ministry was directed by Gen. Juan Pistarini and sponsored directly by President Perón. An important example was the Conjunto General Perón (1948) by Dirección de Arquitectura del MOP.

61 Work was started on September 15, 1947. "Barrio Presidente Perón," *RdA* 365 (February 1952): 23–30.

62 Luigi Piccinato, Francisco S. Dighero, Ernesto S. Gómez, Ricardo J. Morelli, and Óscar J. Stortini, Conjunto 17 de Octubre (1950–1953). See *Historia argentina de la vivienda de interés social. 2da parte: 1943–1955* (Buenos Aires: Arquitectura y Comunidad Nacional, 1985), 58.

63 In the meeting notes for July 20, 1939, Villa is named the group's accountant and at the same time reprimanded because she did not attend the meeting. Folder B7, JFHA. She also found and mailed the aerial photographs of the city that Ferrari and Kurchan used to create Le Corbusier's photomontage for his Buenos Aires plan.

64 On the Bajo Flores project, see Ballent, *Las huellas de la política*, 221; and Itala Fulvia Villa and Horacio E. Nazar, "Urbanización del bajo de Flores: Primer Premio del VI Salón Nacional de Arquitectura," *RdA* 297 (September 1945): 339–357.

65 According to the material saved in her archive, Stern worked as a freelance graphic designer and included several professional women among her clients; the contest layouts for Bajo Flores are also part of her archive. AGS.

66 The complex history of the Buenos Aires plan has been researched by architecture historians Jorge Francisco Liernur and Anahí Ballent. Ballent inserts the EPBA into the broader set of architectural strategies of the Perón regime, while Liernur traces its genealogy through the various connections between modern Argentinian architecture and Le Corbusier.

67 This was a special issue of *La Arquitectura de Hoy*, a short-lived Spanish version of *L'Architecture d'Aujourd'hui*. The publication coincided with Perón's increased interest in urbanism and in the model of the five-year plan. Liernur, *La red Austral*, 341. Le Corbusier had sent a mockup of the proposed publication in 1940, but the project had fallen through. Liernur, *La red Austral*, 192–193.

68 Ferrari to Bonet, December 2, 1947, Folders c1304/160/1, copy, and c1371/249/1, original, FABC. Bonet designed the layout of the resort, the hotel, some residences including his own, and a parallel community for the construction workers. The project included references to vernacular and surrealist projects close to Bonet.

69 Ferrari wrote to Bonet, still in Uruguay, with the details of a rushed, impromptu meeting followed by telegrams to Sigfried Giedion requesting and obtaining an official invitation. In the same letter Ferrari prompts Bonet to send his work on the Artists' Ateliers, Mar del Plata, and Punta Ballena, stating: "I think this congress is important, and we should send a good amount of realized works." Jorge Ferrari to Antonio Bonet, August 24, 1947, Folder c1306.168.5007, FABC.

70 Ferrari to Sert, April 1, 1948, Folder F083, JFHA.

71 To Sert, Le Corbusier boasted how the Argentina team was "team 'Corbusier'" and sent copies of the decree creating the EPBA in Argentina, which he expected to join: "This decree is well made. Perhaps it would be of use in Bogotá?" Le Corbusier to Sert, March 22, 1948, in *Le Corbusier–José Luis Sert Correspondance 1928–1965* (Paris: Éditions du Linteau, 2009), 115. A year later he wrote to Ferrari, comparing the time it had taken to formulate a contract for him in Buenos Aires to the progress made in Bogotá with Sert and Wiener: "In the meantime, I've been to Bogotá a second time and I have signed the contract for the Directing Plan that I established. My work will

then be taken over by Wiener and Sert." Le Corbusier to Ferrari, June 22, 1949, Folder E012, JFHA.

72 The structure was designed in several meetings in July 1948 and was dissolved in August 1948. Enrique Gebhard to Ferrari, April 4, 1949, Folder C151; JFHA.

73 Vivanco was working in Tucumán, a mid-sized city where he had organized the Instituto de Arquitectura y Urbanismo (IAU, Institute of Architecture and Urbanism), a school of architecture intent on teaching the principles of modern architecture. His focus on the IAU eventually distanced him from the EPBA. Vivanco attended CIAM 6 in 1946 (along with Ferrari) and used the trip to recruit Italian architects to teach at the institute, including Ernesto Rogers. The institute functioned briefly as an important pedagogical center for modern architecture in Argentina. Roca was not part of Austral and was left out of many decisions.

74 Gebhard had been published in *Tecné* 1 (August 1942), which featured a Housing Exhibition in Santiago sponsored by health minister Salvador Allende in 1940.

75 Gebhard to Ferrari, April 4, 1949, Folder C151, JFHA. Bonet's absence was likely due to his need to wrap up the work in Uruguay.

76 Gebhard's complaints are confirmed by the copious correspondence archived in the Ferrari Archive: the EPBA presented the appearance of a stratified organization, but it was actually led by Ferrari and Bonet.

77 The architects became aware of its availability in a meeting of March 1948. EPBA Folder C128, JFHA.

78 *RdA* 369 (January–February 1953): 17–75.

79 Part of the conversation focused on the appropriate formats to publicize the plan, dismissing the use of exhibitions and printed material and favoring the production of a promotional film. Minutes of first EPBA committee meeting, February 16, 1948, Folder C069, JFHA.

80 The exhibit *Nuevas Realidades* (New Realities) took its name from the Salon des Réalités Nouvelles, the Paris exhibition of abstract art: after being included in the 1948 edition, the Argentinians used the name for the local iteration. It included *invencionistas* Tomás Maldonado, Enio Iommi, and Claudio Girola, Madí members Arden Quin and Carlos María "Rhod" Rothfuss, Austral architect Eduardo Catalano, and the Italian architects of BBPR (Gianluigi Banfi, who died in 1945 but was kept in the group's name, Ludovico Belgiojoso, Enrico Peressutti, and Ernesto Rogers), due to his presence in Argentina. Rogers's lecture at this event was published by the former surrealists of *CICLO*, bringing together these estranged surrealists with the new generation of *invencionistas*.

81 Various newspaper clippings from May 1948, Folder H010, JFHA.

82 IV Congreso Histórico Municipal Interamericano, Exposición de Urbanismo (Municipalidad de la Ciudad de Buenos Aires, 1949), 24–25.

83 The odd phrase is perhaps due to Gras's Italian origin. Gras to Ferrari, August 22, 1949, Folder C115, JFHA.

84 Stern is addressed as "Mrs. Coppola," although she was already divorced.

85 Argentinian film had been linked to the state since its beginnings in 1933, with the foundation of the Instituto Cinematográfico Argentino (ICA, Argentinian Cinematographic Institute). State supervision increased during Peronism. Clara Kriger, *Cine y peronismo: El estado en escena* (Buenos Aires: Siglo Veintiuno Editores, 2009); Valeria Manzano, *Cine Argentino y peronismo: Cultura, política y propaganda, 1946–1955* (Barcelona: Universitat de Barcelona, 2001).

86 See Kriger, *Cine y peronismo*, 107. Peronism also created annual awards that promoted films with strong moral messages such as family unity and patriotism, and generally supporting the binaries of the Peronist discourse, such as people/oligarchy and profligacy/austerity. Manzano, *Cine Argentino y peronismo*.

87 For details on LUCE and state propaganda in Mussolini's Italy, see Arnold J. Zurcher, "State Propaganda in Italy," in Harwood L. Childs, *Propaganda and Dictatorship: A Collection of Papers* (New York: Arno Press, 1972), 35–57; and Mino Argentieri, *L'occhio del regime: Informazione e propaganda nel cinema del fascismo* (Florence: Vallecchi, 1979).

88 Enrico Gras presented himself as a surrealist filmmaker and never referenced his association with LUCE. However, his name can be found in several films in the archive of this institution. See patrimonio.archivioluce.com (accessed April 4, 2020).

89 In the following days Ferrari sent a telegram. Ferrari to Bonet, September 23, 1949, and telegram, September 24, 1949, Folder E063, JFHA. We know from his correspondence that Bonet was in Italy for CIAM 7 at the end of July, and stayed at least until late September, spending some time in Barcelona.

90 "Memorandum para el arquitecto Bonet, departamento de divulgación y educación urbanística," October 27, 1949, Folder C-114, JFHA.

91 More invitations were sent to architecture journals, newspapers, architects, and academics. Within the photography workshop it was reported that Grete Stern had been assigned to start a methodic work of photographing the city and was supposed to send in weekly reports. October 27, 1949, Folder C-114, JFHA.

92 Bonet, Kurchan, and Ferrari knew Kaufmann through his purchase of their chair, the BKF, for his house, Fallingwater, and for the MOMA.

93 According to the closure decree, the EPBA had spent 1,000,000 Argentinian pesos through 1948 and was requesting 1,500,000 Argentinian pesos for 1950, of which 770,000 had been already spent in salaries and 210,000 in various expenses. "Disuelven una oficina para estudio del plan de la urbe," *La Razón* (November 30, 1949); "Dióse por terminada la actuación de la dirección del plan de Buenos Aires," *La Prensa*, December 1, 1949; "Finalizó la actuación del estudio del plan de Buenos Aires," *La Nación*, December 1, 1949, Folder H016, JFHA.

94 Robert Alexander González, *Designing Pan-America: U.S. Architectural Visions for the Western Hemisphere* (Austin: University of Texas Press, 2011).

95 The event, including inaugural speeches, attendants, and exhibitions, was documented through a publication: *Nuestra Señora de Buenos Aires: Publicación Oficial de la Municipalidad de la Ciudad de Buenos Aires Dirección de Informaciones y Prensa* 1, no. 5 (October 1949): 18–19, Folder L041, JFHA.

96 Inaugural speech by chancellor Roberto Tamagno, published in *Nuestra Señora de Buenos Aires*, 18–19, Folder L041, JFHA.

97 "Discurso del Dr. Hipólito J. Paz," in *Nuestra Señora de Buenos Aires*, 20–21, Folder L041, JFHA.

98 "Arte Popular," in *Nuestra Señora de Buenos Aires*, 29, Folder L041, JFHA.

99 The exhibition was organized by the secretary of culture and municipal police and inaugurated on October 18, 1949; it closed on November 19, 1949. "Clausuróse la Muestra Municipal de Urbanismo," *La Prensa* (November 19, 1949): h-15, JFHA.

100 "Exposición de arquitectura y urbanismo," *RdA* 347 (November 1949): 300–315.

101 "Clausuróse la muestra municipal de urbanismo," *La Prensa*, November 19, 1949, Folder H015, JFHA.

102 See Robert Rydell and Laura Schiavo, *Designing Tomorrow: America's World's Fairs in the 1930s* (New Haven, CT: Yale University Press, 2010).

103 Despite the opposing politics of some of its designers, in particular Edoardo Persico, who designed the Gold Medal room with painter Marcello Nizolli.

104 The aeronautical exhibition was featured in Bardi's journal *Quadrante* 14/15, which included an Argentinian newspaper reporting protests against the fascist stance. Bardi moved to Brazil after the war and eventually became better known as architect Lina Bo Bardi's husband.

105 The rediscovery was prompted by Picasso, *Les métamorphoses* (Lausanne: Albert Skira, 1931), a redrawing of Ovid's *Metamorphoses* (Venice, Lucantonio Giunti, 1497). Daphne appeared on the cover for Dalí's novel *Hidden Faces* (London: Peter Owen, 1944), in which she appears to be burning in the midst of swastikas and other symbols of World War II. In one of his iterations, Dalí transforms Daphne into a motor-tree, for the 1939 World Fair in New York.

106 Spyros Papapetros, "Daphne's Legacy: Architecture, Psychoanalysis and Petrification in Lacan and Dalí," in *Surrealism and Architecture*, ed. Thomas Mical (London: Routledge, 2004). Examining writings and drawings by Jacques Lacan, Salvador Dalí, André Breton, among others, Papapetros follows Daphne as she is transformed into the actualization of pain petrified in stone, to the architecture of Daphne's skirt protecting her genitals from Apollo, to other instances of desire or violence.

107 These halls exhibited the work of the Instituto Superior de Urbanismo (Superior Urbanism Institute), the Dirección de Obras Públicas de la Municipalidad de Buenos Aires (Department of Public Works of the City Hall of Buenos Aires), and the Dirección de Festejos y Ornamentaciones (Department of Festivities and Ornamentations) of the Buenos Aires City Hall. All these institutions displayed their projects using clean modern lines and modular panels.

108 "Exposición de Arquitectura y Urbanismo," *RdA* 347 (November 1949): 300.

109 Original 6 mm film *La ciudad frente al río*, produced by Estudio del Plan de Buenos Aires (EPBA); director, Enrique Gras (one reel, 11 minutes, black-and-white). Box C164, JFHA. Preliminary analysis of this film has been done by Inés Zalduendo, "Buenos Aires: La Ciudad Frente al Río," paper presented at the Society of Architectural Historians Annual Conference, 2010; and Luis E. Carranza and Fernando Luiz Lara, *Modern Architecture in Latin America: Art, Technology, and Utopia* (Austin: University of Texas Press, 2015).

110 The overlapping medical metaphors recall Ivanissevich's discourse against modern art, here applied to modernity rather than to modern art. It also harkens back to a longer genealogy of reactions to urban growth, from Victorian-era urban reform in London to Dziga Vertov's dizzying fascination with the city, here overturned.

111 Luciano Emmer and Enrico Gras, "The Film Renaissance in Italy," *Hollywood Quarterly* 2, no. 4 (July 1947): 353–358. The quotation comes from their biography as authors of the note.

112 Marshall Berman, "Pastoral and Counter-Pastoral Modernism," in *All That Is Solid Melts into Air: The Experience of Modernity* (New York: Simon and Schuster, 1982), 134–142.

113 Perón was firmly opposed to communism.

114 "Sueños de Angustia," *Idilio* (June 1951): 2. Stern often used the images that she had at hand, even those of her ex-husband.

115 Georges Bataille, "Cheminée d'usine," in *Documents* 6 (November 1929): 329; English translation in Bataille, "Factory Chimney," in *Encyclopaedia acephalica: Comprising the Critical Dictionary and Related Texts* (London: Atlas Press, 1995), 51.

116 Libro de Visitas, 14, LO01 JFHA.

117 "El monoblock es la perfecta realización del individualismo carente de personalismo, creador del hombre masa, de la cultura por entregas, de la opinión dirigida y controlada. Como solución de emergencia, es lógica; lo malo que este caso sienta precedente." Carlos Francisco Echenique, November 5, 1949, in Libro de Visitas, 25–26, LO01, JFHA.

118 Max Horkheimer and Theodor W. Adorno, "The Culture Industry: Enlightenment as Mass Deception," in *Dialectic of Enlightenment: Philosophical Fragments*, ed. Gunzelin Schmid Noerr (Stanford, CA: Stanford University Press, 2002), 94–136.

119 Anahí Ballent, "El kitsch inolvidable: Imágenes en torno a Eva Perón," in *Las huellas de la política*.

120 Ballent, "El kitsch inolvidable: Imágenes en torno a Eva Perón"; Ballent, "Unforgettable Kitsch: Images around Eva Perón," in *The New Cultural History of Peronism*, 143–170.

121 Liernur cites a lecture by Ferrari at the Facultad de Arquitectura—Universidad de Buenos Aires (FADU-UBA) in 1964, documented in JFHA: *La red Austral*, 372.

122 "Ciudad Infantil," *RdA* 370 (March–April 1953): 18–27.

123 The architect was Mario Colli.

124 "Urbanización del Bajo Belgrano," *RdA* 369 (January–February 1953), 26–28.

125 Between 1945 and 1946, Disney artist John Hench worked on the storyboards and footage for this movie. It was halted due to financial complications, restarted in 1999, and eventually released in 2003 with Dominique Monféry as director: *Destino* (Walt Disney Pictures).

126 "Así comienza y nuevo y limpido sueño de niño, bajo el techo de la Ciudad Infantil, la urbe maravillosa, poblada de pequeños habitantes que sueñan noche y día, con los ojos cerrados y con los ojos abiertos. En esta ciudad infantil que evoca un cuento de hadas, y que es sin embargo una tierna realidad gracias a Eva Perón, la extraordinaria mujer que no duerme para que los niños de la patria sueñen, y para cumplir el más íntimo anhelo del General Perón: que los argentinos sean un poco mas felices viendo soñar a sus hijos." Parting words in *Soñemos* (SIPP promotional film, 1951).

127 Carl Jung, *The Collected Works of C. G. Jung, Vol. 8: The Structure and Dynamics of the Psyche* (London: Routledge and Kegan Paul, 1960), para. 325.

128 Fredric Jameson, *The Political Unconscious: Narrative as a Socially Symbolic Act* (Ithaca, NY: Cornell University Press, 1981), 9.

129 The exhibition was held from October 18 to November 19, 1949.

130 Bonet to Ferrari and Juan Kurchan, August 1949, Folder E014, JFHA (emphasis in the original).

131 The group included Italians Franco Albini and Ignazio Gardella, Colombian Alberto Iriarte, Castelli (unlisted in the roster, no information available), Frenchman André Wogenscky (Le Corbusier's assistant and eventually his studio manager), Greek G. Candilis, and Bonet, listed as an Uruguayan delegate but representing Argentina. *Documents 7: VIIème Congrès CIAM* (CIAM Archiv, ETH, reprinted by Nedeln, Liechtenstein: Kraus Reprint, 1979).

132 VIIème Congres CIAM, "Séance plénière de cloture [*sic*]" (Bergamo, July 30, 1949), 1–8, in *Documents: 7 CIAM, Bergamo, 1949*, ed. International Congress for Modern

Architecture (Nendeln, Liechtenstein: Kraus Reprint, 1979). Ferrari is listed as the Argentinian delegate, but he did not attend.

133 Meetings between congresses did happen, but only among the small circle of CIAM directors, which operated increasingly like an enclosed, high-ranking group within the expanding base of the group.

134 Bonet to Ferrari and Juan Kurchan, August 1949, Folder E014, JFHA.

135 Ferrari to Sert, April 1, 1948, F083, JFHA.

136 Bonet, "Entrevista al Arq. Bonet," undated, Folder C1305/168/1.2, FABC.

137 Bonet to Ferrari and Juan Kurchan, August 1949, Folder E014, JFHA.

138 Bonet to Ferrari and Juan Kurchan, August 1949, Folder E014, JFHA.

139 Bonet to Ferrari and Juan Kurchan, August 1949, Folder E014, JFHA.

140 Kurchan to Ferrari, July 15, 1948, Folder C155, JFHA.

141 Jorge Vivanco to Ferrari, May 10 (no year, probably 1949), C154, JFHA.

142 The purpose of Vivanco's letter was to notify Ferrari of his decision to focus on the IAU, that is, dedicate himself to teaching and distance himself from the EPBA.

143 Jorge Francisco Liernur, "Vanguardistas versus expertos," *Block* 6 (March 2004): 18–39.

144 Cohen, *Architecture in Uniform*.

145 Henry-Russell Hitchcock, "The Architecture of Bureaucracy and the Architecture of Genius," *Architectural Review* 101 (January 1947), 3–6.

146 Mumford, *The CIAM Discourse on Urbanism*.

CHAPTER FOUR: ETERNAL RETURNS

1 An organized coup d'état occurred in September 1955 and forced Perón to retire.

2 Peronist supporters did not live in San Telmo per se, but they hailed from Barrio Sur at large, that is, from the southern half of the city. By naming his project Barrio Sur, Bonet conflated San Telmo with the larger southern half of Buenos Aires.

3 Borges, "El propósito de Zarathustra," *Diario La Nación* (Buenos Aires), October 15, 1944.

4 Friedrich Nietzsche, *The Gay Science, with a Prelude in Rhymes and an Appendix of Songs* (New York: Vintage Books, 1974), 273.

5 A similar chaotic change of command happened after the 1943 coup d'état. The heads of state were Eduardo Lonardi (1955) and Pedro Eugenio Aramburu (1955–1958).

6 Decreto-ley 3855/55 (6), *Boletín Oficial*, 9.

7 Decreto-ley 4161, March 5, 1956, *Boletín Oficial*, March 8, 1956.

8 Articles in the press directly called for its destruction: see "La residencia presidencial debe ser destruída," *AHORA* 2337 (November 22, 1955). For more on the significance of demolishing this building, see Ana María León, "A Ruin in Reverse: The National Library of the Republic of Argentina, 1961–1992," in *Neoliberalism: An Architectural History*, ed. Kenny Cupers, Catharina Gabrielsson, and Helena Mattsson (Pittsburgh: University of Pittsburgh Press, 2019).

9 Liernur gives a list of the members in "Las políticas de vivienda de la 'Revolución Libertadora' y el debate en torno al proyecto para el Barrio Sur," *Block* 9 (July 2012): 72.

10 Liernur, "Las políticas de vivienda," 71.

11 Federico Deambrosis, "Los temas estructurales en el panorama de las revistas de arquitectura en Argentina de los años cincuenta," *Block* 9 (July 2012): 8–17.

12 In this project Bonet turned his affinity for the curves of the Catalan vault into a repetitive, structurally advanced solution to cover large spans. He worked on this project

under the supervision of Pierre Jeanneret. Bonet, "Testimonio sobre Austral," dated September 18, 1981, Folder c1329–228 Austral, FABC.

13 Liernur, "Las políticas de vivienda," 77.

14 Bonet, Conference at Santiago de Compostela, May 17, 1975, Folder c1305/168/2, 13, FABC.

15 Bonet, Conference at Santiago de Compostela, May 17, 1975, Folder c1305/168/2, 13, FABC.

16 Antonio Bonet, "Plan Remodelamiento Zona Sur," Folder c1303/157/1, FABC.

17 "En este caso, la responsabilidad, me correspondía a mí exclusivamente, y por consiguiente el nuevo enfoque no se discutía." The last phrase is crossed out. Conference in Barcelona, undated, Folder c1305/168/2, 8, FABC.

18 Architects Luis H. Aberastain Oro, Horacio Baliero, Nélida Gurevich, Eduardo Polledo, Próspero E. Poyard, Víctor Sigal, Cesar A. Vapñarsky, Severo A. Yantorno; engineer Jorge A. Martucci; topographer (*agrimensor*) Osvaldo Lauersdorf; model makers Eduardo Bell, Oscar N. Candioti, and Raúl Pastrana; draftspeople Carmen Córdova de Baliero, Carlos Castiglione, Carlos E. Dourge, Justo J. Solsona, and Fernando L. Tiscornia; graphic artist Alfredo Hlito; and photographer Aníbal G. Larumbe. Antonio Bonet, "Plan Remodelamiento Zona Sur" (Buenos Aires: Banco Hipotecario Nacional, 1956), unpaginated, Folder c1303/157/1, FABC.

19 Justo Solsona, interview with the author, October 31, 2012. Solsona remembers that the offices took over one full floor on the first or second level of the central offices for the Automóvil Club Argentino, built in 1941–1943.

20 Antonio Bonet, "Plan Remodelamiento Zona Sur," Folder c1303/157/1, FABC.

21 Antonio Bonet, "Plan Remodelamiento Zona Sur," Folder c1303/157/1, FABC.

22 A small layout of TOSA appears in the crossed-out examples of the literature for Barrio Sur. Bonet has added a fourth housing block, apparently in an effort to disguise the project.

23 The target population was 450,000, or 75,000 units for a city of about 3 million—in later years Bonet admitted that the numbers had been too high.

24 Antonio Bonet, "Plan remodelamiento zona sur," Folder c1303/157/1, FABC.

25 Bonet, "Plan remodelamiento zona sur," Folder c1303/157/1, FABC.

26 See Hilario Zalba, "Homenaje al arquitecto Antonio Bonet," *RdA* 145 (January 1990): 10–18.

27 Bonet, "Plan remodelamiento zona sur," Folder c1303/157/1, FABC.

28 For more on the Chimbote project. see Rovira, *José Luis Sert*, 113–161.

29 Paul Lester Wiener and José Luis Sert, "Can Patios Make Cities?" *Architectural Forum* (August 1953): 124–131.

30 Bonet, "Plan remodelamiento zona sur," Folder c1303/157/1, FABC (the following quotations are also from this source).

31 Jaqueline Tyrwhitt, José Luis Sert, and Ernesto Nathan Rogers, eds., *The Heart of the City: Towards the Humanisation of Urban Life* (New York: Pellegrini and Cudahy, 1952).

32 Bonet, "Plan remodelamiento zona sur," Folder c1303/157/1, FABC.

33 Bonet, "Plan remodelamiento zona sur," Folder c1303/157/1, FABC.

34 Álvaro Blas, "En el camino de la nueva Buenos Aires," *Leoplán* 551 (July 15, 1957): 14–18.

35 Other topics include the life and loves of Cuban dictator Fulgencio Batista, the "industrial spirit" of the United States, the elegant wedding of Aramburu's daughter, and,

tellingly, an article praising the decision to build Brasilia but critiquing its isolation. *Leoplán* 551 (July 15, 1957), 4–8, 18, 50–51, 62.

36 Ramón Gutiérrez, "Luis Morea, el testimonio de una acción cívica 1945–1970," in *Luis Dubois—Paul Pater Alberto y Luis Morea, de la École des Beaux Arts al movimiento moderno* (Buenos Aires: Cedodal 2012), 97–100.

37 "Plan de Remodelación del Barrio Sur," *NA* 330 (May 1957): 76.

38 Comisión Vecinal Defensa Zona Sudeste, "Nos demuelen 105 manzanas," in Gutiérrez, "Luis Morea," 99.

39 The next chapter in the Plaza de Mayo's long history was its occupation by the Madres de la Plaza de Mayo (Mothers of the Plaza de Mayos). For an architectural evaluation of the significance of these protests, see Susana Torre, "Claiming the Public Space: The Mothers of Plaza de Mayo," in *The Sex of Architecture*, ed. Diana Agrest (New York: Harry N. Abrams, 1996), 241–250.

40 The Sociedad Argentina de Escritores (SADE, Association of Writers), over which Borges presided and which Perón had closed, would have been saved.

41 Clorindo Testa, Francisco Bullrich, and Alicia Cazzaniga won the competition in 1962.

42 Carlos Sentís, "Me parece que explotamos a este catalán," *La Vanguardia Española* (September 16, 1960): 14.

43 The CIAM grid system used panels of 33 × 21 centimeters; the photographs show larger panels, but they could have been easily reduced.

44 "Atelier e Residência em Buenos Aires," *Acrópole* 176, no. 15 (December 1952): 282–283.

45 Bonet, Conference in Santiago de Compostela, May 17, 1975, 4–5, Folder c1305/168/2, FABC.

46 I researched Sert's unbuilt plans and complicities in "Sert Goes South: Town Planning in Brazil, Perú, and Colombia," presented at "Architecture and the State, 1940s–1970s," Columbia Graduate School of Architecture, Planning and Preservation (Spring 2010), convened by Marta Caldeira, María González Pendás, and Ayala Levin; Reinhold Martin, respondent.

47 The exhibition, organized by Juan Prats Vellés, Oriol Bohigas, M. D. Orriols, and Roman Vallés, took place between October 6 and November 2, 1960. *Antonio Bonet arquitectura* (Barcelona: Museo de Arte Contemporáneo de Barcelona, 1960).

48 Eamonn Rodgers, "Serra d'Or and the Liberal Catholic Resistance to Francoism, 1960–65," *Journal of Catalan Studies* (Universitat Operta de Catalunya, University of Cambridge, 2000), https://www.uoc.edu/jocs/3/articles/rogers6/index.html (accessed April 5, 2020).

49 For more on the Soca chapel, see Mary Méndez, "Bonet en Soca," *Block* 9 (July 2012): 42–51.

50 Oriol Bohigas, "La nueva ciudad latina de Antonio Bonet," in *Antonio Bonet arquitectura*, unpaginated.

51 "Se trata del replanteo de la 'ciudad latina' con el ser humano como protagonista, calles peatonales y placitas porticadas para el desarrollo del comercio, con separación de la circulación rodada, comunidades semiautónomas con recorridos a pie con un máximo de 15 minutos, y los servicios culturales y de esparcimiento al pie de la vivienda; esplanadas cívicas y espacios verdes autónomos para cada barrio, centrando la vida del mismo, y aparcamientos subterráneos suficientes para liberar la ciudad." Notes for conference at Barcelona University, undated, probably 1987, Folder c1305:165:2, FABC.

52 Bonet, "Plan remodelamiento zona sur," Folder c1303/157/1, FABC.

53 Iñigo de Santiago, "El Barrio Sur de Buenos Aires va a ser totalmente alzado en un plazo de diez años," *Mundo Hispánico* 104 (Madrid, November 1956): 16.

54 Santiago, "El Barrio Sur de Buenos Aires," 17.

55 Geoffrey Jensen, "Dictatorship to Death," in *Franco: Soldier, Commander, Dictator* (Washington, DC: Potomac Books, 2005), 98–116.

56 Raanan Rein, *The Franco-Perón Alliance: Relations between Spain and Argentina, 1946–1955* (Pittsburgh: University of Pittsburgh Press, 1993). For a discussion of Spanish neutrality during World War II, see 12–16.

57 The term *hispanidad* had been proposed in the context of Spanish Catholics living in Argentina in the 1930s to replace "Día de la Raza" (day of the race, to imply the creation of a new race) for the commemoration of Christopher Columbus's arrival in the Americas. *Hispanidad* did not take hold in the Americas but was used in Spain in the 1940s. See Ernesto Mario Barreda, "Día de la Raza, 12 de octubre de 1915," *La Nación* (Buenos Aires, October 12, 1935), cited in Monseñor Zacarías de Vizcarra, "Origen del nombre, concepto, y fiesta de la Hispanidad," in *El Español: Semanario de la Política y el Espíritu* (Madrid, October 7, 1944).

58 "12 de Octubre: Día de América," *Nuestra Señora de Buenos Aires: Publicación Oficial de la Municipalidad de la Ciudad de Buenos Aires Dirección de Informaciones y Prensa* 1, no. 5 (October 1949): 3, Folder LO41, JFHA.

59 Zacarías de Vizcarra, "Origen del nombre, concepto, y fiesta de la Hispanidad."

60 Tamagno had been part of Fuerza de Orientación Radical de la Joven Argentina (FORJA, Radical Orientation Contingent of the Young Argentina), the youth movement of the Unión Cívica Radical (UCR, Radical Civic Union). FORJA had been associated with a discourse of nationalism and opposition to neocolonialism.

61 "Discurso del Dr. Hipólito J. Paz," *Nuestra Señora de Buenos Aires: Publicación Oficial de la Municipalidad de la Ciudad de Buenos Aires Dirección de Informaciones y Prensa* 1, no. 5 (October 1949): 20–22, Folder LO41, JFHA.

62 "Foreign Policy under Franco," in *Spain: A Country Study*, ed. Eric Solsten and Sandra W. Meditz (Washington, DC: Library of Congress, 1990); http://countrystudies.us/spain/24.htm (accessed April 5, 2020).

63 Stanley G. Payne, "The Regime at Mid-Passage 1950–1959," in *The Franco Regime, 1936–1975* (Madison: University of Wisconsin Press, 1987), 413–459, especially 418. According to the Library of Congress report cited above, "During the first ten years of the Pact of Madrid, the United States sent approximately US\$ 1.5 billion in all kinds of aid to Spain": *Spain: A Country Study*, ed. Solsten and Meditz; http://countrystudies.us/spain/24.htm (accessed April 5, 2020).

64 Raanan Rein, "Latinidad Instead of Hispanidad," in *The Franco-Perón Alliance*, 220–223.

65 In 1934 Bonet attended the Universidad Internacional de Verano de Santander, which was an outpost of these groups.

66 Cirici-Pellicer, the author of one of the Bonet catalog essays, would later become one of the founders of the Partido de los Socialistas de Cataluña (PSC, Catalan Socialist Party).

67 Bonet, "Plan remodelamiento zona sur," Folder c1303/157/1, FABC.

68 In 1958 Bonet wrote a letter to *Cuaderns*, the journal of the Catalan College of Architects, with an urban proposal based on an extension of the Cerdá plan. At the time of

the Barcelona exhibition, he was working on a plan for Murcia, still thinking on an urban scale. Bonet, August 1, 1958, letter published in *Cuadernos de Arquitectura* 33 (1958): 419–421.

69 Bonet also designed a few apartment buildings—perhaps the only ones that retain echoes of his urban ideas. Less well known, but also occupying a big part of his time, was the work that he did for the Nuclear Central in Vandellòs in the late 1960s, which included workers' quarters, facilities, and industrial spaces. In this way, his work is a reflection of the policies of the Spanish government under the technocrats.

70 *To return*
With a withered forehead
The snows of time
Have silvered my temples

To feel
That life is a puff of wind
That twenty years is nothing
That the feverish gaze
Wandering in the shadows
Looks for you and names you.

–"Volver" (tango, 1934), lyrics by Alfredo Le Pera and music by Carlos Gardel.

71 Julia Kristeva, *Strangers to Ourselves* (New York: Columbia University Press, 1991), 9–10.

72 Carlos Coire, "Homenaje al arquitecto Antonio Bonet," *RdA* (January 1990): 17.

73 Fernando Álvarez Prozorovich, in conversation with the author, June 18, 2012.

74 See Fernando Bores Gamundi, *Casas de indianos* (Santiago de Compostela: Xunta de Galicia, 2000).

75 See Manuel Enrique Figueroa and María Teresa Rojo, "La palmera, símbolo de poderío o contribución al sistema verde en un escenario de cambio climático," conference paper presented at Arte y Pensamiento, Universidad Internacional de Andalucía (October 2009).

76 Álvarez has worked on the topic of Catalan architects in exile: see Alvarez, "El exilio español en el cono sur," in *Arquitecturas desplazadas: Arquitecturas del exilio español*, ed. Henry Vicente and Fernando Álvarez Prozorovich (Madrid: Ministerio de Vivienda, Secretaría General Técnica, Centro de Publicaciones, 2007), 125–129.

77 Prompted by my curiosity, Álvarez asked Bonet's daughter Victoria whether Bonet had decided on the palm tree. Her response was that this choice was not significant but that it was Bonet's. I choose to interpret the tree differently. Fernando Álvarez Prozorovich, correspondence with the author, October 1, 2019.

CONCLUSION

1 Max Horkheimer, Theodor W. Adorno, and Gunzelin Schmid Noerr, *Dialectic of Enlightenment: Philosophical Fragments* (Stanford, CA: Stanford University Press, 2002).

2 It is not coincidental that the main agent of this development in the United States, Edward Bernays, was Freud's nephew. His mining of his uncle's work for use in advertising also followed parallel developments in Nazi Germany and fascist Italy.

See Adam Curtis, *The Century of the Self* (London: RDF Television and British Broadcasting Corporation, 2002).

3   A rare exception is the living room of the Artists' Ateliers, depicted in the scene of Gras's film in which the children burn the city plan.

4   Bonet, Ferrari, and Kurchan, "Voluntad y acción," 3 (first quotation); Bonet to Ferrari and Juan Kurchan, August 1949, Folder E014, JFHA (second quotation).

5   Hannah Arendt, *The Origins of Totalitarianism* (Cleveland: Meridian Books, 1958), 474.

6   See Beatriz Colomina, *Privacy and Publicity: Modern Architecture as Mass Media* (Cambridge, MA: MIT Press, 1994); Felicity Dale Elliston Scott, *Fuera de lugar = Out of Place* (Santiago, Chile: Ediciones ARQ, 2016); Jordan Kauffman, *Drawing on Architecture: The Object of Lines, 1970–1990* (Cambridge, MA: MIT Press, 2018); Lea-Catherine Szacka, *Exhibiting the Postmodern: The 1980 Venice Architecture Biennale* (Venice: Marsilio Editori, 2017).

7   The Washington Consensus refers to a set of economic policies supported by institutions based in Washington, DC, such as the International Monetary Fund, the World Bank, and the US Department of the Treasury. Policies were issued to countries going through economic crisis and were meant to prioritize economic stabilization by opening these countries to international trade and expanding market forces within the domestic economy. The term was first used by English economist John Williamson in 1989. John Williamson, "What Washington Means by Policy Reform," in *Latin American Readjustment: How Much Has Happened*, ed. John Williamson (Washington, DC: Peterson Institute for International Economics, 1989), 7–20.

INDEX

void, 11–12, 214–215

Wiener, Paul Lester, 110, 146, 174, 190, 253n118, 261n71
"Will and Action" manifesto (Austral), 55–57
Williams, Amancio, 111–112, 118, 120, 174, 182, 240n121, 253nn122–123, 253n125, 254n139

working class, 5–6, 26, 48, 112
World War II, 27, 58, 84, 102–103, 175
Wright, Frank Lloyd, 50, 55, 217

Zalba, Hilario, 51, 53, 121, 181, 239n104, 253n125
Zeppelinfeld (Speer), 74